FORESTLANDS
Public and Private

Edited by
ROBERT T. DEACON
M. BRUCE JOHNSON

Foreword by
B. DELWORTH GARDNER

PACIFIC RESEARCH INSTITUTE FOR PUBLIC POLICY
San Francisco, California

International Standard Book Number: 0-936488-27-1 (CL)
0-936-488-28-x (PB)

Library of Congress Catalog Card Number 84-22699

Printed in the United States of America.

Library of Congress Cataloging in Publication Data

Main entry under title:

Forestlands : public and private.

Includes index.
1. Forest policy–United States.   2. Forest management–United
States.   3. Forests and forestry–Economic aspects–United States.
I. Deacon, Robert T.   II. Johnson, M. Bruce.   III. Series.
HD9756.F67   1985   333.75′0973   84-22699
ISBN 0-936488-27-1
ISBN 0-936-488-28-x (pbk.)

CONTENTS

iii

LIST OF FIGURES

LIST OF TABLES

FOREWORD

This book is an intellectual gem of rare quality and value. It fills a niche that badly needed attention from able scholars. Although the literature demonstrating government mismanagement of public lands has been growing in recent years, the case has never been more convincingly made than in the set of papers comprising this volume.[1]

To provide some perspective of how far we have moved in the direction of skepticism about government management and control of natural resources in the past quarter of a century and why I am so excited about this book, let me briefly describe an anecdote of a personal nature.

I had written a thesis for the Department of Economics at the University of Chicago, and the time came in early 1960 for me to defend it before the faculty. Essentially, the study was a critique of the regulations utilized by the Forest Service and the Bureau of Land Management to define and allocate livestock grazing permits. Typical of nonprice, political allocative criteria, I was able to show that these regulations had misallocated forage among ranchers because they prevented the most efficient operators from acquiring access to the

---

1. Very good examples of this literature are John Baden and Richard Stroup, eds., *Bureaucracy vs. Environment* (Ann Arbor: University of Michigan Press, 1981); idem, *Natural Resources* (San Francisco: Pacific Research Institute for Public Policy, 1983); and Sterling Brubaker, ed., *Rethinking the Federal Lands* (Washington, D.C.: Resources for the Future). (In press.)

allowable grazing. The solution that I proposed was to replace the regulations with a market allocation process that would auction off the permits to the highest bidder.

At Chicago at that time, the student's thesis committee always attended the defense. In addition, any interested faculty member could review the paper and could fully participate in the questioning and discussion of it. The candidates of that time had some forebodings that Professor Milton Friedman would elect to come, since we all knew that he could and likely would trip us up. His general intellectual powers, understanding of economics, and debating skills were (and still are) legendary. Sure enough, when I entered the examination room my worst fears were realized. There was Professor Friedman (and many others) waiting for me.

In discussing Forest Service policy in the thesis, I had written a sentence stating that there were compelling reasons for the federal government to maintain its ownership and management of the national forests. Theories of "market failure," which included technological external effects,[2] public goods,[3] monopoly and monopsony, and especially open access resources,[4] were a part of theory courses at the time, even at Chicago. Perhaps even more important in explaining the remark in the thesis, I had been reared in northwestern Wyoming, immediately adjacent to the Bridger National Forest and south of Yellowstone National Park, and I had come to accept that government ownership and management of the national forests were simply a "natural" fact of life.

Well, to end the story, given the circumstances the inevitable occurred. Professor Friedman nailed me to the wall. I could not defend my statement adequately; neither theory nor empirical data showing "market failure" were convincing. There was nothing I said that Professor Friedman could not easily refute. I remember one or two faculty members entered the discussion on my behalf, but this was not enough. We simply could not make a compelling case. The entire experience remains a vivid reminder that unchallenged ideas

---

2. James E. Meade, "External Economies and Diseconomies in a Competitive Situation," *Economic Journal* 62 (March 1952): 56–67.

3. Paul A. Samuelson, "The Pure Theory of Public Expenditures," *Review of Economics and Statistics* 36 (November 1954): 387–89.

4. H. Scott Gordon, "The Economic Theory of a Common Property Resource: The Fishery," *Journal of Political Economy* 62 (April 1954): 124–42.

acquired in childhood are likely to be replaced sooner or later. For me it was fortunate that it was sooner.

From that day to this, there have been many theoretical and empirical developments that have shed light on the question concerning us that day. It is apparent to me that the case for continuing federal control of the public lands is becoming increasingly weaker and the case for some type of market allocation, and even complete divestiture of the bulk of the federal acreage, is becoming increasingly stronger. Even the political climate appears to be moving this way.

I believe *Forestlands: Public and Private* will accelerate movement in this direction. It is pregnant with cogent argument and sound empirical findings difficult for anyone to refute or ignore. Given time for sufficient reflection and the expenditure of substantial educational capital on a still unconvinced general public, we will witness the decline of what are now essentially political allocations. On the one hand, these allocations confer large benefits to narrow interests, but on the other hand they waste resources as these beneficiary groups compete for the favors bestowed by the political process. In place of these allocations we are likely to see more private market decisions that will be economically efficient and, in addition, will be conducive to a larger degree of economic and political freedom.

This state of "nirvana" will not be painlessly achieved, of course. The interests that benefit from the status quo of public ownership and management are deeply entrenched and have a great amount of political clout. The primary loser group, the taxpayers, are not well organized and do not cut a wide swath in the political arena. Thus, victories will be won slowly.

I would like next to review some ideas I regard as particularly influential that have emerged in the past twenty-five years and have produced the more prevalent critical attitude toward the government's management of the public lands.

Back when I wrote a dissertation, the conventional response from economists and other social scientists whenever market failure could be detected in the private sector was to advise corrective governmental regulation. It was almost accepted as an article of faith that such action would produce more socially optimal outcomes. Likewise, when the public choice theorists in the 1960s demonstrated that "government failure" arises out of political allocations and various forms of nonprice competition, the corrective action usually recommended was to introduce market processes deemed to be more efficient in allocating resources.[5] Therefore, "government failure" became an effective counterweight to "market failure." In most real-world situations, however, examples of both market and government failure are not hard to find. The prevailing opinion now seems to be that whichever type of failure is the most serious in its efficiency implications cannot be settled entirely on a priori grounds. Rather, the question must be resolved by the empirical evidence that can be brought to bear in each situation. Also, no longer can an allegation that a good is a public good be automatically construed to require public intervention. Since the question is open pending empirical evidence, such an approach has been instrumental in producing a large number of case studies in recent years.[6] In these studies some of the merits and demerits of market and political allocations have been evaluated.

On this point I am now satisfied that the definitive work may not have yet been done. What is needed is an evaluative comparison of the actual performances of market and political decisionmakers in situations that closely parallel each other in the types of resources being allocated and outputs being produced.

We know from the recent rent-seeking literature, however, that there is at least a presumption that market processes are likely to be more efficient than nonprice political allocations.[7] If new techniques are found promising improved efficiency by reducing costs, and resources are not impeded from moving into these profitable employments, the resultant shifts in resource allocation will produce a net social gain. This is, of course, the "invisible hand" of Adam Smith, whereby an entrepreneur can do well for himself by doing that which is socially beneficial; that is, he can make profits by reducing costs and attracting resources that would be conducive to greater economic efficiency. This type of activity is decidedly a positive-sum game for society in the sense that more economic output is produced and is available ultimately to be distributed among consumers. By contrast, in public decisions the potential recipients of the benefits from a decision have the incentive to expend resources to make sure

5. See James Buchanan and Gordon Tullock, *The Calculus of Consent* (Ann Arbor: University of Michigan Press, 1962); and William.A. Niskanen, *Bureaucracy and Representative Government* (Chicago: Aldine-Atherton, 1971).

6. B. Delworth Gardner, "Market Versus Political Allocations on Natural Resources in the 1980s," *Western Journal of Agricultural Economics* 8 (2) (1983): 215–29.

7. Anne O. Krueger, "The Political Economy of the Rent-Seeking Society," *American Economic Review* 54 (3) (June 1974): 291–303.

that the decision is made in their favor. These resources may be used to cajole, pressure, or threaten political officials, to contribute to their political campaigns, or to make propaganda to influence public opinion. Of course, if recipient groups are to be successful in this process, they must win out over their competitors who are playing the same zero-sum game.[8] The various groups are fighting for the same fixed bundle of outputs from resources. The inevitable result of this competitive rent-seeking behavior is that valuable economic surpluses are dissipated and lost to society as a whole. When these rent-seeking expenditures are added to production costs, this process turns out to be a negative-sum game that wastes resources and lowers the average per capita standard of living. The introductory chapter in this book by Deacon and Johnson is a very clear statement of these issues.

Another important step forward in understanding the differences between political and market allocations was the development of a theory of property rights.[9] As Demsetz puts it: "Property rights convey the right to benefit or harm oneself or others" and in fact determine "who must pay whom to modify the actions taken. . . ." It is property rights that determine incentives to act in one way or another. Externalities, as a class of market failure, became much less worrisome when it was realized that property rights might be altered in such a way that externalities could be internalized and thus accounted for in ordinary market transactions.

In the same vein, the Coase theorem, first stated in 1960, was immensely influential in pointing out opportunities for mitigating damages arising from external effects.[10] This would be done by bargains struck between the affected parties. The idea is that bargaining may result in side-payments between injuring and injured parties. This may permit an economically efficient action to be undertaken that may have been blocked by the injured party if he/she had not been restored by the side-payment. Since such bargaining involves transactions costs, however, these costs must be included in defining an efficient allocation of resources. Sometimes transactions costs are so

8. Terry Anderson and P. J. Hill, *The Birth of the Transfer Society* (Stanford, Calif.: Stanford University, Hoover Institution, 1980).

9. Harold Demsetz, "Toward a Theory of Property Rights," *American Economic Review* 57 (2) (1967): 347–59. Also see Eirik G. Furubotn and Svetozar Pejovich, eds., *The Economics of Property Rights* (Cambridge, Mass.: Ballinger, 1974).

10. Ronald Coase, "The Problem of Social Cost," *Journal of Law and Economics* (3` (October 1960): 1–41.

high that it does not pay for this bargaining to occur. If so, an efficient allocation does not require the elimination of all external effects. It is quite clear that the Coase theorem also weakened the case for automatic public intervention whenever externalities were observed.

Finally, the theory of regulation provided additional reasons to be skeptical that government bureaucrats, no matter how professional and public spirited, would systematically make decisions in the public interest, assuming the public interest can be defined.[11] Slippage occurs all along the way, from the ultimate consumers to the bureaucrat making the allocative decision. How are the preferences of consumers to be identified in the absence of prices? Even if they were known, what are the incentives for the bureaucrats to give all consumers what they want? Where preferences of various consumers are conflicting, what criteria are to be used to determine which ones will be satisfied? All these are important questions, and to the extent they have been answered, the results are not encouraging. In the real world, the regulators who are charged with looking after the public interest are often captured by those regulated and act to promote the latter's interests rather than the public interest. Again, the reason seems to be that incentives are perverse.

But given that public management is inefficient, isn't it likely that private management will be just as inefficient? Are not corporate bureaucrats in large firms of the private sector just as bureaucratic and blind to the public interest as public bureaucrats in the public sector are? Will not the gains be negligible from trading one set for another? De Alessi has convincingly argued that this is not likely.[12] Private and public organizations differ in the cost of transferring ownership shares. An individual can change his "ownership" portfolio of public benefits only by moving from one jurisdiction to another. This is far more costly than buying or selling securities, his portfolio of private ownership. Thus, property rights in public organizations may be taken to be nontransferable. The owner's incentive to detect and inhibit undesirable managerial behavior is much weaker

11. George J. Stigler, "The Theory of Economic Regulation," *Bell Journal of Economics and Management Science* 2 (1) (Spring 1971): 3–19. See also Richard A. Posner, "Theories of Economic Regulation," *Bell Journal of Economics and Management Science* 5 (2) (Autumn 1974): 335–58.

12. Louis De Alessi, "Implications of Property Rights for Government Investment Choices," *American Economic Review* 59 (1) (1969): 13–24.

in public organizations than in private firms, and gives government decisionmakers greater opportunities to increase their own welfare relative to that of the owners.

It would be difficult to overstate the importance of incentives in directing resources to various employments. But there are other basic differences in the structure of incentives in the private and public sectors. If private entrepreneurs make uneconomic decisions, they tend to pay for them in diminished wealth in the short run, and in possible extinction as a market competitor in the long run. Government bureaucrats normally bear no such risks. The utility functions that motivate their decisions might well be even more complex than those of private decisionmakers, but their own self-interest must be at the center of their concerns just as is the case with private decisionmakers. The relevant point is that they are largely immune from the necessity of making decisions that maximize economic efficiency. It is this fundamental problem of perverse incentives, which militates against economic efficiency, that is so prominently featured in all the papers of this volume.

In the final analysis, economic efficiency in which we all have an important stake is mostly a matter of signals and incentives.[13] Free and competitive market prices convey information essential to an efficient allocation of resources.[14] If goods and services were available to consumers only in the market and equilibrium quantities were purchased at competitive prices, then price would represent the marginal valuations of all consuming agents of any good. If the market itself were in competitive equilibrium, price would also represent the marginal opportunity cost of production. Therefore, how could allocation be efficient with price equal to marginal cost (the acknowledged efficiency optimum) without this essential price information and without market processes to bring about such allocations? The answer is that it is extremely unlikely it ever could be.

I do not wish to encroach upon the territory of the excellent summary of the papers in this volume provided in the introductory chapter by Deacon and Johnson. However, some reinforcement of the overall message, as I see it, might be useful to the reader.

13. Perhaps the best treatment of this subject is Thomas Sowell, *Knowledge and Decisions* (New York: Basic Books, 1980).

14. K. J. Arrow, "The Organization of Economic Activity: Issues Pertinent to the Choice of Market versus Nonmarket Allocation," in Haveman and Margolis, eds., *Public Expenditures and Policy Analysis* (Chicago: Markham, 1970), pp. 59–73.

The essays in this book are replete with examples of inefficient signals, of administered prices (sometimes zero) that represent neither consumer preferences nor producer opportunity costs. Thus, decisions based on these signals, even if they are rational decisions, are bound to be wasteful in allocating resources.

Even when market conditions might have dictated changes in the rate of harvest from the public forestlands, the government agencies have blindly adhered to inefficient harvest rules such as sustained yield and multiple use (Nelson, R. Johnson, Nelson and Pugliaresi, and Deacon).

In order to maintain the support of its constituency groups, and thus the pressure to increase appropriations in its behalf (Dowdle and Hanke), the Forest Service has been reluctant to charge competitive fees for many uses of the forestlands. The resultant use patterns are inefficient and often destructive of environmental quality (R. Johnson).

Failure to charge interest on inventories of standing timber has caused higher stocks of old timber and lower growth rates of new timber than is socially optimal (Nelson, R. Johnson, Nelson and Pugliaresi, and Deacon).

By not collecting the full economic rents that accrue in oil and gas development, the Forest Service and the Bureau of Land Management have no direct incentive to induce the optimal amount of development on the public lands, or even to find out the extent of the deposits of these scarce and valuable fuels (Libecap).

By applying inappropriate valuation techniques to fishing activity, wasteful management of timber and harvests of logs have resulted (Grobey). Faulty procedures used in selling timber have produced both reductions in the harvested volume of timber and less valuable remaining stands for environmental uses (Muraoka and Watson).

By invoking a setaside program to give a break to "small" timber-manufacturing firms under the presumption that communities would be more prosperous, the Forest Service has promoted more costly timber production and manufacturing and has reduced revenues going to the U.S. Treasury (Schniepp). Nonprice restrictions on exports of logs produced on federal lands, again ostensibly in order to help local mills and exporters of logs produced on private lands, have raised the costs of harvesting and transporting timber in aggregate. The sum of these efficiency losses clearly have more than offset any gains to local processors and exporters (Parks and Cox).

The lesson from this book is clear. Even though forestry is a long-term activity, where a timber cycle can be as long as a century, any special treatment in the form of subsidy to users, "low" interest rates, setasides for small businesses, and other distortions of competitive market criteria, will exact a heavy toll in lost economic efficiency. If the government agencies cannot utilize economically efficient management practices, either because of incompetency or because of political constraints, and on the basis of the evidence at hand there are few reasons to believe it ever can, it should get out of the business and leave the job to private markets that will do better.

— B. Delworth Gardner
Professor of Agricultural
Economics
University of California,
Davis

Chapter 1

INTRODUCTION

Robert T. Deacon and M. Bruce Johnson

For over one hundred years the management and use of the nation's forests have been heavily influenced by government policy. In no other natural resource industry has government ownership, particularly at the federal level, been such an important force. In a few western states the federal government now owns over 85 percent of all commercial forestlands, and in ten states federal ownership exceeds 50 percent.[1] Government policy also affects the use of private forestlands. In this realm, public influence is exerted through the regulation of logging practices and road construction, restrictions on the use of herbicides and disease control agents, requirements regarding reforestation, and taxation of private forest holdings.

The nation's forests and the wood-products industries that depend on these forests are in transition. First, private sector forestry is being transformed from a mining to an agricultural activity. Forest industry forests are, for the most part, now operating on second or later generation stocks, and the vast bulk of all remaining old growth timber is located on federal land. Second, the center of industry

1. These and other figures on acreage in forestlands and commercial forests, plus breakdowns by ownership categories, are taken from U.S. Department of Agriculture, Forest Service, *An Assessment of the Forest and Rangeland Situation in the United States*, Forest Resources Report No. 22 (1981), ch. 2; and U.S. Department of Agriculture, Forest Service, *An Analysis of the Timber Situation in the United States, 1952-2030*, Forest Resource Report No. 23 (1982).

activity is shifting away from the Douglas fir regions of the Pacific Northwest toward the pine forests of the south. Finally, the relative price of timber has been rising rapidly, particularly since the mid-1960s.[2] Softwood lumber prices almost quadrupled in nominal terms between 1967 and 1979, and rose more than 60 percent after adjustment for general inflation.[3]

Despite a recent downward turn in prices, the U.S. Forest Service still foresees "growing economic scarcity of timber and associated increases in the relative prices of stumpage and timber products."[4] The importance of timber products in the determination of housing prices makes this a particularly gloomy prospect. To cope with it, the Forest Service, on the one hand, has proposed a variety of remedies. Most of these proposals call for increasing private forest yields and for intensifying management on private lands, an approach that would seem to imply that the source of supply restrictions is in the private sector.[5] A growing chorus of critics, on the other hand, has concluded that the economic difficulties now facing both the forest industry and consumers of forest products are at least partially attributable to federal policy and to the administration of government-owned forests. The critics have charged that as a result of inefficient public management, net growth on government forests is well below its potential and is substantially less than growth rates on private holdings. Various analysts have attributed this poor record to strict adherence to physical principles and to a neglect of economic considerations in the practice of public forest management.

A substantial volume of evidence on the inefficiency of management practices on government-owned forests has now been accumulated. However, a multitude of specific questions remains unanswered. For example, why has public management resulted in this outcome? Is there any reason to expect that past policies and patterns of behavior will change? What efficiencies or inefficiencies accompany the disposal of government timber to the private sector? How large are the gains and losses that result from specific forest policies and regulations? How are these gains and losses distributed among various segments of society?

2. USDA, Forest Service, *An Analysis*, pp. 279, 288.
3. USDA, Forest Service, *An Assessment*, pp. 247–54.
4. Ibid., p. 254.
5. Ibid., pp. 256–65.

These are among the many questions that contributors to this volume were invited to consider. The contributions of individual authors range over a wide array of forest policy issues. But from this diversity of authors, approaches, and views, a common element emerges: outcomes are different when political competition is substituted for ordinary economic or "price competition" in the allocation of resources.

PUBLIC OWNERSHIP OR COMMON PROPERTY?

Anytime an asset enters the public sector, the structure of property rights whereby the asset may be used or acquired is changed. In place of a system of voluntary exchange and "price rationing," access to these assets becomes dependent, at least in part, on the exercise of political power and on other forms of nonprice competition. In general, this nonprice competition will involve activities that use up resources rather than just transferring them among agents. As a result, part of the value of the assets being allocated may be dissipated in the scramble to acquire them.

Dissipation of value, or rent, is a phenomenon that has been widely documented in the allocation of common property resources. In the case of fisheries, for example, an absence of enforceable rights results in excessive costs and levels of fishing effort; thus reducing the net value of any yield obtained. Similarly, if rights governing the allocation of "government-owned" resources are vague and dependent upon the whims and vagaries of politics or administrative discretion, then the inefficiencies associated with the tragedy of the commons may characterize publicly owned resources as well. Competition to obtain public assets may, for example, take the form of lobbying to obtain special access or support for regulations that would reduce their value to the other users. In general, such activities use resources without producing any good or service that benefits society.

The parallel between publicly held resources and common property is drawn explicitly by one of the authors in this volume, John Grobey (see Chapter 7). Implicitly, however, this theme is encountered repeatedly and in a variety of contexts, from historical accounts of public management to the practice of present-day policy and from broad questions of public management to the narrow details of agency procedures. A point very similar to the "public commons" phenomenon has been raised by Gordon Tullock in his analysis of the competition for government grants and public aid.[6] In seeking such prizes, he notes, potential claimants will bear costs up to the expected level of available benefits. As a result of such competition, the net value or rent that the government grant embodies will be partially or wholly dissipated.

The common property and rent dissipation phenomena are manifested in several ways in the case of public forestlands. The most literal example of public property becoming a commons occurred during the midnineteenth century on the vast pine forests of the Great Lakes region. As Robert Nelson points out in his history of public forest management (see Chapter 2), the government claimed vast expanses of timberland, but provided no effective enforcement of property rights. The result was the legendary "plunder of the pineries" in which settlers and lumbermen alike simply helped themselves. The absence of well-defined property rights and commensurate rewards for proper management also created the worst kind of incentives regarding harvest techniques and reforestation. Because those who took part in the trespass could neither exclude other private harvesters nor make any claim to future timber, they had no reason to practice efficient forestry.

The rent dissipation that takes place on modern day public forests is less obvious, and stems in large part from Forest Service practices regarding harvests and reforestation. For example, on many forests the agency's expenditures for intensive management and postharvest replanting exceed the value of timber that can be grown. As Nelson notes, the pressure to manage and harvest such uneconomic resources generally comes from the timber companies, mills, and local communities that stand to benefit from increased employment and incomes. Consequently, a portion of the value that national forests could provide is unnecessarily dissipated; in this case by requiring revenues from productive forestlands to subsidize economically wasteful harvests on unproductive lands. When harvest revenues cannot cover management expenses it is, of course, the general taxpayer who bears the cost.

A striking example of the rent dissipation that results from political competition for the public timberlands is represented by restric-

6. Gordon Tullock, "Competing for Aid," *Public Choice* 22 (Summer 1975): 41–51.

tions that prohibit the export of logs taken from government forests. As Richard Parks and Judith Cox demonstrate (see Chapter 10), the domestic mill owners are the principal beneficiaries and rent seekers in this case. They compete for public timber by supporting political action to restrict its sale to foreign processors. By excluding a potentially efficient set of users, a portion of the value of such timber is lost. The cost of this inefficiency is shared among the taxpaying public in the form of reduced timber revenues. The quantitative results presented by these authors also demonstrate that the losses born by taxpayers more than outweigh any gains received by mill owners and other beneficiaries.

Another example of political competition by a special interest to gain access to public timber is the practice of reserving a portion of public timber for sale to small businesses. As Mark Schniepp observes, this policy significantly reduces government timber sale revenue and encourages inefficiency by rewarding firms for being "small" under the criteria specified in the program. This preference for small firms has parallels in several other industries, particularly energy where oil import quotas, price controls, and federal tax policy have all favored small firms in one fashion or other. All such favors come at the expense of the public treasury, and there is evidence that much, if not all, of the benefits granted are dissipated by the cost increases that accompany inefficient small production units.

Among those best positioned to benefit from publicly owned resources are the bureaucrats charged with managing them. Here again, the system of property rights that defines public ownership severely restricts the role of price competition. Public managers are precluded from appropriating public resources directly, or from exacting dollar payments that reflect the amount by which management efforts increase the value of such resources. Rather, their reward comes in the form of salary, power, prestige, the perquisites of public office, and the control and administrative discretion that such positions can provide. In general, these rewards are related to the size and range of responsibilities undertaken by the management agency. In more specific terms, William Niskanen postulates that all or most of these goals are positively related to the size of the agency budget, and hence offers a theory of bureaucratic behavior based on budget maximization.[7]

7. William A. Niskanen, *Bureaucracy and Representative Government* (Chicago: Aldine and Atherton, 1971.)

Application of this theory to the realm of public resource administration indicates that the agencies involved will tend to dissipate the
rent available from such resources by excessive or redundant management. Public managers obviously do not seek access to the timber
itself, but they do compete for a share of the benefits or rents it is
capable of providing. (Ronald Johnson presents a more detailed discussion of the budget maximization hypothesis and its application to
the Forest Service in Chapter 4.) The impetus for agency expansion
need not come from any monetary self-interested or greedy motivation; it may result from a zealous belief in the righteousness of the
agency's mission—a characteristic of Gifford Pinchot and his followers. Whatever the source, however, the point remains that those bureaus that succeed in expanding their domain of influence and command over resources are most likely to survive and prosper.

With the output or service produced by the U.S. Forest Service
and Bureau of Land Management (BLM) characterized as public
resource management, the preceding theory is consistent with several facets of the behavior of these agencies. For example, the elusive
"timber famines" repeatedly forecast by the Forest Service in the
early part of this century were used to promote a larger public forest
domain and government regulation of private forest practices. In the
same era, scientific evidence regarding forest hydrology and the
effects of fires in forests was ignored and sometimes misstated by the
Forest Service in attempts to increase the acreage under the agency's
control. In both cases, the intended result was to expand the scope
for public management, a mode of behavior that is consistent with
the budget-maximization model. As Nelson explains, such self-serving
claims are common in the history of public timber management. In a
contemporary context, John Grobey (Chapter 7) finds fault with the
economic and biological analysis the Forest Service has employed in
its bid to promote regulation of logging practices and to justify the
agency's program of postharvest stream rehabilitation.

Perhaps the clearest example of inefficiency and rent dissipation
in the bureaucratic management of public timber arises from the
"allowable cut effect" that accompanies nondeclining even-flow harvest schedules. As Barney Dowdle and Steve Hanke explain, this policy makes the harvest of valuable old growth timber contingent upon
increased expenditures for intensive public management. Here, the
Forest Service has made budget increases a precondition for access to
public timber. Policies that govern the sale of public timber offer

additional examples of excessive public management. Each year the Forest Service devotes time and resources to the task of appraising the fair market value of timber to be sold to private harvesters. According to analysis presented by Dennis Muraoka and Richard Watson (see Chapter 8), these appraisals are redundant, and the information they contain is virtually useless. These authors argue that the same function could be served at a fraction of the cost by different appraisal techniques.

These authors also point out that Forest Service stipulations regarding bids and ultimate payments are structured to require intensive Forest Service monitoring of the actual harvest. If replaced by an alternative bidding strategy, this costly activity could be abandoned. Competition between surface and subsurface users of national forests, a subject addressed by Gary Libecap in Chapter 5, presents an additional arena for the dissipation of rents. In Libecap's estimation, choices among these uses have been primarily dictated by the political interests of the managing agencies (the Forest Service and BLM). As a consequence, there is little reason to believe that the resources are being allocated to their highest valued uses.

A SUMMARY OF THE BOOK

The theme that publicly owned forests have many of the allocation problems plaguing common property resources appears throughout the chapters of this book. Yet, it would be misleading to review the contributions of individual authors solely in these terms. Each contributor's insights and analysis are original; collectively they cover a range of issues much broader than the single topic developed above. In the following pages, each author's major findings and interpretations are briefly summarized.

The history of public forest management, with interpretations firmly grounded in the re-emerging discipline of political economy, is recounted by Robert Nelson (Chapter 2). In a thoughtful essay, he traces the beginning of the U.S. system of public forests to the creation of the first forest reserves by Presidents Harrison and Cleveland under the General Reform Act of 1891. As the author points out, the public forest movement was originally preservationist in spirit, and its most effective political support came from easterners who sought to "perpetuate untouched large areas of natural beauty." The rise of the philosophy of "utilitarian conservation" in public forest management, and the eventual triumph of its "gospel of efficiency," were presided over by the Forest Service's founder and first director, Gifford Pinchot. As Nelson notes, acceptance of the utilitarian ethic was not universal, however, and the creation of the National Park Service and the continuing conflict between these agencies underlines the political nature of public forest management.

Efforts by the Forest Service to build political support for its activities are characterized by Nelson as a moral crusade. Pinchot and his followers cast themselves as protectors of society's interests and as promoters of the efficient use of the nation's forests. As they defined it, their task was to remain ever alert in defending public forestlands from the wasteful excesses of stockmen, miners, railroads, and above all, the timber companies. In their crusade, the overriding purpose of federal forests was the provision of housing for the American family. In this light, it is ironic that private timber companies soon surpassed the Forest Service in the application of scientific methods to forestry and in the growth and yields obtained. (Similar points are presented in chapters of this volume by Dowdle and Hanke, Nelson and Pugliaresi, and Deacon.)

The prospect of "timber famines" ever looming on the horizon played an important role in rationalizing public involvement in the allocation of forest resources. Nelson traces such prophesies back to 1876, and notes that Pinchot later used the issue time and again to support extensions of Forest Service activity. In 1910 and again in 1919 he used the famine argument to promote public regulation of private forest practices. During the same era, unsupported scientific claims regarding forest hydrology and the effects of fire in forests were used to argue for an expanded Forest Service domain. In more recent times, the specter of a somewhat less dire sounding "timber shortage" has been raised. Throughout the 1950s and 1960s the Forest Service repeatedly warned that growth in demand would outstrip available supplies, and insisted that the practice of more intensive forestry was the nation's only hope for salvation. The "selling" of the agency's activities in particular and the public role in forestry in general, through the formulation and perpetuation of such myths, is a central theme in Nelson's history.

Following World War II public forests became an increasingly important source of timber supply. Nelson reviews both the major items of public forest legislation and the record of public forest harvest policies during this era. The former are found to be vague and sometimes contradictory, while the latter are often economically wasteful. A striking example of waste in national forest management is the practice of spending more for selling timber and for subsequent reforestation than the timber sale can actually generate in revenue. According to the Forest Service's own calculations, 22 percent of the federal timber harvest in 1978 was uneconomic in this sense. Here, Nelson is careful to dispel the notion that the public somehow gains from such wasteful practices.

In Nelson's view, the true salvation of the nation's public forests lies in the emergence of a new science of forest management, one based on economic analysis of the benefits and costs of alternative management strategies. The author is not, however, optimistic about the chances for its implementation. This lack of optimism on the part of Nelson and other analysts is largely responsible for recent proposals to divest much of the public forestlands to the private sector.

The timber and wood-processing industries in the United States are affected by a variety of government policies, including the direct regulation of logging practices, the taxation of private timber holdings, and harvesting patterns on publicly owned forests. Barney Dowdle and Steve Hanke (Chapter 3) survey this broad range of issues and find that public policy toward this industry has led to uncertainty and instability in overall timber supply; a condition that has fostered a migration of the industry away from the Pacific Northwest where it is heavily dependent on government timber holdings, toward the south where it is not. They point out that since World War II the timber industry has been undergoing a transformation from an extractive to an agricultural industry. This transition from old growth to second-growth supplies is still underway, and during the crucial period until its completion, the nation will be critically dependent on timber from public lands.

Dowdle and Hanke review the legislation that regulates federal forestlands and find that it fails to prescribe management practices in any detail or to limit the discretion of the administering agencies. One result of this is that the management of public forests—particularly harvest levels—has been rendered practically immune to economic considerations. As the authors put it, "the permissiveness of the Forest Service's legislative mandate invites intense political pressure in the determination of what these (harvest) allowances will be."

A major specific flaw in public forest policy is the failure to include interest charges for inventories of standing timber in the formulation of harvest schedules, a practice that results in excessively long rotations. The productivity of federal forestlands is limited further by the "nondeclining even-flow" constraint prescribed for harvests of old growth. Associated with this is the "allowable cut effect," whereby investments that enhance growth are artificially made to appear attractive simply because they permit harvest schedules to circumvent the nondeclining even-flow limitation. The result, as Dowdle and Hanke point out, is a highly convenient situation in which practically any growth-enhancing investment the Forest Service or Bureau of Land Management care to undertake can be justified. The authors also briefly review state and local taxation of private timber holdings and the regulation of logging and reforestation practices.

In response to the poor record of public timber management, Dowdle and Hanke propose limiting the government's role in timber production by selling the most productive public holdings to the private sector. Short of this, they recommend requiring public timber management agencies to incorporate interest charges in planning harvest schedules and to be explicit in the calculation of multiple-use costs and benefits. The result, they conclude, would be national forests that are more productive at providing all of the goods and services demanded of them.

While many have criticized Forest Service policy in the past, few have attempted to explain or rationalize that policy in terms of a consistent set of agency objectives or a coherent theory of government behavior. This important issue forms the basis of Ronald Johnson's chapter (Chapter 4). In traditional theories of government behavior, public servants were viewed as both enlightened and benevolent individuals who immediately shed the cloak of self-interest upon entering the public sector. Both Johnson and other students of modern political economy have rejected this characterization because it assumes that public employees have different goals and motivations than other members of society. Modern political economists, most notably Niskanen, have developed a theory of bureau behavior based on self-interest in which budget maximization becomes the de facto goal of bureaucracies. Within this theory, Johnson finds a model capable of explaining and predicting certain facets of Forest Service policy.

The budget-maximization theory treats the size of an agency's budget as a surrogate for the power, prestige, and perquisites of public office. Hence, the pursuit of these goals indirectly leads to budget maximization as an agency objective. The degree to which this objective is met depends largely on the process whereby agency budgets and policy are reviewed. As Johnson points out, congressional review committees tend to be dominated by representatives of constituencies who have a particularly intense interest in the agency's function, an arrangement that generally predisposes the review committee to be sympathetic to the agency's requests. In a broad sense, Johnson finds Forest Service behavior consistent with this characterization.

The fact that forests can provide a variety of services, however, complicates the pursuit of larger budgets. According to Johnson, the Forest Service's review committees have been dominated by constituents who are primarily interested in timber. When demands for recreational use of national forests rose following World War II, the Forest Service, seeking to expand the scope of its activities into recreation, found itself at odds with its timber-dominated reviewers. During this period, the Forest Service pursued the multiple-use management principle, and lobbied diligently to secure the Multiple-Use and Sustained-Yield Act. Johnson finds this consistent with the budget-maximization theory, since a multiple-use policy is likely to require more intensive planning and regulation than a policy based on dominant use. In examining Forest Service policy toward harvest schedules, Johnson echoes a point made by Dowdle and Hanke that the even-flow constraint makes increased timber harvests contingent upon increased agency funding for intensive management and reforestation. He goes on to point out that the result is a management scheme that holds down timber harvests on national forests, thus satisfying recreationists and preservationists without large reductions in Forest Service appropriations. Johnson provides additional evidence for the budget-maximization theory from an examination of the jurisdictional pattern of forest management expenditures.

The general theory of bureaucratic behavior is explored further by Gary Libecap (Chapter 5) who examines an often overlooked aspect of national forest management — the development of subsurface minerals. In studies by both private and government agencies, the Forest Service and Bureau of Land Management have been criticized for impeding and delaying mineral fuel production on public lands. As Libecap points out, the management of federal lands is characterized by overlapping agency jurisdictions, and the surface management agency responsible for granting leases and permits to drill often has no role in the actual mineral production process if development should take place. As a consequence, Libecap hypothesizes, the surface management agencies will do little to expedite mineral development. Moreover, Libecap postulates, to the extent that mineral development may interfere with surface uses and thus potentially disrupt the interest group relations of surface management agencies, these agencies will actually discourage mineral fuel development.

Libecap presents evidence from a variety of sources to support his case. He notes that the Bureau of Land Management has used administrative discretion vigorously in withdrawing land from mineral development and placing it in protected status. The Forest Service limits mineral production by imposing restrictions on mineral development leases. An example is the prohibition of surface occupancy, a condition that necessitates directional drilling, helicopter transportation, and other costly production practices. Libecap also argues that the use of "contingent rights stipulations" clauses that require environmental review *after* leasing, increases uncertainty to potential leasing firms. He also provides evidence on delays in the leasing process. Evidently, delays of two years are not uncommon in processing Forest Service and BLM lease applications and drilling permits. Libecap further notes that delays tend to be much longer on federal land than on state land. Shorter delays on state land are consistent with the Niskanen model of bureau behavior, since state agencies face competition in leasing mineral rights from other state agencies and from the federal government. The federal agencies, on the other hand, have much larger holdings and are thus in a stronger position to dictate terms to potential developers. Libecap finds further support for his model in comparisons of processing delays between the Forest Service and Bureau of Land Management.

Robert Nelson and Lucian Pugliaresi (Chapter 6) examine alternative harvest strategies on forestlands managed by the Bureau of Land Management. These forests, commonly referred to as the O & C Lands, are located in western Oregon and rank among the world's most productive. The BLM harvest from western Oregon has traditionally been dictated by a nondeclining even-flow policy, and since the early 1960s harvest levels have been roughly constant. Although several analysts have criticized the even-flow strategy, few have attempted to demonstrate the magnitude of its effect on actual harvests. Those who defend the even-flow doctrine have typically argued that it stabilizes job opportunities in communities dependent on timber harvests. To date, however, this point has largely been offered as an article of faith without hard analysis to indicate how efficient it is in promoting this goal.

Nelson and Pugliaresi employ a model of the BLM forestlands to quantitatively examine the harvest policy issue. They compare four timber harvest schedules: the first simply replicates the nondeclining even-flow policy used by the BLM. The second, termed a "demographic harvest option," schedules harvests from the O & C Lands to match changes in the demand for housing. The third alternative plans public timber harvests to offset swings in private harvests, thus dampening overall employment shocks from harvests on public and private forestlands. It thus represents a comprehensive community stability approach. The final alternative accelerates harvests temporarily, and then allows them to decline to the maximum sustainable yield available with intensive forest management. Notably, none of the alternatives were designed to maximize a narrowly defined economic objective such as net present value, and all alternatives were constrained to prevent yields from ever falling below levels attainable with the traditional even-flow policy.

The results of these comparisons strikingly demonstrate the shortcomings of present BLM harvest strategies and, by implication, the use of similar strategies by the Forest Service. The demographic harvest option, for example, yielded simulated timber supplies that significantly exceed the even-flow policy, and simultaneously provided a closer match to future demands. When the community stability option was simulated and compared to existing policies, the result was a significant increase in timber supply and timber-related job opportunities, with no sacrifice in overall community stability. A partial analysis of the accelerated harvest option also yielded results that dominated the even-flow approach.

Despite such evidence and mounting criticism from other analysts, federal timber management agencies have shown little inclination to adopt policies in closer accord with the public interest. As Nelson and Pugliaresi point out, these agencies are "trustees for resources owned by the American public"; as such, it is their obligation to "plan their harvests to maximize the value of timber holdings, including commodity and environmental values." As the authors' analysis demonstrates, the policies now in force are not fulfilling this obligation.

John Grobey (Chapter 7) addresses the debate regarding the effect of timber harvesting on salmon yields and the regulation of logging practices to protect salmon runs. In his evaluation of this controversy, attention is focused on the state of scientific knowledge regarding the relationship between logging and salmon stocks, and the way in which scientific evidence has been interpreted by those responsible for making forest resource management policy. To date, claims that logging severely impairs salmon production, together with estimates of dollar losses involved, have formed the basis for reductions in harvests from public lands, costly restrictions on private harvesting practices, and expenditure of public funds for stream rehabilitation.

Grobey separates the issues in the debate into two categories — biological and economic. Despite the superficial plausibility of an interaction between salmon yields and logging activity, direct attempts to demonstrate and quantify this relationship have been largely unsuccessful. This stems in part from the complex life cycle of the species and from the possibility that an increase in mortality at one life stage may be fully or partially offset by compensating decreases at other stages. The potential effects of logging on spawning and propagation of juvenile salmon stem from increased erosion and sedimentation, amplification of low flow conditions, changes in stream temperature and chemistry, and other factors. However, reductions in survival of juvenile salmon cannot be directly translated into proportional reductions in eventual harvests. In fact, the two may not even be directly related, since reductions in spawning in one area may relax food or habitat constraints elsewhere, and thus permit compensating increases to occur.

The economic issues addressed by Grobey primarily concern the use of average rather than marginal values to represent losses. The failure of policymakers to recognize the common property or open access nature of fisheries tends to result in the exhaustion of any net economic benefits they are capable of providing. The use of average values in evaluating fishery habitat protection tends to bias estimated benefits upwards, thus overstating the costs that result from logging. Estimates of economic losses are further complicated by the nonmarket nature of recreational fishing values and by the likelihood that such values are not proportional to the sport catch.

Grobey concludes by drawing attention to the asymmetry between consumptive (timber) uses of public forests and nonconsumptive uses such as recreation. The former are price rationed while the latter are offered free of charge. Since they preclude the use of the forests for producing timber, these nonconsumptive uses are clearly not without costs. Predictably, the absence of an explicit price gives rise to an excess demand for such uses and necessitates some other (nonprice) form of rationing. As Grobey points out, the process of gaining "access to private benefits at public expense exhibits many characteristics strikingly similar to the characteristics of open-access resources of a commons such as a fishery." This is, of course, precisely the point developed in the preceding section of this chapter.

The process whereby federal timber is sold to private harvesters is evaluated by Dennis Muraoka and Richard Watson (Chapter 8). Their analysis focuses on Forest Service procedures, although methods used by the BLM are broadly similar. As a criterion for their evaluation, the authors propose maximization of the net economic value of all the resources provided by publicly owned forests. As the authors point out, timber sale procedures may fail to maximize net value if they fail to select the most efficient harvester, artificially distort the timing of timber harvests, or require unnecessarily high administrative or contract monitoring costs.

Muraoka and Watson examine, in turn, four important components of the timber sale process: the appraisal of public timber, the method of sale, the bidding procedure, and the timing of payments to the government. Prior to each sale the Forest Service undertakes a costly series of appraisals designed to estimate the stumpage value of the timber subject to sale. The appraisals are intended to serve as a floor for acceptable bids from private harvesters. As Muraoka and Watson point out, however, such appraisals are redundant and wasteful in the presence of competition and an efficient sale method. Their empirical analysis also indicates that government revenues could be increased by using sealed bids rather than oral bids for final contract determination.

Current bidding procedures require firms to submit separate bids for each major species represented in the sale. The authors argue that this process may fail to select the most efficient harvesters and may also encourage inefficient and wasteful logging practices. Payments to the government are computed as the product of bid price times the volume of timber removed for each species. This form of "species bidding" can induce harvesters to abandon valuable timber if its bid price is high. Furthermore, since the procedure requires the Forest Service to monitor contracts closely in order to measure the volume of timber removed, it is costly for the agency to administer. The timing of payments for public sales is an additional source of inefficiency in the sale process. Payments are made not when contracts are awarded, but when the harvesting actually takes place. Because the government does not charge interest for delayed revenue, this practice reduces the present value of government receipts and encourages harvesting firms to delay harvests in the hope that prices will rise.

A variety of recommendations to correct these inefficiencies are offered by Muraoka and Watson. To reduce the costs due to appraisals, they suggest a system of postsale appraisals for only a sample of sales, and the use of statistical techniques to estimate fair market value. They also recommend scrapping the existing system of species bidding in favor of a single overall bid for the entire volume of timber in each sale, and for replacing the oral auctions with a sealed bidding procedure. To avoid the inefficiencies due to improper timing, the authors argue in favor of lump sum payment due either at the time of sale or in installments with interest charged at competitive rates.

Each year a program instituted by the U.S. Forest Service and the Small Business Administration reserves a predetermined share of timber sold from national forests for firms having 500 or fewer employees and meeting other small business criteria. This small business setaside program is addressed by Mark Schniepp (Chapter 9). If, in a given year, small businesses fail to secure a predetermined share of federal timber in open sales, then special sales are set aside for bidding by qualifying small firms only. The share of federal timber affected by this program is potentially very large. In early 1983 the small business share exceeded 50 percent in all but one marketing area in the far west, and exceeded 70 percent in six marketing areas. Critics of the program have argued that it earmarks higher quality timber sales to setaside status, that it results in lower winning bids for federal timber than open sales would yield, and that it discriminates against ineligible firms and the communities that depend on them for employment and income. In this chapter, Mark Schniepp describes the setaside program in detail and subjects these charges to empirical scrutiny.

The first hypothesis, regarding bias in the selection of sales for the setaside program, is examined by comparing sale characteristics in setaside versus open timber sales. In a statistical model, such sale attributes as timber quality, logging, and road construction costs, the volume of timber per acre and other factors are related to the Forest Service's choice of sale status. The results of Schniepp's quantitative analysis indicate that setaside sales typically involve higher quality timber, lower logging costs, longer contract durations, and generally more economically attractive timber resources than do open sales.

To assess the impact of setasides on federal timber sale revenues, the author constructs a statistical model that relates many of the sale attributes listed above, plus other factors, to the amount of the winning bid. Included in the set of additional sale characteristics is a variable indicating whether or not the sale was in the setaside program. Thus, taking into account quality differences, Schniepp was able to determine whether and to what extent the setaside program affected levels of winning bids. His results indicate that the program significantly reduced federal timber sale revenue over the period 1973–1981. When expressed in 1982 dollars, timber revenue losses for the Douglas fir region of the Pacific Northwest (Westside Region 6) totalled to $180 million during this period.

The federal government and the governments of most western states presently prohibit the export of logs harvested from public lands. Furthermore, important nonsubstitution provisions in these laws are designed to prevent firms from exporting private timber and replacing it with timber purchased from government lands. The economic effects of these export bans, and the pattern of resulting gains and losses among affected groups, is addressed by Richard Parks and Judith Cox (Chapter 10). At present, Washington is the only Pacific coast state that permits logs to be exported from government lands. However, an export ban has been proposed for Washington's publicly owned timber, and the analysis of its potential impact is the focus of their analysis.

The authors demonstrate that the proposed export ban would have two distinct effects. The first arises from a shift in timber supply away from the export market and toward the domestic market. As a result of this supply shift, the export price would rise and the domestic price would fall. As Parks and Cox explain, a strong preference for high quality logs in the export market permits differences between domestic and export prices to persist. The second effect of the proposed ban would be felt in the market for processed lumber and other wood products. With a restriction on the available supply of exportable logs and a resulting increase in their price, exports of lumber from the United States would be made more attractive to foreign consumers. Because there is no ban on exports of lumber, the unmet demand for log exports would be partially rechanneled into a demand for lumber and wood product exports.

Using data and market conditions for the year 1978, Parks and Cox estimate the impact of such an export ban on prices and trade flows, and then use these estimates to compute the gains and losses to various participants in the log and lumber markets. Because the ban would partially convert a foreign demand for U.S. logs into a demand for finished wood products, domestic processors would be among the major beneficiaries of such a policy. Those private timber producers who sell primarily to the export market would also gain from higher export prices. Losses, on the other hand, are borne almost entirely by the taxpayers and citizens of the state. These losses stem from the diversion of public timber away from the high-priced export market and toward the domestic market. Other losers are the public and private timber producers who sell exclusively to the domestic market, and thus suffer when domestic log prices are reduced.

It is significant that the losses suffered by those harmed greatly exceed the gains to potential beneficiaries. The annual sums involved were estimated at $42 million in gains and $63 million in losses. Thus, in the process of transferring wealth from the taxpayers and citizens of Washington State to wood processors and private log exporters, a sum of $21 million is lost to pure waste. Moreover, this loss estimate excludes any costs imposed on our trading partners abroad. In reflecting on the political economy of the policy, Parks and Cox note that, on the one hand, the domestic mill owners — those who stand to gain most from a log export ban — represent a small group with a highly concentrated interest in the outcome. As such, the costs of organizing lobbying efforts and eliminating free riders appear sufficiently low to permit them to influence policy in their favor. The interests of taxpayers, on the other hand, are much more widely dispersed, and are evidently not well represented by the agencies given responsibility to manage publicly owned resources in their behalf.

Because private forestry decisions are affected by a variety of government programs, an understanding of private forest practices and the forces that shape them is necessary for the evaluation of public policy. To this end, the final chapter in this book presents a nontechnical guide to the economics of forest management. In this chapter, Robert Deacon develops the general principle of comparing benefits and costs, and adopts this principle as a unifying theme for analyzing a variety of forest management decisions. The classic forest rotation problem, which involves the choice of an optimal harvest age for current and future stands of trees, is analyzed in terms of the decision of whether to harvest a currently growing stand of trees or to wait for an additional year of growth. As the general solution to this problem demonstrates, the rotation age that maximizes present value will depend, in predictable ways, upon such economic factors as stumpage prices, real interest rates, and reforestation costs.

Use of the benefit-cost framework to evaluate policy issues is exemplified by the analysis of private sector responses to alternative forms of forest taxation. As the author shows, the imposition of severance taxes tends to extend rotation times and to result in the withdrawal of marginal land from future reforestation. Because harvest costs are typically not deductible, such taxes can also lead to the abandonment of marginal lands prior to harvest. A property tax, levied annually as a fraction of the market value of standing timber, acts in much the same way as an increase in the interest rate in that it tends to reduce rotation ages and prevents the reforestation of marginal forestlands.

The general benefit-cost approach also provides an appropriate vehicle for the analysis of policy on forestlands managed by the government. Although the proper goals for private and public sector managers may differ due to the presence of externalities, the principle of comparing benefits and costs is appropriate in both realms. The author notes that divergences in private allocations and socially efficient outcomes might differ if, for example, market prices fail to reflect marginal social benefits or if the presence of standing forests confers nonmarket benefits or costs. If such differences were demonstrated and quantified, then the benefit-cost framework used to analyze private decisions could be used to design efficient public policies to cope with these problems.

The management agencies actually responsible for carrying out policy on public forests apparently make little attempt to compare the costs and benefits of alternative courses of action. As Deacon notes, this disregard for economic considerations and the strict adherence to physical principles in managing the public forests unnecessarily reduce the value of timber production without generating offsetting increases in nontimber benefits.

CONCLUSIONS

Several of the contributors to this volume have pointed to a "timber supply problem" in the United States, and have recommended ways in which it might be resolved. The public officials responsible for carrying out federal policy on the nation's forests apparently agree that a problem exists, but take a much different view of the inherent causes and potential remedies. In 1981 the Forest Service summarized the recent history and current status of the forestlands of the United States, and reached the following conclusion:

> The rising trends in net annual timber growth illustrate a striking success story in American forestry. In the late 1800s and extending through the early decades of the 1900s, when the nation's timber resources were being rapidly depleted, concern about future supplies led to the development of a broad array of policies and programs, such as fire protection, tree planting, research, and public ownership. The large increases in net annual growth since 1952 are presumably a result of these policies and programs.[8]

Later in the same report, the authors cited as cause for concern rising real timber and lumber prices and projections that future rates of growth of demand will exceed growth of supply. In the Forest Service's estimation, we are entering an age of "growing economic scarcity of timber and associated increases in the relative prices of stumpage and timber products."[9]

To resolve this pending economic crisis, the Forest Service has proposed a variety of measures intended to enhance timber supplies. Among these are recommendations to reforest currently vacant lands; to clear and restock some sites with more valuable species; to increase use of genetically improved stock, precommercial thinning, fertilization, and advanced harvest techniques; and to improve fire management and insect control. Notably absent from the list of possible supply remedies is any mention of policy and management changes on government-owned forests. In particular, the possibility of increased harvests from the old growth forests of the west is summarily dismissed.

In the agency's opinion, opportunities for enhancing growth and supplies are now confined almost exclusively to private forest hold-

8. USDA, Forest Service, *An Assessment*, p. 234.
9. Ibid., p. 254.

ings.[10] According to the Forest Service's analysis, private sector own-ers, particularly in the nonindustrial category, often pass up such opportunities because they lack the necessary capital, are not suffi-ciently knowledgeable of proper timber practices, or have planning horizons that are too short. Accordingly, the agency concludes that "there is a strong justification for publicly supported cost sharing and technical assistance programs . . . [because] existing economic opportunities for management intensification on the farmer and other private ownerships are not likely to be realized in any substan-tive way without such programs."[11]

To those who have studied federal forest policy and the behavior of agencies responsible for carrying it out, this is quite obviously a plea for business as usual. We now have over a century of experience with federal forest ownership, and almost eighty years of experience with management by the Forest Service and the Bureau of Land Management. With the weight of evidence that has now accumulated regarding the inefficiency characterizing this regime, it would seem the burden of proof should now be shifted to those who would de-fend the present set of policies and institutions.

The contributors to this volume have, in their findings and recom-mendations, sketched out the elements of an alternative national for-est policy. Several authors have recommended divesting the most productive timber-producing forests to the private sector while re-moving from timber production entirely those areas that are best suited to noncommodity uses. Short of such divestiture, a policy of timber management that explicitly imputes interest charges to stand-ing stocks and evaluates old growth harvest policies on the basis of net present values rather than a set of arbitrary physical rules, would better serve the interests of taxpayers and consumers. Similarly, the substitution of economic criteria for such administrative slogans as "multiple use" in the allocation of forestlands among surface versus subsurface uses or recreation versus timber generation, hold the pros-pect for increasing all of the valuable outputs that forests can pro-vide. Additional areas for economic improvement lie in the design of policies that govern the disposal and ultimate use of timber from government lands. Recommended policy changes in this realm would reduce government expenses for timber sale management, encourage selection of the most efficient harvesters for federal timber, and

10. Ibid., pp. 256–64.
11. Ibid., p. 255.

ensure that supplies are ultimately allocated to those users—whether domestic or foreign—who value them most highly.

It is, perhaps, a bit quixotic to recommend an infusion of new thinking and analytical skills into agencies that have exhibited resistance to change and have been plagued by institutional inbreeding in leadership since the turn of the century. Yet, even the remotest chance of reform makes the effort worthwhile because the economic stakes are so large. The nation's forestlands, public and private, are *potentially* among its most valuable assets. Without a more enlightened national forest policy, however, one that truly represents the interests of the American public, the full potential of these resources will remain unrealized.

Chapter 2

MYTHOLOGY INSTEAD OF ANALYSIS
The Story of Public Forest Management
Robert H. Nelson

INTRODUCTION

The national forests, administered by the Forest Service in the Department of Agriculture, contain 142 million acres of forestlands located in forty states.[1] Around 80 million of these acres hold sufficient timber and have other characteristics to qualify as commercial timberland. In the Department of the Interior, the Bureau of Land Management (BLM) manages around 2 million acres of prime timberland on the Oregon and California grant lands and Coos Bay Wagon Road lands in western Oregon (the "O & C Lands"), plus limited amounts of timber in other states. Combined, timber harvests from Forest Service and BLM lands in recent years have constituted a little more than 20 percent of the nation's total timber supply. Federal forests contain a much higher proportion of the total standing timber inventory—in excess of 40 percent. Federal forests also contain some of the most scenic areas in the United States. Every year millions of Americans hike along trails and camp in these areas. In 1980

Disclaimer: The author is a member of the Office of Policy Analysis, U.S. Department of the Interior. The Interior Department does not necessarily agree with the analysis or conclusions of this chapter.

1. For basic forestry statistics, see U.S. Department of Agriculture, Forest Service, *An Assessment of the Forest and Rangeland Situation in the United States* (January 1980).

a total of 234 million visitor days were spent in the national forests. Though fees are charged for only a small fraction of these visits, a conservative estimate shows the value of recreational activities to exceed the revenue from timber sales. In short, the management of public forests is a matter of major national concern.

This paper tells the story of public forest management, focusing on the conflict between two very different outlooks – that of the professional forester and that of the professional economist. The former perspective has dominated public forest management, which partially accounts for the wide tendency to see trees, wood, and other forest products as ends in themselves. Foresters have sought to formulate physical output goals and then to manage public forests to achieve these goals. By contrast, economists have emphasized that the products of public forests should be seen as inputs to the end of maximizing the total value of public forests to society. Where marketable outputs are produced, market prices usually provide a good estimate of their social value. During the past two decades the economics perspective has posed a basic challenge to professional forestry and public forest management, a challenge that has not yet been resolved.

Since the days of Gifford Pinchot, founder of the Forest Service, foresters have been taught to believe, first, that a technically correct answer exists to forest management questions and, second, that society should defer to such answers once they are shown by professional forestry experts. Indeed, acceptance of this viewpoint has been equated with public virtue and morality; those who challenged it have often been portrayed as special interests seeking to undermine the public interest. Especially in its early days, the high morale of the Forest Service rested at least as much on a strong sense of moral righteousness as on technical proficiency in forest management. Economists and other observers have found in such attitudes a virtual gospel for which the forestry profession has been the keeper of the faith.[2] Public forest management is seen as having been dominated by a set of myths, which offered great emotional appeal but which were lacking in scientific qualities. The history of public forest management shows many examples of a clash between an urge to create

2. See William A. Duerr and Jean B. Duerr, "The Role of Faith in Forest Resource Management," in Fay Rumsey and William A. Duerr, eds., *Sciences in Forestry: A Book of Readings* (Philadelphia: W. B. Saunders Co., 1975).

forestry myths with wide public appeal and the demands of more rigorous analytical thinking.

THE FIRST FOREST RESERVES

When the United States first acquired the public lands, they seemed to possess limitless amounts of timber, far more than the nation would require within the forseeable future. In fact this impression was largely valid; even in 1980 there still remain large areas of virgin "old growth" timber in the Pacific Northwest and Alaska. The Forest Service currently obtains about 85 percent of its harvest from old growth forests and does not expect to harvest the last old growth stands for at least another fifty to one hundred years.

The rapid economic growth of the United States in the nineteenth century created heavy new demands for timber. Although much of the available timber was found on public lands, the public land laws had not been designed with timber production in mind. The Preemption, Homestead, and other key land laws were intended to promote agricultural settlement by small farmers. In most cases, they limited the sale or other disposal of land to 160 acres per individual. Originally, there were no special provisions for sale of timber.

Not surprisingly, when the nation's requirements for timber collided with the land laws, the laws gave way. When settlers needed timber, they simply took it from nearby public lands. Over a huge expanse of public domain, the government lacked any effective means to prevent timber trespassing, and in many cases not only settlers, but lumber companies and mill operators, helped themselves. The federal government shifted back and forth between periods of acquiescence, with little effort to prevent timber trespass, and periods of active, if generally futile, attempts at enforcement.

The absence of any satisfactory way of obtaining public timber created incentives of the worst kind for those who actually harvested such timber. There was no reason for trespassers to be concerned about employing proper harvesting techniques or reforestation, since they would have no claim on future timber from the site. In essence, the public forests were a giant timber commons and the failure to establish property rights created the usual adverse incentives of the commons—to rush out to get ahead of others in exploiting the resource. Even without this problem, the huge supplies and very low price of timber provided little incentive to reforest. Like air or water, timber on the stump was close to a free good.

These factors were at work in the harvesting of timber from the vast pine forests of the upper Great Lakes states of Michigan, Wisconsin, and Minnesota. The story of the "looting" or "plunder" of the pineries is a classic in American forestry lore—generally interpreted as a moralistic tale in which public good loses out to private evil. The retelling of this lore has exerted an influence on federal timber policy continuing to the present day. One writer recalls the "thievery on a monumental order, organized and financed by business interests that did not hesitate to use bribery, intimidation, and violence to make a dishonest dollar."[3]

By the 1860s and 1870s the widespread uncontrolled harvesting of timber on public lands had begun to attract national attention. An 1869 report of the Michigan legislature warned that "generations yet unborn will bless or curse our memory according as we preserve for them what the munificent past has so richly bestowed upon us, or as we lend our influence to continue and accelerate the wasteful destruction everywhere at work in our beautiful state."[4] Commissioner Williamson of the General Land Office stated that "a national calamity is being rapidly and surely brought upon this country by the useless destruction of the forests."[5] The warnings of George Marsh's famous study, *Man and Nature*, including the critical influence of forests in controlling erosion and preserving water flow, were widely discussed.[6] Reflecting such concerns, the Timber Culture Act of 1873 provided that settlers could acquire title to 160 acres by planting and sustaining trees for ten years on a quarter of this acreage. In 1875 growing public interest in forestry led to the founding of the American Forestry Association.

By this time there was also considerable recognition of the need for new laws to control the disposal of public lands chiefly valuable for timber. In 1878 Congress finally passed such a law—the Timber and Stone Act. The Act allowed sale of 160 acres of timberland in

3. Henry Clepper, *Professional Forestry in the United States* (Baltimore: Johns Hopkins University Press, 1971), p. 8.

4. Samuel T. Dana, *Forest and Range Policy: Its Development in the United States* (New York: McGraw-Hill, 1956), p. 77.

5. Ibid.

6. George Perkins Marsh, *Man and Nature* (1864; reprint ed., Cambridge, Mass.: Harvard University Press, 1965).

the states of California, Nevada, Oregon and Washington, but limited use of the timber to the purchaser. Not surprisingly, this limitation proved virtually impossible to enforce; there was instead widespread acquisition of timberlands for speculation and sale to timber companies. In some cases, timber companies would round up a crowd from a tavern or other gathering place, shepherd the enlistees down to the land office, and have them sign over the timberlands immediately thereafter. Around 15 million acres were eventually sold under the Timber and Stone Act, most of it ending up in the hands of timber companies. The Preemption Act and the commutation provision of the Homestead Act were also subject to similar manipulations.[7]

The failure of timber disposal laws would lead eventually to the retention of public timber in the national forests. The first small step in this direction occurred in 1876 when a rider was slipped through attached to an appropriations bill providing $2,000 for the Agriculture Department to collect statistics and report on forestry problems to the Congress. Also in 1876, legislation to set aside national forest reserves was first introduced. In 1882 the third report on forestry by the Agriculture Department recommended that "the principle bodies of timber land still remaining the property of the government . . . be withdrawn from sale or grant under the existing modes for conveying the public lands, and that they be placed under regulation calculated to secure an economical use of the existing timber, and a proper revenue from its sale."[8] Finally, after years of inaction, a short section was added at the last moment to the General Reform Act of 1891, providing for the creation by the President of forest reserves. The section attracted little notice and was passed with little debate. The foremost early historian of federal forest policy, John Ise, was of the view that "it is fairly certain that no general forest reservation measure, plainly understood to be such, and unconnected with other measures, would ever have had the slightest chance of passing Congress."[9]

Within two years President Harrison had established the first forest reserves containing 13 million acres. President Cleveland added an-

---

7. For histories of the public lands, see Paul W. Gates, *History of Public Land Law Development* (Washington, D.C.: Government Printing Office, 1968); Benjamin H. Hibbard, *A History of Public Land Policies* (1924; reprint ed., Madison: University of Wisconsin Press, 1965); and Roy M. Robbins, *Our Landed Heritage: The Public Domain, 1776-1970* (1942; reprint ed., Lincoln: University of Nebraska Press, 1976).

8. Dana, *Forest and Range Policy*, p. 82.

9. Cited in ibid., p. 101.

other 4.5 million acres in 1893. At this point, however, additions were halted until the question of management policy for the reserves could be decided.

THE CREATION OF THE FOREST SERVICE

Until 1891 the only lands set aside in reserves had been for the purpose of preserving them in their natural condition. Indeed, much of the support for the 1891 forest reserves legislation had come from preservationists seeking to enlarge the area in which timber harvesting and other commercial activities were precluded. According to one observer, the main forces behind the creation of the forest reserves were "the drive by wilderness groups to perpetuate untouched large areas of natural beauty, by eastern arboriculturists and botanists to save trees for the future and by western water users, both large corporations and small owners, to preserve their water supply by controlling silting."[10]

However, in a forerunner of current wilderness controversies, many in the west strongly opposed the withdrawal from productive use of large new acreages in forest reserves. In 1896 the National Academy of Sciences appointed a study commission to consider the future of the forest reserves. The commission included Gifford Pinchot, then a young little-known forester. Pinchot strongly opposed pure preservation and instead favored a policy of maximum use; the forest reserves, he believed, were "made to be used, not just to look at."[11] The commission supported Pinchot's ideas and issued a report in 1897 firmly backing the management of the reserves for productive uses including timber harvesting. Moreover, it considered that users of the forest might be made to pay an appropriate charge.

In June 1897 President McKinley signed the Forest Reserve Act, the "organic" act of the Forest Service. The Act provided authority to establish necessary rules and regulations for forest reserves in order to "regulate their occupancy and use." Sale of timber was specifically allowed for the appraised price, although limited to "dead, matured or large growth of trees." Gradually, as Forest Service har-

10. Samuel P. Hays, *Conservation and the Gospel of Efficiency: The Progressive Conservation Movement, 1890-1920* (Cambridge, Mass.: Harvard University Press, 1959), p. 264.

11. Gifford Pinchot, *Breaking New Ground* (New York: Harcourt, Brace and Co., 1947), p. 125.

vesting increased, this restriction was to be interpreted very flexibly by the Forest Service until sued on the matter in the 1970s. Further forest reserves could be created where the creation served the purpose either of "securing favorable conditions of water flows" or "to furnish a continuous supply of timber." [12]

Administration of the forest reserves was assigned to the General Land Office in the Interior Department, which had a staff possessing little knowledge of forestry. Pinchot became Chief of the Division of Forestry in the Agriculture Department in 1898, and he soon decided that efficient administration of the forest reserves could be achieved only by their transfer to his division.

When Theodore Roosevelt became President in 1901, he quickly set about defining the themes of his administration. Pinchot obtained an audience with Roosevelt and persuaded him to propose in his first message to Congress that timber management "should be united in the Bureau of Forestry" in the Agriculture Department. [13] But Congress was not yet ready to go along with this idea, in part, because it was not yet prepared to agree with Pinchot that the national forests should be given over to such intensive forestry management. Pinchot thereupon embarked on an energetic campaign to secure transfer of the reserves. At Pinchot's suggestion, Roosevelt created a committee to study the organization of government scientific efforts, on which Pinchot served and which endorsed the transfer. In 1905 the American Forest Congress was held in Washington, D.C., and provided the final impetus. The Congress brought together a wide range of leading citizens, including the president of the Northern Pacific Railroad and the National Lumber Manufacturers. Strong support across a wide spectrum of opinion spurred passage of the Transfer Act, signed on February 1, 1905.

In a famous statement actually drafted by Pinchot, Secretary of Agriculture James Wilson laid out the broad directions of the new Forest Service. The letter captures much of the spirit and philosophy that have guided the Forest Service to the present day:

> In the administration of the forest reserves it must be clearly borne in mind that all land is to be devoted to its most productive use for the permanent good of the whole people, and not for the temporary benefit of individuals or companies. All the resources of forest reserves are for use, and this use must

12. 30 Stat. 34–36, 43, 4 (1897).
13. Pinchot, *Breaking New Ground*, p. 190.

be brought about in a thoroughly prompt and businesslike manner, under such restrictions only as will insure the permanence of these resources. The vital importance of forest reserves to the great industries of the Western States will be largely increased in the near future by the continued steady advance in settlement and development. The performance of the resources of the reserves is therefore indispensable to continued prosperity, and the policy of this department for their protection and use will invariably be guided by this fact, always bearing in mind that the conservative use of these resources in no way conflicts with their permanent value.

You will see to it that the water, wood, and forage of the reserves are conserved and wisely used for the benefit of the home builder first of all, upon whom depends the best permanent use of lands and resources alike. The continued prosperity of the agricultural, lumbering, mining and livestock interests is directly dependent upon a permanent and accessible supply of water, wood, and forage, as well as upon the present and future use of their resources under businesslike regulations, enforced with promptness, effectiveness, and common sense. In the management of each reserve local questions will be decided upon local grounds; the dominant industry will be considered first, but with as little restriction to minor industries as may be possible; sudden changes in industrial conditions will be avoided by gradual adjustment after due notice; and where conflicting interests must be reconciled the question will always be decided from the standpoint of the *greatest good of the greatest number in the long run.*[14]

SCIENTIFIC FORESTRY MANAGEMENT

Many of the basic issues of federal timber management had already emerged by the time the Forest Service was created in 1905. The leading controversy of the 1890s had been whether the forest reserves should be preserved in their natural state or utilized for various productive purposes. Preservation had seemed for a moment to win out; but Pinchot stood solidly for utilization and under his leadership, this philosophy was firmly established. A separate organization, the National Park Service, was eventually formed in 1916 to manage the most scenic and wild areas for recreational and other noncommercial uses.

Pinchot himself had little interest in recreational use of the national forests. His belief that timber in the national parks should be harvested embittered many preservationists as did his support for the

14. Ibid., p. 261.

construction of Hetch Hetchy Dam in Yosemite National Park. He considered forestry to be "tree farming," and the basic purpose of the forests to be provision of wood for homes: "The object of our forest policy is not to preserve the forests because they are beautiful . . . or because they are refuges for the wild creatures of the wilderness . . . but the making of prosperous homes. . . . Every other consideration comes as secondary."[15]

Pinchot considered the preservationist cause to be romantic sentimentalism. He portrayed himself instead as a hardboiled scientist. He was in fact among the first practitioners of the science of forestry in the United States. As a young man Pinchot had studied forestry in France, and upon his return to the United States, sought to promote the lessons he had learned. He was a founder in 1900 of the Society of American Foresters, whose mission was to spread scientific forestry.

In his scientific orientation, Pinchot was very much a man of his time. Frederick Taylor was spreading the principles of scientific management to the business and government world. Belief in the great powers of science to solve the problems of mankind was widespread. Faith in science had become much like a religion for many, and Pinchot was the apostle of this faith for forestry. Samuel Hays, in particular, has emphasized the critical role played by science in the conservation movement:

> Conservation, above all, was a scientific movement, and its role in history arises from the implications of science and technology in modern society. Conservation leaders sprang from such fields as hydrology, forestry, agrostology, geology, and anthropology. Vigorously active in professional circles in the national capital, these leaders brought the ideals and practices of their crafts into federal resource policy. Loyalty to these professional ideals, not close association with the grass-roots public, set the tone of the Theodore Roosevelt conservation movement. Its essence was rational planning to promote efficient development and use of all natural resources. The idea of efficiency drew these federal scientists from one resources task to another, from specific programs to comprehensive concepts. It molded the policies which they proposed, their administrative techniques, and their relations with Congress and the public. It is from the vantage point of applied science, rather than of democratic protest, that one must understand the historic role of the conservation movement.[16]

15. Hays, *Conservation and the Gospel of Efficiency*, pp. 41–42.
16. Ibid., p. 2.

Science is of course not the domain of the layman; it requires special training to acquire technical knowledge. Politics should not become involved; rather, scientific knowledge is to be applied by the experts in the field. Such a vision underlay not only the development of the Forest Service, but much of growth of government under the progressive banner during the first two decades of this century.

The conservationists saw in science the ability to provide objective answers to social issues. Conflicts should be resolved, not through political combat among special interests, but by appeal to what was right, that is to say, what science and technical expertise determined. Theodore Roosevelt, one of the most optimistic of all progressives, epitomized this philosophy. He believed that "social and economic problems should be solved, not through power politics, but by experts who would undertake scientific investigations and devise workable solutions."[17] The view that forestry was a science meant such objectivity could be obtained, and could serve as a guide for, managing the national forests in the public interest.

These convictions have motivated the Forest Service to fight fiercely to retain political independence. Their wide acceptance has also made outsiders much more willing to grant such independence. Since 1910 all the chiefs have come from within the Forest Service and have served through changes in the presidency. Pinchot proudly remarked that "from the day I entered the Division of Forestry under President McKinley till I was dismissed from the Forest Service by President Taft, not one single person in the office or the field was appointed, promoted, demoted, or removed to please any politician, or for any political motive whatsoever."[18]

The scientific influence also explains other features of the Forest Service. It has included three basic divisions: the best known division is for management of the national forests; the other two are for the conduct of forestry research and the provision of technical forestry assistance to state and private forest owners. The Forest Service has collected and distributed information on trends in timber markets, and has promoted adoption of more scientific forestry practices. In general, it has functioned as the leading planner for long-run timber production in the United States.

The creation of the Forest Service can, in fact, be seen as one of the important steps in a much broader social development—the dis-

17. Ibid., p. 267.
18. Pinchot, *Breaking New Ground*, p. 284.

placement of small decentralized competitive institutions (such as individual lumbermen) by larger, scientific, planned institutions. In most cases, this occurred within the private sector as a small number of large corporations took the place of many smaller firms. This happened, for example, to some degree in timber with the assembly of the Weyerhaeuser holdings. The Forest Service was unusual for its time primarily in that it was a public agency.

THE O & C LANDS

Although the primary concern of this chapter is the national forests, it should be recognized that they are not the only important federal holdings of timber. The Oregon and California (O & C) lands in western Oregon, under management by the Bureau of Land Management, also provide major supplies. These lands were originally granted to railroads. Under the terms of the grants, land was to be sold only to legitimate settlers in blocks of no more than 160 acres. Responding to widespread allegations that these terms had been violated, Congress in 1908 moved to recover the lands. The Supreme Court in 1915 agreed that the original grant had been violated, and in 1916 Congress revested the 2.9 million acres still owned by the railroad to the federal government. Even though the lands were intermingled with national forest lands, they were placed under the jurisdiction of the Interior Department, one indication of the widespread western discontent with the Forest Service at that time.

The intent was that the land should eventually be disposed for private agricultural development. However, the O & C Lands were mostly forests; attempts to farm them generally proved unsuccessful. The O & C Lands produced few revenues and imposed a continuing drain on the federal treasury. In 1937 Congress enacted the O & C Act, providing for long-run federal retention and management for timber production. Additional management purposes included "protecting watersheds, regulating stream flow, and contributing to the economic stability of local communities and industries." The management of timber production was to be based on the "principle of sustained yield."[19] Notably, this was the first time that sustained yield was mandated by law for the management of federal timberlands.

19. Dana, *Forest and Range Policy*, p. 266.

THE MORAL CRUSADE

Good science constantly questions old answers, challenging conventional wisdom. On the one hand, the best scientists maintain an attitude of habitual doubt and skepticism; strict requirements must be met for scientific proof before any final answer will be accepted. On the other hand, these same characteristics are at odds with the successful conduct of politics. A good politician typically must maintain a posture of certainty even when he may harbor many private doubts. Confessions of doubt are likely to be seen as signs of weakness and inability to lead. They erode the commitment of supporters, undercutting the necessary solidarity.

Although Gifford Pinchot considered himself a scientist, most of his life was spent in the political arena where he was a great success. Similarly, while conservationists promoted scientific management, they sought to incorporate its use by restructuring political institutions, enlarging the role of government. In essence, the conservation movement espoused a set of political rather than scientific ideas; conservationism was, in short, a political ideology. Like other ideologies, it faced the need to attract and sustain popular support. The political requirements of conservationism were bound to conflict with the scientific methods that conservationists sought to advance.

Indeed there was a religious quality to the progressive and conservationist faith in applied science, a point that Waldo has stressed.[20] Hays later echoed this theme in characterizing conservationism as the "gospel" of efficiency. According to conservationist tenets, improvement would occur steadily in the human condition, eventually making it possible for all mankind to achieve "the good life." This vision of human progress—leading toward a secular "heaven on earth"—produced a widely held sense of virtue and important purpose. In the progressive era, a new ethic of human progress replaced the Protestant ethic as the motivator of good works. From the very beginning, Pinchot instilled such attitudes in the Forest Service. He himself commented that Forest Service employees were not to be motivated by "the desire to earn good money"; rather, they were doing "good work in a good cause."[21]

20. Dwight Waldo, *The Administrative State: A Study of the Political Theory of American Public Administration* (New York: Ronald Press, 1948), p. 30.
21. Pinchot, *Breaking New Ground*, p. 284.

The Forest Service was all the more virtuous when contrasted with the self-seeking, mercenary attitudes of its opponents. In the service of the good cause, the Forest Service had to overcome the "special interests" who "go on creating baronies for themselves out of the resources that belonged to all the people. We denied and opposed their profound conviction that money and profits are all important and must control."[22] Pinchot and the men of the Forest Service saw themselves as fending off the "vast power, pecuniary and political . . . [of the] . . . railroads, the stock interests, mining interests, water power interests, and most of the big timber interests."[23] The basic reason that the Forest Service could win, Pinchot stated, was that "in the long run our purpose was too obviously right to be defeated."[24]

The elevation of applied science from a practical tool into a new form of religious faith was characteristic of the progressive era. But the roles of science as practical problem-solving technique and as theology are much different. The future of the Forest Service was to see much tension between these elements. The demands of political mobilization as well as organizational discipline and morale were often to place a greater premium on the theological than on the problem-solving role of science.

CRYING WOLF

Predictions that the country would soon run out of timber—experience a "timber famine"—have recurred throughout American forestry history. The Commissioner of the General Land Office in 1868 predicted that "in forty or fifty years our own forests would have disappeared and those of Canada would be approaching exhaustion."[25] Matters appeared to be getting worse when, in 1876, a forestry student purported to prove that within ten years there would be "a clean swoop of every foot of commercial wood in the United States east of the Pacific slope."[26] In 1889 former Secretary of the

22. Ibid., pp. 258–60.
23. Ibid., p. 260.
24. Ibid.
25. Cited in Clepper, *Professional Forestry in the United States*, p. 135.
26. Cited in John Ise, *The United States Forest Policy* (New Haven, Conn.: Yale University Press, 1920), p. 30.

Interior Carl Schurz feared that "if the present destruction of forests goes on for twenty-five years longer, the United States will be as completely stripped of their forests as Asia Minor is today."[27]

This refrain was taken up by Pinchot who, by 1910, was sure that a timber famine was imminent: "The United States has already crossed the verge of a timber famine so severe that its blighting effects will be felt in every household in the land."[28] Counseled by Pinchot, President Theodore Roosevelt warned, "If the present rate of forest destruction is allowed to continue, with nothing to offset it, a timber famine in the future is inevitable."[29] It was not until the "energy crisis" of the 1970s that public alarms over natural resource depletion were again driven to such heights.

The specter of timber famine was raised anew in the battle over public regulation of private timber harvests. A committee of the Society of American Foresters, chaired by Pinchot, forecast in 1919 that "within less than 50 years, our present timber shortage will have become a blighting timber famine."[30] To prevent such an occurrence, the committee advocated federal regulation of private timber harvesting. The report of this committee set off a bitter struggle over public regulation of private forests that was to go on for thirty years.

The possibility of running out of timber naturally aroused strong public fears, and playing to these fears was an effective way of mobilizing public support. But one cannot give false alarms too many times; a timber famine cannot forever be looming. By the 1930s it was becoming necessary to explain where the timber famine had gone. Although Pinchot still raised the cry, for many others "the bogey of timber famine was ceasing to be a pivotal issue and was even becoming an embarrassment."[31]

The timber famine episode raises the question, How could an organization based on special expertise and the application of science go so far wrong? The hallmark of science is an accurate prediction; to make an unqualified prediction that does not materialize casts serious doubts on the scientific credentials of the predictor. Pinchot and others in the Forest Service concluded that a timber famine was in-

27. Cited in Clepper, *Professional Forestry in the United States*, p. 135.
28. Cited in ibid., p. 136.
29. Cited in Michael Frome, *Whose Woods These Are: The Story of the National Forests* (Garden City, N.Y.: Doubleday, 1962), p. 59.
30. Clepper, *Professional Forestry in the United States*, pp. 137–38.
31. Ibid., p. 145.

evitable on the basis of their projections of future timber demands that were greatly in excess of projected timber supplies. But demand, of course, is not independent of price, a matter then generally neglected. As timber comes into shorter supply and prices rise, purchasers find new ways to economize on the amounts they use. Similarly, the effective supply is not independent of price, but can be increased by better utilization, shifts to lower grades of wood, wood treatments, and various other means.

Pinchot believed the only way to avoid a timber famine was through more scientific management of the forests to produce much greater supplies of timber. As Olson observed, however, the actual historical solution to the timber problem was achieved mostly by lowering demand through conserving on wood use.[32] Wood users learned how to substitute other materials for wood and how to utilize available wood supplies more efficiently. For example, pushed by rising timber costs, the railroads in the decade from 1900 to 1910 developed a host of new conservation techniques; among the most important of which were the adoption of wood-preserving methods, substitution of new species and materials, and the more efficient allocation of timbers to various uses. Railroad foresters had initially looked to the Forest Service for help, but gradually were put off by the "dogmatic character of their publications. . . . They were advised to adopt practices in line with an idealized concept of 'good forestry,' instead of forest practices that would actually promote railroad economies."[33]

Indeed, the Forest Service was apparently preoccupied with its moral crusade to the extent that it actually neglected, in many cases, the scientific management of the nation's timber supplies. The Forest Service was often more concerned with a favorable public reaction and expanding its domain than with scientific research. Pinchot believed the answers basically were already known and "research was practically eliminated in the first few years of his administration."[34] Pinchot's role in almost single-handedly bringing about creation of the national forests has established his place in history. But in this task his greatest skills, ironically, were as a propagandist and politician. By selling the idea of scientific management of the forests

32. Sherry H. Olson, *The Depletion Myth: A History of Railroad Use of Timber* (Cambridge, Mass.: Harvard University Press, 1971), p. 104.
33. Ibid., p. 96.
34. Ibid., p. 75.

to an enthusiastic public and by promoting the virtue of the Forest Service, Pinchot succeeded in gaining the influence needed to overcome that agency's many determined opponents.

SCIENCE IN THE FOREST SERVICE

Schiff has conducted a major study focused on the question of whether the Forest Service was a suitable agency for the management of forestry research.[35] The Forest Service was often faced with strong opposition, and it had to fight strenuously for its political aims. Could the Forest Service afford to show a scientific questioning attitude toward its own policies in the face of strong outside challenges? Instead, the tendency might well be to circle the wagons and defend established policy. Science would be enlisted for the defense rather than left free to inquire in any direction.

The highly moralistic tradition of the Forest Service was likely to enhance this tendency. As a former chief declared, the Forest Service was "born in controversy and baptized with the holy water of reform."[36] As a result, according to Schiff, there was a "danger . . . that moral righteousness when embroidered with scientific technology would be too attractive in a science worshipping age. Moral appeals might even lead 'researchers' astray by encouraging tendencies to oversimplify and overgeneralize complex problems. Worse yet, their thinking might become rigidified, thereby losing the best qualities of the research mind."[37]

The tendency to make unrealistic and exaggerated claims has been most in evidence when the Forest Service has sought to expand the scope of its authority—usually in the face of much resistance. In the debate prior to the passage of the Weeks Act in 1911, which authorized acquisition of private lands for eastern national forests, a question arose as to whether the federal government actually had constitutional authority to make such purchases. In fending off this challenge, the Forest Service argued that forests were a critical factor in determining river flows; thus, forestland purchases by the federal

---

35. Ashley L. Schiff, *Fire and Water: Scientific Heresy in the Forest Service* (Cambridge, Mass.: Harvard University Press, 1962).

36. Ibid., p. 5.

37. Ibid.

government could be justified under the federal power to regulate navigation in waterways.

The public then, as now, was greatly concerned about the problem of flooding; severe floods in the Ohio, Mississippi, and other river valleys had caused damage on a vast scale. Pinchot, abandoning scientific caution, agreed that "the great flood which has wrought devastation and ruin in the Upper Ohio Valley is due fundamentally to the cutting away of the forests on the watersheds of the Allegheny and the Monongahela Rivers."[38] The Weather Bureau and the Corps of Engineers immediately challenged Pinchot's claim, but with little consequence. The Weeks Act passed with the inclusion of the provision that new forestlands could be acquired for the purpose of improving downstream navigation. Not surprisingly, the Forest Service was unreceptive toward scientific studies that questioned the actual importance of forest influences on river flows.

During the New Deal, the Forest Service sought to expand its domain by acquiring large new public holdings of private forests and by imposing Federal regulation on private forests. Once again there was wide opposition, and again the Forest Service responded with a campaign of exaggerated claims. Scientific objectivity had to make way for the political advantages of strong emotional appeals. The National Plan for American Forestry, released in 1933, repeated the claim that denuded forests were "major contributing causes of excessively rapid runoff and destructive floods."[39] Such statements of the Forest Service again were severely criticized by other scientific organizations. According to the Geological Survey, the leading government agency for hydrologic research,

> the changes which have been brought about by streamflow regulation through agricultural and forestry practices over broad areas are in general, so insignificant and tenuous that they are indeterminate. . . . It is a sad commentary on a so-called scientific organization like the Forest Service that during its existence it has never published a report on the role played by vegetal cover on the hydrologic cycle which was in accord with well-established hydrologic principles.[40]

38. Ibid., p. 120.
39. Cited in ibid., p. 139.
40. Ibid., p. 146.

Confronted with such statements, the Chief of the Division of Silvics replied, "All that may be true, but I think with my heart as well as my head."[41]

Schiff suggests the Forest Service may have actually recognized that its position lacked scientific merit, but deliberately failed to conduct its own research as a way of delaying the necessity of a formal acknowledgment of the situation. By the mid-1940s it was widely recognized that the Forest Service had greatly overstated the importance of forest condition in controlling floods. Acceptance of such views within the Forest Service could be achieved only because the old guard was now leaving. Pressed to return to the old crusading spirit, a representative of a newer era, Forest Service Chief Richard McArdle, responded in 1955:

> We live in different times. We cannot recreate the initial crusade for forestry anymore than we can rediscover America. That crusade was pointed toward creating a widespread public awareness of our need for the products and services of forestlands. . . . I think our task in the next half century is more concerned with action than with publicity.[42]

Fire prevention is another area in which the Forest Service refused for many years to accept scientific evidence conflicting with its policies. From its inception, the Forest Service had promoted this issue as another moral crusade. In the 1920s, however, scientific evidence began to accumulate that in the south use of fire was necessary to promote regeneration of the longleaf pine. The Forest Service refused to heed this evidence, insisting that its policies were correct; yet, the longer the agency ignored its critics, the more difficult a later reversal became. In the end, outside scientific opinion became so united that the Forest Service had to give in.

Based on the fire and water cases as well as other Forest Service history, Schiff concludes that the Forest Service was often all too willing to sacrifice scientific objectivity for public appeal. This produced not only poor science, but much less effective management of public forests. "In the end, therefore, administration itself suffered because research was too closely identified, from a spiritual and structural standpoint, with 'the cause.' "[43]

41. Ibid., p. 144.
42. Ibid., p. 162.
43. Ibid., p. 169.

AN ERA OF CUSTODIAL NATIONAL
FOREST MANAGEMENT, 1905-1945

Pinchot had envisioned that the Forest Service would intensively manage the national forests for timber and other uses. He also expected that the national forests would be profitable, that their revenues would exceed their costs. In his view, the main reason for creating the system of national forests was to introduce greater efficiency in forest management. In each of these beliefs, events were to prove otherwise.

For the first forty years, management of the national forests was mainly custodial. The effect of creating a national forest in an area was to curtail timber harvesting rather than to stimulate it. In the earlier part of this century, there were still huge supplies of timber available on both private and public lands. Timber prices were held at low levels by this vast supply, and many timberland owners found it difficult to cover payments on their land. The private sector thus pressured the Forest Service to limit harvesting in order to avoid depressing prices further. Seeking to create greater stability in the timber industry and not wanting to antagonize western timber interests, the Forest Service generally obliged. Among the objectives of its policy, the Forest Service sought to "avoid competing with private enterprise by withholding federal timber until private supplies were exhausted; sell only to meet purely local shortages; protect the national forests from fire and other disasters."[44]

In 1910 the timber harvested from Forest Service lands was around 500 million board feet, less than 2 percent of national lumber production. By 1929 the Forest Service harvest had risen to around 1.6 billion board feet, but this was still small compared with national lumber production of 36.9 billion board feet. At the time the total timber inventory on Forest Service lands was 552 billion board feet, around a third of the national timber inventory. The Forest Service harvest never exceeded a few percentages of national timber production until heavy demands in the aftermath of World War II forced the nation to turn to the national forests for timber supplies.

---

44. Harold K. Steen, *The U.S. Forest Service: A History* (Seattle: University of Washington Press, 1976), p. 113.

The pattern of harvesting private lands first and Forest Service lands later was politically popular because "harvesting it would have lowered stumpage prices on private lands."[45] Nevertheless, it was also economically rational. The private lands were generally the better timberlands, having higher volumes of timber per acre and located closer to roads and other transportation. Because future returns are discounted, the long-run value of timber is maximized by taking the lowest cost timber first, just as the highest grade and lowest cost mineral deposits are taken first.

While timber was being harvested on private lands, the national forests were becoming a major source of recreation, a use in which Pinchot had shown little interest. The national forests contain much of the higher elevated scenic areas west of the Mississippi, as well as many other attractions. Although mountainous terrain and steep slopes made the lands less valuable for timber production, these features made them more desirable for recreation. In contrast to the circumstances of timber production, the national forests held the most desirable recreational areas and were appropriately brought into recreational use ahead of private lands. The numbers of recreational visits to the national forests grew rapidly from 4.7 million in 1924 to 16.2 million in 1940. By 1950 recreational visits had further climbed to 27.4 million, more than five times the level twenty-five years earlier.

Despite the rapid growth in recreational use of the national forests, Pinchot and his successors in the Forest Service were unsympathetic to the idea of setting aside certain lands solely for recreation. They contended that recreation and other uses could be accommodated together without great loss to either. They generally resisted creation of any areas in which one or another use was automatically precluded. Rather, it was thought that the land manager should exercise his professional judgment in deciding the best overall use of the land in light of the particular circumstances at hand. In some cases, a use such as timber harvesting might prove to be incompatible with recreation, but why prejudge the issue?

The Forest Service thus showed little sympathy toward the creation of national parks, and found it difficult to understand that park

45. Remarks of Murl Sturms, Chief of Forestry, Bureau of Land Management, cited in Daniel R. Barney, *The Last Stand: Ralph Nader's Study Group Report on the National Forests* (New York: Grossman Publishers, 1974), p. 19.

proponents distrusted the exercise of professional judgment and wanted ironclad guarantees that an area would be protected. In retrospect, it is ironic that one of the most important functions of the national forests for their first forty years was to serve as a holding zone from which the national parks and monuments, wilderness areas, back country areas, and other special recreational areas could later be formed. A host of important national parks—including Olympic, Grand Canyon, Grand Teton, Glacier, North Cascades and others—were created entirely or in part from land originally in the national forests. If these lands had previously passed into private ownership, many of these parks and recreation areas might never have been created or might have been much smaller; in any case, the task would have been much more difficult, as the recent problems in assembling the land for the Redwood National Park have demonstrated.

The Forest Service greatly resented the loss of some of its most attractive lands to the national park system, and it resisted the formation of most of the national parks noted above. Eventually, however, it perceived that it would have to move with the tide, if for no other reason than to protect its domain. Moreover, some Forest Service staff were becoming strong enthusiasts for wilderness protection—the young Aldo Leopold, for one. (Wilderness areas receive protections and management more in the spirit of the national parks, but are retained within the national forests under the management of the Forest Service.) The first wilderness area was established in 1924 and by 1939 about 13 million acres had been set aside in "primitive areas" with restricted commercial use.

In short, up until World War II the guiding principles of the Forest Service concerning the proper management of the national forests had not been put to much of a test. The Forest Service espoused active management to maximize use, but actual management activities to that point had been fairly minimal. The public saw the national forests as a vast recreation area, a lot like a national park, although lacking the natural wonders of the world. The Forest Service had become popular making available its 180 million acres for public pleasure and promoting good causes such as fire prevention. But matters would become much more complicated after World War II. New economic pressures would bring about a shift to a much more intensive use of the national forests.

THE CAMPAIGN FOR FEDERAL
FOREST REGULATION

For most of American history, timber companies simply cut and moved on to the next virgin stands. This pattern made much economic sense at the time. There were vast forests rich in timber; transport costs might rise, but it would still be cheaper to move to new stands, as long as they were available, than to regrow the forest. The long time required for timber to reach harvesting age—forty to one hundred years—made it especially difficult to achieve an adequate return from reforestation.

Pinchot and other early members of the forestry profession had learned their forestry in the European tradition. There was little old growth timber available in Europe; instead, European forestry was conceived for circumstances in which harvesting had gone on for centuries. The forests had typically been through many cycles of cutting, regrowth, and cutting once again. Given these circumstances, it was logical that maintenance of a sustained yield of timber was a central principle in European forestry.

Pinchot and most others in the new American forestry profession directly adopted the idea that sustained-yield forestry represented proper and "truly scientific" forest management. Other forestry practices were considered wasteful and unscientific. Accordingly, the Forest Service released a continuing flow of data and statistics on the number of forest acres that had been harvested but not reforested. In graphic terms it described the extent of "forest devastation" on these lands.

Given private unwillingness to reforest, Pinchot came to the conclusion that either public ownership or public regulation of private forests was necessary to achieve sustained-yield timber management for the United States. Recognizing that public acquisition of private timberlands would be extremely expensive, and on any wide scale would be likely to generate fierce resistance, Pinchot came to advocate federal regulation of private timber harvests.

As noted earlier, in 1919 the President of the Society of American Foresters designated Pinchot to be chairman of a committee whose purpose was "to recommend action for the prevention of forest devastation of privately owned timberlands in the United States."[46]

---

46. Clepper, *Professional Forestry in the United States*, pp. 137–38.

The committee subsequently reported that drastic steps were required to head off a timber famine. It proposed the federal government be authorized "to fix standards and promulgate rules to prevent the devastation and to provide for the perpetuation of forest growth and the production of forest crops on privately owned timberlands for commercial purposes."[47]

The necessity of government regulation was widely accepted among professional foresters. However, there was strong disagreement as to whether the federal government or the states should be the primary regulator. Pinchot favored federal regulation, but his two successors as chiefs of the Forest Service, Henry Graves and William Greeley, both favored state responsibility. In the American tradition of decentralization, many other professional foresters agreed that, whenever possible, the state level was the better choice. The timber industry itself did not dispute the fact that private owners were not reforesting. The National Lumber Manufacturers Association, in fact, supported public reforestation.

The concerns about forest devastation and the drive for regulation did not produce much legislative movement toward direct regulation. However, these pressures spurred the passage of the Clark-McNary Act in 1924 and the McSweeney-McNary Act in 1928. These two acts created the basis for federal assistance to state and private forestry and a major federal program of forestry research. Rather than compulsory regulation, voluntary cooperation became the byword.

The depression of the 1930s encouraged radical views, and in many fields the New Deal brought about major changes in policy and legislation. This failed to occur in forestry, but not for lack of Forest Service effort. In 1933 the Forest Service released its most comprehensive study of forestry up to that time—the National Plan for American Forestry (also called the Copeland Report). The plan recommended a massive acquisition program to more than double the area of public forests. In the spirit of the times, the Forest Service made a harsh attack on the effects of private ownership and profit incentives:

> Laissez-faire private effort . . . has seriously deteriorated or destroyed the basic resources of timber, forage, and land almost universally. It has not concerned itself with the public welfare in protection of watersheds. It has felt little or no responsibility for the renewal of the resources on which its own

47. Ibid., p. 138.

industries must depend for continued existence and much less for the economic and social benefits growing out of the perpetuity of resources and industry.[48]

The Forest Service also argued that public ownership of the forests was required to expedite forestry planning for the whole nation. At that time, the idea of public ownership and national planning was being widely proposed not only for the forests, but for much of the U.S. economy. During the 1930s and 1940s the Forest Service also campaigned vigorously for federal regulation of private forests where public ownership was not achieved. In 1935 the Chief of the Forest Service, Ferdinand Silcox, set the official Forest Service position, which was not changed until the early 1950s:

1. The primary objective of forestry is to keep forestland continuously productive. This must take precedence over private profit.
2. Forest devastation must stop, and forest practice must begin now, not in the nebulous future.
3. Public control over the use of private forest lands which will insure sustained yield is essential to stabilize forest industries and forest communities. The application of the required practices on private lands must be supervised by public agencies and not left to the industry.[49]

The drive for public regulation was gradually being undercut, however, by the spread of private industrial forestry. Industry reforestation and management for long-term sustained yields emerged in the 1930s and spread rapidly. One of the earliest full-fledged "tree farms" was on the Clemons Tract of the Weyerhaeuser Company, set up in 1941. By 1950 a University of Michigan forestry professor remarked, "Millions of tree farm acres are already getting more intensive forest management than is available to most of the publicly owned lands."[50]

Surprisingly, the Forest Service sometimes reacted to this development with suspicion and distrust, even though it had promoted it for many years. The Forest Service feared improvements in private

48. *A National Plan for American Forestry: The Report of the Forest Service of the Agriculture Department on the Forest Problem of the United States.*(Washington, D.C.: Government Printing Office, 1933), vol. I, p. 41.
49. Cited in Clepper, *Professional Forestry in the United States*, p. 150.
50. Ibid., p. 291.

forestry practices might be an industry ploy to defeat Forest Service objectives of regulation or large scale public forest acquisition. Lyle Watts, Chief of the Forest Service, complained in 1943 by stating, "It is unfortunate that a well-financed publicity campaign sponsored by the forest industries during the recent past should tend to cultivate public complacency when the situation with respect to our forest resources is so unsatisfactory."[51]

Any real prospects of federal forestry regulation passed with the coming of World War II. The nation was too absorbed with war to embark on major domestic reforms. In the next several decades, private industry would surpass the Forest Service in the sophistication of its timber management. Ironically, after the Forest Service finally began to harvest timber on a large scale in the 1950s, one of the main criticisms aimed against it would be a failure to achieve reforestation.

The Forest Service made another pitch for federal regulation in the early 1950s. As expressed in 1951 by the Assistant Chief of the Forest Service, Edward Crafts, one argument for public regulation was a sophisticated version of the old timber famine theme: "Latest surveys show—and practically all authorities agree on the basic figures—that the drain of sawtimber trees substantially exceeds growth. . . . Thus, we have a situation in which we are gradually using up our capital growing stock of the larger and better trees."[52]

However, the Forest Service proposals for regulation were incompatible with the philosophy of the Eisenhower administration then coming into office. The Forest Service was concerned that the new administration might abandon the traditional, nonpolitical tenure of its chiefs and, more broadly, feared compromise of its traditional freedom from heavy-handed political interference. To head off this threat, the Forest Service modified some of its positions to fit the views of the new administration, most notably dropping the idea of establishing federal forest regulation.

This campaign for regulation once again showed the Forest Service making strong, unqualified predictions only to be proved wrong by actual events. It officially stated for many years that private forest owners could never be expected to practice sustained-yield manage-

51. Ibid., p. 290.
52. Edward C. Crafts, *Forest Service Researcher and Congressional Liaison: An Eye to Multiple Use.* An interview conducted by Susan R. Schrepfer (Santa Cruz, Calif.: Forest History Society, Oral History Office, 1972), p. 125.

ment and other forms of intensive forestry. Yet within a few decades, industry was, in many cases, applying a more scientific forestry than was found on the national forests.

As in other cases, the Forest Service's miscalculation can be traced to a lack of interest and sophistication in using economic analysis. The Forest Service viewed sustained-yield management as a desirable end in itself, not something to be employed because it made economic sense. Private industry had a more pragmatic view; it would practice good forestry when it could make money in this way. The Forest Service, however, failed to grasp that industry behavior was dependent on economic calculation. Because it tended to see actions in terms of good and evil, it viewed early industry failure to reforest as a moral failing. The private sector was portrayed as irresponsible and destructive in its refusal to save the forests from "devastation." With this outlook, the Forest Service did not recognize that when old growth became less available and timber prices rose, reforestation would become economically profitable and industry would move rapidly to undertake it.

DEMANDS FOR FOREST SERVICE TIMBER AFTER WORLD WAR II

As noted above, in meeting national timber demands, the highest quality and most accessible timber was the first to be cut. Timber production in the United States thus started in the east and moved westward. By 1870 the Great Lakes states with their vast forests of white pine had displaced the middle Atlantic region as the most important timber-producing region. In 1889 the Great Lakes states produced 35 percent of the nation's lumber. But then, as these supplies became depleted, new sources had to be found. By 1899, with 32 percent of the nation's production, the south had already passed the Great Lakes states as the largest lumber producer. The Pacific coast and Rocky Mountain regions were just beginning to become important; their combined lumber production had not yet reached 10 percent of national production. Thus, at the time the national forests were being established, the west was not a major source of timber supply. This was no doubt an important factor facilitating creation of the national forest system.

By 1929, however, the Pacific coast region, along with the south, had become one of the two major sources of timber for the nation. As production shifted westward, the national forests in the west became a potentially important source of timber. But, as noted earlier, public timberlands were generally the poorer timber-producing lands. In the Pacific coast region, for example, the old growth forests owned by private industry contained more than twice as many board feet per acre as publicly owned forests. Moreover, public forests tended to be located further from transportation, on steeper slopes, and in otherwise more difficult terrain. In 1929 the total Forest Service harvest was still only 4 percent of national lumber production, and during the depression years the overall Forest Service harvest declined.

World War II marked a turning point; between 1939 and 1945 the harvest from the national forests doubled and continued to rise thereafter. In 1952 the Forest Service harvest reached 6.4 billion board feet, 13 percent of the U.S. timber supply. It rose further to 10.7 billion board feet in 1962, supplying 22 percent of the national timber supply. At this point the Forest Service harvest stopped growing and has since remained roughly at the same level.

The Forest Service's share rose rapidly because, while Forest Service harvests themselves were increasing steadily, there were only modest increases in total national timber production. In 1976 total U.S. lumber production was 36 billion board feet, 8 billion less than it had been in 1909. Likewise, per capita use of lumber has fallen steadily from 539 board feet in 1900 to 199 board feet in 1976. Although plywood and veneer have replaced lumber in many wood uses, combined use of lumber and plywood is still well below the levels of wood use per capita reached earlier in this century.

The need to draw upon progressively more difficult to harvest and more costly stands of old growth, together with a gradual dwindling of these supplies, has caused the real price of timber to rise rapidly. Between 1900 and 1954 the nominal price of lumber rose nine times, and the real (inflation-adjusted) price almost tripled. The continuing rise in prices largely explains the sharp reductions in per capita use of timber as well as mounting pressures for greater timber production on the public forests.

In 1952 the Forest Service began a major study of the timber situation, eventually to be released in 1958 as *Timber Resources for*

America's Future.[53] The report described the much greater efforts being made to utilize Forest Service timber. For example, whereas very little road construction for timber harvesting had occurred prior to 1940 in the west, from 1940 to 1951 construction rose to almost 800 miles of roads per year. Then in 1952 and 1956, respectively, construction reached 1,650 and 2,600 miles; a further need for 30,000 miles of new roads was projected. The study also warned that a major commitment of new resources to forestry was necessary to avoid future timber shortages.

In the late 1950s the Forest Service was prepared to shift its timber harvesting into high gear, but it did not anticipate the strong opposition among recreationists that was about to develop. It still tended to regard recreation as an incidental activity—a natural use of large areas of often scenic forestland, but not requiring much special attention. Whereas the dominant event of the fifteen-year period from 1945 to 1960 was the major expansion in timber production, the next twenty years would be dominated by a counterthrust of recreational users of the national forests that prevented further harvest increases.

FOREST SERVICE TIMBER PREDICTIONS

After so many false alarms, the term "timber famine" came into disrepute in the 1930s, and few predictions of a timber famine have been made since. But to some extent the mentality did not really disappear but rather took on new, albeit less extreme, forms. Instead of a famine, the prediction is now of a "timber shortage," and the suggestion is made that unacceptable social consequences—such as rapidly rising timber prices—will afflict the nation.

Since 1933 the Forest Service has undertaken a number of comprehensive studies of future demands and supplies for timber in the United States.[54] The most recent are the two assessments mandated

53. U.S. Department of Agriculture, Forest Service, *Timber Resources for America's Future* (January 1958).

54. See U.S. Department of Agriculture, Forest Service, *A National Plan for American Forestry; Timber Resources for America's Future; Timber Trends in the United States*, (February 1965); idem, *The Outlook for Timber in the United States* (October 1973); U.S. Department of Agriculture, Forest Service, *The Nation's Renewable Resources—An Assessment, 1975* (June 1977); and U.S. Department of Agriculture, Forest Service, *An Assessment of the Forest and Rangeland Situation in the United States* (January 1980).

Table 2-1. Comparison of Predicted and Actual Total U.S.
Sawtimber Growth, Volume, and Harvest (billions of board feet).

	1933 Prediction for 1950	*Actual 1952*	*1958 Prediction for 1975*	*Actual 1976*
Timber growth	12.8	47.2	58.6	74.6
Inventory volume	1,207.2	2,507.0[a]	1,934.0	2,578.9
Timber harvest	33.7	48.8	65.4	62.9

a. Inventory data are for 1953.
*Sources: A National Plan for American Forestry: The Report of the Forest Service of
the Agriculture Department on the Forest Problem of the United States* (Washington, D.C.:
Government Printing Office, 1933); USDA, Forest Service, *Timber Resources for America's
Future* (Washington, D.C.: Government Printing Office, 1958); and USDA, Forest Service,
An Assessment of the Forest and Rangeland Situation in the United States (Washington,
D.C.: Government Printing Office, 1980).

under the Forest and Rangeland Renewable Resources Planning Act
of 1974 (RPA), prepared for 1975 and 1980. Each of these timber
studies has concluded that a major shortage of timber was likely to
develop—sooner in some cases than in others.

Sufficient time has passed that some of the earlier predictions of
timber shortages can be assessed in retrospect. It is significant that in
light of actual events, all were too pessimistic. The shortage has
proved to be almost as elusive as the earlier famines were. Table 2-1
shows Forest Service predictions for two years, 1950 and 1975, plus
actual figures for the nearest years available.

The difficulties of projections become greater as the projections
become more disaggregated. This is an important point because current public land planning appears headed toward greater use of projections broken down in considerable detail, especially in the RPA
effort. The predictions in 1958 for 1975 and the actual 1976 outcomes are shown in Table 2-2 for some highly specific items. As can
be seen, in one case the prediction proved almost exactly correct,
but in most cases the predictions were far off, in two cases by as
much as a factor of six.

Relying on its future demand projections, the 1958 Forest Service
study estimated needed forest growth and showed it to be much
above projected growth, leading to a major shortage. The study reported "the interpretations given to these projections of future
growth are perhaps the most important in the entire timber resource
review. The projections indicate that if medium levels of timber demand are met each year, sawtimber growth by 1965 would show a

14 percent deficit in relation to needed growth and a 76 percent deficit by the year 2000."[55] The study then warned that

> prompt and very substantial expansion and intensification of forestry in the United States is necessary if timber shortages are to be avoided by 2000. . . . The necessary intensification in forestry will have to be in addition to what could be expected by extending the trends in forestry improvements in recent years. This acceleration in forestry will have to come soon, and very largely within the next two decades, because otherwise it will be too late for the effects to be felt by 2000. The degree of forestry intensification needed is much larger and far greater than the general public or most experts are believed to have visualized.[56]

Only seven years later a third set of future projections for timber were made by the Forest Service as shown in Table 2-3. Once again the Forest Service did not anticipate future timber growth. Projecting only five years ahead, the Forest Service underestimated 1970 growth by 11 percent. By 1976 actual timber growth already exceeded the Forest Service projection for 1980 by 16 percent. Somewhat smaller differences between the predicted and actual results occurred for timber harvests.

Regarding the underestimation of growth potential, Marion Clawson has commented that "timber growth potential has been repeatedly and seriously underestimated" by the Forest Service. The agency failed to take proper account of the impact of ongoing harvesting on future growth; the "great increase in annual net growth of timber was a direct consequence of the decline in standing volume. . . . Net growth was possible only as original stands of timber were opened up by harvest."[57] The older stands grew little if at all; harvesting them more quickly made way for rapidly growing young stands.

The agency's tendency to overstate projected timber shortages again displayed its weak understanding of economic forces. Price changes operate to bring demand and supply into equilibrium; an impending shortage calls forth a higher price, which both reduces demand and stimulates additional supply.

55. USDA, Forest Service, *Timber Resources for America's Future*, pp. 96-97.
56. Ibid., p. 102.
57. Marion Clawson, "Forests in the Long Sweep of American History," *Science* (June 15, 1979), pp. 1171-72.

Table 2-2. Comparison of Predicted and Actual Total U.S. Demands for Selected Items.

Item	Units	1958 Predicted for 1975 (millions)	Actual 1976 (millions)
Cooperage	board feet	600	94
Piling	linear feet	59	39
Poles	pieces	6.5	6.3
Posts	pieces	400	60
Mine timbers	cubic feet	105	24

Sources: Timber Resources for America's Future, Department of Agriculture, Forest Service (Washington, D.C.: Government Printing Office, 1958); and *An Assessment of the Forest and Rangeland Situation in the United States*, U.S. Department of Agriculture, Forest Service (Washington, D.C., January 1980).

Table 2-3. Comparison of Predicted and Actual Total U.S. Sawtimber Growth, Volume, and Harvest (billions of board feet).

	1965 Prediction for 1970	Actual 1970	1965 Prediction for 1980	Actual 1976
Timber growth	59.6	66.2	64.5	74.6
Inventory volume	2,586.0	2,538.6	2,645.0	2,578.9
Timber harvest	53.6	58.5	60.4	62.9

Sources: Timber Trends in the United States, U.S. Department of Agriculture, Forest Service (Washington, D.C.: Government Printing Office, February 1965); and *An Assessment of the Forest and Rangeland Situation in the United States*, U.S. Department of Agriculture, Forest Service (Washington, D.C., January 1980).

THE MULTIPLE-USE SUSTAINED-YIELD ACT OF 1960

Recreation does not necessarily conflict with timber harvesting; many game animals, for example, require a diversity of habitat, which timber harvesting can provide. Timber harvesting substitutes to some degree for fire, insects, and disease in providing areas of brush and browse. For the bulk of recreation, however, especially ordinary hiking and camping, most recreationists prefer uncut old growth forests to the much smaller, less imposing trees in reforested areas. Almost all recreationists find the immediate aftermath of clear cutting to be visually unattractive or worse.

When demands for recreational uses arose, there was little in the background of the Forest Service to prepare it for the problem of resolving competing uses. Pinchot had been concerned with building political support for the Forest Service. He sought the backing of all national forest users, and preferred to avoid what were then only abstract questions of allocation among competing uses.

When conflicts began to arise, the Forest Service did not respond with fresh thinking. Rather, it continued to employ the basic tactics of Pinchot, to give a commitment in very general terms to accommodate all the different kinds of uses, but to leave the specifics for later resolution. This approach was embodied in the Multiple-Use Sustained-Yield Act of 1960.

The act did not actually create any new authority, as the Forest Service conceded; nevertheless, key members of the Forest Service argued that an explicit congressional endorsement of its previous practices was needed. The main content of the act was its requirement that the national forests be managed according to the principles of "multiple use" and "sustained yield." These terms were defined in the legislation as follows:

"Multiple use" means: The management of all the various renewable surface resources of the national forests so that they are utilized in the combination that will best meet the needs of the American people; making the most judicious use of the land for some or all of these resources or related services over areas large enough to provide sufficient latitude for periodic adjustments in use to conform to changing needs and conditions; that some land will be used for less than all of the resources; and harmonious and coordinated management of the various resources, each with the other, without impairment of the productivity of the land, with consideration being given to the relative values of the various resources, and not necessarily the combination of uses that will give the greatest dollar return or the greatest unit output.

"Sustained yield of the several products and services" means the achievement and maintenance in perpetuity of a high-level annual or regular periodic output of the various renewable resources of the national forests without impairment of the productivity of the land.[58]

Clearly, the Multiple-Use Sustained-Yield Act in practice provided little specific guidance to Forest Service land managers. Due to its vagueness, the definition of multiple use is subject to many interpre-

---

58. Public Law 86–517. See 16 U.S.C. sec. 531 (1976 ed.). For the history of this law, see Edward C. Crafts, "Saga of a Law: Part I," *American Forests* 76, no. 6 (June 1970) and Edward C. Crafts, "Saga of a Law: Part II," *American Forests* 76, no. 7 (July 1970).

tations. The Public Land Law Review Commission concluded from its investigations that the term "multiple use has little practical meaning as a planning concept or principle."[59]

Even Edward Crafts, one of the key Forest Service officials responsible for the Multiple-Use Sustained-Yield Act, later conceded, "Everything fell under multiple use, and who can argue against multiple use because it is all things to all people. They used it as a justification for whatever they wanted to do."[60]

The definition of sustained yield in the act similarly allows many interpretations. For example, the question of area is critical. Obviously, sustained yield is not achieved in a small area that is clear cut. Then how large must the area be? Can sustained yield include yields from nearby private or other public agency lands? Must a sustained yield be achieved every day, year, decade, or century? The legislation provides little guidance on these and other critical questions.

The true significance of the Multiple-Use Sustained-Yield Act is symbolic. It gave a boost to recreation and certain other uses by providing explicit "authority to manage the lands for recreation and other purposes for which prior authority was lacking or unclear."[61] The act also represented for the Forest Service a congressional pat on the back for its traditional ways of doing things. The Forest Service hoped to fend off attempts by outside groups—both industrial and recreational—to box the Forest Service into specific policies in particular areas. The Forest Service instead preferred its traditional administrative discretion, which allowed it to deal equally with all the multiple uses in each forest area.

At the time, the Forest Service was upset by losses of its land to the National Park Service, and was also unhappy with the loss of administrative discretion entailed in proposals for statutory designation of wilderness areas. According to some observers, the Multiple-Use Sustained-Yield Act was an attempt to forestall creation of further national parks. The Forest Service agreed to go along with formal congressional wilderness designations only "in exchange for congressional ratification of its long standing multiple use philosophy

59. *One Third of the Nation's Land: A Report to the President and to the Congress by the Public Land Law Review Commission* (Washington, D.C.: Government Printing Office, 1970), p. 45.

60. Crafts, *Forest Service Researcher and Congressional Liaison*, p. 80.

61. *One Third of the Nation's Land*, p. 43.

in the Multiple-Use Sustained-Yield Act of 1960."[62] The Sierra Club, in fact, was about the only prominent organization to oppose the bill because it saw multiple use possibly limiting further creation of national parks and wilderness.

AN ECONOMIC INTERPRETATION
OF MULTIPLE USE

Under the pressure of increasing use conflicts, an attempt has been made in the past few years to give the multiple-use concept a more concrete meaning. The impetus has come also in part from the need to work out the implications of the Forest and Rangeland Renewable Resources Planning Act of 1974 and the National Forest Management Act of 1976.

John Krutilla, a leading environmental economist, has criticized the Forest Service, and in fact the whole forestry profession, for never facing up to the question of multiple use. Where foresters have "appreciated that there is need to provide the 'correct' level and mix of the various resource services which the national forests are capable of producing, up until the present the instincts and proper impulses of the profession expressed themselves somewhat more as high motives and sincere exhortations than as the application of operational criteria."[63] Partly because objective criteria for allocating the services of the national forests were never developed, the forestry profession has been forced to suffer "indignities at the hands of one or another group insisting that the national forests satisfy their mutually incompatible demands."[64] To resolve this undesirable situation, the Forest Service must recognize the "need to bring into its management frame of reference the developments which have advanced in other scientific or management disciplines which, while not required of the forester during the 'golden age of forestry,' have elements of direct applicability to national forest management today."[65] In

62. Glen O. Robinson, *The Forest Service: A Study in Public Land Management* (Baltimore: Johns Hopkins University Press, 1975), p. 16.
63. John V. Krutilla, "Adaptive Responses to Forces for Change" (Paper presented at the Annual Meetings of the Society of American Foresters, Boston, Massachusetts, October 16, 1979), p. 6.
64. Ibid., p. 5.
65. Ibid., p. 7.

short, in Krutilla's view the time has come to make good on the original promise of Gifford Pinchot, who preached only scientific management.

In developing a more scientific approach, the critical first step is to define a precise goal. Krutilla considers that there might be three basic types of goals for the Forest Service: (1) to promote economic efficiency, (2) to improve the distribution of income, and (3) to help stabilize the economy. There is little disagreement that the third of these is not the job of the Forest Service. But he also goes on to dismiss social equity as a legitimate Forest Service mission; as a practical matter, "it is a bit quixotic for the Forest Service to attempt to ensure 'community stability' when the means to do so are not available to it."[66] Krutilla is also concerned that public participation may cause forest outputs to be distributed not on the basis of economic efficiency, but to the greatest number of votes. As a consequence, then, Krutilla argues that the goal should be "to manage the national forests . . . in order to maximize benefits"—in short, to "pursue economic efficiency."[67]

To pursue efficiency in this sense means seeking the maximum possible net value of the outputs of the national forests. Where market prices exist, outputs would be valued at these prices. Where no markets exist, estimates must be formed of the prices that would otherwise have existed—simulated market prices. Clearly, such prices may be difficult to estimate; yet according to Krutilla, the difficulties are not so great as to preclude this approach. Economics thus provides a specific definition of multiple use. Given different combinations of possible outputs, the only way to compare apples and oranges is to establish a set of relative values, that is, prices. Using these prices, the agency course of action is that which maximizes total net value.

Despite some very substantial difficulties in estimating nonmarket values, this approach represents the most scientific way currently available to make management decisions for public forests. Yet, until very recently, the Forest Service never considered such a procedure. While the term "multiple use" was offered as a "principle" for making public forest decisions, it was essentially left undefined. Thus, as noted above, multiple-use decisionmaking, in practice, has meant

66. John V. Krutilla and John A. Haigh, "An Integrated Approach to National Forest Management," *Environmental Law* 8, no. 2 (Winter 1978): 383.
67. Ibid., p. 383.

decisionmaking by administrative discretion—the absence of any binding objective standards.

The implementation of the Multiple-Use Sustained-Yield Act illustrates once again the consequences of Forest Service resistance to economic concepts. Rejecting economic analysis, the agency has not offered any other type of analysis in its place. Instead, the Forest Service recipe has been to muddle. In the end, this has left decisions to be determined mainly by the forces of interest-group politics, ironically, the very antithesis of the original conservationist ideal. Multiple-use decisionmaking might more accurately be described as multiple-interest-group decisionmaking.

THE WILDERNESS ACT OF 1964:
A CONTRADICTORY STEP

The Forest Service began creating wilderness areas in 1924 when Aldo Leopold persuaded the local forest supervisor to designate 700,000 acres of the Gila National Forest in New Mexico as the first wilderness area. The early designation of a wilderness area (then often called "primitive area") was not very restrictive. Roads were not necessarily excluded and timber harvesting was often allowed. In 1939 new wilderness regulations were issued that greatly tightened the restrictions. A procedure was established to review existing wilderness areas for permanent inclusion in a new wilderness system. Subsequently, however, the Forest Service moved very slowly, and in 1960 many areas still had not been reviewed.

After 1939, wilderness designation effectively committed an area to one particular use. Except where other nonwilderness uses were already present, these uses were allowed only to the extent that they did not detract seriously from the wilderness character. The explicit identification of one primary use, of course, violates the multiple-use principle. In fact, the purpose of wilderness designation was precisely to eliminate the discretion to consider all uses. Wilderness proponents wanted a formal and permanent commitment of each wilderness area; they were not willing to trust the discretion of individual Forest Service field managers.

With tighter restrictions, little acreage was added to the wilderness system after the 1930s, and in some cases areas with high timber or other commercial value were taken out of wilderness status. This created opposition, both within and outside the Forest Service, to the agency's wilderness policies.

> Not only the pace of reclassification but its results were challenged by preservationists. . . . There was, too, growing skepticism among preservationists that the Forest Service would, or even could, maintain permanent reservation for lands classified as wilderness. The mounting public demand for forest products and forest use increased the anxiety which a natural distrust of the bureaucracy instilled.[68]

Following almost a decade of discussion and debate, the Wilderness Act was finally passed in 1964. Timber harvesting and mechanized recreation were barred from wilderness areas. As a concession to the mining industry, mineral exploration was allowed to continue until 1984. No new livestock grazing or major new range improvements would be allowed, but existing grazing could continue. The act gave statutory confirmation to the status of 9.1 million acres that had already been administratively designated as wilderness by the Forest Service. The Wilderness Act also created procedures for review of additional lands for wilderness designation. Wilderness was said to be "an area where the earth and its community of life are untrammeled by man, where man himself is a visitor who does not remain." For the purposes of the act, wilderness was defined by a set of characteristics. But as with the term multiple use, the language left great latitude for interpretation.

In practice, the best definition of wilderness is probably a roadless remote area that in some way is of recreational and environmental concern to the whole nation. Wilderness areas offer a federal parallel to the state creation of "critical areas" under state land use legislation of the 1970s. The National Parks might be considered early federal critical areas; the creation of a wilderness system allowed the Forest Service to retain its own management control over newer federal critical areas—rather than having to surrender them to the Park Service.

The history of public land legislation is one of conflicting signals; Congress has seldom acted with clear objectives and events have often produced reversals or contradictions of previous policies. Here again, although Congress enacted a major public land law in 1960 stating its commitment to multiple use, four years later it passed an-

68. Robinson, *The Forest Service*, p. 158.

other significant public land law effectively ignoring the multiple-use philosophy and establishing a new single purpose management category. As one observer put it, "The Wilderness Act is the antithesis of some conceptions of multiple use management and in a sense the Act expressed a lack of faith in the ability of the Forest Service to implement the multiple use requirement."[69] By 1982, 25 million acres of national forests, greater than the total area of the national parks in 1964, had been designated as wilderness. An additional 55 million acres of wilderness had been designated within the National Park System and the National Wildlife Refuge System, most of this acreage located in Alaska.

Vagueness in congressional directions to administrative agencies often reflects the necessity for political compromise and the fact that congressmen themselves are unsure how to proceed. Vague legislation often amounts to a push for the agencies to move in a general direction, but it is up to the agency and the affected interests to work out the details. The Multiple-Use Sustained-Yield Act and the Wilderness Act both fit this pattern. The Wilderness Act, especially, precipitated a major controversy over its implementation that is still being waged.

RARE I AND RARE II

The Wilderness Act required that the Forest Service review 5.4 million acres of primitive areas then under consideration for wilderness and make a recommendation to Congress as to whether these areas should be placed within the wilderness system. The Forest Service subsequently determined that almost all such areas were in fact suitable and should be designated as wilderness.

Although not required, the Wilderness Act also included provision for further wilderness review of roadless areas in the national forests. In 1967 the Forest Service decided to inventory such areas, the initial step in the first Roadless Area Review and Evaluation (RARE I). There was little follow-up, however, until 1971 when outside pressures finally forced the Forest Service to act. Having moved very slowly for four years, the Forest Service now rushed to complete the

---

69. James L. Huffman, "A History of Forest Policy in the United States," *Environmental Law* 8, no. 2 (Winter 1978): 277.

inventory. A total of 56 million acres were identified as roadless. Of this acreage, 10.7 million acres were selected in 1972 by the Forest Service for intensive wilderness study.

The study procedures followed by the Forest Service provoked outcries from the environmental and recreation communities. The Forest Service had used a strict standard of judging signs of previous human presence in an area; minor structures or roads were enough to exclude an area from any consideration for wilderness, no matter how otherwise isolated and wild the area might be. Large potential wildernesses were sometimes cut up into pieces by the presence of old and barely discernible roads. In 1972 the Sierra Club and other environmental organizations brought suit against the Forest Service to prevent any commercial activity in roadless areas until an acceptable environmental impact statement for them had been completed. Apparently having doubts about its own position, the Forest Service agreed to this request rather than fight it. The effect was to bar timber harvesting and other development activities from nearly one third of all Forest Service land.

By the time the Carter administration entered office in early 1977, the wilderness review had bogged down. Large acreages were left in limbo, available neither for wilderness nor for other uses. To resolve questions more rapidly and at a national level, a new wilderness review procedure was established—RARE II. The new review began by redoing the basic inventory. This time, the Forest Service granted wider flexibility in allowing evidence of previous development, so long as these signs of human presence did not too severely impair the potential for wilderness experience. For example, areas previously cut over for timber could be included if they had returned to a condition characteristic of areas that had never been cut. Special standards were provided for the eastern national forests, a step much sought by recreationists. This process eventually resulted in the identification of 2,919 individual roadless areas containing a total of 62 million acres. Also, the review sought to ensure that the overall wilderness system included adequate representation of different types of ecosystems and land forms, and that wilderness was distributed so as to provide adequate accessibility for different populations.

In January 1979 the Forest Service released a final environmental impact statement that recommended 15 million acres of new wilderness, 36 million acres of nonwilderness (to be managed under multiple-use principles) and further planning on 11 million acres.[70] Although recreationist critics considered RARE II an improvement over RARE I, they were still harshly critical. The Sierra Club and the Natural Resources Defense Council (NRDC) attacked it as inadequate, biased, and illogical. In their view, the Forest Service had decided to emphasize "speed before quality."[71] Both groups argued that the only thing to do was to put most of the land into the further study category.

The tribulations of the Forest Service in conducting its wilderness review were no doubt partially due to management mistakes. But they were also due significantly to deficiencies in the agency's basic approach to wilderness, which reflect broader problems of public forest management as discussed earlier.

In his insightful book on the Forest Service, Glen Robinson examined closely the problems the Forest Service had experienced in conducting RARE I.[72] The issue was an emotional one; every little battle tended to be elevated to a grand contest of ideology; "contention between preservationists and multiple-use advocates is quickly escalated into a grand debate over wilderness vs. nonwilderness values, which in turn becomes an even more wide-ranging debate over the character of modern civilization. For some preservationists, each battle is but a larger holy war and has a symbolic significance far beyond any measurable objective. So, too, for some of the opposition."[73] Another factor making things difficult for the Forest Service was the strength of local feelings accompanying each wilderness dispute.

Partially because the wilderness concept is vague, it is not possible to say definitively that one area is wilderness and another not. Among potential wilderness preserves, there are large differences in the other resource values foregone by wilderness designation; some potential wilderness areas in the overthrust belt of the Rocky Mountains may contain extremely valuable oil and gas, while others have

70. U.S. Department of Agriculture, U.S. Forest Service, *Roadless Area Review and Evaluation: Final Environmental Statement* (January 1979).

71. "Comments of the Sierra Club and the Natural Resources Defense Council on the United States Department of Agriculture, Forest Service's Draft Environmental Statement on the Roadless Area Review and Evaluation (RARE II)," in USDA, *Roadless Area Review and Evaluation*, p. V–141.

72. Robinson, *The Forest Service*, pp. 161–89.

73. Ibid., p. 167.

little if any commercial potential. These factors make the wilderness issue, at least in part, a question of resource allocation; that is to say, an economic question. According to Robinson, the Forest Service's reluctance to employ economic analysis has been a serious impediment to a satisfactory wilderness review. In this regard, he finds that "the Forest Service has not made much use of economic analysis in its primitive area review process until recently. Even now [1975] one senses it is groping somewhat in deciding just how and how much an economic analysis (beyond crude thumbnail calculations) will aid in decisionmaking." [74] The record does not show much change in this regard.

Some observers consider that the designation of a wilderness area actually constitutes a religious statement — that wilderness areas are "churches" or "cathedrals" in modern civilization. Indeed, a strong religious motive is explicit in the writings of John Muir, founder of the Sierra Club in 1892. Muir often referred to the wilderness as his "temple" where he sought refuge from the trials of urban life. [75] Partially for this reason, some proponents contend that wilderness is "priceless" and cannot be subject to economic valuation. Nevertheless, such contentions must be taken as largely rhetorical; society obviously has a limit on the sacrifices it will make to create more wilderness. Indeed, medieval society similarly could not afford unlimited expenses for its religious statements; many other benefits of wilderness are of a much more mundane sort — hiking, fishing, hunting, and so forth.

In short, wilderness does have a value, if one more difficult to fully determine than many other values. Some portions of the value can be estimated in a formal way despite the fact that the benefits have a nonmarket character. It is often easier to determine the costs of wilderness — loss of timber harvests, minerals, intensive recreation, and other excluded activities. These costs may well be minimal in many potential wilderness areas, greatly simplifying the task of deciding whether wilderness designation is appropriate.

---

74. Robinson, *The Forest Service*, p. 173.

75. See Roderick Nash, *Wilderness and the American Mind* (New Haven, Conn.: Yale University Press, 1967); also William Dennis, "Wilderness Cathedrals and the Public Good" (Paper presented at a symposium on "Natural Resource Economics and Policy: Explorations with Journalists," Center for Political Economy and Natural Resources, Montana State University, Bozeman, Montana, June 15–June 19).

The Forest Service's unwillingness to subject wilderness decisions to economic analysis has further politicized these decisions – the same consequence seen elsewhere of a lack of economic analysis. Decisionmakers have been required to proceed with little hard information, exacerbating the pressures to make wilderness decisions as a symbolic – perhaps even religious – gesture.

THE ECONOMICS OF TIMBER HARVESTS

Harvesting timber makes a positive contribution to national economic output only if the value of the timber is greater than the costs of harvesting it. On lands where this is not the case, more resources are used up in obtaining the timber than the output is worth. The social loss is increased when valuable recreation and other nonmarket uses of forest land are displaced by uneconomic timber harvesting.[76]

It is sometimes suggested that unprofitable timber should nevertheless be harvested in order to restrain increases in (or help drive down) the price of timber. However, production of unprofitable timber will act to raise the prices of other goods. By drawing off resources that would more economically be used in nontimber sectors, less production takes place in these sectors; the supply declines and prices rise. Timber price rises are thus simply displaced to price rises of other goods.

Clawson, among many others, finds that Forest Service timber investments and harvests have often been economically irrational – that "the pattern of expenditures by regions and by forests strongly suggests that too much money is being spent on poor sites and not enough on good ones."[77] In particular, Clawson reports that "the Forest Service has made timber sales on poor sites, where continued timber management is uneconomic, and has incurred costs for cleaning up the site (more for aesthetic than for silviculture reasons), which were in excess of the value of the timber sold. It is difficult to justify timber management that costs more than it returns, especially

---

76. See John Baden and Richard L. Stroup, eds., *Bureaucracy versus Environment: The Environmental Costs of Bureaucratic Governance* (Ann Arbor: University of Michigan Press, 1981); and Richard L. Stroup and John Baden, *Natural Resources: Bureaucratic Myths and Environmental Management* (San Francisco: Pacific Research Institute for Public Policy, 1983).

77. Marion Clawson, *The Economics of National Forest Management* (Baltimore: Johns Hopkins University Press, 1976), p. 78.

since nontimber values are as likely to be reduced as to be increased thereby."[78]

By concentrating timber management efforts on the best areas and sites and adopting other measures to use its resources more effectively, Clawson concluded that the Forest Service could simultaneously increase greatly the volume of timber, wilderness, and other outputs. Indeed, he has estimated—perhaps somewhat optimistically—that with more efficient management of national forests, the wood grown annually could be increased on an economic basis by a factor of two or three, wilderness areas expanded by a factor of three or four, and outdoor recreation visits by a factor of two or three.[79] The conflict between timber harvesting and recreation thus could be greatly reduced simply by ceasing to harvest timber on uneconomic lands. In fact, the Sierra Club proposed in 1977 to intensify harvests on some highly productive timberlands in exchange for abandoning harvesting altogether on much lower productivity lands.[80]

The response of the Forest Service to these criticisms has been to acknowledge that many timber sales are uneconomic, but to defend them nevertheless. Assistant Secretary of Agriculture Rupert Cutler reported that Forest Service calculations showed almost 22 percent of the volume of timber harvested in 1978 did not generate enough public revenues to cover public costs.[81] Cutler, however, cited the Multiple-Use Sustained-Yield Act provision that the goal of Forest Service management is "not necessarily the combination of uses that will give the greatest dollar return or the greatest unit output." Moreover, timber harvesting may promote multiple uses and recreational benefits from wider road accessibility. Cutler also made the argument that even unprofitable timber sales increase the supply of timber, lower timber prices, and maintain employment. The same could, of course, be said for any form of production, public or private, no matter how wasteful or unprofitable.

78. Ibid., p. 86.

79. Marion Clawson, "The National Forests," *Science* 191, no. 4227 (February 20, 1976), p. 763.

80. Statement by Brock Evans, Director, Washington office, Sierra Club, before the Senate Subcommittee on Interior of the Appropriations Committee regarding the Forest Service budget for fiscal year 1978 (April 19, 1977).

81. Rupert Cutler, Assistant Secretary of the Department of Agriculture for Natural Resources and Environment, to James G. Dean, Editor of *The Living Wilderness*, March 13, 1980.

The Forest Service defines its main timber objectives in terms of volume of wood harvested. The absence of an economic orientation leaves a vacuum that instead is filled by physical output measures. Harvesting of uneconomic timber allows the Forest Service to reach its timber harvest goal for the year. Field personnel often believe they will be judged by the volume of timber harvested, not by its quality or profit. This is a problem widely observed in large bureaucracies of all kinds.

But the chief explanation for the maintenance of uneconomic timber harvests is political pressure from local timber areas. Local timber companies bid what the timber is worth; it is the Forest Service—and indirectly the national taxpayer—that absorbs the harvest deficits. Local communities and mill workers also benefit from income and jobs generated by timber harvests. Hence, local pressures typically offer strong support for the continuance of uneconomic harvests, although some local recreationists and environmentalists may object.

In a political context, economic analysis tends to serve as pressure for a national perspective. The reluctance to employ economics is partially a reflection of a long tradition in public land agencies of deference to local concerns. Traditionally, the Forest Service has proclaimed a management philosophy to decentralize decisionmaking as much as possible to the field. In an earlier era, when public management costs for national forests were small and many decisions concerned solely the allocation of land among local uses, this local delegation may have made good sense. More recently, however, the rapidly growing costs of forest management require the assertion of outside constraints, especially since local areas pay so few of the costs. The local incentive is simply to press for further services whose costs will be borne by someone else.

HARVESTING OF OLD GROWTH TIMBER

As discussed previously, the role of the Forest Service as supplier of last resort, left it after World War II with large inventories of old growth timber, in the case of softwoods much larger than those of any other type of ownership. Facing strong pressures to increase supplies, the Forest Service did raise its harvest levels substantially, and would have gone further had it not encountered strong opposition from recreational users.

The possession of large old growth forests required the Forest Service to decide how best to draw down this one-time inventory. Traditional forestry principles, however, offered little guidance. Going back to Pinchot, forestry principles were derived from European circumstances in which few old growth forests existed. The chief issues for European foresters had been the level of timber investment and how long to let the forest grow before harvesting—the rotation age. The management of a huge stock of timber in vast virgin forests was a wholly unfamiliar problem.[82]

The Forest Service—indeed the entire forestry profession—proved very slow in recognizing the differences between the European and American circumstances. Having learned a particular gospel, foresters attempted to apply it in all circumstances. Thus, the allowable cut was set by the Forest Service at the level of long-run sustained yield, even on forests where a large old growth inventory was found. This harvest policy was eventually enshrined as the "nondeclining even flow" policy. Specifically, it required timber harvests from a national forest be set at the maximum level achievable that would never allow future harvests to fall below this level.

The Forest Service initially defined the long run as the period of the first rotation—usually about one hundred years. The nondeclining even-flow policy then set the allowable cut to equal the maximum sustainable harvest over the duration of the rotation. However, because there was so much old growth timber on the national forests, much higher harvesting levels could be sustained for the first rotation than for subsequent rotations. Studies by the Forest Service in the late 1960s revealed that a significant drop off in harvests at the end of the first rotation would occur.

Because this seemed to violate the spirit of the nondeclining even-flow policy, even if it would not occur for one hundred years, in 1973 the Forest Service decided to adopt an even more strict harvesting standard: harvests must equal the maximum nondeclining even flow of timber that could be sustained indefinitely. In areas with ample supplies of old growth timber, this resulted in a constant even flow of timber at the level of long-run sustained yield. In other forests, the harvest might start off lower and then rise to the long-run sustainable level. But a harvest higher than long-run sustained yield

82. See R. W. Behan, "Forestry and the End of Innocence," *American Forests* 81, no. 5 (May 1975); and idem, "Political Popularity and Conceptual Nonsense: The Strange Case of Sustained Yield Forestry," *Environmental Law* 8, no. 2 (Winter 1978).

was precluded, even where the subsequent drop might only be to the level of long-run sustained yield. This was in fact feasible in a number of federal forests with large inventories of old growth timber.

The public land agencies have justified the even-flow policy partially as a means of promoting community stability. However, this implicitly assumed that private and state timber harvests were also being maintained at an even flow. As will be recalled, private timber has generally been harvested ahead of federal timber—indeed, for good economic reasons. But private supplies in the Pacific Northwest are now rapidly being depleted and will decline sharply until second growth forests become available. In such circumstances, an even-flow policy for public forests perversely becomes a destabilizing rather than a stabilizing influence.

Forest Service harvest policies for old growth timber were questioned as early as the late 1950s. A study prepared by the Forest Service examined harvesting issues for the forests in the Pacific Northwest (the so-called Duerr report).[83] One alternative provided for a five-decade acceleration of timber harvests to twice the levels that would be achieved under the even-flow policy. Over the full rotation (eleven decades), total timber harvests would be increased 27 percent over the even-flow policy. The only liability would be that in decades six through eight, harvests would drop to half the even-flow levels. Although this drop might be made up by private harvest acceleration, it created the possibility—however far in the future—of substantial local income and employment instability. The Forest Service considered this alternative to be so heretical that it required the alternative be dropped from the final version of the study eventually published in 1963.

By the early 1970s timber supplies had tightened further, prices had risen sharply, and Forest Service harvest policies were receiving much wider attention. The price of timber was identified as an important contributor to a surge then occurring in housing costs. Timber prices were one of the few housing cost elements that the federal government might directly influence. Pressures thus grew to find additional supplies of public timber, and resulted in the creation of the President's Advisory Panel on Timber and the Environment. The

83. U.S. Forest Service, Pacific Northwest Forest and Range Experiment Station, *Timber Trends in Western Oregon and Western Washington*, Portland, Oregon, August 1960. (Unpublished.)

panel examined the even-flow issue, and in one of its reports concluded that timber harvests could be accelerated by 30 percent on
certain forests heavily stocked with old growth timber. The panel
reported, "Even flow restrictions clearly result in a substantially lowered allowable cut than would be the case if full recognition were
given to the fact that a typical western national forest is frequently
overstocked with old growth timber and the fact that this overstocking can be harvested over a period of time without any reduction in
the amount of second growth timber that can be grown in subsequent rotations."[84] Similar concerns that conservative federal timber
harvesting policies were driving up timber prices unnecessarily were
expressed in 1977 by the Council on Wage and Price Stability.[85]

Further concern for the inflationary effects of federal harvest policies was expressed in the spring of 1978 when inflation rates again
jumped suddenly. In April President Carter announced a new inflation program, including as one element new efforts to contain rising
housing prices through expanded federal timber sales. The Secre-
taries of Agriculture and Interior were instructed to report on ways
of increasing federal timber harvests. In preparing the report, internal administration debate focused on the possibilities for departing
from even flow as a way of increasing timber supplies. To make such
a departure more acceptable, a constraint was proposed that future
harvests never decline below the even-flow level. Even-flow proponents were put on the defensive because they were forced to argue
that current timber harvest increases should be rejected even where
they did not require any future declines in timber harvests below
those already planned (under even flow).

The strongest opposition to departures from an even-flow policy
came from the Council on Environmental Quality. The council and
to a lesser extent the Forest Service argued that the National Forest
Management Act of 1976 did not allow departures from an even
flow. The greatest support for departures came from the economic
agencies (Council of Economic Advisors and the Council on Wage
and Price Stability) and the Interior Department. Interior Secretary
Cecil Andrus had himself been in the timber business and took this
issue into his own hands to an unusual degree. In June 1979 the

84. *Report of the President's Advisory Panel on Timber and Environment* (Washington,
D.C.: Government Printing Office, April 1973), p. 80.

85. U.S. Council on Wage and Price Stability, *Interim Report: Lumber Prices and the
Lumber Products Industry* (October 1977).

President announced that he was directing the Departments of Agriculture and Interior to "use maximum speed in updating land management plans on selected . . . lands with the objective of increasing the harvest of mature timber through departure from the current nondeclining even-flow policy."[86]

Once again, the Forest Service had found itself being overriden by an outside institution. In the case of wilderness and environmental protection of fragile areas, it was by environmentalists and the courts; on even flow and the harvesting of old growth timber, it was by other agencies in the executive branch and by the president. In each instance, the Forest Service had proven unable to adjust to new ideas and had clung to ill-conceived policies until finally outside forces compelled change. Although the Forest Service had been conceived as a vanguard agency, it had long since become defensive and reactive, slow to see new requirements and forces being brought to bear on it.

As in so many other cases, the fundamental problem in its approach to harvesting old growth timber lay in the absence of an analytical and skeptical tradition. For bureaucratic and other reasons, the agency found it very difficult even to ask the right questions about the harvesting of a large one-time timber inventory. The Forest Service also promoted even flow partially because it saw this policy as a popular and easily explainable interpretation to the public of sustained yield management; in short, it sounded good. An even-flow policy was also easy to administer since the guidance to the field for determining timber harvests followed a simple mechanical rule. The fact that even flow produced nonsensical results was perhaps not initially recognized; in any case, once the policy was officially decreed, the Forest Service stubbornly defended it against all criticism, as though it were defending the one true faith.[87]

PUBLIC FOREST MYTHOLOGY

An examination of the track record of public forestry in the United States—now more than three quarters of a century old—reveals some

86. Memoranda to the Secretary of Agriculture and the Secretary of the Interior from the White House, June 1979. For further details on this policy debate, see Robert H. Nelson and Lucian Pugliaresi, "Timber Harvest Policy Issues on the O & C Lands," in this volume.

87. See Thomas Lenard, "Wasting Our National Forests," *Regulation* (July/August 1981).

major shortcomings. There is no contesting that the public forests contain natural assets of high value, which have conferred many wonderful benefits on the American public. The nation has succeeded in harvesting large amounts of valuable timber and in creating a system of national parks and wildernesses. The national forests have become prime recreational grounds for millions of hikers, fishermen, hunters, and other recreationists. However, these impressive gains have often been achieved by surmounting the main precepts of public forestry, rather than with their assistance.

The Forest Service for years issued dire warnings about timber famines that in every case proved to be false alarms. It warned that public regulation of private harvests was the only way to achieve forest regeneration, only to see parts of industry exceed the Forest Service itself a few years later in regeneration success. The Forest Service persisted for years in promoting scientifically inaccurate and misguided information about the impacts of water and fire in the national forests. The agency also misread the future by almost always resisting creation of new national parks from national forestlands, arguing against preservation of large areas from commodity uses.

After pushing the Multiple-Use Sustained-Yield Act through to enactment, the Forest Service did little to give this vague concept more substance; instead, it used the act as an ever handy justification for just about any Forest Service policy or action. After initially appearing to promote wilderness, the Forest Service cooled to the idea when the concept appeared to limit the agency's prerogatives. In the face of rapidly growing public demands for more recreation, the Forest Service instead has persisted in harvesting timber in roadless and other recreationally valuable areas even when that timber is uneconomic to cut. The nondeclining even-flow policy advocated by the Forest Service led to obviously silly and unreasonable timber harvesting implications.

The Forest Service still reflects in many ways the character initially given to it by Gifford Pinchot, who saw his role as one of promoting scientific forest management in the United States. But in achieving his mission, he behaved not as a scientist but as a proselytizer. When challenged, Pinchot did what was necessary to advance his aims, and scientific caution did not necessarily get in his way. Those who agreed with him would later argue that his actions were necessary means to defeat the powerful and self-seeking forces that opposed him—the timber companies, stockmen, and others; Pinchot was a man of action who should be judged by his success in creating the Forest Service, not the consistency of his thought. As one friendly observer puts it, his "genius lay not in silviculture but in progressive reform politics."[88] It took a man of immense political talent because Pinchot, after all, was trying to sell "a socialist approach to forestry—public ownership in operation—in an age when rugged individualism, laissez-faire capitalism, and minimal federal regulation were the accepted political norms."[89]

But as so often happens, the means became the end. The Forest Service has never adopted the highly self-critical and questioning attitude characteristic of science; it has shown declining fervor, but never really called off the moral crusade. To skeptical outsiders, Forest Service policymaking often seems to bear a closer resemblance to moral affirmation than to hard analysis.

In reviewing the history of Forest Service policies, it seems clear that a prime criterion has often been to create a suitable image in the public eye. Early opponents were portrayed as villainous perpetrators of "forest devastation" who were pushing the country into a "timber famine." In setting its own policies, the Forest Service characterizes itself as following the principles of "multiple use," "sustained yield," and "even flow," all of which may sound laudible, but in practice are vacuous or even misconceived. Until recently, the Forest Service had shown a genius for favorable publicity such as the Smokey the Bear campaign, which had great public appeal. In reciprocation, until recently at least, the public has showered good will on the Forest Service, which ultimately has been translated into large budgets and congressional deference.

The fact that the Forest Service was a purveyor of very appealing myths did not make much difference so long as Forest Service management remained largely custodial, a situation that lasted up until World War II. One might even say the Forest Service performed a noble public service in this regard, storing the lands for future, more important uses. But in the past thirty-five years there has been a widening discontent with the management of the national forests. The earlier foundations satisfactory for a custodial role proved inadequate to meet a new era of intense competition among valuable uses of the public lands.

The criticisms of Forest Service mythology are part of a wider criticism of the ideas of the conservation movement. The term con-

---

88. Behan, "Forestry and the End of Innocence," p. 38.
89. Ibid., p. 38.

servationist has great popular appeal. As Gordon noted, it is "replete with honorable and admirable connotations, designating one who is unselfish, and forward-looking, rational and public spirited, energetic and self-denying." Nevertheless, this critic concludes, much as others have, that "a great deal (perhaps the greater part) of what has been done in the name of 'conservation policy' turns out, on subjection to economic analysis, to be worthless or worse."[90]

The Forest Service has never found a satisfactory alternative to its founding conservationist gospel. As support for conservationist ideas has eroded, the defenses against political intervention in national forest affairs have fallen. Indeed, as previous discussion has indicated, over the past thirty years management decisions regarding the national forests have become more political. The criterion for a good decision now typically is to achieve a satisfactory balance of user pressures. Some political scientists contend that this is as it should be. Rejecting a scientific basis for government policies, the proponents of "interest-group liberalism" see the governing process as appropriately and inevitably one of interest-group bargaining and agreement.[91]

For those who find such a view unsatisfactory, the chief hope to revive scientific forest management lies in economics. Economics seeks to provide an objective measure of the value of each forest resource use. Then, rather than weighing the claims of public forest users by their political power and influence, economic decisionmaking would weigh these claims by their market prices or estimated social values. Similarly, the use of economics would attempt to put management of the public forests on a business-like basis. Instead of managing to produce a maximum profit, however, the wider standard of total social value would be maximized, taking account of nonmarket outputs as well as ordinary commodity outputs.

RETHINKING PUBLIC FOREST MANAGEMENT

One cannot be optimistic, however, that a vision of a new economically sophisticated Forest Service is achievable. There are both internal agency obstacles and external political constraints. Either alone is

90. Scott Gordon, "Economics and the Conservation Question," *Journal of Law and Economics* 1, no. 1 (October 1958): 110–11.

91. See Theodore J. Lowi, *The End of Liberalism: Ideology, Policy and the Crisis of Public Authority* (New York: W. W. Norton, 1969).

probably sufficient to ensure that future decisionmaking for the federal forests will continue to rely primarily on factors other than economic analysis.

It would not be enough simply to introduce some economists into the Forest Service. There have, in fact, previously been economists in the agency, but they have had a small influence. In order to make economic concerns a central element in agency decisionmaking, more drastic steps are necessary. The leadership positions of the agency must be occupied by people who are either economists themselves or for whom economic reasoning is second nature. This would amount to a revolution in the selection and advancement processes of most public agencies. Short of extreme outside pressures, it is hard to imagine how the existing leadership would make way for such a new economist cast—most of whom would have to be brought in from outside.

To be sure, skills in economic analysis have not traditionally commanded much of a premium in public forestry because the rest of the world has not asked for them. Under the original conservationism, public forestry was to be practiced by expert professionals insulated from politics. But it never turned out that way. Rather, the Forest Service has always operated in a highly charged political environment. Much of the appeal of forestry mythology has been as a way of rallying support to protect Forest Service independence. This effort achieved some success in the early history of the agency, but has become less feasible over time. Now, like most government agencies, the Forest Service is pushed and shoved by the many interest groups that stand to benefit or lose from its policies. Indeed, it may be that the Forest Service has ended up with the worst of both worlds; it frequently abandoned scientific analysis for popular imagery, but still could not achieve the independence from politics prescribed in the conservationist design.

Hence, even if the Forest Service were to decide to base its management on a much greater use of economics, there would still be no guarantee that its policies eventually adopted would closely reflect this change. If a new economically sophisticated Forest Service were also less popular and therefore politically weakened—indeed, perhaps as a direct consequence of its turn to economic calculations—the Forest Service might have less ability to implement its newly efficient plans. The ultimate consequence might be a further breakdown of the barriers to political interference and an even less efficient set of actions carried out on the national forests.

Public forest management thus represents an illustration of a basic dilemma facing natural resource management in the public sector.[92] Professional management is impossible without substantial autonomy from the political forces that characterize democratic government. Yet the achievement of such autonomy is itself a highly political task; the necessary political actions compromise both the claim to independent professionalism and the professional quality of management decisions. Progressives sought to establish the idea of management by experts as a generally accepted governing principle. However, this effort had to concede defeat long ago to the pressures of interest-group politics.

The failure of the progressive prescription, combined with grave doubts as to the efficiency or equity of interest-group politics, raise the possibility of more radical solutions.[93] One option would be to dispose of at least the prime timber growing lands to the private sector.[94] Private management would have much more of the autonomy from politics necessary to implement scientific management of the forests. Indeed, rather than the modern Forest Service management, Weyerhaeuser forest management is probably much closer to what Gifford Pinchot and other conservationists originally had in mind. Private management of divested public timberlands would probably not mean a group of small timber firms; rather, it would probably involve creating one or more new major corporations (or expanding existing ones).

However, the accountability of the large corporation to market forces is not always very great — especially in the short run. Nor are the political mechanisms for regulating corporate behavior always efficient in achieving social goals not reflected in market incentives. These concerns seem particularly important on lands with marginally

92. Further treatment of these issues with respect to federal coal policy is found in Robert H. Nelson, *The Making of Federal Coal Policy* (Durham, N.C.: Duke University Press, 1983).

93. See Robert H. Nelson, "Ideology and Public Land Policy: The Current Crisis," in Sterling Brubaker, ed., *Rethinking the Federal Lands* (Washington, D.C.: Resources for the Future – distributed by the Johns Hopkins University Press, 1984).

94. See Richard Stroup and John Baden, "Externality, Property Rights and the Management of our National Forests," *Journal of Law and Economics* 16, no. 2 (October 1973); Phillip N. Truluck and David J. Theroux, eds., *Private Rights and Public Lands* (Washington, D.C.: Heritage Foundation; San Francisco: Pacific Research Institute for Public Policy, 1983); and articles on "Land Use and Resource Development" in *The Cato Journal* 2, no.: (Winter 1982).

profitable timber, but which have high recreation and environmental values.

Such public forest issues have not been fully aired since the progressive era. The time is overdue for a re-examination of fundamental assumptions and purposes with respect to public forest ownership and indeed public land management more broadly. The chief options would seem to be revitalization of federal forest management, transfer of federal forestlands to the states, or disposal of forestlands to the private sector. The ultimate resolution might well involve a combination of these options; each land tenure would be applied on the public forestlands to which it is most suited.[95]

95. See Robert H. Nelson, "The Public Lands," in Paul R. Portney, ed., *Current Issues in Natural Resource Policy* (Washington, D.C.: Resources for the Future–distributed by the Johns Hopkins University Press, 1982). See also Robert H. Nelson, "Making Sense of the Sagebrush Rebellion: A Long-Term Strategy for the Public Lands" (Paper prepared for presentation at the Third Annual Conference of the Association for Public Policy Analysis and Management, Washington, D.C., October 23–25, 1981). A shortened version of this paper is found in Robert H. Nelson "A Long-Term Strategy for the Public Lands" in Richard Ganzel, ed., *Resource Conflicts in the West* (Reno: Nevada Public Affairs Institute – University of Nevada, March 1983).

Chapter 3

PUBLIC TIMBER POLICY AND THE WOOD-PRODUCTS INDUSTRY

Barney Dowdle and Steve H. Hanke

INTRODUCTION

The wood-products industry, which produces lumber, plywood, and various other wood products, is an important sector of the overall economy. Numerous regional and local economies are highly dependent upon the production of wood products, which are also important inputs to other industries, especially housing. It has been estimated that 14 percent of the cost of a new single-family home consists of expenditures on lumber and wood products.[1] The slump in housing starts that accompanied the recent recession severely impacted the wood-products industry. This impact was most serious in western states where many producers are dependent upon public timber supplies. A number of important policy questions have been raised because of apparent causality in this relationship between the public and private sectors.

Public timber policy, which, broadly defined, encompasses a number of specific federal and state timber management, tax, and regulatory policies, is increasingly being identified as the source of industry problems. Particular attention has been focused on federal timber management policy; the primary goal of which is to stabilize commu-

---

1. *Forest Service Timber Sales: Their Effect on Wood Product Prices* (Washington, D.C.: Congressional Budget Office, 1980).

nities that are dependent upon timber and wood-products industries. The economies of these communities are among those most seriously impacted by the recent recession. Public timber-marketing practices, for example, encouraged speculative bidding for federal timber, and this in turn led to a curtailment of production beyond that caused by depressed demand. Subsequently, a bailout was granted to holders of federal timber-cutting contracts.

Federal timber management policy, as well as some state tax and regulatory policies, also appears responsible for the migration of the wood-products industry from the Pacific Northwest, where over 70 percent of the total timber inventory is owned and managed by various agencies of government, to the south, where most forestlands and timber are privately owned. It is worthy to note that the federal government owns and manages 554 billion board feet of softwood sawtimber inventory in Idaho, Oregon, and Washington—63 percent more than the entire south.[2] Private investors appear to be increasingly reluctant to invest in wood-conversion facilities significantly dependent upon this federal timber inventory.

Even though the wood-products industry is recovering from its recent economic difficulties, it still faces serious economic problems. This is especially so in the west where the industry appears to be suffering the chronic economic anemia characteristic of a declining industry. Moreover, a direct correlation exists between the severity of the industry's condition and its dependence upon public timber supplies. State and local tax and regulatory policies merely make a bad situation worse.

To be more specific, faulty timber management and timber marketing policies and the political-bureaucratic practices associated with the implementation of these policies create uncertain and unstable timber supplies. Private producers will not operate in an environment of this kind if alternatives exist.

A number of perverse federal and state policies threaten both the short- and long-term health and viability of wood-products and timber production. Federal timber management policies are the most seriously defective and most urgently in need of correction. Certain state tax and regulatory policies are likely to affect private timber production over the long run as are specific counterproductive policies; yet there are some prescriptions for effective policy changes.

2. USDA, Forest Service, *Forest Statistics of the United States*, unnumbered publication (1980).

TIMBER OWNERSHIP PATTERNS

The nation contains 488 million acres of commercial forestland, about 25 percent of the total land area of the continental United States. Commercial forestlands, as listed in Table 3–1, are classed by regions and types of ownership and do not include forestlands within national parks, wilderness areas, or other exclusive-use areas.

Publicly owned commercial forestlands are concentrated in the Pacific and Rocky Mountain states, where 63 and 75 percent of the forests, respectively, are in some form of government ownership. In the north and south only 18 and 9 percent, respectively, of commercial forestlands are public.

The concentration of public forestlands in the west is a result of land disposition policies designed to implement private ownership during the nation's formative years, when heavy settlement following the westward movement was taking place. These policies were changed to promote public ownership, especially of timberlands, around the turn of the century.

The rows in Table 3–1 show millions of acres and percent of total U.S. commercial forestlands by region and owner. In the northern region, for example, 121.6 million acres or 71 percent of the total

Table 3–1. Commercial Forestland Ownership in the United States by Region and Ownership, Million Acres, 1977.

Region	National Forest	Other Public	Forest Industry	Other Private	Total Percent[a]
North	10.1	21.2	17.8	121.6	170.7
Percent	6	12	11	71	35
South	11.0	6.7	35.8	134.9	188.4
Percent	6	3	19	72	38
Pacific	31.5	12.9	12.3	14.1	70.8
Percent	45	18	17	20	15
Rocky Mountain	36.4	6.8	2.1	12.5	57.8
Percent	63	12	4	21	12
U.S. Total	89.0	47.6	68.0	283.1	487.7
Percent[b]	18	10	14	58	100

a. Percent of U.S. total by region.
b. Percent of U.S. total by ownership.

Source: USDA, Forest Service, *Forest Statistics of the United States*, unnumbered publication, review draft (1978), pp. 3–8.

170.7 million acres of commercial forestland is owned by the "Other Private" class of owners. Forestland owners in this class grow and sell timber, but in general do not engage in wood processing. Total commercial forest acreage in the northern region comprises 35 percent of the U.S. total.

Figures in the columns of Table 3-1 indicate regional acreages by ownership. For example, the column under "National Forests" first indicates that total commercial acreage on the national forests is 89.0 million acres, or 18 percent of the U.S. total and second, that 45 and 63 percent of the forestland areas in the Pacific and Rocky Mountain regions, respectively, are in the national forests.

Commercial forestlands, while important from the standpoint of future timber supplies, do not necessarily indicate where lumber and plywood will be produced in the near term. Sources of supplies of these solid wood products will be determined for the next several decades by the location of existing inventories of mature softwood sawtimber (see Table 3-2). Timber supplies from these inventories are, in turn, importantly affected by timber management policies.

The contrast between the ownership patterns of commercial forestland and softwood sawtimber inventories is evident by comparing Tables 3-1 and 3-2. While most of the commercial forestland is in private ownership (72 percent), the public sector currently owns most of the mature softwood sawtimber (63 percent). The national forests alone, as noted in Table 3-2, contain over half (51 percent) the total inventory.

The disparity between the public ownership of commercial forestland (28 percent) and the public ownership of mature timber (63 percent) arises because past timber harvests were concentrated in the private sector. During the first fifty years of their existence (1905-1955), the national forest contributed about 3 percent to total softwood timber output.[3]

As a result of past timber harvests originating primarily in the private sector, much of the private timber inventory now consists of immature timber established on previously cut over lands. Much of this timber will not reach maturity and be ready for harvest for several years. In the interim, the wood-processing industry will be heav-

3. Marion Clawson and Burnell Held, *The Federal Lands: Their Use and Management* (Baltimore: Johns Hopkins University Press, 1957); and USDA, *The Outlook for Timber in the United States.*, F44-20 (1970).

Table 3–2. Softwood Sawtimber Inventories, by Region and
Ownership, Billion Board Feet, International 1/4-inch Log Scale,
1977.

Region	National Forest	Other Public	Forest Industry	Other Private	Total Percent[a]
North	7.1	12.8	23.1	54.2	97.1
Percent	7	13	24	56	5
South	33.8	13.9	87.3	204.9	340.0
Percent	10	4	26	60	17
Pacific	706.4	166.1	175.8	116.9	1,165.4
Percent	61	14	15	10	59
Rocky Mountain	260.8	42.7	23.3	53.5	380.4
Percent	69	11	6	14	19
U.S. Total	1,008.1	235.6	309.5	429.5	1,982.8
Percent[b]	51	12	16	21	100

a. Percent of U.S. total by region.
b. Percent of U.S. total by ownership.
Source: USDA, Forest Service, *Forest Statistics of the United States*, unnumbered publication, review draft (1978), pp. 39–40.

ily dependent upon public timber supplies. Likewise, public timber policies, which played a minor role in the past, will play a significant role in the future in determining the health and viability of these industries and the prices that consumers pay for lumber, plywood, and other wood products.

HISTORICAL SEQUENCE OF TIMBER HARVESTING

The reasons underlying the historical sequence of timber harvesting by region and ownership provide insights into the emergence of current timber supply problems. Privately owned timber inventories were generally more favorably located with respect to wood-processing facilities and final markets than public timber inventories. Their initial exploitation was therefore economically efficient — superior resources were being used first.

Lumber production was concentrated in the New England states during the early years of the nation's development. As timber inventories there were depleted, production shifted to the Great Lake states, then to the south, and finally to the Pacific Northwest. The Pacific Northwest did not become the center of lumber and plywood production until after World War II.

In spite of the fact that the Pacific region has a timber inventory more than three times as large as the south (Table 3-2), the center of production is now shifting from the Pacific region back to the south. As noted, most of the Pacific region's inventory is in public ownership, hence the implication that policy deficiencies rather than a lack of wood is the cause of the industry's departure.

During the initial settlement and developmental stages of economic growth, the timber industry was effectively a "mining" industry. Natural endowments of mature "virgin" timber provided raw materials for the production of wood products. Timber prices were low during this period, reflecting the vastness of virgin timber inventories and the ample timber supplies these inventories were able to sustain relative to demand. Timber prices did not rise appreciably until after World War II. The trend in prices for Douglas fir, the predominant species in the Pacific Northwest, is shown in Figure 3-1.

During the "mining" era of timber exploitation, the United States had an "excess" inventory of timber. Until this excess was reduced at prices which reflected an "inventory reduction" sale, it was to be expected that the lumber industry would migrate in the direction of low-priced virgin timber. As noted by the trend shown in Figure 3-1, rising timber prices did not signal that this process was nearing completion until the 1940s. From 1940 to 1980 the rate of real price increase was about 3 percent per year. Predictably, the market responded by directing resources into growing timber. Timber companies retained cut over lands; the latter were reforested, and tree "farming" developed into an important industry.

A significant intraregional sequence of timber harvesting occurred in the west from 1950 to 1980. Private inventories of mature timber were depleted and, as was expected, private timber supplies were reduced. As private supplies fell, demand increased for public timber.

The Douglas fir region of the Pacific Northwest (western Oregon and western Washington) provides a good example of this transitional process, especially when compared to changes that took place in the ownership of the timber inventory in the south. Both regions are important sources of lumber and plywood products. Reduced output in one region, therefore, tends to result in increased output in the other.

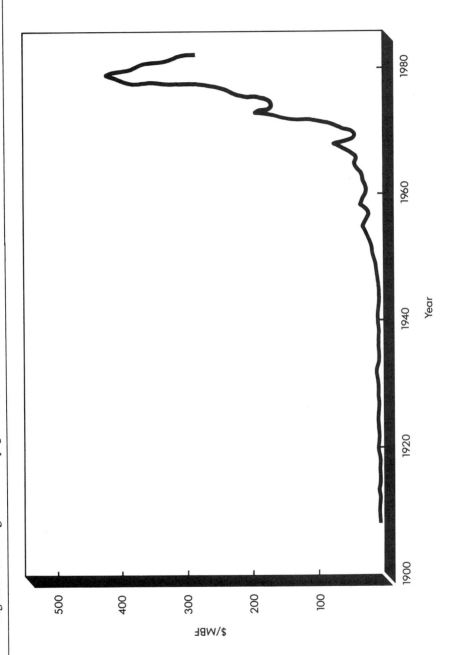

Figure 3-1. Douglas Fir Stumpage Prices, 1910–1982.

The timber inventory in the Douglas fir region was estimated to be 544 billion board feet in 1977. The south had 340 billion board feet at that time.[4] Timber outputs in the two regions for that year were 15.5 and 18.9 billion board feet, respectively. Twenty-five years earlier in 1952, the timber inventory in the Douglas fir region was estimated to be 657 billion board feet, and annual output was 12.9 billion board feet. The south had 197 billion board feet, and annual output was 11.9 billion board feet. During the twenty-five-year period from 1952 to 1977, the timber inventories in the Douglas fir region were declining at a rate of 0.8 percent per year; in the south they were increasing at a rate of 2.2 percent per year. Both trends were to be expected.

The Douglas fir region was producing timber from virgin timber stands that, because of their advanced age, were characterized by large volumes of timber per acre. Net growth rates in some of these stands are commonly negligible or even negative. reflecting the fact that physically overmature timber is subject to rot and decay. As virgin timber was liquidated, inventories fell.

The increase in timber inventories that occurred in the south reflected the region's transition from the exploitation of virgin timber to the production of timber as a crop. As young timber stands on previously cut over timberlands grew to maturity, the timber resource base expanded and the south was able to support increased rates of timber harvest and lumber production. As noted, annual output in the south rose 7 billion board feet (59 percent) in the twenty-five-year period from 1952 to 1977.

Privately owned virgin timber was harvested first in the Douglas fir region for reasons similar to those that dictated the regional location of lumber production historically: private timber was more favorably located with respect to wood-conversion facilities and timber markets. Economic incentives also existed to increase timber growth rates on private lands by harvesting stagnant stands of overmature timber and establishing new timber stands. Idle capital was replaced by productive capital.

Current political pressures to increase harvest rates of public timber are a reversal of what occurred in the past. Historically, private timber owners did not want to compete with public timber supplies,

---

4. USDA, Forest Service, *Forest Statistics.*

and this fact was clearly evident in the positions the owners took in the political arena.

During the 1952 to 1977 period, private sawtimber inventories in the Douglas fir region were reduced from 252 to 165 billion board feet, or 35 percent. Public timber inventories during the same period were reduced from 405 to 379 billion board feet, or only 6 percent. The ending inventory in the private sector included substantial volumes of young timber growing on previously cut over lands; the public timber inventory in 1977 still consisted of mostly virgin timber, much of which was overmature and subject to high rates of mortality and decay.

FEDERAL TIMBER MANAGEMENT POLICIES

Changing patterns of ownership of mature timber inventories will have important implications for timber supplies to the lumber and plywood industries in the Douglas fir region over the next several decades. The reason is that an entirely different set of institutional arrangements will be dominating the amount of timber sold annually. Private timber supplies are determined by economic considerations. The conventional tools of supply and demand analysis (price theory) are useful in predicting the magnitudes of these supplies.

The size and timing of public timber supplies are dictated by policies largely devoid of economics. Economic theory has limited usefulness in estimating what these supplies will be. Political considerations, including agency budgeting processes and pressures to withdraw commercial forestlands for parks or wilderness areas, play an important role.

Government agency policies—such as the Forest Service's legislative mandate, the Multiple-Use Sustained-Yield Act of 1960—that affect timber supplies are commonly labelled "sustained yield" and "multiple use."[5] As the phrase implies, the assumption of sustained yield is that production will be continuous; multiple use means that a variety of goods and services will be produced. Some of these goods, such as timber, are marketed. Others, such as hunting, fishing, and other types of recreation, are not.

5. 16 U.S.C. 528–531.

Under the provisions of the Multiple-Use Sustained-Yield Act, the Forest Service is not required to produce a profit. Moreover, relative prices and costs are not used formally in determining levels and mixes of outputs. These decisions are largely administrative, and are based primarily on ad hoc political considerations. The permissiveness of the Forest Service's legislative mandate invites intense political pressure in the determination of what these allowances will be.

An important analytical concept used in implementing sustained-yield timber production is "even flow," and a recent variant called "nondeclining even flow." The essence of even flow is that the quantity of public timber entering the marketplace is determined by timber inventory volumes and timber growth rates. Information pertaining to both volumes and rates, and constraints imposed to facilitate the production of nonmarketed multiple-use benefits, are used to determine "annual allowable cuts" (AACs).

AACs for public timber are analogous to "bag limits," which are used in the management of fish and wildlife. The nondeclining even-flow variant of even flow merely means that future timber output must never fall below an originally adopted AAC. Increases in output are permissible, but "falloffs" are not.

The assumed objective of even flow is to promote local community "stability." The historical roots of this assumption lie in the belief that if even flows of timber outputs are maintained in local areas, this would then preclude the migration of the lumber industry. Lumbering ghost towns were a common feature of the nineteenth century landscape as virgin timber inventories from which supplies for local mills were being drawn were depleted and industry moved to new locations. Public ownership of timber and management based on the sustained-yield (even-flow) concept were believed to be a means of preventing this occurrence.

The Forest Service, the BLM, and state timber management agencies sell most of their timber under the terms of "pay-as-cut" timber-cutting contracts, which are awarded on the basis of high bids in auction markets. Bids are usually restricted to timber species that comprise the largest proportion of the total volume of timber in the sale. Down payments on these contracts are typically a small percentage of the total bid price, ranging among agencies from about 2 to 10 percent. Volumes of timber in individual sales are relatively small, and contract terms average three to four years. The announced purpose of selling timber in this manner is to enable small firms to compete against larger firms. Empirical evidence demonstrating that existing sales practices are serving this policy purpose is lacking.

ANALYSIS OF PROBLEMS CREATED
BY PUBLIC TIMBER POLICY

Economic problems are created by federal timber policy primarily because relevant economic information is neglected in planning how much timber to supply. Second, timber-marketing practices encourage speculative bidding, and as recent events have demonstrated, speculation in public timber markets has produced some pathological economic effects.

The even-flow concept is the focal point of many of the economic problems that arise, largely because it is not consistent with the economic concept of "supply." Even flow is a relationship between physical output and timber inventory volumes, timber growth rates, and ad hoc environmental constraints. Economic information, such as production costs and market demands, does not enter directly into AAC calculations.

If economic information is not heeded in determining the output of timber producers as large as the Forest Service or the BLM, then it would be coincidental if outputs from those agencies were consistent with maintaining economically efficient timber markets. Disruption would be expected, and this has, in fact, occurred.

Viewed differently, the Forest Service and the BLM are attempting to manage timber, which is a capital asset, without using the accepted rules of optimal capital management. The most conspicuous error in their planning process is improper use of the interest rate.

Misuse of interest occurs in three important areas: (1) capital-carrying charges are not counted on timber inventories, which results in holding too much inventory and the corollary problem of too little current output; (2) timber harvest ages that are too long; and (3) distortions in investment analyses made by public agencies. The latter distortions are not a direct result of even-flow policies, but of the use of faulty investment analyses made in conjunction with these policies. Each of these areas merits discussion, especially the first. The latter two are largely by-products of the first.

The Omission of Capital-Carrying Charges

Capital-carrying charges on timber inventories are omitted from Forest Service management planning as a matter of agency policy. No statutory language exists that sanctions this neglect of interest charges, with the exception of determining optimal timber harvest age, which is discussed later. In fact, it would appear that the relevant statutory language mandates the inclusion of interest charges in the management of federal timber, but the Forest Service is either willfully or unknowingly neglecting this congressional directive.

The National Forest Management Act, for example, mandates that the Secretary of Agriculture shall report on "economic constraints," among other things, in making assessments of the timber supply situation.[6] Additionally, the Forest and Rangeland Renewable Resources Planning Act of 1974 specifically states that management plans for individual forests should be based on "a systematic interdisciplinary approach to achieve integrated consideration of physical, biological, *economic*, and other sciences."[7]

Capital-carrying charges are important "economic constraints" in the management of any kind of inventories, including timber, and their neglect will predictably result in the production of nonoptimal timber supplies. Moreover, any meaningful "consideration" of economics in planning timber management would require that inventory holding costs be considered.

According to current Forest Service regulations for management planning, "economic costs should not include *explicit charges for interest* computed on the value of existing National Forest land and other resources. . . . "[8] This regulation clearly appears to conflict with relevant laws.

Moreover, this regulation is in direct conflict with the position of John B. Crowell, Jr., who is currently Assistant Secretary of Agriculture for Natural Resources and Environment and has responsibility for supervising Forest Service planning activities. In a recent speech Mr. Crowell stated,

---

6. U.S. Senate, National Forest Management Act of 1976. *Report of the Senate Committee on Agriculture and Forest*, Report No. 94–893.

7. Forest and Rangeland Resources Planning Act of 1974, Sec. 6 (b). Emphasis added.

8. Federal Regulation 47 (80): 17947, 4–26–82, para. 1971.53 (10). Emphasis added.

Some 121 administrative units of the National Forest System are currently in the process of preparing plans for all the national forests. . . . A key part of that [planning] analysis is economics. . . .

Not only is this a businesslike way to approach planning, but it is also mandated by law. The Resources Planning Act and the National Forest Management Act both contain numerous references to the need for economic evaluation. I personally believe that economic efficiency must be a principal criterion for decisionmaking in the forest planning process. That doesn't mean it is the *only* criterion or even the overriding criterion. But economic consequences of alternative decision possibilities *must* be laid out if managers are going to identify the most cost effective courses of action.[9]

Disregard of interest-carrying charges on timber inventories in planning timber management perpetuates a practice of long tradition in the Forest Service. The extent to which this tradition has been institutionalized by the Forest Service and the collectivist philosophy on which it is founded, can be better appreciated by a brief digression into its historical background.

Forest Service Traditions

Bernhard Fernow, the first Chief of the Division of Forestry, which was later to become the Forest Service, argued for state ownership of commercial forests on grounds that "the time element, together with the large capital required in timber-wood production, renders the forestry business undesirable to private enterprise of circumscribed means."[10] According to Fernow, forests should be owned by the state. In his words, "the maintenance of continued [timber] supplies . . . is possible only under the supervision of permanent institutions with whom present profit is not the only motive. It calls preeminently for the exercise of the providential functions of the state to counteract the destructive tendencies of private exploitation."[11]

In a 1925 *Journal of Forestry* article, Ward Shepard, an Assistant Chief of the Forest Service, observed that "under sustained yield

9. John B. Crowell, Jr., "Current Public Policies on Natural Resources," Oklahoma State University, Nat Walker Lectureship, 1983, p. 2.

10. Bernhard E. Fernow, *Economics of Forestry* (New York: Thomas Y. Crowell, 1902).

11. Ibid.

[forest management] there is not compound interest."[12] It was sufficient, Shepard argued, if annual revenues from timber sales exceeded annual costs for planting, protection, taxes, and forest administration. "The reverse of this," he said, "is that where compound interest does apply, sustained yield cannot at present be obtained."[13] Since the national forests were being managed on the basis of sustained yield, Shepard felt that "compound interest is not rationally chargeable."[14]

The issue over proper use of the interest rate also arose in the 1934 Copeland Report, which resulted from a congressionally mandated study of the U.S. forestry situation. Prepared by the Forest Service, the report concluded that private forestlands in the United States should be nationalized or, at minimum, strictly regulated.

In a symposium sponsored by the Society of American Foresters to discuss the Copeland Report, Alfred Gaskill, a private forester from Vermont, cautioned the forestry profession "to avoid the risk of discrediting itself and the forestry movement, through giving blind and unintelligent support to doctrines and policies not based on sound interpretation."[15] Gaskill's general comment was partially based on his specific observation that the Forest Service did not count interest charges on forestry investments.

The response to Mr. Gaskill's criticism by the Chief of the Forest Service, Mr. F. A. Silcox, is indicative of the philosophy that continues to dominate Forest Service thinking:

> Why should public investments in forestry be expected to earn compound interest, or even simple interest? Government is not in business, and in spite of popular slogans to the contrary it should not pursue the same objectives. For government to seek a profit on its undertakings is contrary to the underlying philosophy of either socialism or capitalism. In the one, profits have no place; in the other, profits are supposed to be left to private enterprises.[16]

Over the next forty years the Forest Service changed its rhetoric, but the substance of its position regarding interest-carrying charges has remained the same. This is evident in a 1976 exchange of corre-

---

12. Ward Shepard, "The Bogey of Compound Interest," *Journal of Forestry* 32 (1925): 251-59.

13. Ibid.

14. Ibid.

15. Alfred Gaskill, "Whither Forestry?," *Journal of Forestry* 32, no. 2 (1934): 196–201.

16. F. A. Silcox, "Forward Not Backward," *Journal of Forestry* 32, no. 2 (1934): 202–07.

spondence between Senator James A. McClure of Idaho and John R. McGuire, who was then Chief of the Forest Service. Chief McGuire wrote that the Forest Service's interpretation of the proposed National Forest Management Act was that "investment costs would not be capitalized, and that the initial harvest of a stand of trees would normally bear the cost of roading and revegetation including reforestation." [17] This interpretation, he indicated, was based on the report of the Senate Committee on Agriculture and Forestry. [18] The report addressed issues pertaining to S. 3091, the Senate version of the proposed National Forest Management Act.

A careful reading of the Senate committee report suggests the Forest Service may be falling short on its interpretation of the mandate. The relevant language in the committee report stated that

> In determining whether *certain lands* should be managed for timber production, only direct timber production costs should be evaluated. Costs and benefits attributable to other resource values should be excluded because of the lack of certainty involved in assigning values to other benefits derived and the impact on multiple-use goals. On *areas where timber production is not practical as a land management objective*, the costs of revegetation following harvest, access, protection, and administration for other multiple-use purposes are extended. The Committee also excluded the *economic cost of carrying trees for the rotation cycle*. [19]

The question arises whether or not the "economic cost of carrying trees for the rotation cycle" was to be excluded on all lands managed by the Forest Service, or on only "certain lands," those "areas where timber production is not practical as a land management objective."

It is understandable that Congress may have felt that counting carrying charges on timber inventories on lands submarginal for timber production might conflict with the production of multiple-use benefits. As mandated in the National Forest Management Act, "lands once identified as unsuitable for timber production shall continue to be treated for reforestation purposes, particularly with regard to the production of other multiple-use values." [20] Capital costs, it would seem, would be charged to the production of these

17. Congressional Record, Senate. Chief McGuire to Senator James A. McClure, August 24, 1976.

18. Ibid.

19. United States Senate, National Forest Management Act of 1976, p. iii. Emphasis added.

20. Ibid., Sec. 6 (k).

values; however, it is not obvious that Congress intended the neglect of capital-carrying charges on timber inventories to apply to lands that were supramarginal for timber production.

If inventory costs are not counted, then predictably they will not be heeded and, as noted earlier, excess inventories will be carried. The purpose of maintaining inventories, it should be emphasized, is to supply the market and meet existing demands.

An important consequence of the Forest Service's faulty inventory policy is that supplies of timber are not being made available in sufficient quantities to meet timber demands during the private sector's transition from virgin timber to "second-growth" timber supplies. By restricting supplies, the Forest Service and the BLM are creating, and apparently will continue to create, an artificial timber shortage. This is a major reason for the migration of the wood-processing industry from the Pacific Northwest to the south. Private ownership in the south provides a more secure timber supply.

Determination of Optimal Timber Harvest Age

In the management of federally owned timber, optimal timber harvest age is reached at "culmination of mean annual increment of growth."[21] Technically this means that average annual growth (total volume per acre divided by timber stand age) has reached a maximum. Physical outputs of timber are thereby maximized over time. Exceptions to harvest age at culmination are permissible under existing law.

Within the framework of capital theory, permitting timber to grow to the age of culmination implies the use of a zero interest rate.[22] Optimal (timber) capital management requires that timber be harvested at the age that maximizes the present net worth of the joint investment in forestland and timber inventory. The rate of return on this joint investment is, thereby, expected to equal the discount rate used in determining present net worth.

Optimal harvest age based on the economics of capital management will be shorter than harvest age based on culmination of mean

21. Ibid., Sec. 6(m)(1).
22. Paul A. Samuelson, "Forestry Economics in an Evolving Society," *Economic Inquiry* 47 (1976): 273–300.

annual increment. Optimal timber inventories therefore will be lower. The inventory differential between the two approaches represents the quantity of capital that will earn a rate of return less than the specified interest rate.

The effect of changing from a policy of determining harvest age on the basis of optimal capital management as opposed to culmination of mean annual increment would be to reduce excess timber inventories. As this excess is reduced, timber supplies would be increased.

Distortions in Investment Analyses

Within the framework of even-flow scheduling of timber harvests — or more correctly, timber sales — increases are permissible if investments are made to increase timber growth rates. This corollary of even flow is known as the "allowable cut effect" (ACE).

The Forest Service, the BLM, and state timber management agencies have steadfastly defended ACE interpretations of their mandates. They are, therefore, vulnerable to the charge that excessive inventories of timber are being held hostage to bigger agency budgets. Bigger budgets, they maintain, are necessary to increase timber growth rates such that they can "earn the right" to increase the quantity of timber being sold for current harvest.

This situation has given rise to seriously faulty investment accounting. Expected rates of return, or benefit-cost ratios, on investments to grow more timber not to be harvested until the distant future, are based in part on expected revenues from increased sales of timber from existing inventories.[23] Benefit-cost ratios are calculated, for example, by dividing the present net worth of expected revenues from increasing the rate of timber harvest by the present net worth of investments in timber growth that permit these increases to be made. This procedure gives uneconomical investments a deceptive appearance of being economical. Expected rates of return on investments that, when conventionally evaluated, would not be justifiable,

---

23. USDA, Forest Service, *Douglas Fir Supply Study*, Pacific Northwest Forest Region Experiment Station, 1969; and Francis J. Horak, "An Economic Analysis Series for Screening Proposed Timber Management Projects," Report No. 1, "Analytical Consideration," BLM Technical Note (1977).

commonly exceed 100 percent.[24] Alternatively, benefit-cost ratios based on discount rates of 6 percent may exceed 5.0.[25]

The absurdity of investment accounting that incorporates ACE can be demonstrated with a simple example. Suppose that an AAC is calculated for an overmature timber stand in which the timber growth rate is negligible. Further suppose that part of the overmature inventory is destroyed by a forest fire, and that a new rapidly growing timber stand is established on the burned acreage. The effect of increased growth on the AAC could exceed that caused by lost inventory; hence the net effect of the fire would be to increase the AAC. The rate of return on the forest fire is positive.

Losses to society that are occasioned by the use of the anachronistic even-flow formula for calculating timber outputs and by the use of faulty accounting in conjunction with this formula, are clearly indefensible. Public timber management agencies should be required to report accurately the real rates of return expected on investments in growing timber. This would provide the general public with information regarding the unjustifiably high cost of practicing even-flow timber management.

ADVERSE EFFECTS OF EVEN FLOW
ON TIMBER OUTPUT

Adverse short-run effects are caused by even flow because of the resultant timber supply rigidity and by resultant price instabilities. Additional price instabilities are caused by timber-marketing practices that encourage speculative bidding. As noted above, "pay-as-cut" sales with minimal down payments result in bid prices for public timber that are based on anticipated future market prices. Recent bailouts for holders of public timber-cutting contracts by both the federal and state governments are a direct consequence of speculative bidding on these contracts as timber prices were rising. When prices declined sharply, holders of these contracts predictably made pleas for government relief.

Given the greater than "normal" price fluctuations of raw timber inputs in regions dominated by public ownership and associated even

24. USDA, Forest Service, *Douglas Fir Supply Study*.
25. Horak, "An Economic Analysis Series."

flow, timber processors face greater than normal risks. As a result, costs are higher. Higher costs of these kinds, in addition to those caused by unnecessarily restrictive timber supplies, have also contributed to the redirection of timber-processing capital to the south where timber markets are not impacted by the vagaries of state and federal timber sales policies.

A good example of the long-run economic waste inherent in even-flow forestry has been provided by Cartwright.[26] His example is based on the Quinault Ranger District in the Olympic National Forest in Washington State. The facts and assumptions used in his example are as follows:

1. The Quinault Ranger District consists of 151,000 acres, of which 110,000 acres is designated for timber production.
2. The timber inventory contains 6.5 billion board feet of timber; 41 percent of this timber exceeds 280 years of age; 78 percent is over 96 years of age. Because of the overmature age of most of the timber on the district, the net growth rate is negative.
3. Annual timber sales on the Quinault have averaged 71 million board feet per year.
4. Optimal harvest age on the forest, based on optimal capital management, is assumed to be 45 years; average annual growth would be 800 board feet per acre per year.[27]

Based on the assumption that the existing timber inventory will continue to be sold at the Forest Service's AAC rate of 71 million board feet per year, 91 years would be required to complete the sale of timber currently in inventory. If cut over lands are reforested immediately following harvest, then at the end of 91 years the timber inventory would consist of 3.3 billion board feet of timber, most of which would still be economically overmature. During this ninety-one-year period, the forest would produce 9.8 billion board feet of timber; the current inventory of 6.5 billion board feet would be liquidated, and a new inventory of 3.3 billion board feet would exist in its place.

26. Philip W. Cartwright, "The Management of Federal Timberlands," in *Agenda for the 80s: A New Federal Land Policy.* Proceedings of the National Conference on States' Rights, the Sagebrush Rebellion, and Federal Land Policy. Salt Lake City, November 20–24, 1980.
27. Ibid.

Suppose now that the 110,000 acres were managed on the basis of economic criteria. The overmature inventory would be liquidated as quickly as possible, the cut over lands would be replanted, and the forest would be harvested again in forty-five years. The present inventory, plus two timber crops, would therefore be harvested sooner that the Forest Service would finish liquidating the present inventory under its even-flow policy. Total output over the ninety-year period under economic management would be 14.5 billion board feet; 48 percent more than the Forest Service would be expected to produce.

Viewed differently, first suppose that the 110,000 acres consisted of a forest in a "regulated" condition; that is, it contained a uniform distribution of timber age classes. And second, suppose it was managed on the basis of economic criteria. Based on these assumptions, the forest could sustain a harvest of 88 million board feet per year; 24 percent more than the Forest Service's AAC of 71 million board feet per year. Cartwright's conclusion, based on his example, was that "the Forest Service, which espouses concern over the availability of timber for future generations, may be creating a future shortage by permitting timber stands that are either not growing or growing at rates far less than the real rate of interest to remain standing."[28]

STATE AND LOCAL TAXATION OF PRIVATE FOREST PROPERTY

State policies for the taxation of forest property may adversely affect long-term timber supplies because they have the potential for discouraging investments in growing timber. This situation arises from the fact that (1) timber inventories in a number of states are subjected to an annual ad valorem property tax or (2) an excise (yield) tax is levied on gross timber harvest receipts. States that use a yield tax in forest taxation generally use it in lieu of the annual ad valorem property tax on timber inventories. All states have an annual ad valorem property tax on forestland.

It is a well-known fact that inventory taxes have resulted in production moving to taxing jurisdictions where these taxes are not

28. Ibid.

applied, and that they discriminate against those productive activities characterized by lengthy periods of production. The reason is that taxes must be paid "out-of-pocket" prior to the receipt of sales income; hence they must carry interest charges until final sales are made. Timber production commonly requires that inventories of maturing timber be carried for as long as fifty to seventy-five years.

An historical perspective is useful in explaining why inventory taxes, or yield taxes in lieu thereof, exist in timber production. Additionally, why are they not an immediate problem, yet may be a problem in the long run?

The tax problem arose because of the historical dependence of the timber industry on naturally endowed (virgin) timber stands classified and taxed as real property. This classification was consistent with the nature of the timber resource, but taxation of inventories of these kinds encourages their rapid liquidation in order to escape the property tax.

A similar problem had arisen in the mining industry; "out-of-pocket" tax payments, plus interest, on nonproducing properties had the potential of confiscating mineral wealth before the property was developed and producing income flows. The mining industry dealt with this situation by successfully promoting policy changes that substituted severance taxes on production (income) for annual ad valorem property taxes on wealth (asset values).[29]

During the "mining" stages of virgin timber exploitation, the timber industry was encouraged to liquidate timber inventories to escape property taxes; it was also encouraged to abandon cut over lands following the harvest. The reason for abandoning land was that a tax system including both forestland and timber inventories in the tax base created expectations that property tax burdens would exceed net income. Cut over land had negative value.

This situation was exacerbated by low timber prices that prevailed during the period when virgin timber inventories were being reduced. The long wait required to carry maturing timber inventories from the time a new stand was established until it reached maturity and was ready to harvest was, however, the principal reason for a forest tax "problem." During the first four decades of the 1900s this problem

---

29. Charles W. Nelson, "Broader Lessons from the History of Lake Superior Iron-Ore Taxation," in Richard W. Lindholm, ed., *Property Taxation—USA* (Madison: University of Wisconsin Press, 1969), pp. 237–61.

was to result in the abandonment of millions of acres of privately owned cut over forestlands.[30]

Many of these tax delinquent lands eventually reverted to state and local ownerships. Some were recycled back into private ownership, but many of these lands are now included in publicly owned state and local forests. Moreover, the widespread belief that markets did not work in timber production was reinforced by the pathological effects of these faulty property tax policies.

The federal government mandated a study of the forest tax problem in the 1924 Clark-McNary Act. The results of this ten-year study, which was called the Fairchild Report (1935), concluded that timber production was subjected to a "deferred yield" tax bias.[31] A number of proposals were suggested for alleviating the situation; many states substituted the yield tax on gross timber harvest income for the annual ad valorem property tax on timber inventories.[32]

The upward trend in timber prices, which began in the 1940s, effectively masked the discriminatory effects of the inventory tax on timber or its substitute, the yield tax on gross timber harvest income. As prices were rising, harvest rates were increasing, and cash flows to the industry were rising. State legislators were not predisposed to reform tax policies while this was occurring. A discriminatory tax was operating as an excess profits tax.

The recent collapse of timber prices does, however, call attention to state policies for taxing timber once again. If price expectations are pessimistic, then many cut over forestlands will have negative values because of tax burdens. Additionally, if these lands cannot be converted to alternative uses, then in the absence of tax policy reform they are likely to be abandoned. In either case, economic inefficiencies will arise and less timber will be produced.

The remedy for this situation is obviously to repeal state and local taxes on timber, including annual ad valorem property taxes and their substitute, yield taxes on gross timber harvest income. Timber inventories may be "milked" in the short run by faulty taxes, but in the long run domestic timber production can be expected to shift

30. Fred R. Fairchild and Associates, *Forest Taxation in the United States*, USDA Misc. Pub. 218 (1935).

31. Ibid.

32. Samuel Trask Dana and Sally K. Fairfax, *Forest and Range Policy* (New York: McGraw-Hill, 1980).

in the direction of jurisdictions where discriminatory taxes are not encountered.

FOREST PRACTICES REGULATIONS

Forest practices regulations in timbered states have as their objective the mitigation of a number of environmental impacts associated with timber production and the maintenance of the "productivity" of forestland. Four major areas of regulations are: (1) road construction, (2) timber-harvesting operations, (3) the use of chemicals, and (4) reforestation.

The regulation of road construction and timber-harvesting operations is undertaken for the purpose of controlling the adverse effects of these operations on soil erosion, water flows, and water quality. The principal benefits from these regulations are reduced water pollution and protection of fishery resources.

Regulating the use of chemicals is undertaken to prevent pollution of water and the environment in general. Chemicals are used in timber production primarily for two purposes. Herbicides or silvicides are used to control vegetation ("weeds") that would otherwise compete with timber crops, and insecticides or pesticides are used to control destructive insects. Chemicals are also used to control forest fires. However, this use has not been subjected to the same level of criticism as other uses, for the adverse environmental effects of fire are often worse than the adverse effects of the chemicals.

Finally, most forest practices regulations require that cut over timberlands be reforested within a relatively short period of time following timber harvests, usually three years. The objective of this regulation is to maintain the "productivity" of forestland. Productivity is defined as the volume of timber growth per acre per year. Aesthetics are commonly mentioned as adjunct benefits to maintaining forest productivity.

Some means of controlling the adverse external effects ("externalities" or "neighborhood effects") of timber production are obviously necessary. Legitimate questions do arise, however, regarding the extent to which these means should be applied. It should also be recognized that a number of means are available for achieving this objective. These means include legal actions (torts), regulations or standards enforced by the police power of the state, and various kinds of incentive (and disincentive) systems.

An example of the latter would be the "bubble" concept introduced as a means of controlling the quality of air. For example, existing patterns of pollution ("rights to pollute") can be taken as given, and then a new entrant into the area whose activities would lead to increased pollution must buy a right to do so from existing polluters. If the cost of reducing air pollution to the latter is less than the market price of the right, pollution control equipment would be installed and the right sold.

Means of controlling external effects of timber production and other economic activities are continually evolving, and there is considerable room for improving existing means. There are also good reasons for believing that existing regulations in many industries, including timber production, are not cost effective. Costs may be imposed on producers that are higher than benefits being produced. Since producers pay these costs, and benefits accrue to those who do not, political pressures from the latter persist not to adopt more cost effective measures.

The reforestation requirement, which appears in most forest practices regulations, is potentially counterproductive from the standpoint of long-term timber supplies from the private sector. As noted, land owners are required to reforest cut over timberlands.

If a reforestation investment is profitable relative to other investment alternatives, then land owners can be expected to reforest and the law is redundant. On the other hand, if reforestation investments do not yield a competitive rate of return, then forcing landowners to reforest merely results in foregoing more productive investments elsewhere in the economy. Unless forestland can be converted to a higher value use, forest practices laws have the potential of wasting resources.

Aside from timber production, there may be compelling reasons for maintaining forest cover on an area. Examples would include the maintenance of game habitat, the prevention of erosion, or the provision of aesthetics. These are separable issues from the production of timber per se, however, which raise questions of equity if forestland owners are forced to bear the costs of providing these social benefits.

The history of the development of forest practices legislation for most states indicates a primary concern for future timber supplies. More simply stated, lawmakers and the general public were haunted by fears of a timber "famine." Game habitat and soil erosion were secondary considerations, while aesthetics were hardly mentioned. These obsolescent and potentially counterproductive laws are clearly in need of review, and the reforestation requirement of these laws in need of repeal.

CONCLUSIONS

Public timber policy, which is broadly defined to include a variety of state and federal policies, is currently in a state of disarray. The most seriously defective of these policies, and in most immediate need of change, is public timber management policy at the federal level.

The most defective state policies are those that pertain to the taxation of timber and the forest practices regulations that require reforestation of cut over forestlands. State laws in both these categories should be repealed. Timber production should be taxed as any other crop, that is, on land only, and forestland owners should not be required to reforest if it is uneconomical to do so. Wasteful cross-subsidization of timber production is being forced.

Public timber sales are scheduled on the basis of noneconomic criteria; hence timber is not being supplied to markets in a manner that provides buyers secure supplies. Markets are disrupted, and timber-processing capital is flowing away from dependency upon public timber supplies. Prices of wood products are, therefore, higher than they need be.

The most obvious reform for faulty public timber management policies would be to remove governments from the business of timber production. This could be achieved simply by selling commercial public timber holdings into private ownership. By privatizing these lands, and establishing an incentive system based on free enterprise, the unnecessary waste associated with government timber management could be eliminated. This would also eliminate inequities that accompany politicized management.

If privatization is not politically feasible, then at minimum, public timber management agencies, especially the Forest Service and the BLM, should be required to report interest-carrying charges on timber inventories and to incorporate these costs into timber-management planning. If the high cost of carrying excess federal timber inventories were reported, and the general public made aware of the enormous cost that it must bear to continue the economically dubious policy of even-flow timber harvest scheduling, almost assuredly more timber would be made available. Indeed, the reporting of these costs would create considerably more interest than now exists in privatizing public timberlands.

Neither the sale of public timberlands nor increased rates of harvest if they are maintained in public ownership would conflict unduly with the production of nonmarketed multiple-use benefits. Selling these lands, or, if they are retained in public ownership, correctly reporting interest charges on asset values, would ensure that the costs of producing multiple-use benefits would get reported. This would help to ensure that the value of nonmarketed benefits exceeded production costs.

Contrary to the arguments of public foresters, who are defensive of their multiple-use and sustained-yield policies, and many environmentalists, who view policy reforms as a possible dismantling of environmental programs, the issue is not a tradeoff between more timber and fewer environmental amenities (more disruption from increased timber harvesting). Both more timber and environmental benefits could be produced if public timberlands were used more efficiently. This would be made possible by reducing the waste of resources currently being induced by faulty policy.

In summary, the United States has ample supplies of timber to meet wood-products demands for the next several decades, for housing, and all other uses. Our problem is not lack of timber, but faulty institutional arrangements. Moreover, the cost of these defective arrangements is becoming increasingly burdensome. This is evident in both the movement of wood-processing industries to the south even though the south has a much smaller commercial timber inventory than the west, and the government bailouts recently granted to the timber industry. An unfortunate side effect of these bailouts, which apply to firms dependent upon public timber, is likely to be disruption of private timber markets in the south.

Sooner or later, society will react to the accumulating adverse effects of faulty public timber policy. The sooner this occurs, the more likely policy reforms can be made that will be based on a reasonably objective assessment of existing problems and what might best be done to correct them. The alternative is to wait until a crisis occurs, and then to adopt crash reforms that might make things worse. Recidivism is not unique to private behavior. Existing faulty timber policy suggests that this has happened before, and there are no assurances it will not happen again.

Chapter 4

U. S. FOREST SERVICE POLICY AND ITS BUDGET

Ronald N. Johnson

INTRODUCTION

Criticism of the land management policies of the U.S. Forest Service has become epidemic. Attacks have come from timber interests who see their harvest levels being restricted and from environmental groups who are convinced that the agency strongly prefers traditional commodity use over wilderness use. While these positions may appear to be self-serving and contradictory, both have merit. There is growing evidence that the Forest Service has promoted timber harvesting in areas where no private firm could profitably operate.[1] At the same time, the agency has restricted the harvest on more productive sites, such as those in the Pacific Northwest. By emphasizing multiple use and designing timber management programs based on biological rules, the Forest Service has managed to disregard economic efficiency criteria, choosing instead to spread harvesting activities across political

---

1. William F. Hyde, "Compounding Clear-cuts: The Social Failures of Public Timber Management in the Rockies," in John Baden and Richard L. Stroup, eds., *Bureaucracy vs. Environment* (Ann Arbor: University of Michigan Press, 1981). Hyde offers strong evidence that harvesting operations in the Rocky Mountains are often uneconomical. See also Marion Clawson, *The Economics of National Forest Management* (Baltimore: Johns Hopkins University Press, 1976), and Thomas Barlow, Gloria Helfand, Trent Orr, and Thomas Stoel, *Giving Away the National Forests: An Analysis of U.S. Forest Service Timber Sales Below Costs* (Washington, D.C.: Natural Resources Defense Council, Inc., 1980).

jurisdictions and reducing the amount of de facto wilderness in the process.

At first glance, adherence to biological rules may seem to constitute a conservative approach to resource management, but harvesting timber in areas where costs exceed returns contradicts most notions of conservation. Since economic criteria are not used to select harvest sites and schedules, Forest Service land management policy also appears to be inconsistent with increasing aggregate national wealth.

The Forest Service's land management policy is simply the result of a political compromise with neither commodity users nor environmental groups successfully capturing the agency.[2] Even though political pressures from competing interest groups have influenced Forest Service policy, focusing on them would ignore the Forest Service itself and the ways in which it has influenced its own environment.[3] For example, the Forest Service successfully lobbied for the Multiple-Use Sustained-Yield Act of 1960,[4] which, although considered vague and contradictory,[5] provides the agency with a statutory framework for controlling competing demands and avoiding capture. The act also gave the Forest Service a means for increasing its budget. Even though adhering to the concept of multiple use has left the agency besieged by competing groups, its budget does not appear to have suffered. In a recent study of seven natural resource-oriented federal bureaus, the Forest Service ranked at or near the top in terms of budgetary growth over the period 1950–1980.[6]

2. Paul J. Culhane, *Public Lands Politics* (Baltimore: Johns Hopkins University Press, 1981). Culhane provides an excellent discussion of interest group pressure on the Forest Service. He also argues that the Forest Service does not conform to the capture hypothesis.

3. For an historical account of the Forest Service, see Marion Clawson and Burnell Held, *The Federal Lands: Their Use and Management* (Baltimore: Johns Hopkins University Press, 1957); Samuel T. Dana and Sally K. Fairfax, *Forest and Range Policy* (New York: McGraw-Hill, 1980); Clifford Pinchot, *Breaking New Ground* (New York: Harcourt Brace, 1947); Glen O. Robinson, *The Forest Service* (Baltimore: Johns Hopkins University Press, 1975); and Harold K. Steen, *The U.S. Forest Service: A History* (Seattle: University of Washington Press, 1977).

4. 74 Stat. 215 (1960), 16 U.S.C. #528–31.

5. See, for example, George R. Hall, "The Myth and Reality of Multiple Use Forestry," *Natural Resources Journal* 3 (October 1963): 276–90.

6. Jeanne Nienaber and Daniel McCool, "For Richer or for Poorer: A Comparative Approach to the Study of Bureaucracies." Paper presented at the Western Political Science Association meeting, Denver, Colorado, 1981. The other six agencies studied were the Bureau of Land Management, the National Park Service, the U.S. Fish and Wildlife Service, the Soil Conservation Service, the U.S. Army Corps of Engineers, and the Bureau of Reclamation. For a comparison of the Bureau of Land Management and Forest Service with

The Forest Service's budgetary success does not, of course, imply that individuals in the Forest Service are strictly motivated to enhance the agency's budget. Those individuals may well hold a strong preference for preservation and may believe in the merits of intensive forest management, but other factors such as salary, promotional opportunities, and the power of office are also likely to influence their behavior. Niskanen has argued that those factors motivate the agency toward budget maximization.[7] While strict conformity with the budget maximization model will not be advocated here, evidence of the agency's responsiveness to incentives and its attempts to influence the process suggest a strong consistency with the maximization hypothesis. Such a finding indicates that the agency would resist proposals to adopt decisionmaking criteria that would have a significant negative impact on its budget.

THE BUDGET-MAXIMIZATION HYPOTHESIS

Theories of governmental output and budgetary practices either explicitly or implicitly incorporate postulates as to the behavior and motivation of elected representatives who establish the demands for governmental service and bureaucrats who provide the output. Theories that relegate bureaucrats and politicians to the role of enlightened servants carrying out the public weal implicitly assume that those individuals will not attempt to alter outcomes for their own benefit. But, here the Niskanen argument that bureaucrats seek to maximize their budgets applies.[8] That argument can be refined to encompass the incentives that a bureau such as the Forest Service has for spreading activities across numerous political jurisdictions and why the bureau would seek to broaden its mission and also limit the level of certain activities on the national forests.

---

special emphasis on the 1974 Resource Planning Act, see Dennis C. Le Master, "Forest Service Funding Under RPA," *Journal of Forestry* 80 (March 1982): 161–63; and Christopher Leman, "Resource Assessment and Program Development: An Evaluation of Forest Service Experience Under the Resources Planning Act, with Lessons for Other Natural Resources Agencies." Discussion paper, U.S. Department of the Interior, 1980.

7. See William A. Niskanen, *Bureaucracy and Representative Government* (Chicago: Aldine & Atherton, 1971); and idem, "Bureaucrats and Politicians," *Journal of Law and Economics* 18 (December 1975): 617–44.

8. Niskanen, *Bureaucracy and Representative Government.*

The budget-maximization hypothesis builds on the premise that bureaucrats maximize their own utility functions. Niskanen argues that "among the several variables that may enter the bureaucrat's utility function are the following: salary, perquisite of the office, public reputation, power, patronage, output of the bureau."[9] In the strict version of that model, such variables are considered to be a positive monotonic function of the bureau's total budget and the agency is seen as offering the legislative body a promised output in exchange for that budget. The budget the agency can expect to receive is defined as being a positive, but concave, function of the promised output. The parameters of the budget function are the outcome of the political process.

Under majority rule, where voting occurs on each budget item, the desires of the median voter act as the binding constraint on the bureau's attempts to maximize its budget. In the Niskanen approach to representative government and bureaucratic behavior, it is the "representative" legislator who acts as the median voter. Representatives are ultimately subject to the approval of their local constituencies, and in their endeavors to gain reelection will seek legislation and provide appropriations for particular interest groups. Concerned primarily with the desires of their local constituency, legislators seek membership on committees that are most closely associated with those preferences.[10] Each representative is aided in that attempt by colleagues' desires to also serve on certain committees. With varying intensities of preferences, representative government characteristically becomes specialized. While legislative specialization can improve the efficiency of monitoring agency behavior, it can also facilitate legislative logrolling or vote trading.[11] The end product is service-specialized committees dominated by representatives of the group with the highest relative demand for the agency's output.

9. Ibid., p. 38.

10. In *The Federal Lands*, p. 145, Clawson and Held note that "For many years a substantial proportion of the representatives from the eleven western states, in which most of the federal lands lie, have sought membership on the House Committee on Interior and Insular Affairs." Some legislative matters and especially the budget come before that committee.

11. For a theory of logrolling, see James M. Buchanan and Gordon Tullock, *The Calculus of Consent* (East Lansing: University of Michigan Press, 1962). For a discussion and rationale of logrolling between high demand review committees, also see Bruce L. Benson, "Why Are Congressional Committees Dominated by 'High-Demand' Legislators? – A Comment on Niskanen's View of Bureaucrats and Politicians," *Southern Economic Journal* 48 (July 1981): 68–77.

The committees, however, are not unconstrained since budget approval must be obtained from a majority of the legislature. Since the legislature does not face the same degree of pressure from local interest groups as does the committee, it will have a lower demand for the particular service or output. But the committee, in concert with the appropriate bureau, has an advantage in dealing with the entire legislature since it conducts the review process and has superior information about the cost of producing the bureau's output. When this information is coupled with the quasi-territorial rights granted to committees by the logrolling process, challenges to the committee's recommendations will be few. Wildavsky, for example, notes that "Appropriations Committee recommendations in both houses are accepted almost nine out of every ten times."[12]

A budget-maximizing bureau with the support of the high demand review committee seeks the largest budget and, hence, output, which is subject to the condition that total costs will not exceed the approved budget. Following Niskanen's choice of quadratic functional forms, the budget and cost functions faced by the bureau can be written as

$$\text{Total Budget } (B) = aQ - bQ^2$$
$$\text{Total Costs } \quad (C) = cQ + dQ^2 \tag{1}$$

where Q is the output level and a, b, c, and d are the parameters of the appropriate functions. Here, the budget function represents the amount of appropriations that a majority of the entire legislature would approve for various promised output levels. It is assumed that the review committee will recommend passage of a bill providing for the largest output possible. The solution (as shown in Figure 4–1) is $Q^* = (a - c)/(b + d)$. That solution yields the largest possible budget to the bureau.

Critics have pointed out that budget maximization in the Niskanen framework implies output maximization.[13] If the agency sought to maximize its budget, it could do so only by minimizing costs and producing a larger output. A tendency on the part of bureaucrats to

12. Aaron Wildavsky, *The Politics of the Budgetary Process* (Boston: Little, Brown, 1964), p. 54.

13. See, for example, Earl Thompson, "Book Review," *Journal of Economic Literature* 11 (September 1973): 950–53, and Jean-Luc Migue and Gerard Belanger, "Toward A General Theory of Managerial Discretion," *Public Choice* 17 (Spring 1974): 27–47.

Figure 4-1. The Budget-Maximization Model.

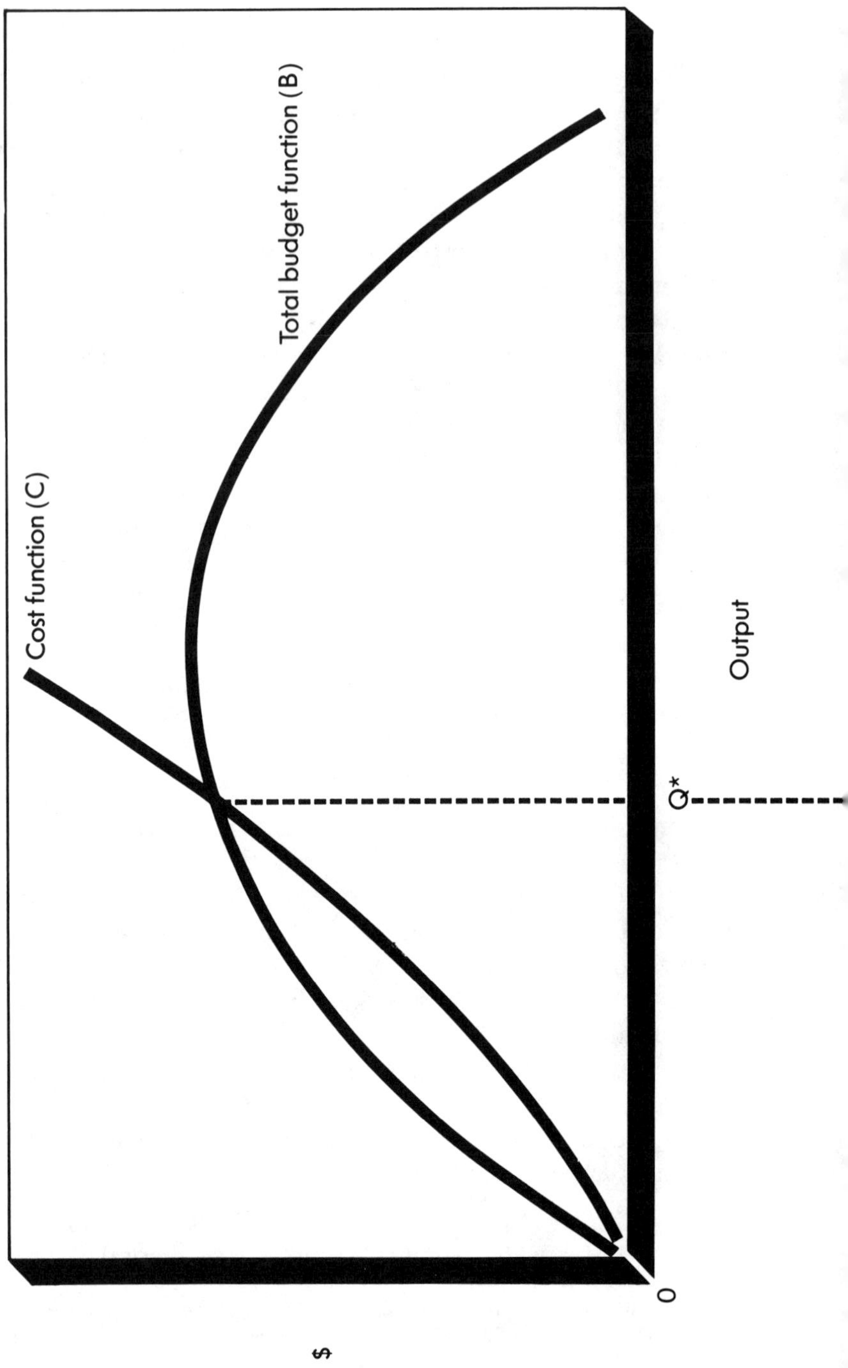

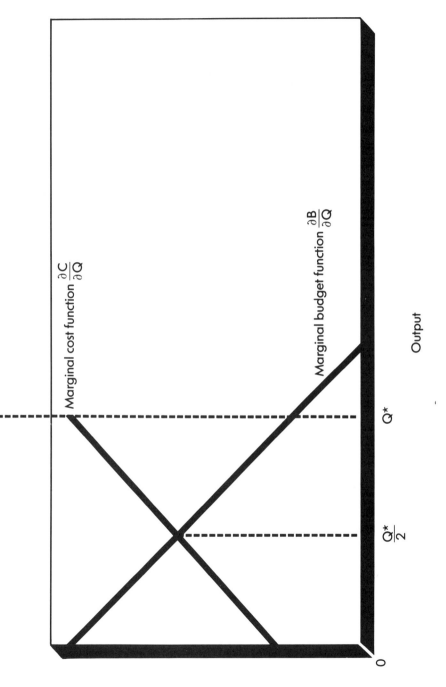

Marginal cost function $\frac{\partial C}{\partial Q}$

Marginal budget function $\frac{\partial B}{\partial Q}$

Output

Q^*

$\frac{Q^*}{2}$

0

$

inflate costs would reduce output and, hence, the total budget. The budget-maximization model would then suggest that bureaucrats place no value on discretionary budgets.[14] At first glance it would appear that efficiency in production is inconsistent with most perceptions of bureaucratic behavior. Nevertheless, while some deviation from strict output and budget maximization can be expected, certain forces will reduce the amount of slack evident in the cost of producing the bureau's output.

Recall that the political interests of the high demand review committee are not served by budget excesses.[15] The committee seeks the largest output it can obtain from the bureau. As is observed in ordinary business practices, the review committee can design a reward structure and invest in control devices designed to reduce inefficiencies. If cost comparisons with similar operations in the private sector or other agencies are available, the chances for effective monitoring are increased. Furthermore, if the agency were to develop a reputation for inefficiency, the legislature would likely be less willing to approve budget requests. Bureaucrats whose careers are tied closely to the success and reputation of a single agency are less likely to engage in discretionary budget making that may be detected than those that have greater mobility. That is not to say that political appointees whose tenure in the agency may be short will necessarily engage in discretionary budget making. Indeed, the appointee's reputation and future career opportunities may be enhanced by budget slashing. Rather, a bureaucrat whose career opportunities are closely tied to an agency has an incentive to avoid damaging the agency's reputation in order to maximize its budget and indirectly enhance that individual's career. These circumstances fit the Forest Service.

While the Forest Service is in a monopoly position regarding management of the national forests, it does not have a monopoly on major commodities such as timber. Cost comparisons are available from the private sector and from other federal and state agencies. Competition between agencies exists and the history of the Forest Service is replete with examples of jurisdictional disputes with other

---

14. The discretionary budget is the difference between the maximum budget that would be approved by a government review committee and the minimum cost of producing the output. See Niskanen, "Bureaucrats and Politicians," p. 619.

15. Niskanen, "Bureaucrats and Politicians," p. 626. Niskanen notes that "In general, a high demand committee is 'in the bureau's pocket' only with respect to the output decision."

federal agencies over guardianship of the public domain.[16] Disputes with agencies with similarly stated conservation objections, such as the Bureau of Land Management (BLM), also suggest that Forest Service personnel are not concerned only with the establishment of a resource management creed. Moreover, highly specialized bureaus often have personnel whose expertise is relatively restricted, with possibilities for advancement residing mainly within the agency.[17] As the agency grows, there are more opportunities for rapid advancement and salary justifications. Specialization in the Forest Service can be seen in the large proportion (approximately 90 percent) of the agency's top personnel who are trained foresters,[18] many of whom have come up through the ranks.[19] All of these conditions — internal promotion, competition from other agencies, and the availability of cost comparisons — reduce the potential for discretionary budgets and drive the agency toward budget maximization.

The argument that there are controls that can mitigate discretionary budget making does not imply that the output level Q^* (in Figure 4–1) represents an optimum from the standpoint of society taken in the aggregate. If, for example, the budget function were thought of as representing a benefit function based on the political process, it follows that the output is too large. Efficiency would call for equating marginal costs with marginal benefits. In the example given, that criterion would call for setting $Q = (a - c)/2(b + d)$, or half of Q^*. Whether the budget function can be taken to represent an aggregate benefit function is a complex question, and no attempt will be made here to answer it. The model does, however, provide an initial framework for analyzing the behavior of an agency attempting to maximize its budget.

16. For a discussion of the Forest Service's conflict with the Bureau of Land Management, see Gary D. Libecap, *Locking Up the Range: Federal Land Controls and Grazing* (San Francisco: Pacific Research Institute for Public Policy, 1981), p. 46. For a history of the Forest Service and its frequent conflict with other agencies, also see Dana and Fairfax, *Forest and Range Policy,* and Steen, *The U.S. Forest Service: A History.*

17. Albert Breton and Ronald Wintrobe, "The Equilibrium Size of a Budget-Maximizing Bureau: A Note on Niskanen's Theory of Bureaucracy," *Journal of Political Economy* 83 (February 1975): 195–207. Breton and Wintrobe argue that where mobility is restricted, budget maximization is more likely.

18. Culhane, *Public Lands Politics,* p. 68. The fact that the Forest Service's top management is composed mainly of foresters may seem quite natural. However, the agency has long advocated the multiple use concept and there are few range or recreational types at the top.

19. For a discussion of the Forest Service bureaucracy, see Herbert Kaufman, *The Forest Ranger* (Baltimore: Johns Hopkins University Press, 1960), and Robinson, *The Forest Service,* pp. 21–47.

Consider the agency's incentive for influencing the parameters of the budget function. If the agency could spread its activities across numerous localities, it would likely have greater support from the entire legislature. More representatives would be confronted by constituents who benefit from the agency's activities. The effect would be to increase the budget function (shown in Figure 4-1).

The agency's objective in spreading activities across political jurisdictions, however, need not serve the interests of the members of the review committees. While the total budget will be higher as a result of spreading activities, there is no guarantee that the amount of appropriations going to committee members' constituents will increase. Accordingly, conflict between the bureau and its review committee could arise. The bureau, however, is not defenseless and could aggressively seek statutory approval from the legislature that would encourage the spread of its activities. The history of the Forest Service indicates that it actively sought statutory approval for multiple-use and sustained-yield management, which fosters the dispersal of land management activities. The possibility for conflict between the bureau and the review committee complicates the basic Niskanen model of budget maximization.

In a simple setting where the bureau produces a single, well-defined output, it would appear from Niskanen's description that the objectives of the bureau and the review committee would be commensurate. Output maximization implies budget maximization. Niskanen argues that high demand review committees reduce the review process to a "stylized farce" and suggests that "the primary purpose of the review is to check whether the bureau has accurately estimated the largest program that would be approved by a majority of the legislature."[20] Niskanen's argument leads to the conclusion that a budget-maximizing bureau and a high demand review committee seek compatible objectives. As already argued, however, the act of spreading services and outputs across localities can cause conflict. Conflict can also arise when the agency produces a mix of outputs and services and when the production of some of those outputs reduces or impairs the quality of other outputs or services and, indirectly, appropriations for them. Accordingly, the mix of outputs preferred by the review committee need not provide the largest budget obtainable. In that setting, domination by a review committee

20. Niskanen, *Bureaucracy and Representative Government*, p. 148.

can suggest a form of capture that will not be in the bureau's best interest.[21]

Consider what happens when the review committee's primary concern is with commodity uses of the national forests, such as mining, grazing, and timber harvesting. Appropriations for other activities, such as recreation and wildlife, are likely to be neglected and deemed incompatible with commodity uses. In that environment, the agency has an incentive to stimulate demand for the neglected activities and seek statutory approval that would mandate a broadening of the agency's mission. Where uses of the national forests conflict, the Forest Service can also be expected to seek a means for controlling the intensity of uses rather than allowing the review committee to dictate the outcome.[22]

The act of seeking a broader mission and attempting to balance competing demands does not by itself imply that the agency is self-serving. The argument made here suggests, however, that such actions are more likely if they have a favorable impact on the budget. In the following section, actions of the Forest Service are analyzed. Con-

21. Robert J. MacKay and Carolyn L. Weaver, "On the Mutuality of Interests Between Bureaus and High Demand Review Committees: A Perverse Result," *Public Choice* 34 (Fall/Winter 1979): 481–91. MacKay and Weaver have also reconsidered the mutuality of interests between a bureau and its high demand review committee. They demonstrate that where a single government bureau undertakes two activities and the review committee has a relatively high preference for only one of those outputs, the bureau's potential budget will not be maximized.

22. The complications that can arise for a budget maximizing bureau where there are numerous interrelated outputs can perhaps best be stated within the framework of a nonlinear programming model. The objective is to maximize the total budget (B):

$$\text{Max } B = \sum_{i=1}^{n} b_i (Q_1, Q_2, \ldots, Q_n) \text{ subject to}$$

$$b_i - C_i (Q_1, Q_2, \ldots, Q_n) \geq 0, i = 1, 2, \ldots, n.$$

Here, b_i and C_i are the respective budget and cost functions for output Q_j. Furthermore:

$$\frac{\partial b_i}{\partial Q_j} \gtrless 0 \text{ and } \frac{\partial C_i}{\partial Q_j} \gtrless 0; \ i \neq j$$

There is no reason to suspect that in the above setting the Q's preferred by the review committee will be the same set of Q's that maximizes B. In *Bureaucracy and Representative Government*, pp. 106–12, Niskanen, in presenting a model of a multiservice bureau, utilized a single budget constraint as opposed to the n constraints here. His constraint would imply that funds can be freely transferred between accounts and the allocation for one activity used to subsidize another. While the Secretary of Agriculture may approve minor transfers between accounts, any significant reallocations must be approved by Congress and transfer is largely restricted.

sideration is given as to whether the Forest Service's behavior is consistent with the budget-maximization model prescribed here or more in line with either economic efficiency criteria or the agency's espoused conservation ethic.

FOREST SERVICE POLICY AND ITS BUDGET

An agency's ability to foster support in the political arena and influence its growth depends in part on how the agency perceives its own mission and how well it convinces the electorate of the benefits of that mission. Gifford Pinchot, a leading conservationist and the first head of the Forest Service, showed uncanny talent in this regard. Pinchot[23] argued that the goal of forest management was no less than "the greatest good for the greatest number for the longest time."[24]

Since its official designation in 1905, the Forest Service has maintained that timber resources should be managed according to the biological principle of maximum sustained yield. Scientific management based on biological rules was the cornerstone of the alternative proposed by early conservationists who observed a too rapid harvest of the nation's virgin timber. Despite evidence to the contrary, conservationists alleged that private timber was being harvested without regard to the needs of future generations;[25] implanting in the minds of many voters the notion that private ownership would result in timber famine. Pinchot envisioned an agency that would bring scientific management not only to federal lands but to private lands, as well.[26] While the principle of multiple use was recognized, Pinchot's

23. Pinchot, *Breaking New Ground*, p. 353.
24. Despite observations such as Scott Gordon's in "Economics and the Conservation Question," *Journal of Law and Economics* 1 (October 1958): 113, that "even the 'felicific calculus" of Jeremy Bentham which had contented itself with only the first two of these maxima, fell to the ground upon realization that the 'greatest good' may be conflicting and indeed incompatible objectives," the slogan has received wide popular support and repeated use.
25. Whether the private sector harvested at "too" rapid a rate is debated by Ronald N. Johnson and Gary D. Libecap in "Efficient Markets and Great Lakes Timber: A Conservation Issue Reexamined," *Explorations in Economic History* 17 (1980): 372–85.
26. For a short history of the early years of the Forest Service and Pinchot's emphasis on scientific management, see Robinson *The Forest Service*, pp. 7–10. Also see Dana and Fairfax, *Forest and Range Policy*, pp. 74, 83–86.

main thrust was scientific timber and land management with recreation and wilderness preservation being secondary.

Prior to World War II the Forest Service acted mainly as a custodian of the national forests. Range and timber management were its primary activities. Postwar increases in recreational and other uses of the national forests, however, offered the Forest Service an opportunity to expand its mission. The multiple-use principle provided the platform for expansion, and the sustained-yield concept offered a way to control outputs.

Changing the Agenda Through Advocacy of Multiple Use

The years 1898 to 1910 have been viewed as the golden era of the conservation movement.[27] The Forest Service grew rapidly during this period; and even though some saw preservation as the main objective, Pinchot directed the agency toward scientific land management. Timber harvesting on the national forests, while minor compared to the total national harvest, grew from 68 million board feet in 1905 to 525 million board feet in 1908 (see Figure 4–2). As part of the basic land management program, Pinchot viewed revenues from the leasing of mineral lands and grazing rights and the sale of timber as sources of funding to be used for the administration and development of national forests.[28] By 1907 revenues from the national forests reached nearly $1 million and "were much higher than the Congress had expected."[29] Westerners were generally hostile to the continued expansion of the national forests, and independent funding made the Forest Service a powerful force to contend with.

In 1907, at the urging of western representatives, Congress revoked the Forest Service's authority to spend receipts without reappropriation.[30] In 1908 Congress went even further and enacted legislation on the distribution of timber receipts: 25 percent to counties in lieu of taxes, 10 percent to the Forest Service for roads and trails, and

27. See Dana and Fairfax, *Forest and Range Policy*, ch. 3.
28. Ibid., p. 73, and Pinchot, *Breaking New Ground*, p. 257.
29. Clawson and Held, *The Federal Lands*, p. 236.
30. For a discussion of the events surrounding the revoking of the Forest Service's control over receipts, see Dana and Fairfax, *Forest and Range Policy*, pp. 90–92.

Figure 4-2. Volume of Timber Cut on, and Total Recreational Visits
to, National Forests, 1905-1980.

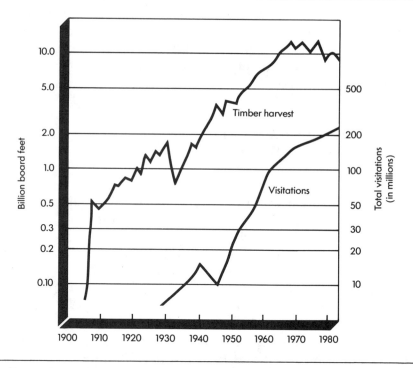

Sources: (1905-1955) Clawson and Held, *The Federal Lands*, tables 3 and 4.
(1955-1975) *U.S. Forest Service Report of the Chief*, various years.
(1976-1980) U.S. Forest Service, *Report of the Forest Service*, various years.

the remainder to the U.S. Treasury.[31] That distribution remains
essentially intact.

Removing timber revenues as a direct source of funding can be
expected to alter the incentives faced by the agency. In 1909 the
volume of timber cut fell to 458 million board feet, suggesting that
the Forest Service does respond to incentives and is not anchored
to a rigid scientific management scheme. A general upward trend in
demand for Forest Service timber was evident, however, and harvests
began to increase, reaching 1,769 million board feet in 1930. Con-

31. 35 Stat. 259, 260, 267 (1908).

tributing to that demand was pressure from states and counties, which received 25 percent of the receipts from timber sales.

As the demand for wood products increased after World War II, pressures mounted for expanding the cut on national forests. The period of drawing down the stock of old growth timber on western private lands was coming to an end, and many members of the lumber industry viewed the Forest Service stock as the next logical sequence in the harvesting cycle. While it would be incorrect to view the timber industry as a homogeneous group, since those who owned vast holdings of old growth timber were not likely to support an increase in the harvest on public lands, there was sufficient pressure mounted for increasing the cut, and construction of access roads on the national forest was funded. The Forest Service supported the effort to expand its road system, not only for timber harvesting but also for fire and insect control and the newly emerging demands for recreational use.[32] The volume of timber harvesting increased from 3,623 million board feet in 1950 to 6,434 million board feet in 1955.

The postwar years brought increasing conflict to the Forest Service and the agency showed no signs of attempting to avoid it. There were, for example, numerous encounters with stockmen over livestock grazing permits on the national forests. The grazing industry wanted increased tenure rights to the Forest Service lands and a halt to increases in grazing fees and reductions in the stipulated carrying capacity of the range. The Forest Service, in arguing for reductions in the number of animal units on the range, stressed that the national forests were set aside for multiple use and grazing was only one of many considerations for land use.[33] During the 1950s recreational use on the national forests began to increase significantly (see Figure 4-2), and stockmen responded by threatening to have the Forest Service budget slashed if their demands were not met. Since grazing interests had managed to cut the BLM's budget over similar disputes, the threat was not an idle one.[34]

Even though the Forest Service managed to win some disputes with the timber, mining, and grazing interests by aligning with conservation and wilderness groups, in the mid-1950s its everyday functioning and budget allocations were related mainly to traditional

32. See Steen, *The U.S. Forest Service*, p. 284.

33 Ibid., pp. 272-77.

34. For an analysis of the Bureau of Land Management conflict with grazing groups, see Libecap, *Locking Up the Range.*

commodity users. Clawson and Held, in discussing the political environment of federal land management in the 1950s, note that the Senate and House Committees on Interior and Insular Affairs (the main budgetary review bodies for the Forest Service) were dominated by representatives from the eleven western states that contain most of the federal lands.[35] While stressing that western representatives have an interest in promoting recreational use, Clawson and Held went on to state, "It is true that in the west the grazing and mining interests are stronger politically, compared with recreation and conservation groups, than they are elsewhere in the nation."[36]

The evidence of burgeoning recreational use in the 1950s was not wasted on the Forest Service, which began to promote its recreation potential under "Operation Outdoors."[37] There was also a threat that if the Forest Service did not provide for recreational demands, it could lose acreage to the National Park Service. During the 1950s the Park Service engaged in a conflict with the Forest Service over which agency was better suited to serve recreational users and administrate lands primarily used for recreation.[38] The Park Service was supported by preservation groups who wanted an increase in the wilderness designation of Forest Service lands and who felt the Forest Service had become too timber oriented. Although the Forest Service recognized the threat and saw the opportunities, there were still obstacles to overcome. Dana and Fairfax note that "traditional users were not going to welcome another 'mouth to feed' at the Forest Service table."[39]

With mounting pressures for recreational use and with timber and grazing industries becoming increasingly wary of Forest Service objectives, the agency actively sought a compromise solution that would also increase its budget. The solution was a legislative one and was to be based on the principle of multiple use. To this point, the main statutory base for operation was the Organic Act of 1897, which stated: "No public forest reservation should be established except to improve and protect the forest within the reservation, or for the pur-

---

35. Clawson and Held, *The Federal Lands*, pp. 145–47.
36. Ibid., p. 147.
37. For a discussion of the Forest Service's "Operation Outdoors" and its reorientation toward recreation, see Dana and Fairfax, *Forest and Range Policy*, pp. 193–94. Also see Steen, *The U.S. Forest Service*, p. 312.
38. Dana and Fairfax, *Forest and Range Policy*, p. 194.
39. Ibid., p. 193.

pose of securing favorable conditions of waterflows, and to furnish a continuous supply of timber for the use and necessities of citizens of the United States.[40] The Forest Service wanted a legislative mandate that would explicitly recognize other uses of the national forests and provide that forests and range resources would be operated under the principle of sustained yield. In explaining why the Forest Service needed statutory provision for the principle of multiple use, Forest Service Chief Richard McArdle stated, "We believe it to be both timely and desirable to recognize in a single statute these multiple-use objectives. . . . Such recognition would also serve as protection against excessive advocacy of single use. With the growing value of national forest resources, their increased use and accessibility, the pressures for single use of large areas of national forest land are growing tremendously."[41]

The agency obtained its objective when the Multiple-Use Sustained-Yield Act was passed in 1960. In Section 1, the uses recognized under multiple use are explicitly listed: "the national forests are established and shall be administered for outdoor recreation, range, timber, watershed, and wildlife and fish purposes." Furthermore, as stated in Section 4, the various uses were not to be ranked or given particular preference just because they generated receipts: "the various resources, each with the other, without impairment of the productivity of the land, with consideration being given to the relative values of the various resources, and not necessarily the combination of uses that will give the greatest dollar return or the greatest unit output."

The order of listing the multiple uses caused considerable debate. The timber and grazing industries saw the act as negatively affecting their interests and sought to have the language of the bill altered to emphasize traditional commodity uses. The best those interest groups could accomplish was an insertion in Section 2 noting that the "purposes of this Act are declared to be supplemental to, but not in derogation of, the purpose for which the national forests were established as set forth in the Act of June 4, 1897 (16 U.S.C. 475)." Throughout the debate, the Forest Service insisted that the listing did not imply ranking of priorities. Dana and Fairfax suggest other-

---

40. 30 Stat. 35; 16 U.S.C. 475.

41. U.S. Congress, House Hearings, Subcommittee on Forests of the Committee on Agriculture, *National Forests — Multiple Use and Sustained Yield*, 86 Cong., 2nd sess. (1960), p. 38.

wise: "If there was any doubt that the Forest Service was pushing to emphasize recreation, this litany resolved it. In order to get recreation first on the list, they had to modify it with 'outdoor,' change fish and wildlife to 'wildlife and fish,' and call forage 'range.' "[42]

Opposition to the Multiple-Use Sustained-Yield Act also came from groups advocating an increase in Forest Service wilderness lands, but wilderness usage would clearly disallow a justification for intensive management and other uses and was unlikely to provide a budget increase. The threat of increased wilderness also tempered the opposition to the act, as many traditional commodity users saw multiple use as a way of keeping the lands open. The Forest Service successfully balanced competing demands by emphasizing the consequences if a particular group prevailed. Hearings before the House and Senate Subcommittees on Forestry of the Committees on Agriculture (neither body had a majority from the eleven western states) revealed almost unanimous support for the multiple-use concept.[43]

The passage of the Multiple-Use Sustained-Yield Act was the result of an effort started by the Forest Service in the mid-1950s. Throughout the 1950s the agency had pushed recreation and other nontraditional uses and Congress had responded with budget increases. The act would amplify those increases and establish a base for future growth.

An examination of the budget line items for the Forest Service from 1955 to 1961 indicates just how successful the agency was in gaining support for a broader mission and increasing its budget. Table 4–1 shows the history of appropriated funding in constant 1967 dollars for major line items for the years 1955, 1961, and 1980 along with total appropriated funds. The latter includes provision for the construction of roads by the Forest Service from appropriated funding, road and trail maintenance, and fire fighting and protection along with miscellaneous expenditures. While the appropriated funds constitute the major portion of the Forest Service budget, the grand total is much larger. In addition to the appropriated or "controllable" funds that are the main subject of congressional review, there are trust funds (e.g., the Knutson-Vandenburg program authorizing

---

42. Dana and Fairfax, *Forest and Range Policy*, p. 202.

43. For example, of ten members of House Subcommittee on Forests of the Committee on Agriculture, only three came from the eleven western states. See U.S. Congress, *National Forests*, p. II.

the Forest Service to require timber purchasers to make deposits in addition to payments for timber to pay for reforestation),[44] a budget item for road construction by timber purchasers, and permanent appropriations, which include the 25 percent payments to states and counties, the 10 percent fund for roads and trails, and collections from timber purchasers for brush disposal. For example, in 1980 total appropriated funding amounted to 1.26 billion dollars, while the grant total amounted to $2.64 billion.[45]

As argued, the Forest Service sought via the multiple-use concept to increase appropriations for nontraditional commodity uses. As Table 4–1 reveals, the appropriations for recreational use increased significantly over the period 1955–61. The major increase came with the appropriations act for 1961 when recreation received an increase of 43 percent over the 1960 appropriation. Furthermore, the appropriations for recreation actually understate that activity's effect on the budget. For example, Forest Service roads are, in part, justified on the basis of recreational usage, and the construction of recreational sites is generally included under other headings.[46] In addition, wildlife plus soil and water management, two categories listed in the Multiple-Use Sustained-Yield Act, have received large increases since passage of the act. On the other hand, budget items for range management and administration of mineral claims have not kept pace with the general increase in appropriations. These categories were not large items in the agency's budget in the 1950s, and were viewed with hostility by conservation groups and as an obstacle to expanding recreational usage.

It could be argued that the Forest Service was merely responding to the demands placed on it and that a larger budget was incidental to meeting those demands. But the agency was not passive. It actively lobbied for recreational use and sought to control the mix of appropriations for line items under the principle of multiple-use management. The Forest Service's behavior is consistent with the argument

44. For a discussion of the use of funds under the Knutson-Vandenberg Act, see Robinson, *The Forest Service*, pp. 74–75.

45. See footnotes in Table 4–1 for sources on the Forest Service budget. Also see Le Master, "Forest Service Funding Under RPA," for a discussion of the Forest Service budget and treatment of purchaser road credits.

46. Dana and Fairfax, *Forest and Range Policy*, p. 194. Dana and Fairfax note that the Forest Service "allocates its basic infrastructure expenses (roads, housing for rangers, personnel training programs) across a wide variety of expenditure categories. . . ."

Table 4-1. Forest Service Appropriations and Rates of Growth Over the Long Run (in thousands of 1967 dollars).[a]

	Appropriations			Annual Rates of Growth		
	1955	1961	1980	1955–61	1961–80	1955–80
1) Timber sales administration and management	9,097	22,517	70,464	16.3	6.2	8.5
2) Reforestation and stand improvement	1,309	4,944	40,434	24.8	11.7	14.7
3) Recreation use	2,797	16,289	42,071	34.1	5.1	11.4
4) Range management	4,962	7,885	14,330	8.0	3.2	4.3
5) Forest research	8,153	19,344	44,082	15.0	4.4	7.0
6) State and private forestry, cooperative and general	13,320	13,768	29,530	0.6	4.0	3.2
7) Wildlife and fish habitat management	621	1,713	15,713	18.4	12.4	13.8
8) Soil and water management	400	2,319	19,147	34.0	11.8	16.7
9) Minerals area management	2,105	5,229	6,257	16.4	0.9	4.4
10) Total appropriated funds	93,747	172,194	510,076	10.7	5.9	7.0
11) Total appropriated funds (10) less 1–9	50,983	78,186	228,048	7.4	5.8	6.2

a. Current values were adjusted to constant 1967 dollars using the consumer price index.

Sources: U.S., Congress, Senate, *Congressional Record,* 86th Cong., 2d sess., 1955 and 1961, 106, pt. 9: 12077–87. U.S. Forest Service, "Appropriations Estimates, Historical Summary Fiscal Year 1980" (1980). In 1980 the Forest Service included forest roads constructed by timber purchasers as part of total appropriated funds. That item was not included as part of appropriated funding in 1955 or 1961. Accordingly, 1980 appropriations reported here exclude purchaser roads funds. See also Dennis C. Le Master, "Forest Service Funding Under RPA," *Journal of Forestry* 80 (March 1982): 161–63.

that an agency providing interrelated services and outputs would not necessarily find control by a review committee in its best interest. The budget-maximization model also implies that the agency would not be guided by economic efficiency criteria. Clawson has attempted to estimate a balance sheet for the Forest Service that includes imputed values for nonpriced outputs of the national forest as well as the opportunity cost of timber stocks. Based on his findings, the Forest Service was operating at a loss of nearly $2 billion annually around 1974.[47]

Clawson's results should not be surprising since matching receipts with expenditures is not in the Forest Service's best interest. The agency's budget does not depend on receipts, and there are no strong incentives to seek them in the current framework. For example, while one could argue that user fees may be appropriate for recreational use, the Forest Service has shown little interest in fees. With negatively sloping demand curves, user fees would reduce the number of visitations and the political support recreationists give the Forest Service. Furthermore, multiple-use management requires considerably more planning and service-related activities than would be needed if areas were designated on the basis of a dominant use. Since 1964 the annual harvest on the national forests has not increased, but appropriations for timber sales administration have more than doubled in real terms. That increase is largely attributable to increased monitoring and planning necessitated by multiple-use considerations.[48]

Regulating the Timber Harvest

The actions of the Forest Service during the 1950s were directed at gaining control over the agenda and expanding recreational services. Ostensibly, however, the agency's traditional priorities were not altered. From 1955 to 1961 timber harvesting on the national forests increased from 6.4 to 8.4 billion board feet with commensurate

---

47. Clawson, *The Economics of National Forest Management*, p. 56.

48. Ross Gorte, "An Analysis of Forest Service Timber Management Costs" (Washington, D.C.: National Forest Products Association, 1982). (Unpublished.) Gorte attributes higher administration costs of public forest sales as compared to private to environmental analyses required on Forest Service timber sales.

increases in appropriations for timber sales administration (see Figure 4–2 and Table 4–1). Increasing the timber harvest, however, meant cutting on lands where wilderness groups had long advocated protection. Those groups began to argue that the Forest Service was approaching the point where the rate of harvest exceeded the "allowable cut."

Regulating the cut on the national forests according to the biological principle of sustained yield had always been a cornerstone of Forest Service policy and was the major justification for creation of the forest reserves in the first place. Allegations that the private sector had cut in an abusive manner and at too rapid a rate were continually advanced by the Forest Service, as were forecasts of impending timber famine. The agency received strong support for sustained-yield management from conservation groups that were also advocates of the Forest Service's attempts to regulate forestry on private lands as advancing scientific management through the agency's research activities and cooperative work programs.[49] Expanding the cut on national forests would not only reduce the support of conservation groups, but it would lower timber prices and reduce demand for the intensive management techniques offered through the Forest Service's extension programs. Restricting harvest rates, on the other hand, could increase support from the wood-products industry for reforestation and timber stand improvement. Under the sustained-yield principle, harvest rates can be increased if the growth potential of the forest is improved. However, restricting the current harvest rate would have a negative impact on budget items for timber sales administration and related activities such as road construction. The Forest Service was faced with a trade-off with the current harvest rate acting as the control variable.

The Multiple-Use Sustained-Yield Act gave the Forest Service a basis for controlling the demands for an accelerated harvest schedule. The act did not specify the method of computing the allowable cut, only that sustained yield "means the achievement and maintenance in perpetuity of a high-level annual or regular periodic output."[50] The allowable cut is calculated by the Forest Service and is a function of timber growth and the standing volume of "over mature tim-

---

49. Forest research and state and local cooperative work are not minor elements in the Forest Service budget: see Table 4–1. In *Public Lands Politics*, p. 336, Culhane notes that environmentalists support those programs.

50. 74 Stat. 215 (1960).

ber," but sustained yield can be increased if investments in silvicultural practices are undertaken.[51] While current investment in reforestation or timber stand improvement would not immediately result in an increase in timber volume, it would increase potential growth and under the allowable cut formula would allow a subsequent increase in the rate of harvest of the overmature stock. An increase in timber harvests could be accomplished under sustained-yield management only by increasing appropriations for silvicultural practices.

From 1950 to 1960 the allowable cut on the national forest advanced from 5.6 to 9.8 billion board feet largely because of construction of access roads, improved inventory data, and changes in utilization standards.[52] In the early 1960s, however, increases in the allowable cut essentially ceased. Confronted by the expansion of wilderness areas, which adversely affected the allowable cut and the demand for national forest timber, the wood-products industry pressed for an increase in appropriations for silvicultural practices. In 1969 the National Timber Supply Act was submitted with the intent of establishing a "high yield timber fund" to be collected from the receipts of timber sales.[53] All timber receipts not already designated were to go into a fund directed exclusively toward augmenting the allowable cut. In testimony before Congress, the chief of the Forest Service stated that with the funding the agency could increase the allowable cut by 5.8 billion board feet.[54]

The 5.8 billion board feet plus an increase in timber salvage operations would augment harvests on the national forests by 50 percent. The Forest Service recognized that preservationists would not welcome such an increase and proposed a substitute bill that left the timber fund intact, but restated the Forest Service's multiple-use mandate. The substitute bill also proposed to eliminate a provision of the original bill (Section 7): "The Secretary of Agriculture shall immediately establish programs to carry out the policy and purpose of this Act."[55] Testifying in support of the bill, former Forest Ser-

51. For a discussion of how sustained yield or allowable cut is calculated, see William F. Hyde, *Timber Supply, Land Allocation, and Economic Efficiency* (Baltimore: Johns Hopkins University Press, 1980), pp. 12–42. In recent years the Forest Service has relabeled allowable cut to mean potential cut.

52. See U.S. Congress, House Hearings, Subcommittee on Forests of the Committee on Agriculture, *National Timber Supply Act of 1969*, 91st Cong., 1st sess. (1969), p. 85.

53. Ibid.

54. Ibid., p. 97.

55. Ibid., p. 3.

vice Chief Edward C. Crafts explained that Section 7 could be interpreted "to pressure the Forest Service to increase its cut beyond the safety levels even if it does not get the money to handle the job."[56]

The testimony of the Forest Service during the hearings on the act shows that the agency was willing to increase harvest rates provided there were significant increases in the budget. While most of the bill's opponents supported intensive management, conservation groups were alarmed by the proposed large increase in the cut of old growth timber and a timber fund based on receipts. The bill was defeated.

With defeat of the act, the timber lobby sought relief by enlisting the aid of the White House. The Executive Office of the President was used with apparent, but temporary success, to obtain an increase in timber sales in 1970.[57] While that action was not accomplished without a promised increase in appropriations for reforestation, it was apparent that White House pressure could have an impact on timber harvest rates. Throughout the 1970s the Forest Service continued to claim that the harvest rate could be increased only if yields were improved. In 1976, with passage of the National Forest Management Act, that constraint was further defined and strengthened.[58] Section 6(m) directs the Secretary of Agriculture to ensure that "prior to harvest, stands of trees throughout the National Forest System shall generally have reached the culmination of mean annual increment of growth."[59] It is widely recognized that rotation age, when determined by the biological criteria of maximum physical sustainable yield (culmination of mean annual increment), results in higher rotation periods than that given when the criteria of maximizing net present worth are utilized.[60] When applied to the Forest Service's method of calculating the rate of converting old growth stands to a regulated forest, a high rotation age increases the conversion period and, hence, reduces the current allowable cut. In addition, Section 13 provided that harvest rates with some minor exceptions

56. Ibid., p. 172. Crafts also stated that, "The Forest Service has been pushed and pushed under tremendous pressures during the last 10 or 20 years to increase the cut on the National Forests." See U.S. Congress, *National Timber Supply Act of 1969*, p. 175.

57. See Daniel R. Barney, *The Last Stand* (New York: Grossman, 1974), p. 89. Also see Culhane, *Public Lands Politics*, p. 18.

58. 90 Stat. 2949 (1976).

59. Ibid., p. 2956.

60. See, for example, Paul A. Samuelson, "The Economics of Forestry in an Evolving Society," *Economic Inquiry* 14 (December 1976): 466–92.

were to be nondeclining over time.[61] The combination of a high bio-logically determined rotation age and the nondeclining harvest flow regulation gives the Forest Service a strong statutory basis for re-stricting the rate at which old growth timber can be harvested.[62] Like the Multiple-Use Sustained-Yield Act, the 1976 act leaves the actual determination of the allowable cut to the Forest Service, which con-ducts the inventory and classification scheme.

A budget-maximizing bureau would seek to control the flow of outputs through statutory reform. In particular, the bureau would constrain output levels where those outputs negatively affected the demands for other outputs or the overall political support the agency receives. For timber harvesting, the Forest Service has an incentive to constrain output below that which a high demand review committee that supported the timber industry would seek. By controlling the harvest rate, the Forest Service can influence support for silvicultural practices and càn continue to receive tacit approval from conserva-tion groups for adhering to sustained-yield management. There is evidence that the agency has been successful (see Table 4-1). Appro-priations for reforestation and timber stand improvement have in-creased at double the annual rate of total appropriations over the period 1955 to 1980. In addition to the appropriations, the Forest Service also collects funds for reforestation under the Knutson-Vandenburg program. Those funds have increased at a similar rate and were approximately equal in magnitude to the appropriated funds in 1980.

The ability to constrain the total timber harvest under the manage-ment principles of multiple use and sustained yield has also allowed

61. 90 Stat. 2957 (1976). In the U.S. Department of Agriculture, *An Assessment of the Forest and Rangeland Situation in the United States* (Washington, D.C.: Government Print-ing Office, 1980), p. 413, the Forest Service readily admits that harvest rates could be increased, but argues that "the sustained yield level could not be maintained with present and planned management programs and the dependent industries and communities would sooner or later be faced with a drop in harvests." The community dependency argument ignores the impact of constrained harvests on other sectors of the economy.

62. Clawson, *The Economics of National Forest Management*, p. 11. Clawson stresses the point that "harvest must take place, if growth is to be possible." Under the usual dynamic optimization rules where there is a large stock with current low growth rates, opti-mal harvest rates decline over time until the excess stock is liquidated. See, for example, R. G. Cummings and Ronald N. Johnson, "Welfare Analysis of Long-Term Forest Products Price Stabilization: Note," *American Journal of Agricultural Economics* 60 (November 1978): 689-90. Also see U.S. Comptroller General, "Projected Timber Scarcities in the Pacific Northwest: A Critique of 11 Studies," EMD-79-5 (December 12, 1975).

the Forest Service to spread its activities across the national forest system. By adhering to biological rules for determining timber harvest programs, the agency has designated areas capable of growing as little as twenty to fifty cubic feet of wood per acre annually as harvestable sites. Even though intensive management of such areas cannot be economically justified, the Forest Service continues to spend more on timber harvesting and related activities than the timber is worth.[63]

In comparing related expenditures with receipts across national forests, Clawson finds considerable variation.[64] The Pacific Northwest and California regions, which account for most of the Forest Service inventory of valuable high quality old growth timber, frequently show receipts in excess of expenditures. The Rocky Mountain and southwestern regions, on the other hand, have expenditures considerably in excess of receipts. Furthermore, the associated costs of timber management, including sales administration, reforestation, and timber stand improvement, are lower in California and the Pacific Northwest than in other regions. Clawson's results are supported by Hyde, who has shown that in the Rocky Mountain region the Forest Service has permitted harvesting of timber in areas where it could not be "justified by a free timber market," and by Barlow et al., who indicated that the practice is widespread.[65]

The spreading of agency activities would be across political jurisdictions. Table 4-2 contains data on activities in twelve western states. These twelve states made up about 85 percent of the total harvest from the national forests in 1970-71.[66] The period 1970-71 is utilized because site class data (Table 4-2, column 8) are readily available for that period. Column 1 of Table 4-2 shows the proportion each state has of the region's total timber receipts. Column 2 is the proportion of the region's total harvested volume. Comparing columns 1 and 2 indicates that the harvested volume is directed away

63. In *The Economics of National Forest Management*, p. 8, Clawson argues that "Site Class V forests . . . are not commercial in the sense that they can be managed economically to grow wood."

64. Clawson, *The Economics of National Forest Management*, pp. 65-77.

65. Hyde, "Compounding Clear-cuts," p. 200; Barlow, Hefland, Orr, and Stoel, *Giving Away the National Forests.*

66. While the bulk of Forest Service lands are in the western part of the United States, the agency manages lands in almost every state. In 1970 harvesting operations on Forest Service land were carried out in forty-one states. See USDA, *Report of the Chief Forest Service, 1970-71*, p. 85.

Table 4-2. Activity Spreading on National Forests in Twelve Western States, 1970-71.

State	(1)	(2)	(3)	(4)	(5)	(6)	(7)	(8)
Oregon	.451	.344	36.39	.274	.898	.311	.272	.573
California	.211	.219	26.66	.283	.686	.184	.175	.573
Washington	.191	.162	32.77	.093	.923	.081	.144	.521
Idaho	.054	.101	14.66	.118	.530	.044	.209	.596
Montana	.053	.080	18.45	.088	.369	.101	.106	.451
Arizona	.017	.030	15.85	.024	.175	.157	.017	.969
Colorado	.008	.021	10.42	.024	.090	.019	.044	.924
New Mexico	.008	.016	13.12	.036	.051	.057	.003	.975
Wyoming	.003	.013	7.17	.014	.138	.007	.018	.981
South Dakota	.002	.008	8.78	.004	.111	.015	.002	1.000
Utah	.001	.006	6.36	.030	.025	.023	.009	.992
Nevada	.001[a]	.001[a]	5.00	.007	.000	.002	.001[a]	.981

Definitions: Column (1) – Proportion of total timber receipts
Column (2) – Proportion of total harvested volume
Column (3) – Average dollar value per thousand board feet
Column (4) – Proportion of total appropriated road funds
Column (5) – Expenditures for road construction by timber purchasers divided by appropriated funds
Column (6) – Proportion of total acres receiving timber stand improvement
Column (7) – Proportion of total acres planted
Column (8) – Proportion of commercial timberlands in site classes IV and V.

Sources: Columns (1) to (7) – USDA, Forest Service, *Report of the Chief Forest Service, 1970-71* (1971). Column (8) – USDA, Forest Service, *The Outlook for Timber in the United States* (1973), appendix I, table 5.

a. Actually less than .001.

from the higher valued timber in Oregon, California, and Washington toward lower valued timber in the remaining states. In 1970-71 the average value of harvested timber (column 3) in Oregon was $36.39 per thousand board feet while in Nevada it was only $5.00; an outcome that is the direct result of adherence to the biological rules inherent in the sustained-yield concept. Once an area is designated as "commercial timber," it becomes part of the timber harvest plan and can be sold to private timber purchasers. The volume sold annually tends to be proportional to the inventory of sawtimber on each national forest.[67]

67. The volume sold annually is also influenced by even flow constraints, rotation age, and the planning process.

The harvesting operation will generally require constructing access roads, often built by timber purchasers. Larger system roads are constructed by the Forest Service. The estimated value of the roads constructed by purchasers is applied toward the payment of the timber harvested. Clearly, if the value of the timber is less than the cost of constructing the specified roads, there would be no sale. If the Forest Service wanted to sell timber in areas where the value of the timber was low it would have to subsidize the operation by constructing the roads out of appropriated funds. When column 4 of Table 4–2 – the proportion of the region's total appropriated funds for road construction going to each of the twelve western states – is compared with columns 1 or 2 the relationship is not proportional. That is, there is a statistically significant disproportionate share of funds going to the states with lower harvest receipts or lower harvested volumes.[68] While factors such as recreational usage can influence the result, it should be pointed out that Oregon, California, and Washington had considerably more recreational use in terms of visits per day than did the remaining nine states.[69]

There is additional support for the contention that the Forest Service uses appropriated funding for roads to further the harvesting of low-valued timber. The figures in Table 4–2, column 5 are the ratios of expenditures for road construction by timber purchasers (P) to Forest Service appropriated funding for road construction (A). Since the Forest Service does not retain timber receipts, it has an incentive to use those funds indirectly by requiring timber purchasers to construct a greater share of roads where timber values are higher. The data in Table 4–2 bear this argument out. The simple correlation

68. A simple test of proportionality is to run the regression $Y = a + bx$ where Y is the proportion of total appropriated road funds and x is either the proportion of total timber receipts or proportion of total harvested volume. The constant is included because even in the absence of harvesting, some road construction can still be expected. Proportionality would be indicated if b were equal to unity. The results are:

		Estimated Coefficient		
	Constant	Proportion of Receipts	Proportion of Volume	R^2
eq. 1	.0308	.6306 (.1083)		.772
eq. 2	.0116		.8609 (.0973)	.887

Numbers in parenthesis are standard errors. In both equations the coefficient b is significantly less than unity at the .10 level.

69. See USDA, *Report of the Chief*, p. 69.

coefficient between the ratio P/A and the average value per thousand board feet is 0.95. This last result would also imply that as timber values rise in real terms over time the ratio P/A should also increase. From 1970 to 1980 the average value per thousand board feet for the entire Forest Service system went from $22.95 to $69.98 in constant 1967 dollars. The ratio P/A went from 0.42 to 1.15 over the same period.[70]

Columns 6 and 7 show the proportion of the total acres in the region receiving timber stand improvement and acres planted (acres treated are used because expenditures by states are not readily available). Once again, when those columns are compared to columns 1 and 2 there is a disproportionate relationship. Activities such as timber stand improvement appear to be directed away from higher valued timber. More striking, however, is the relationship of columns 6 and 7 to column 8. The latter represents the percentage of total commercial timber acreage in site classes IV and V. These site classes are considered marginal to submarginal in terms of potential economic returns to intensive management. Yet, those sites are the subject of intensive silvicultural practices. Once those areas are harvested, Forest Service regulations require that they be regenerated.[71]

Standard models of resource exploitation generally call for the better or lower cost resources to be used first. The dense old growth forests of the Pacific Northwest have lower harvesting costs than are found in other regions of the country and contain sufficient volumes to offset substantial reductions in the harvest rates on national forests in higher cost areas. Despite the regions' potential for timber harvesting and future growth, it is in the Pacific Northwest where the Forest Service appears to exercise the most restraint. The Forest Service, which espouses a conservation ethic, has fostered the harvesting of timber in areas where economic criteria would argue against it. As a consequence, the environment has been unnecessarily degraded.

In considering a rationale for Forest Service behavior, Clawson offers the following:

> All too often in national forest management, 'multiple use' has meant a little of everything, everywhere, regardless of costs and of results. The tendency to invest too much capital in poor sites, at the expense of more rewarding invest-

---

70. Data for 1980 are from USDA, *Report of the Forest Service: Fiscal Year 1980*, 1981, tables B.7.3 and B11.1 and B11.2.

71. For a discussion of the impacts of those regulations, see Hyde, "Compounding Clear-cuts," p. 192.

ment on better sites, the tendency to practice timber management on sites when timber cannot be grown economically, and other similar actions have been noted. Each national forest supervisor and ranger has wanted a diversified program. He has especially wanted to include timber management in his territory, fearing that in its absence his work would not be properly appreciated or that the funds available to him would be inadequate.[72]

Clawson's description of the motives is consistent with the budget-maximization model, but it must be remembered that the agency is not always free to do as it pleases. The political process is an integral part of and constraint on the agency's behavior. The Forest Service has worked within that process to alter the rules and has successfully spread activities across political jurisdictions since there was an initial constituency to be served. Timber-harvesting activities generate employment and local communities often become dependent on national forest timber supplies—and the Forest Service has utilized those constituencies.[73] It is the outcome of this process that Clawson describes. Conflict will undoubtedly arise during such a process, but it does not appear to have reduced the Forest Service budget.

CONCLUSION

Three fundamental facts emerge from the analyses. First, Forest Service policy is not guided by economic efficiency criteria. Second, the agency's behavior is often at odds with its espoused conservation ethic. Third, the agency has not been passive; it has sought to expand its operations under the guise of multiple-use and sustained-yield management and has been successful in that endeavor. While it has been argued that the agency's behavior is consistent with the budget-maximization hypothesis, the analysis does not permit the conclusion that the agency does seek to maximize its budget. In the absence of the budget-maximization model, however, it is difficult to imagine why the Forest Service would not support a move away from the principle of multiple use toward dominant use with emphasis on high productivity sites. The result would be an increase in timber growth

---

72. Clawson, *The Economics of National Forest Management*, p. 108.

73. The Forest Service admits to selling below costs but, in part, attempts to justify its actions by arguing that such sales stabilize communities dependent on Forest Service timber. See USDA, *Report of the Forest Service*, p. 16.

and supplies as well as an increase in wilderness areas. A move toward dominant use coupled with economic efficiency criteria, however, would likely reduce Forest Service appropriations.

Budget items for timber sales and related activities on a per thousand board foot basis are generally higher in other regions than for the Pacific Northwest. A shift in harvest activity to regions where appropriations on a thousand board foot basis have been historically low would make it difficult for the Forest Service to justify current levels of appropriations for timber-related activities, let alone expansion. Furthermore, a dominant use philosophy could place the justification of Forest Service custodianship in jeopardy. If an area is to be used primarily for timber growing, the argument for public ownership would be significantly reduced. Analysis suggests that the Forest Service can be expected to resist changes that reduce its budget and, more importantly, that the Forest Service will be supported in its resistance efforts by negatively affected constituencies.

Chapter 5

REGULATORY CONSTRAINTS ON OIL AND GAS PRODUCTION ON FOREST SERVICE AND BLM LANDS

Gary D. Libecap

INTRODUCTION

There is growing conflict over oil and gas development on federal lands between private firms and the Forest Service and the Bureau of Land Management (BLM). Private exploration for and production of oil and gas are authorized by the Mineral Leasing Act of 1920 as amended.[1] Under that statute, firms can obtain leases to federal land subject to conditions applied by the two agencies and to monitoring by the BLM (formerly postlease monitoring was by the Minerals Management Service and before that, by the Geological Survey). Between 1979 and 1982, however, there have been at least five General Accounting Office (GAO) reports, one Office of Technology Assessment study, and three reports by the American Petroleum Institute critical of the Forest Service and BLM for impeding mineral fuels production.[2] In particular, the agencies are charged with widespread

---

1. 30 U.S.C. 181.

2. GAO, *Federal Leasing Policy—Is the Split Responsibility Working?* EMD-79-60, 1979; idem, *Actions Needed to Increase Federal Onshore Oil and Gas Exploration and Development*, EMD-81-40, 1981; idem, *Minerals Management at the Department of the Interior Needs Coordination and Organization*, EMD-81-53, 1981; idem, *Accelerated Onshore Oil and Gas Leasing May Not Occur as Quickly as Anticipated*, EMD-82-34, 1982; idem, *Interior's Minerals Management Programs Need Consolidation to Improve Accountability and Control*, EMD-82-104, 1982; American Petroleum Institute, *Analysis of the*

administrative withdrawals of land from exploration and production, long delays in processing leases and applications for permits to drill, and the use of restrictive stipulations as a condition for lease development. The potential negative effects of these agency actions are large. Of the 770 million acres owned by the federal government, over 600 million acres are administered by the Forest Service and BLM, and are thereby subject to regulatory controls.[3] The GAO estimates that as many as 261 million acres of federal land outside Alaska have prospective oil and gas deposits.[4] Of particular concern is the overthrust belt running from Idaho and Montana to Arizona and New Mexico, which has favorable geologic characteristics but which lies almost wholly on federal land.

The empirical evidence of administrative delays and land withdrawals can be analyzed with a model of self-interested bureaucratic behavior. Neither the Forest Service nor the BLM has direct incentive to promote oil and gas development on the lands under their administrative control. Indeed, they have the counterincentive to sharply constrain the activities of petroleum firms and to limit the information released on oil and gas values.

ADMINISTRATIVE STRUCTURE FOR LEASING: MULTIPLE JURISDICTIONS AND FIRM INITIATIVE

The regulatory structure controlling private exploitation of petroleum deposits on federal lands contains overlapping jurisdictions among and within federal agencies. Moreover, the initiative for development lies with the firm, not with the surface management agency. These are key points in understanding the behavior of the

---

Processing of Permits to Drill on Federal Lands, Research Study 029 (Washington, D.C.: American Petroleum Institute, 1982); Everett and Associates, *Withdrawal of Public Lands from Access to Minerals and Fuels* (Washington, D.C.: Everett & Associates, 1980); idem, *Analyses of Delays in the Processing of Applications for Permit to Drill and Prestaking Clearance Applications* (Washington, D.C.: Everett & Associates, 1981); and U.S. Congress, Office of Technology Assessment, *Management of Fuel and Nonfuel Minerals in Federal Land*, 1979. A related though earlier study is an intradepartmental analysis by U.S. Department of the Interior, *Final Report of the Task Force on the Availability of Federally Owned Mineral Lands*, 1977.

3. U.S. Department of the Interior, *Public Lands Statistics*, 1980.
4. GAO, *Actions Needed to Increase Federal Onshore Oil and Gas Exploration and Development*, p. 40.

Forest Service and BLM. The principal governing legislation is the Mineral Leasing Act of 1920, which authorizes the Secretary of the Interior to issue oil and gas leases on most federal land. The Bureau of Land Management is the leasing agent for onshore development, postlease monitor, and the largest manager of surface land (427 million acres). The Forest Service is the next largest surface manager (188 million acres), but it has no direct legislative responsibility for leasing. As lease administrator, the BLM awards leases for two types of land. Where there are known geological structures (due to past development), competitive bids are accepted. A royalty of at least 12.5 percent of gross production is required for the lease, which runs for five years or as long as commercial production continues. For lands outside of known producing areas, leases are assigned on a first come basis for a 12.5 percent royalty and rental of $0.50 per acre per year for ten years or the length of production.

Before approving leases, the office of the BLM Assistant Director for Onshore Energy and Minerals coordinates with the surface agency—the Forest Service or the BLM Assistant Directors for Renewable Resources and Lands. Coordination is at the National Forest or BLM district level. The surface management agency can specify terms and conditions for leases or request that particular areas be withdrawn from leasing. Access restrictions are most often applied under the Wilderness Act, the Wild and Scenic Rivers Act, and the National Environmental Policy Act.[5] In 1979, 12,000 new leases were issued for approximately 13 million acres; 97 percent were assigned noncompetitively. By the beginning of fiscal year 1980, there were over 118,000 active oil and gas leases involving some 100 million acres of land.[6]

Actual lease supervision to ensure compliance with lease requirements and the stipulations added by the surface agency is provided by the BLM as lease monitor. The lease does not automatically assign the right to develop. Before an operator can drill a well, the BLM must be notified, and the agency may then grant a Pre-Stake Clearance (PSC) after conferring with the surface management agency and conducting a preliminary environment review. If the PSC is granted, the operator follows with a formal Application for Permit to Drill

5. 16 U.S.C. 1131–36; 16 U.S.C. 1280; 42 U.S.C. 4321–47.
6. GAO, *Actions Needed to Increase Federal Onshore Oil and Gas Exploration and Development*, p. 18.

(APD) with location maps, access proposals, technical development plans, bonding for surface rehabilitation, and operator designation. The BLM reviews the APD for completeness and submits it to the surface agency, either another BLM division or the Forest Service. At this point, the latter can add site specific stipulations as a condition for development. The stipulations may address various surface qualities affected by drilling such as archeological sites and wilderness and wildlife areas. The nature of the imposed stipulations importantly affects production costs and the incentive to drill. The surface agency can also request more extensive environmental impact analysis before considering the APD. If the Forest Service or BLM approves the APD, the permit will be issued with any necessary stipulations. Monitoring of drilling and production to see that APD obligations are met is provided by the BLM for all federal land. These stipulations are the means by which the surface agencies maintain some jurisdiction over leased areas. This complex jurisdictional arrangement affects the behavior of the Forest Service and BLM toward mineral fuels production of federal land.

ANALYTICAL FRAMEWORK: AGENCY BEHAVIOR AND ITS IMPLICATIONS FOR OIL AND GAS DEVELOPMENT ON FEDERAL LAND

The Forest Service and BLM as surface management agencies have incentives to discourage the use of federal lands for oil and gas development. To see why, a model of bureaucratic behavior is employed as presented by Niskanen, Breton and Wintrobe, and others which postulates budget maximization as a primary agency goal.[7] No direct tests of that model are provided here, yet the model is used to establish self-interest behavior by agency officials as a motivation for discretionary policies regarding oil and gas development. The model asserts a direct link between budget size and utility maximization for bureaucrats. Budget expansion provides for increased salaries, staffing, perquisites, political power, and ability to implement professionally

---

7. William A. Niskanen, *Bureaucracy and Representative Government* (Chicago: Aldine & Atherton, 1971); Albert Breton and Ronald Wintrobe, "The Equilibrium Size of a Budget-maximizing Bureau," *Journal of Political Economy* 83 (1975): 195–207.

desired programs. The latter may be particularly important for the Forest Service and, to a lesser extent, for the BLM because of long-standing professional forestry and range management emphasis within the agencies.

The model argues that in making land use decisions, Forest Service and BLM officials will select those options that are consistent with budget growth. A key characteristic of bureaucratic discretionary decisionmaking is that bureaucrats are not residual claimants. Unlike firm managers, their pecuniary rewards are not tied to profits or the surplus between revenues and costs. Accordingly, officials do not have the same incentive to seek out new land uses to maximize economic returns. For example, any increases in the rental value of federal land due to the discovery of commercial oil and gas deposits do not accrue to the Forest Service or BLM. Under current law, royalty payments from oil and gas production go to general treasury revenues. Permanent staff income and advancement depend instead upon GS ratings and overall agency jurisdiction and managerial activities. While administration of oil and gas leases is primarily under the BLM, neither the Forest Service nor the BLM, as *surface management agencies*, has a broad functional role in energy development comparable to surface uses such as forestry or grazing. Hence, energy provides little justification for budget growth. Because of split jurisdictions, any budget gains from oil and gas activity will be difficult for the surface agency to predict.

Indeed, oil and gas development may have the opposite effect if it disrupts established resource management programs and interest group relations. The Forest Service and BLM make land allocation decisions both to build and maintain favorable political support for budget requests from interest groups and Congress and to meet internal bureaucratic management goals. These allocations imply broad discretionary authority by the agency over its output. Accordingly, the resource uses selected will be those that maintain or enhance bureaucratic control, ceteris paribus. The initiation of leasing and minerals production, however, is with firms, and the surface management agencies are respondents, which diminishes their discretionary authority over land use. This establishes that the Forest Service and BLM find it in their interest to restrict private minerals exploration and production to maintain regulatory control. To do so, they will limit the information revealed on land value to emphasize agency-preferred uses. Because information on oil and gas deposits depends upon drilling, it can be controlled through constraints on exploration. Through suppressing information on the value of lost potential output, political criticism of current allocation arrangements can be minimized. Because the Bureau of Land Management has a greater role in administering oil and gas leases than the Forest Service, there will be greater internal pressures within the BLM to adopt less restrictive policies toward leasing than within the Forest Service.

THE RELATIONSHIP OF OIL AND GAS TO ESTABLISHED POLICIES, CONSTITUENCIES, AND PAST BUDGET GROWTH

The traditional focus of both the Forest Service and the BLM has been on renewable resource management, specifically of timber and rangeland, and has been molded by staffing, interest group relations, and budgeting patterns. This focus affects the response of the agencies toward oil and gas activities. The long-standing emphasis of the Forest Service on the conservation of forest resources and disinterest in subsurface land values is noted in nearly every study of the agency. For instance, Dana and Fairfax detail the broad commitment of the Forest Service to scientific timber management, and point out a bias against minerals because of the lack of agency authority over them.[8]

In drafting the Multiple-Use and Sustained-Yield Act of 1960, the Forest Service singled out only renewable surface uses of the National Forests as multiple-use categories and did not include mining or minerals.[9] Frome noted that mining, in general, constituted a challenge to the land-planning efforts of the Forest Service because of the private patenting and leasing activities of firms.[10] Forestry is the dominant profession within the Forest Service and the agency relies more than most on internal promotion from within the ranks, which gives the agency a cohesive stand toward forest management.[11]

8, Samuel T. Dana and Sally K. Fairfax, *Forest and Range Policy*, 2d ed. (New York: McGraw-Hill, 1980), pp. 297–330.

9. 16 U.S.C. 528–31.

10. Michael Frome, *The Forest Service* (New York: Praeger, 1971), pp. 108–117

11. Glen O. Robinson, *The Forest Service* (Baltimore: Johns Hopkins University Press, 1975), pp. 260–62; Jeanne Nienaber and Daniel McCool, "Agency Power: Staking Out Terrain in Natural Resources Policy" (Tucson: University of Arizona, Department of Political Science, 1980), p. 56.

Its forestry and budgeting aims have been assisted by close ties to the forest products industry, forestry schools, and professional forestry societies.[12] The forestry tie has been disrupted somewhat by the emergence, since the mid-1960s, of environmental groups as influential interest groups; they have advocated restrictions on all surface use including forestry.[13] Their lobbying in Congress and through the courts has forced both the Forest Service and BLM to adopt increasingly cautious programs for surface development. The emphasis of Forest Service policy and staffing on renewable forest management is reflected in budget data. Johnson details Forest Service appropriations from 1955 through 1980.[14] The data show that minerals management is a small and declining portion of total Forest Service appropriations. While overall agency funding grew at an annual rate of 7.0 percent over the twenty-five year period, minerals management grew at 4.4 percent annually and was only 1 percent of the 1980 appropriation.

The renewable resource orientation of the BLM, its interest group links, and budgeting patterns are similar to those of the Forest Service. Professionally trained range specialists are a major share of the agency's permanent work force.[15] Moreover, its strongest interest group ties have been with ranchers who hold grazing permits.[16] Clawson contrasts the management of range and forestlands, where the BLM formulates policies for sustained yield, and mineral resources, where the initiative for development lies instead with private firms through leasing or patenting.[17] Similarly Culhane describes the limited control both the Forest Service and BLM have over mining and oil and gas activities as follows:

When the agencies have a chance to officially approve mining rights by patenting mining claims or issuing minerals leases, those decisions are the formal

12. Dana and Fairfax, *Forest and Range Policy*, p. 306; and Nienaber and McCool, "Agency Power," p. 42.

13. Paul J. Culhane, *Public Lands Politics* (Baltimore: Johns Hopkins University Press, 1981), p. 169.

14. Ronald N. Johnson, "Budget Maximization and Agencies Control: The Case of the U.S. Forest Service" (Bozeman: Montana State University, 1982), p. 24.

15. Nienaber and McCool, "Agency Power," p. 57.

16. Dana and Fairfax, *Forest and Range Policy*, pp. 341–43; and Gary D. Libecap, *Locking up the Range: Federal Land Use Controls and Grazing* (San Francisco: Pacific Research Institute for Public Policy, 1981).

17. Marion Clawson, *The Bureau of Land Management* (New York: Praeger, 1971), p. 122 and n. 2.

Table 5-1. Total BLM Appropriations and Funding for Surface
Resources and Energy and Minerals Management.

	1955	1965	1975	1980	Annual Rate of Change 1955-1980
	(thousands of constant 1967 dollars)				
Total appropriation	61,762	152,705	247,646	371,794	7.4%
Surface resource management[a]	15,665	67,531	116,442	141,493	9.2%
Energy minerals management[b]	3,035	10,500	20,483	36,391	10.4%
Energy share of total appropriation	4.9%	6.9%	8.3%	9.8%	

a. Includes the budget classifications, management of lands and resources, construction, and range improvements less energy management and payments to states for O & C Lands and grazing permit receipts.
b. Includes funding for leasing OCS and onshore as well as disposal of lands for all purposes (except in 1980).
Source: U.S. Budget.

responsibility of BLM state offices, not local Forest Service or BLM administrators. Postlease monitoring and administration are conducted by the Conservation Division of the U.S. Geological Survey, not by Forest Service rangers or BLM area managers. The agencies have evolved informal administrative practices for consulting with local land managers over mineral management decisions. . . . But such procedures are a far cry from the formal control that local BLM and Forest Service officers have over other uses of lands under their jurisdiction.[18]

Table 5-1 outlines budget appropriations for the BLM from 1955 to 1980. Because of the agency's dual role as surface manager and leasing agent, energy programs receive larger allocations than in the Forest Service. Nevertheless, the overriding budget appropriation for the BLM, as with the Forest Service, is for surface resource management.

Existing constituent relations, budgeting patterns, and surface resource management programs, then, provide the BLM and Forest Service with incentives to curtail oil and gas exploration and production on the lands under their respective jurisdictions.

18. Culhane, *Public Lands Politics*, p. 123.

DISCRETIONARY POLICIES OF THE FOREST SERVICE AND BLM THAT CONSTRAIN OIL AND GAS DEVELOPMENT ON FEDERAL LAND

Land Withdrawal

Of the 410 million acres of federal land in the lower forty-eight states, 65 million acres (about 16 percent of the total) have been withdrawn from mineral leasing for various reasons. One quarter of the 65 million acres, some 16 million acres, have been removed through informal administrative decisions, while the remainder has been formally set aside by Congress in national parks, military reservations, and wildlife refuges.[19] Because of the concern that as much as 55 percent of the withdrawn lands may contain commercial oil and gas deposits, the GAO investigated land withdrawals in 1980 in five states: Colorado, Mississippi, Nevada, New Mexico, and Wyoming. In 1980 in those states, 20 million acres were removed from leasing; 14 million by formal statute and 6 million primarily through discretionary actions by the Forest Service and BLM.[20] BLM and Forest Service withdrawals were largely for wilderness reviews.

Such reviews are extensive since an additional 16.5 million acres are under consideration by the two agencies for wilderness designation in the five states. The GAO found that the Forest Service and BLM used their administrative discretion to be more restrictive in their policies regarding mineral leasing than Congress authorized in the Wilderness Act of 1964. That act specifically allowed for exploration and development of mineral deposits under the mining laws for twenty years. That period was designed to prevent the permanent locking up of unknown deposits in wilderness areas.

The BLM and Forest Service, however, have implemented policies that prevent firms from taking advantage of that provision of the Wilderness Act. In conducting wilderness studies, the BLM has applied, instead, the nonimpairment clause of the Federal Land Policy and Management Act to close areas from minerals exploration by firms.[21] While Section (603e) of the Act directs the Secretary of the

---

19. GAO, *Federal Onshore Oil and Gas Exploration*, p. 27.
20. Ibid., p. 48.
21. 43 U.S.C. 1782.

Interior not to impair areas formally preserved as wilderness, it does not necessarily apply to lands only under review by the BLM for possible wilderness designation by Congress. Similarly, the Forest Service has used its discretion to restrict access by firms to federal lands. The Federal Land Policy and Management Act does not apply to the Forest Service; hence, it cannot use the nonimpairment clause.

Instead, the Forest Service approves leasing in review areas only with extremely restrictive stipulations. An example is the no-surface-occupancy stipulation that affects nearly 1 million acres in the five states studied by the GAO, including at least 345 thousand acres of the potentially rich overthrust belt in Wyoming.[22] The text of the stipulation illustrates the constraints placed on oil firms:

> Surface occupancy on these lands for the purpose of oil and gas exploration or development is prohibited. The underlying oil and gas resources may be developed so long as no portion of the surface of the described lands is occupied or disturbed. The provisions of this stipulation may be modified only with mutual consent of the Lessee, Surface Management Agency, and Area Oil and Gas Supervisor.[23]

When applied, the no-surface-occupancy stipulation requires directional drilling, use of helicopters for access, and other special production techniques that raise costs and effectively remove many areas from oil and gas development.

In both cases, the BLM and Forest Service have adopted the most guarded approach to wilderness review and imposed restraints on mineral activity, despite contrary provisions of the Wilderness Act. Those restraints, however, maintain agency control over the surface land area during wilderness studies. While wilderness is not necessarily an agency goal, administrative control allows the agencies to respond to the demands of environmental groups who are influential wilderness advocates, while limiting the interference of oil and gas exploration and development by private firms. Exploratory activities also affect other lands besides those under wilderness review through multiple drilling site development and the construction of and heavy traffic on access roads. Hence, the stipulations serve to maintain bureaucratic control beyond wilderness sites. The economic costs of the stipulations and foregone petroleum production are borne by neither the Forest Service nor the BLM.

22. GAO, *Federal Onshore Oil and Gas Exploration*, p. 57.
23. Quoted in ibid., p. 56.

A related administrative policy that both raises the costs of oil and gas development and effectively removes land is the contingent rights stipulation (CRS). The CRS was adopted by the Forest Service and BLM in 1982 for leasing in areas outside known geologic structures where most leasing occurs.[24] With it, the right to lease is separated from the right to develop. The CRS is placed in leases, notifying the operator that the right to develop is subject to environmental review. The text of the Forest Service CRS is as follows:

> All operations on this lease are subject to Government approval with such site-specific stipulations as may be necessary to assure reasonable protection of or mitigation of effects on other values. A plan of operations shall not be approved if it results in unacceptable impact on other resources, land uses, and/or the environment. If for these reasons a plan of operations cannot be approved, the lease term may be suspended for up to 5 years . . . or . . . terminated . . . without recourse for compensation.[25]

The CRS reverses the past policy of conducting environmental reviews prior to leasing. Under the former policy, once the reviews were completed oil and gas firms could apply for leases subject to any stipulations imposed by the surface management agency. Since the nature of the constraints was then known, firms had the information to determine which areas to lease. Since the CRS calls for environmental review only upon development, firms obtain leases for exploration in areas where development may be subsequently denied or subjected to unknown production controls. Accordingly, the CRS shifts additional uncertainty to the firm. Given the inherent risks of exploration, the added uncertainty of the regulatory environment further discourages private leasing activity. On the other hand, the CRS allows the surface management agency to comply with the requirements of the National Environmental Policy Act for environmental reviews and to respond to pressure from environmental groups while controlling oil and gas development on federal land.

Administrative Delays in Processing Lease Applications

In addition to land withdrawals by administrative agencies, there are significant delays in lease processing that further increase uncertainty

---

24. Federal Register, vol. 47, no. 82, April 28, 1982.
25. Ibid.

and raise the costs of private exploration and development of federal land. In its five-state analysis, the GAO found that 10 percent (7,233) of the leases applied for under the Mineral Leasing Act of 1920 between 1971 and 1979 were still pending December 31, 1979. Of those 3,995, or 55 percent, had been in processing for over four months.[26] Processing delays were most often associated with noncompetitive lease applications for areas outside known geologic structures. A related finding was reported by the Mountain States Legal Foundation for Idaho, Montana, Wyoming, and Colorado. Of 2,295 noncompetitive leases pending in November 1977, well over half, or 1,541, were still unprocessed nearly two years later in September 1979.[27] To determine the causes of delay, the GAO sampled 868 leases in processing for over four months. Of those sampled, 90 percent were held up by regulatory policies of the BLM and Forest Service as surface management agencies. Delays included processing for environmental impact studies, wilderness reviews, and lease stipulations.[28]

The focus of administrative delays on noncompetitive leases is straightforward. Since noncompetitive leases are in areas previously undeveloped for oil and gas, information on the potential surface impact is lacking, justifying more detailed agency review. Because such leases imply potential new development, however, they also are most likely to conflict with established surface management programs. While in most cases the surface management agency cannot deny leases, it can raise entry costs through processing delays and application of stipulations.

Delays in Processing Applications
for Permit to Drill

As described earlier, actual lease operations cannot occur until an Application for Permit to Drill (APD) is submitted and approved. Processing of the APD requires coordination between the BLM as lease administrator and the surface management agency. While thirty days is the usual guideline for processing, the GAO, Everett and

---

26. GAO, *Federal Onshore Oil and Gas Exploration*, p. 69.
27. Everett and Associates, *Withdrawal of Public Lands from Access to Minerals and Fuels* (Washington, D.C.: Everett & Associates, 1980), pp. 111-17.
28. GAO, *Federal Onshore Oil and Gas Exploration*, pp. 74, 75.

Table 5-2. **Mean Approval Times and APD Requirements.**

Area	Number APD's Processed	Mean Approval Time (days)	Requirements
Federal: Northern Rocky Mountain Area	1,367	67	Preliminary environmental review, APD application, map, bond, 10-point technical plan, 13-point surface use plan, archeological clearance, final environmental study
Wyoming	2,468	18	APD application, map, bond
Montana	780	1	APD application, map, bona
Pennsylvania	7,043	6	APD application, map, owner and lessee identification

Source: API (1982, tables 1, 2).

Associates, and API cited significant and increasing regulatory delays in handling APDs.[29] For instance, in its study of the northern Rocky Mountain area (Montana, Wyoming, Colorado, Utah, North Dakota, South Dakota, Nebraska) where 60 percent of all federal APDs are filed, the API reported a mean approval time between June 1979 and January 1980 of sixty-seven days.[30] Table 5-2 lists mean approval times for drilling applications for federal and state lands during 1979-1980 and processing requirements. The table shows that with more complex APD conditions, processing took over three times longer on federal lands as for state lands.

Major delays occurred during APD review by the BLM and Forest Service where permits were held from fourteen to fifty-four days.[31] Those agencies duplicated functions and repeated studies completed for earlier wells on the same lease. Indeed, only 26 percent of the wells drilled and requiring APDs were the first well on the site.[32] Of the six district offices in the northern Rocky Mountain area, the longest processing times were at Salt Lake City with a mean 113 days versus fifty days for the rest of the area.[33] The Salt Lake City

29. GAO, *Federal Onshore Oil and Gas Exploration*; Everett and Associates, *Analyses of Delays*; and American Petroleum Institute, *Analysis of the Processing of Permits to Drill on Federal Lands.*
30. American Petroleum Institute, *Processing of Permits*, p. 1.
31. Ibid., p. 44.
32. Ibid., p. 66.
33. Ibid., p. 19.

District had the largest portion of Forest Service land, and the Forest Service required more stipulations and environmental reviews than did the BLM, which coincides with the administrative roles and the past budgeting patterns of the two agencies and is predictable given the arguments outlined in the Analytical Framework section. These processing delays raise the development costs borne by firms since drilling crews and rigs must be retained but cannot be used until the APD is approved. The added costs of regulatory delays may be sufficient to lead to the abandonment of marginal sites.

CONCLUSION

Bureaucratic restrictions and delays of oil and gas development on federal land neither are random nor follow from specific congressional directive; instead, they are consistent with a model of self-interested bureaucratic behavior by the BLM and Forest Service. Both agencies have long-standing professional staffing, budgeting, and interest-group focus in the management of surface renewable resources. Oil and gas activities offer important obstacles to those arrangements and provide the agencies few political or budgetary rewards.

Importantly, the initiative for development lies with private firms that apply for leases under the Mineral Leasing Act of 1920. Once leases are granted, supervision is transferred to the onshore minerals and energy division of the BLM. Petroleum operations require access roads, storage sites, and in some cases, pipelines, all of which potentially disrupt surface management plans and established constituent relations. The only way the BLM and Forest Service can control the pace of oil and gas development in order to coordinate it with agency management plans and the demand of other interest groups is through land withdrawal, regulatory restrictions, and delay. Since the agencies have little incentive to promote optimal economic development of their lands, the continued conflict between them and private oil firms may well be predicted. Because information on oil and gas depends upon drilling, the regulatory constraints will block the information needed for weighing the social value of alternate land uses, which will deny the United States unknown amounts of oil and gas production from the huge federal estate.

Chapter 6

TIMBER HARVEST POLICY ISSUES ON THE O & C LANDS

Robert H. Nelson and Lucian Pugliaresi

INTRODUCTION

The Bureau of Land Management (BLM) is responsible for management of major timber holdings on the Oregon and California Grant Lands and the Coos Bay Wagon Road Lands in western Oregon (commonly referred to as the O & C Lands). These holdings are among the most productive timberlands in the world. The BLM timber inventory consists of 50 billion board feet of mostly Douglas fir on about 2 million acres—an important part in "old growth" forests that have never been cut.[1]

The total timber harvest in recent years from O & C Lands has been about 1.2 billion board feet, which is about 2 percent of the total national harvest of timber. The value of O & C timber sold was $302.5 million in 1979 and $365.7 million in 1980. Although the Forest Service typically harvests ten times as much timber as BLM, the O & C timber accounted for 23 percent of all federal timber revenues in 1980, reflecting the relatively high value of the BLM holdings. BLM supplies are not only an important national source of timber, but their harvesting plays a major role in the local economy of western Oregon.

---

1. Bureau of Land Management, *Final Environmental Statement for Timber Management* (Washington, D.C.: Government Printing Office, 1976), p. I-1.

Federal timber harvests are large enough to affect the price of timber and in turn the price of housing and other wood-using products. An estimated 45 percent of national softwood production is used to provide lumber for construction of new housing. Rising timber prices have been one of the important factors contributing to past rises in the cost of housing. Since World War II the price of timber has grown at an annual rate nearly 2 percent above the general inflation rate. Approximately 15 percent of the selling price of a home can presently be attributed to the price of lumber. Concerns about the effects of timber prices on housing costs are heightened by the prospect of increased needs for new housing. The primary cause is the arrival in the prime home buying ages of the post–World War II baby-boom generation. Although much of the expected growth in numbers in the age group thirty to forty has already occurred, further increases are expected to continue into the 1985–1995 decade.

A second area of major concern for public timber policy is the predicted reduction in private timber harvests over the next few decades in some of the prime timber growing areas of the United States. In particular, because of past heavy private cutting, western Oregon is expected to experience a 40 percent reduction in private timber harvests between 1980 and the year 2000.[2] This will contribute to already strong trends toward higher timber prices nationally at a time of rising housing needs. At a regional level, it could cause a major reduction in employment and income in Oregon. Direct and indirect employment generated by the timber industry accounts for more than 40 percent of total employment in the state.

It is partially because of these expected problems that proposals have arisen to increase significantly the rate of harvest from public lands. Slow rates of public timber harvest in the past, and the resulting existence of large stands of old growth timber on public lands, make it possible to increase public harvests substantially in the next few decades. However, changes in the harvest policies of the public timber agencies would be required to achieve these increases.

Debates concerning federal timber harvest policies are nothing new; they have been going on for several decades, particularly since federal timber became a significant source of supply after World War II. The history of harvest policy debates with respect to BLM and

2. John Beuter, Norman Johnson, and Lynn Scheurman, *Timber for Oregon's Tomorrow: An Analysis of Reasonably Possible Occurrences*, Research Bulletin 19 (Corvallis, Ore.: Oregon State University, Forest Research Laboratory, January 1976), p. 19.

Forest Service lands are examined in this paper, making use of the results of a computer modelling effort conducted in 1976. This 1976 study simulated long-term timber supplies from the O & C Lands under a variety of harvesting policies. As these simulations show, increases in harvests from public lands could be obtained without sacrificing community stability or the long-term interests of the American consumer.

PAST O & C HARVESTING POLICIES

By the turn of the century, most of the commercially productive forest lands in the United States were either in national forests or in private hands. However, in 1908 the federal government began legal action to repossess lands in western Oregon originally granted to the Oregon and California Railroad in 1866, but on which the terms of the grant had been violated. After considerable legal and legislative action, most of the lands were eventually placed under the jurisdiction of the Department of the Interior. The Coos Bay Wagon Grant Lands have a similar history and are managed as part of the O & C Lands. The O & C Lands are currently administered by the Bureau of Land Management under authority granted to the Secretary in the Revestment Act of 1916 and the O & C Act of 1937. This latter act provided for recreational as well as timber use of the lands and directed that timber production should follow the principle of maintaining a long-run sustained yield.[3]

The harvest from BLM western Oregon timber lands has traditionally been set equal to the maximum level that can be sustained over the long run—a so-called nondeclining even-flow policy. Under such a policy, an increase in the present harvest level can occur, but only if it can be sustained over the long run; decreases in harvests thus are not allowed. To help smooth out short-term fluctuations in lumber demands, the requirement that the harvest should never decline is usually interpreted to mean decade-long harvests.

Until the 1960s, allowable harvest levels on BLM lands did not receive much attention. Private industry forests still contained ade-

3. For this history, see Marion Clawson and Burnell Held, *The Federal Lands: Their Use and Management* (Baltimore: Johns Hopkins University Press, 1957), pp. 82–84. See also Elmo Richardson, *BLM's Billion-Dollar Checkerboard: Managing the O & C Lands* (Santa Cruz, Calif.: Forest History Society, 1980).

Table 6-1. Average Annual Allowable Cut and Sales (millions of board feet per year).

	1946-50	*1951-55*	*1956-60*	*1961-65*	*1966-70*	*1971-75*
Allowable Cut[a]	603	700	679	1131	1289	1172
Sales	371	529	729	1256	1324	1206

a. Includes thinning and mortality salvage.

quate supplies of old growth timber and industry efforts were concentrated on harvesting these supplies. In some years, the allowable harvest was not fully taken. In Table 6-1, allowable cuts and actual sales in past years are shown.

During the 1960s, however, it became apparent that the forest industry's private timber inventories were shrinking. In addition, timber demands to meet national housing needs were increasing, and in the latter part of the decade lumber prices began to rise rapidly. These factors created strong pressures for BLM to increase harvests. At the same time, environmental concerns were receiving much greater emphasis, and strong new pressures were exerted on BLM to limit its harvests to protect the environment and to provide for greater recreational opportunities.

In 1966 the BLM initiated a major study of harvest policies for western Oregon lands, an effort that resulted in a comprehensive inventory of timberlands. The study was undertaken between 1967 and 1970. The purpose was to determine the total commercial forestry base (lands to be devoted principally to timber use) and the distribution of these lands among quality—"site"—classes. A benefit-cost study of possible timber investments such as thinning, fertilization, and genetic improvement, was also made.

Another product of this study was a computer model that allowed the agency to simulate the growth of timber on BLM lands over long periods and under varying harvest policy assumptions. It was, in part, due to this new simulation capacity that BLM decided to change its basis for calculating the allowable cut. Previously, the requirement that harvests should not decline below existing levels had been interpreted to mean that they should not decline over the duration of the next full rotation—about eighty to ninety years for Douglas fir on

BLM lands. For this period, existing old growth inventories with large amounts of wood per acre were available, and hence the harvest for this rotation exceeded levels that would be sustainable for rotations after that. However, in the late 1960s BLM changed its interpretation of long-run sustained yield. With the new definition, the yield to be sustained was the level of harvest that could be maintained in perpetuity, after existing old growth inventories had been exhausted. Given the even-flow requirement, this immediately reduced the current allowable cut, and effectively barred the option previously available of maintaining a harvest above perpetually sustainable yields in the near term.

Two other actions also affected the calculation of sustained yield, and hence the allowable cut. A major reassessment of the commercial timberland base resulted in the removal of large areas from this base. On the one hand, these lands were regarded as environmentally vulnerable, or as areas where the regeneration of harvested land would be difficult. On the other hand, the BLM determined as a result of its benefit-cost studies that most of the proposed investments to enhance forest productivity were economically justified. The expectation of increased future investments tended to raise long-run sustainable yields, and hence to increase the allowable cut.

The net effect of these diverse actions on the allowed harvest was apparent in 1970 when BLM issued allowable cuts for the next decade in each of its thirteen western Oregon master units. Overall, the permitted harvest for western Oregon was reduced by 10 percent and, as a result, a controversy arose. A report prepared for the Oregon Governor's Office asserted that the even-flow policy followed by BLM was far too inflexible,[4] that it did not take sufficient account of lower expected harvests on private lands, and that it raised the potential for timber shortages, possible depressions in local economies, and higher timber prices.

The report also noted that if the private sector does not practice even flow, the public sector's adoption of such a policy may actually have a destabilizing influence on communities.[5] Local officials in the O & C Lands were equally critical of BLM for ignoring harvests on

---

4. State of Oregon Executive Department, *An Economic Assessment of the BLM's Allowable Cut Plan for Western Oregon*, Salem, Oregon, p. A–4. Contains a measure of the State's criticism of the BLM and the limited range of policy alternatives it considered.

5. Ibid., p. A–4.

private lands and, more generally, for the low productivity of the agency's even-flow policies.[6]

At the same time, however, others in Oregon and elsewhere criticized BLM for allowing excessive harvesting. BLM's investment assumptions were assailed as too optimistic, regarding both the levels of investments that would actually take place in the future and the increases in timber production that would actually result from them. Environmentalists argued that damage to the environment from timber production was much greater than BLM acknowledged. Assumptions about the total commercial forestry base and regeneration rates in cutover areas were also questioned. Others argued that the provisions made for recreation were inadequate in light of rapidly increasing recreational needs and values.

On another front, some economists were critical of BLM's benefit-cost study methods. As noted, the long-run sustained yield on timberlands can be raised by making higher investments. Although increased yields may not actually be realized for eighty years or more, under a nondeclining even-flow policy the higher sustained yield allows an immediate increase in the current harvest level. This is the much discussed "allowable cut effect." Investments often show artificially high benefits because the investment allows the government to raise the level of harvesting from the existing stock of overmature timber. This is, in effect, a benefit attributable to circumventing an unproductive policy.[7] The real investment benefits, those that actu-

---

6. In *Timber Abundance or Scarcity? It's Up to Us* (Proceedings of the Timber Supply Conference sponsored by the Industrial Forestry Association, Portland, Oregon, November 1975), p. 15, Ray Doerner, a Douglas County Commissioner and president of the Association of O & C Counties, stated:

> Now, I do not fault the even-flow principle, but in my County it's not doing the job. I, as a County Official interested in maintaining employment, want even flow from all the timberlands, not merely from one owner. As the private lands take the necessary breather to re-grow to harvestable size, the public lands continue merrily on their less productive even-flow course.
>
> A planned increase in harvest on public lands above their even-flow level for a period with a planned decrease when the private lands again make their heavy contribution offers a more certain solution.

7. Reflecting the views of a number of economists, Professor Jack Hirshleifer of UCLA commented:

> The following metaphor may shed some light on the "allowable cut" issue. Suppose that instead of a "no-drop-off" constraint on harvest there was a "Druid-agreement" constraint. Before a tree could be cut, a Druid wizard would be hired to perform an incantation. Assume further the tree is worth $200, and the wizard charges $100 per incanta-

ally result in increased future physical yields, might be small by comparison.

PAST FOREST SERVICE
HARVESTING POLICIES

Because the Forest Service holds a much larger inventory, its timber management policies have received much more study than those of BLM. Prior to the National Forest Management Act of 1976, primary guidance for the Forest Service was provided by the Multiple-Use and Sustained-Yield Act of 1960. It stated that timber management policies should follow principles of sustained yield, defined as "the achievement and maintenance in perpetuity of a high level annual or regular periodic output of the various renewable resources of the national forests without impairment of the productivity of the land." To translate this very general guidance into specific allowable cuts for the various national forests, the Forest Service has had to deal with many of the same issues faced by BLM. In the 1950s and the 1960s allowable cuts for the national forests were generally calculated in a manner similar to that used by BLM. In most cases, the allowable cut was the estimated maximum harvest level that could be sustained at an even flow for one rotation (about one hundred years for Douglas fir on Forest Service land).

As explained earlier, one result of an even-flow policy is a loss of potential timber production due to slow growth of old growth timber. In the late 1950s a study was prepared by the Forest Service to examine this issue for forests in the Pacific Northwest (the Duerr Report). In a preliminary draft, the study showed that accelerated cutting could increase Forest Service harvest levels over the next five decades by 100 percent above their current harvest trends and by 27 percent over the next full rotation (eleven decades). The main cost of this policy would be a drop in harvest level to 50 percent of

---

tion. Simple arithmetic shows the rate of return on hiring the Druid to perform his incantation and then cutting the tree is 100 percent, a very profitable investment it would appear. We could do even better, of course, by dispensing with the wizard and just getting on with our timber harvesting.

See J. Hirshleifer, "Sustained Yield versus Capital Theory" (Paper presented at the symposium, "The Economics of Sustained-Yield Forestry," at the University of Washington, Seattle, Washington, November 1974), p. 8.

planned harvests for the sixth through eighth decades.[8] Because of its controversial nature, the Forest Service eliminated discussion of this alternative from the final report published in 1963,[9] However, the questions it had raised regarding harvest acceleration were the subject of widespread discussion both within and outside of the Forest Service during the next few years.

Partially as a result of this controversy, the Forest Service prepared a new study for release in 1969.[10] This study did not examine the possibility of an accelerated harvest because it would have involved a departure from the then existing version of even-flow policies. However, it did examine possibilities for accelerated harvests as an indirect result of higher investment levels and lower rotation ages. The study showed that current allowable cuts could be increased by as much as 36 percent by increasing investment levels. Reductions in rotation ages could increase harvests by up to 30 percent. However, the study also revealed that there would be substantial reductions in timber harvests at the end of one rotation of even-flow production.

During the early 1970s a number of allowable cut plans were in preparation for national forests. At the time, the Forest Service had not established a single central procedure for making allowable cut calculations, leaving considerable discretion with individual national forest managers.

In 1973 the Forest Service established the same basic harvesting policy that BLM was already following—nondeclining even flow. As BLM had done earlier, the Forest Service adopted as its interpretation of long-run sustained yield the maximum yield that could be sustained in perpetuity. One justification given by the Forest Service was that it conformed to a strict interpretation of the legal requirement for sustained yield. A second justification, one which is often raised in discussions in Congress and in other public forums of the desirability of even-flow policies, is the need to prevent abrupt declines in harvest levels and thereby to maintain community stability.

---

8. "Timber Trends in Western Oregon and Western Washington," Pacific Northwest Forest and Range Experiment Station, Portland, Oregon, August 1960, p. 188. (Unpublished review draft.)

9. *Timber Trends in Western Oregon and Western Washington*, U.S. Forest Service Research Paper PNW 5 (Portland, Ore.: Pacific Northwest Forest and Range Experiment Station, October 1963).

10. See *Douglas Fir Supply Study* (Portland, Ore.: Pacific Northwest Forest and Range Experiment Station, 1969), pp. vi, vii.

An additional consideration was that increased harvest levels might cause excessive environmental damage.

The adoption of a strict even-flow policy by the Forest Service generated considerable controversy. In 1973 the President's Advisory Panel on Timber and the Environment criticized the Forest Service for the wastefulness of its policies with respect to old growth timber, and recommended that the Forest Service "seek to increase the output of timber from the national forests. . . . This will involve some acceleration in harvest of mature old growth timber. . . . "[11] The panel also was critical of the low investment levels in national forests and recommended that "the level of appropriations for national forest management be sharply stepped up."[12]

The Forest Service has also drawn criticism from professional economists who have attacked the agency's policies for wasting timber resources,[13] and from the timber industry, which has been unhappy with even-flow and low-investment policies. Partially in response to these criticisms, the Forest Service undertook the *Timber Harvest Scheduling Issue Study*.[14] Released in 1976 this study did not reach any conclusions, but described harvest projections that would result from adopting various harvest policy alternatives. Several of the alternatives studied were specifically designed to provide for accelerated harvests, and after reviewing these the Forest Service concluded that substantially accelerated harvests were technically feasible. However, the study did not evaluate options that would allow an accelerated cut yet avoid ever dropping below the long-run sustained-yield level. The report did examine the effects of higher investments on long-run sustained yields. For the two Douglas fir forests considered, the long-run sustained-yield level was shown to increase by more than 50 percent with higher investment levels.

11. *Report of the President's Advisory Panel on Timber and the Environment* (Washington, D.C.: Government Printing Office, April 1973), p. 80. As the Panel noted:

. . . even-flow restrictions clearly result in a substantially lowered allowable cut than would be the case if full recognition were given to the fact that a typical western national forest is frequently overstocked with old growth timber and the fact that this overstocking can be harvested over a period of time without any reduction in the amount of second growth timber that can be grown in subsequent rotations.

12. Ibid., pp. 84, 87.

13. Perhaps the most widely known critic has been Marion Clawson, who served on the President's Panel. For a more complete understanding of Clawson's criticism, see: Marion Clawson, *The Economics of National Forest Management* (Baltimore: Johns Hopkins University Press, 1976), pp. 99–100.

14. U.S. Forest Service, *Timber Harvest Scheduling Issues Study* (October 1976).

While the basic position of the Forest Service during the 1970s was to reaffirm even-flow policies, the agency did indicate a willingness to accelerate harvests. To accomplish such increases without violating even-flow policies, however, would require major increases in investment on national forests. As a former director of Timber Management for the Forest Service put it;

> ...on our national forests the Government has the opportunity to assume the role of a responsible landowner for a modest investment that through the allowable cut effect can be repaid in a short period of time. An investment that will create thousands of tax-paying jobs, enable people to more easily own their own home, raise the standard of living for thousands of people and be a positive factor in our balance of payments.[15]

The National Forest Management Act of 1976 mandated the strict Forest Service interpretation of long-run sustained yield, requiring that the Secretary of Agriculture "shall limit the sale of timber from each national forest to a quantity equal to or less than a quantity which can be removed from such forest annually in perpetuity on a sustained-yield basis." However, the law provided a loophole that allowed the Secretary of Agriculture to disregard this requirement if "in order to meet multiple-use objectives" such a departure would be warranted. The act also provided for expanded investment levels and stipulated that the rotation age for national forests be set at the "culmination of mean annual increment" (i.e., the age that maximizes total physical, as opposed to economic, yield).

The National Forest Management Act remains the leading statement of federal policy regarding the management of timber on public lands. However, since 1976, new studies of federal timber policy have been conducted, changes in policy have been recommended, and some alterations in harvest schedules have occurred.

O & C TIMBER HARVESTS UNDER ALTERNATIVE HARVESTING POLICIES

In 1976 the Office of Policy Analysis of the Department of the Interior conducted a series of harvest simulations for the O & C Lands in

---

15. Remarks of Richard Worthington, in *Timber Abundance or Scarcity? It's Up to Us*, Proceedings of the Timber Supply Conference sponsored by the Industrial Forestry Association (Portland, Ore.: Industrial Forestry Association, November 1975), p. 24.

western Oregon. These simulations were carried out with a model constructed for the Oregon State Board of Forestry by researchers at Oregon State University.[16] The alternatives examined permitted comparison of the BLM's traditional nondeclining even-flow policy to other strategies designed to achieve newly specified objectives. One of the objectives examined sought to match public timber harvests to the expected growth in housing. This "demographic harvest option" will be described in more detail.

A second alternative aimed to promote community stability by dampening employment shocks that arise from variations in the total (public and private) level of harvest. The last alternative evaluated the possibility of temporarily raising harvest levels sharply, followed by a steep decline and then a return to a higher level of long-term sustained yield.

For purposes of this chapter, these simulations provide a natural context in which to compare and quantify the outcomes of alternative harvest policies. Recall that each of the alternatives examined sought to maximize an objective other than strict economic value. In part, this reflected the difficulty of projecting demand and supply functions many decades into the future. Moreover, the alternatives were further constrained to prevent harvests from falling below the long-run yields sustainable under an even-flow policy; harvest declines were, however, permitted within these bounds. The results reported here indicate that each of these alternative policies outperforms nondeclining even flow in terms of volumes of timber harvested and the present value of receipts.[17]

NONDECLINING EVEN FLOW

The first option considered was a standard nondeclining even-flow policy. It provided a benchmark against which gains or losses resulting from alternative harvest policies could be compared. The first step in implementing nondeclining even flow is to calculate the long-run sustained yield. If existing inventories are sufficient, this harvest level is maintained indefinitely. Otherwise, to whatever extent pos-

16. Beuter, Johnson, and Scheurman, *Timber for Oregon's Tomorrow.*

17. The results of the study were originally reported in Robert Nelson and Lou Pugliaresi, *Timber Harvest Policy Issues on the O & C Lands*, U.S. Department of the Interior, Office of Policy Analysis, March 1977.

Table 6-2. Harvest Levels Under Nondeclining Even Flow (millions of cubic feet per decade).

	Existing Investment Level	High Investment Level
1975-1985 Harvest	1844	2033
1985-1995 Harvest	1858	2042
1995-2005 Harvest	1871	2079
2005-2375 Harvest	1881	2102
Present Value (millions)	$3462	$3822

Note: These results are totals for the seven master units in the BLM O & C Lands. For some master units, the 2005-2375 simulated harvests were actually computed for the period 2005-2015. Results for individual timbersheds are reported in Nelson and Pugliaresi. Present values are computed under an assumption of constant price ($150 per thousand board feet) and an interest rate of 5 percent.

sible, harvests are steadily increased over time until the long-run sustained yield is reached.

In Table 6-2, harvest levels projected for an even-flow policy are shown. These figures represent totals for the seven major timbersheds on the O & C Lands. The even-flow harvest level depends on the level of future investments assumed. The higher investment levels shown in this table include such practices as precommercial thinning, fertilization, and genetic improvement. Estimates of present values of the timber sales under a nondeclining even-flow policy are also shown. These values include only the value of the timber sales and do not take costs into account (cost estimates were not available). The price of timber was simply assumed to remain constant at $150 per thousand board feet in making the estimates. As a result, the present values shown are considered minimum values and are of primary use in indicating general magnitudes and making relative value comparisons of income streams under different harvest policies.

As Table 6-2 shows, higher investment levels result in significant increases in the present value of the harvest flow. The apparent high rate of return on timber investments results largely from the "allowable cut effect," however. As explained, under an even-flow policy the most important benefits of new investments are the increases in current harvests of mature timber, allowed due to a higher calculation of long-run sustained yield. To this extent, these apparent returns to investment are illusory in that they are actually attributable to the relaxation of an inefficient harvest policy. The even-flow policy artificially makes larger current harvests a "captive" to the provision of funds for higher timber investments.

DEMOGRAPHIC HARVEST OPTION

The period through 1995 is expected to be one of substantial increase in new housing demand as the post-World War II "baby boom" generation continues to form new households. According to U.S. Bureau of Census projections, the number of persons in prime house-buying age groups will continue to rise through 1995, after which it will fall off. These demographic trends indicate that unusually large timber supplies will be needed during 1985–1995.

As explained, some BLM lands have large old growth inventories, and could thus allow accelerated harvests for a few decades followed by reductions to a level commensurate with long-run sustained yield for all subsequent decades. To examine this possibility, the 1976 simulations included calculations of the maximum BLM harvest level that could be sustained for three decades without ever subsequently dropping below the long-run sustained yield. These levels are referred to as the "demographic harvest option" in Table 6–3. Much larger departures would be feasible if the departure period were limited to one decade.

For existing investment levels, when compared to even flow, the demographic harvest option resulted in increased harvests over the next three decades of 17 percent or 945 million cubic feet for all the BLM lands in western Oregon. After 2005, harvests were identical under the two policies at the long-run sustained yield (except in some timbersheds where this yield could not be achieved). The long-

Table 6–3. Harvest Levels Under Demographic Harvest Option (millions of cubic feet per decade).

	Existing Investment Level	High Investment Level
1975–1985 Harvest	2159	2114
1985–1995 Harvest	2173	2133
1995–2005 Harvest	2186	2150
2005–2375 Harvest	1881	2114
Present Value	$3916	$3943

Note: See notes accompanying Table 6–2.

run present value of the demographic option exceeded the value of the nondeclining even-flow policy by 13 percent or $454 million.

At higher investment levels, the projected gain from adopting the demographic harvest option is reduced. This, again, is substantially due to the allowable cut effect. As shown in Table 6–3, with higher investment levels the harvests projected over the next three decades for western Oregon under the demographic option were 243 million cubic feet (4 percent) greater than the harvests under a nondeclining even-flow option.

Assuming existing investments, the demographic option yielded higher harvests on five of the seven timbersheds. For those timbersheds alone, the first-decade harvests under the demographic option exceeded nondeclining even-flow harvests by 27 percent under existing and 8 percent under high investment assumptions. The corresponding increases in total present value for these timbersheds were 21 and 7 percent, respectively. The highest three-decade gains for a single timbershed were 35 and 11 percent for existing and high investments, respectively, for the mid-Willamette Valley. These harvest increases generated present value increases for that timbershed of 28 and 9 percent.

COMMUNITY STABILITY OPTION

One of the primary responsibilities of the Secretary of the Interior under the 1937 O & C Act is to promote community stability by avoiding fluctuations in employment due to variations in public harvests. The desire to promote community stability has been a basic rationale for maintaining nondeclining even-flow policies, and has been reiterated in many contexts, including congressional debate on the National Forest Management Act of 1976.

To achieve community stability, as previously indicated, would require that total public *and* private harvests be maintained at an even flow. When private harvests are uneven, the adoption of an even-flow policy for public harvests would do nothing to stabilize the total harvest. A truly stabilizing policy would instead seek to counter private harvest fluctuations.

Simulation of the community stability option in 1976 set public harvests in an attempt to achieve this aim. Estimates of future declines in private harvests were taken from an independent study.

Table 6-4.   Harvest Levels Under the Community Stability Option
(millions of cubic feet per decade).

	Existing Investment Level	High Investment Level
1975-1985 Harvest	1844	2058
1985-1995 Harvest	1945	2100
1995-2005 Harvest	2213	2149
2005-2015 Harvest	2266	2179
2015-2025 Harvest	2229	2191
LRSY Harvest	1902	2155
Present Value (millions)	$3689	$3896
Percent of private harvest decline filled	11%	2%

Note: See notes accompanying Table 6-2.

Under the community stability option, the BLM was assumed to increase harvests in each of the next five decades to make up the maximum percentage possible of private harvest declines. The increase in BLM harvest was constrained, however, by the requirement that future harvests must never fall below the long-run sustained yield (i.e., the nondeclining even-flow harvest level).

As shown in Table 6-4, the simulations demonstrated that with existing investments a departure from even-flow policies would allow BLM to increase its harvests by enough to make up 11 percent of the expected decline in private harvests in western Oregon over the next five decades. This could directly save 1200 jobs in the timber industry and indirectly an additional 1800 jobs in western Oregon. Assuming existing investments, the present value of the community stability option exceeded the present value of the even-flow option by $272 million (8 percent).

Assuming high investments, a higher long-run sustained yield would permit an immediate increase in allowable cut under a nondeclining even-flow policy. With this increase, BLM could make up part of the expected declines in private harvests in future decades without departing from even flow. Beyond that, as shown in Table 6-4, a departure from even-flow policies would have allowed harvest increases sufficient to make up an additional 2 percent of the expected private harvest decline in western Oregon, and would have yielded a present value that exceeded the even-flow option by $74 million.

HIGH INVESTMENT–ACCELERATED HARVEST OPTION

Imposing a constraint that the harvest must never drop below the long-run sustained yield obviously limits the extent to which harvests can be increased in future decades to meet housing, community stability, and other needs. A greater degree of acceleration might well be desirable. For example, it might be beneficial to cut public timber supplies heavily for a few decades in anticipation of a large rise in private harvests in following decades. Similarly, if increased investments are planned, harvests might be accelerated in the short run, subject to a less restrictive constraint never to reduce harvests below the current yield levels. Under this scenario, after the first rotation is completed, harvests would then rise to the higher even-flow level and the long-run sustained yield associated with the higher investments.

A high investment, high harvest acceleration option of this nature was examined in the 1976 simulations. It selected the maximum harvest attainable for the next three decades without later declining below existing harvests, subject to the further requirement that the long-run sustained yield for high investments be maintained after the first rotation. Because of limitations on computing resources, this harvest option was not calculated for all the western Oregon timbersheds. However, it was developed for two of them, the mid-Willamette and Medford timbersheds.

In the mid-Willamette timbershed, the current long-run sustained yield was 105 million cubic feet per decade. With existing investments, it would be possible to increase the harvest to 142 million cubic feet per decade for three decades, and then drop to a sustained level of 105 million cubic feet. Assuming high investments instead, the long-run sustained yield was determined to equal 125 million cubic feet per decade. Under the high investment-accelerated harvest option, the harvest for the Willamette timbershed was calculated to be 165 million cubic feet for three decades. After dropping to the sustained-yield level of 105 million cubic feet in the fourth decade, the harvest would then rise to, and eventually be maintained indefinitely at, the long-run sustained-yield level of 125 million cubic feet per decade. The present value of this option exceeded the present value of the nondeclining even-flow option with high investments by 22 percent.

For the Medford timbershed, similar calculations showed that under the high investment-high harvest acceleration option, harvesting could be increased to 617 million cubic feet per decade for the next three decades. By comparison, with high investments and under the even-flow option, the harvest was 464 million cubic feet during this period. Selecting the high investment-accelerated harvest option increased the present value of the harvest 23 percent when compared to the high investment even-flow policy.

HARVEST POLICIES SINCE 1976

The preceding simulations, carried out by the Interior Department in 1976, gave concrete examples of points that had been made by many previous critics of even-flow policies. Indeed, if timber production were the sole criterion, the even-flow policy was indefensible. When it is possible to sustain a high level of timber production for several decades and then drop to a lower planned level, no one could argue seriously that it would instead be preferable to restrict harvests to the lower level for the entire period. Moreover, the even-flow policy takes no account of long-term fluctuations in total demands for timber or in timber supplies from other landowners. It thus tends to accentuate instabilities of timber prices and timber employment, just the opposite of the expressed intent in adopting even-flow policies.

Responding to criticisms of the even-flow policy, in January 1977 the Interior Department Office of the Assistant Secretary for Land and Water Resources directed that "the scheduled EIS's for the Western Oregon Master Units should include at least two accelerated timber harvest options." One of these options would have to be "an accelerated harvest at a level which will allow increased cutting of mature stands without resulting in an eventual decline or drop off in harvest below the current even flow level."[18] By June 1977 the BLM State Director for Oregon had followed up these instructions in his guidance for the first timber EIS then getting under way for the Josephine sustained-yield unit. The State Director specified that two alternatives to the even-flow doctrine be included in the Josephine EIS. The first alternative would accomplish "the sale of the maxi-

18. Memorandum from Deputy Assistant Secretary for Land and Water Resources to Director, Bureau of Land Management, "Timber Harvest Options for Western Oregon Environmental Impact Statements," January 3, 1977.

mum amount of timber possible during the first, or first two, dec-
ade(s), without diminishing the sustainable harvest of 90 MMBF in
the decades beyond"; the second alternative was "designed to provide the Josephine [unit's] pro-rata share of BLM timber harvest
called for in the recent State publication, 'Forestry Program for
Oregon.'"[19]

The effect of studying these new alternatives on actual harvests
has been minimal, however. In 1980 the BLM did announce a small
departure from even-flow policy for the Josephine unit in southwest
Oregon. This announcement was important for symbolic reasons as
the first formal departure from even-flow harvest adopted by the
federal government. But a year later, the Bureau developed new calculations that showed insufficient old growth timber to sustain the
announced departure.

In 1977 the Federal Council on Wage and Price Stability (COWPS)
under the Carter Administration became interested in federal timber
harvest policies because of their impact on the price of timber and
housing costs. In October 1977 COWPS issued a report critical of the
even-flow policy, noting that "the accelerated harvest of mature forests is limited by a requirement that forbids a production decline in
the future, even if that decline is to a level which is not below the
long-run sustainable yield."[20] In April 1978 President Carter formed
a study group to examine ways to expand overall U.S. timber harvests. The group identified four main alternatives for raising federal
timber supplies; two of which were to "accelerate old growth harvest
for one to several decades, then return to but not below the current
even-flow/sustained-yield level" and to "accelerate old growth harvest for one to several decades, then reduce below current even-flow
sustained-yield levels."[21] The Forest Service made estimates that on
some national forests increases of 12 percent, 7 percent, and 2 percent might be achieved above the even-flow level in successive decades, then dropping to the even-flow level in the fourth decade. The
BLM estimated that it could achieve a 15 percent harvest increase for
a decade and then permanently drop to the even-flow level after
that.

19. Memorandum from State Director for Oregon to Director, Bureau of Land Management, "Alternatives – Josephine ES," June 15, 1977.
20. Council on Wage and Price Stability, *Lumber Prices and the Lumber Products Industry: Interim Report*, Executive Office of the President, October 1977, p. X.
21. "Options for Dampening Softwood Timber Products Price Increases, 1978–1990,"
May 10, 1978. (Unpublished.)

The Carter administration was sharply divided on the merits of departing from even-flow policies. The Council on Wage and Price Stability and the Office of Management and Budget, reflecting the heavy influence of economists on their staffs, strongly supported departures. The Council on Environmental Quality and, to a lesser extent, the Forest Service and Agriculture Department opposed such a change. However, in June 1979, more than a year after the study group was formed, President Carter finally issued a memorandum directing the Departments of Agriculture and Interior to update their management plans on selected federal forests "with the objective of increasing the harvest of mature timber through departure from the current nondeclining even-flow policy."[22]

No immediate increases in timber harvests were required as a result of the presidential directive.[23] Rather, the agencies were told to proceed as rapidly as possible to conduct the planning and environmental studies that would be necessary before actual harvest increases could be realized. As of this writing more than three years later, the 1979 presidential directive has still had very little impact on federal timber harvests. The Forest Service has been slow to complete land use plans that examine the possibility for accelerated timber harvests. More generally, it has shown little enthusiasm for any departures from even-flow policies, although the Reagan administration appointees in the Agriculture Department have criticized the even-flow policy.

So long as long-run sustained yield remains a lower bound on harvest levels, the gains in gross harvest levels achievable by departing from an even-flow policy do not now appear as large as they did in 1976. A key reason is the high level of timber investments being planned on federal lands. As shown in the 1976 simulations, increases in planned investments raise immediate harvest levels through the allowable cut effect. It was noted earlier, however, that this apparent return to investments in advanced forestry is illusory. To a large degree these investment outlays pay off by permitting a departure from the even-flow regime. Thus, many of the gains now attributed to these investments might well be available without increased investment expenditures if alternative harvest policies were insti-

22. Memorandum to the Secretary of Agriculture and the Secretary of the Interior from the President, June 1979.
23. Statement of Alfred E. Kahn on the President's anti-inflation decision to depart from even-flow timber harvest on federal lands, June 1979.

tuted. This is apparent from a comparison of "high investment" even-flow yields and "existing investment" noneven-flow yields in Tables 6–2 and 6–3.

Recent critics of the even-flow policy have often focused on the ability to harvest timber temporarily above the long-run sustained yield without any sacrifice to future harvests. Showing this potential has proved an effective way of demonstrating the logical deficiencies of the even-flow policy. However, the constraint never to go below the long-run sustained yield is itself artificial. It makes no more sense to treat the long-run sustained yield as an absolute lower bound than an absolute upper bound (the even-flow policy).

In their role as trustees for resources owned by the American public, federal timber agencies should plan their harvests to maximize the value of timber holdings, including commodity and environmental values. This may well require that they accelerate timber harvests when total timber demands are high or when alternative nonfederal timber supplies are low. In many cases, harvests may well need to fluctuate so that they exceed sustained yield for a time and then at other times fall below the sustained-yield level. Sustained yield should refer to the long-term maintenance of the productive capacity of the land and to its continuing reforestation, not to an artificial and rigid constraint that inhibits the flexibility needed to meet varying harvest requirements.

Chapter 7

POLITICS VERSUS BIOECONOMICS
Salmon Fishery and Forestry Values in Conflict

John H. Grobey

INTRODUCTION

The alleged effect that logging has on anadromous salmon stocks plays a major role in the political storm over forest management policies on public forestlands and the ever-tightening regulation of private forest practices in the western United States. The focus of attention by policymakers on the logging-salmon linkage is due to the superficial plausibility of the case for curtailing timber harvest in the interest of protecting salmon stocks. Justification of the case for curtailment on economic grounds rests on the ability to compare the economic costs of environmental damage with the primary net economic benefits of logging activity. The economic costs of environmental damage are estimated by applying a unit economic price to the reduction in physical units of environmental assets. The central attention of timber regulators to the alleged logging-salmon tradeoff may be related to several facts: (1) published estimates of unit prices of commercially-caught salmon are readily available; (2) published values for recreational salmon catches have been uncritically accepted or misused, and; (3) the adverse effects that logging is alleged to have on the physical yield of salmon has gone largely unchallenged and has thus served as the remaining basis for stating salmon damages in economic terms. Estimates of environmental damage associated with logging, other than salmon, are harder to obtain. Comparison of the alternative values in the alleged tradeoff between timber and salmon in turn simplifies the justification of policies curtailing the harvest of timber. Fisheries biologists who claim to have identified the physical tradeoff need merely assert that the forgone net salmon fishery values are higher than the net values flowing from timber harvest.

Much excellent and valid scientific research has been and is being done in the areas of inquiry pertinent to the logging-salmon linkages, but in the formulation of regulatory policies, valid findings are frequently overlooked or misapplied. Evidence is insufficient at the present time to allow the statistical estimation of salmon-yield-function parameter differences attributable to logging. Rather, physical yield effects have been guessed at, or hypothetical yield effects have been advanced as if they were documented scientific facts. The value of the fish, presumably lost, has been estimated using improper economic valuation techniques such as the application of average values to marginal changes. The erroneous results have been used to justify reduced timber harvests and changes in harvesting techniques that greatly increase logging costs with no identifiably concomitant benefits.

The most striking misuses of biological and economic analyses of the logging-salmon issue have been committed by the U.S. Forest Service. More stringent forest practices legislation governing private forestlands may have been inspired by the incorrect Forest Service analyses. Such legislation is thus based on the false notion that more restrictive logging practices serve to protect, rehabilitate, or enhance salmon stocks. The result is significantly increased logging costs without any measurable attendant benefits. For example, Henry Vaux, a member of the California Board of Forestry, at a Resources For the Future conference on forest policy in 1981, estimated the annual cost of compliance with the California Forest Practice Act at 55 million dollars.[1] He asserted that the Act is efficient, implying the existence of at least 55 million dollars worth of benefits resulting from the restrictive and costly practices required under the Act. If the conclusions in this chapter are correct, the fishery benefits received by the public for these increased costs are statistically indis-

1. Henry Vaux, "State Intervention in Private Forests in California," (Paper delivered at National Conference on Coping with Pressures on U.S. Forest Lands, sponsored by Resources For The Future at the Brookings Institute, Washington, D.C., March 30–31, 1981), Table 5.

tinguishable from zero. Thus the incorrect Forest Service analysis is capable of producing a very costly error.

The increased costs and benefits forgone through reductions in the landbase devoted to timber harvest on the national forests are probably much larger than Vaux's estimate. Each of the national forests in the salmon-producing regions has published a study of the estimated economic value of anadromous fisheries attributable to streams contained therein. These studies have employed an algorithm originally developed by Fred Everest, a fishery biologist for the U.S. Forest Service.[2] This algorithm represents a gross overestimate of salmonid values, and together with other studies alleging to represent the salmon losses due to logging, e.g., the *Timber Harvest Scheduling Study, Six Rivers National Forest*, has formed the basis for estimation of damages accruing to the fisheries. These studies will be examined in more detail later.

Careful scientific studies have documented the effect of sedimentary fines in the spawning substrate on the reduced survival to emergence of fry. The results, however, have not always been unequivocal. Reduction in the percent survival to emergence due to suspended sedimentary fine loads has been statistically insignificant in a few of the controlled studies carried out.[3] The influence of sediments on incubating salmon eggs appears functionally related to hydrological and biological variables, especially in the stream gradient and, hence, water velocity. Higher velocity flows prevent the precipitation of fines into the substrate.

To demonstrate that logging-induced accelerated soil erosion adversely affects a salmon fishery, it is not sufficient to show how sedimentary fines reduce salmonid juvenile production. It must further be shown how locally reduced juvenile production influences the eventual recruitment of adult salmon native to the entire watershed. Research must focus on life-cycle population dynamics, for there is

2. F. Everest, *An Economic Evaluation of Anadromous Fishery Resources of the Siskiyou National Forest* (Grants Pass, Ore.: USDA, Forest Service, Siskiyou National Forest, 1975). See also C. Kunkle and P. Janik, *An Economic Evaluation of Salmonid Fisheries Attributable to Siuslaw National Forest*, USDA, Forest Service, Siuslaw National Forest, Region 6, Pacific Northwest, April 1976; and Dean Smith, *The Economic Value of Anadromous Fisheries for Six Rivers National Forest*, USDA, Forest Service, Region 5, February 1978.

3. C. J. Cederholm, R. Stokes, and E. Salo, "Salmonids, Forestry, and Economics on the Clearwater River, Washington" (Paper delivered at the Western Economic Association Meeting, University of Washington, July 3, 1981), pp. 14–16.

a compensation mechanism whereby an increase in mortality in one phase of the life cycle is partially or completely offset elsewhere in time and space. There is no other way to explain why replicated pre-logging and postlogging studies of adult escapement reveal no statistically significant differences. The absence of such differences is reported by Brian Edie and by Dave Gibbons and Ernest Salo, whose studies will be examined in greater detail later.[4] Furthermore, the use of average values, even if properly estimated, to price out short-term and marginal effects is clearly inappropriate. Marginal values are invariably less than average values.

The open-access or "common property" character of fish stocks leads a priori to systematic overfishing of the stocks and the well-known tendency for dissipation of economic rent to the point of exhaustion of net economic benefits accruing to the fishery. The fact of overfishing is established in a study by Jeff Cederholm, Robert Stokes, and Salo, who report a catch-to-escapement ratio of about sixteen to one in the Sol Duc River runs compared with a normal, biologically sound ratio of five to one.[5] Such high catch-to-escapement ratios have been typical of runs for other Pacific Northwest streams. This tendency toward systematic overfishing strongly overpowers any conceivable effect of logging on the stocks. Furthermore, until the problem of irrational regulation of the fishery itself to prevent excess entry is resolved, the regulation of logging in the attempt to protect the stocks will be an exercise in futility, even if the physical linkage of reduced yields to logging can be demonstrated.

The issues, then, can be treated according to the physical-biological effects of logging on salmon stocks, the questions that revolve around the valuation of salmon fishery yield reductions, assuming the reductions can be identified, and environmental ethics and the political process.

---

4. B. G. Edie, "A Census of the Juvenile Salmonids of the Clearwater River Basin, Jefferson County, Washington, in Relation to Logging" (M.S. thesis, University of Washington, Seattle, 1975); and Dave R. Gibbons and Ernest O. Salo, *An Annotated Bibliography of the Effects of Logging on Fish of the Western United States and Canada*, USDA, Forest Service General Technical Report PNW-10 (Portland, Ore.: Pacific Northwest Forest and Range Experimental Station, 1973). The report resulted from a workshop on logging and fisheries held at the University of Washington, Seattle, November 1972.

5. Cederholm, Stokes, and Salo, "Salmonids, Forestry, and Economics," p. 19.

THE HYDROLOGICAL AND BIOLOGICAL EFFECTS OF LOGGING ON SALMON STOCKS

A study entitled *Timber Harvest Scheduling Study, Six Rivers National Forest* is typical of the approach taken by all national forests in that region in formulating management plans pursuant to implementation of the Resources Planning Act as amended by the National Forest Management Act of 1976.[6] There are serious errors in the treatment of the linkages between timber harvest and anadromous fish losses and in the treatment of the alleged resulting economic losses. The errors invalidate the treatment of the linkages and serve to illustrate the disregard by the Forest Service for life-cycle population dynamics.

Six Rivers National Forest investigators are not entirely to blame for errors contained in their report, for some of the errors can be attributed to the literature on which the linkages were based. But other errors constitute misapplication or misrepresentation of research findings.

Critique of the Fishery Aspects of the Six Rivers National Forest Timber Harvesting Scheduling Study and Related Documents

The Six Rivers Forest study employs evaluation techniques related to anadromous fisheries that rest heavily on the work of hydrologists William Brooks, Richard Cline, William Platts, and Walter Megahan.[7] Fishery valuation effects were drawn from a study by a forester,

6. National Forest Management Act, P. L. 94–588 (*United States Statutes at Large*, 1976), Vol. 90, Part 2, p. 2949.
7. William M. Brooks and Richard G. Cline, *Linear Program Management Alternatives Using Literature-Land-Form-Based Sediment Values: A Method*, Notes, United States Forest Service R-1, February 1979; and W. S. Platts and W. F. Megahan, "Time Trends in Riverbed Sediment Composition in Salmon and Steelhead Spawning Areas: South Fork Salmon River, Idaho," in *Transactions of the Fortieth North American Wildlife and Natural Resources Conference* (Bethesda, Md.: American Fisheries Society, 1975). See also W. S. Platts, "Time Trends in Riverbed Sediment Composition in Salmon and Steelhead Spawning Areas: South Fork Salmon River, Idaho," USDA, Forest Service, Intermountain Forest and Range Experiment Station, n.d.

Dean Smith.[8] These documents were used by Six Rivers investigators as the basis for employing an algorithm that links acres of timberland harvested annually within the streamside zone to reduction of fishery production due to the disturbance of the streamside and the increase of delivered sediment.

A functional relationship between percent increase of delivered sediment and "percent decrease of fish population" ascribed to Platts was produced and incorporated into the Everest algorithm.[9] The procedure thus provided a functional relationship presuming to show that increased timber production reduced salmon yield. This model was then employed to analyze a number of possible alternative timber harvest schedules on Six Rivers National Forest with respect to expected fishery valuation losses. The results were compiled in table C–11 of the Forest Service study.

The Sediment Output Index employed in the construction of table C–11 was reviewed and discredited by both forest hydrologist Dave Wooldridge and fisheries biologist John DeWitt.[10] The Six Rivers investigators erroneously made the implicit assumption of a linear and proportional relationship between reductions in the populations of fry and adult recruitment in the cycle year. That is, the "percent decrease in fish population" identified as fry by Platts was applied directly to adult salmon escapement estimates contained in Smith's research.[11]

Furthermore, the alleged decreases in fish population were not made site specific, but were assumed to apply to the entire forest; nor was the duration of the effect examined, leading the policymakers untrained in fisheries biology and population dynamics to conclude irreversible and permanent damage to salmon habitat. These same errors seem to pervade the treatment of the effects of logging on salmon throughout the region.

8. Smith, *The Economic Value of Anadromous Fisheries.*

9. Everest, *An Economic Evaluation of Anadromous Fishery Resources.*

10. D. Wooldridge, "Review–Timber Harvest Scheduling Study: Six Rivers National Forest," USDA, Forest Service, Pacific Southwest Region, May 1979; and John DeWitt, "Fishery Aspects," in B. F. Emad et al., *Review and Analysis of Smith River Draft Management Plan and Appendices* (Eureka, Calif.: Terrascan, 1980).

11. Smith, *The Economic Value of Anadromous Fisheries.*

A Review of the Linkages Between Timber Harvest
and Anadromous Salmon Populations

The effects of timber harvest on salmon populations operate through various hydrological effects. The in-stream deposition of logging debris that might block the upstream passage of spawners is the most obvious damaging effect. However, for anadromous stocks the essential relationship must show the influence of timber harvest not simply on incubating eggs, alevins, and fry, but also on the resultant recruitment of adult salmon in the cycle year when they enter the commercial and recreational fisheries. Hydrological effects of timber harvest that influence fry production and survival include accelerated erosion leading to increased sedimentation, reduction of watershed evapotranspiration losses and hence low-flow augmentation of stream flow, modification of the stream-flow temperature, and dissolved oxygen regimes. Other effects include changes in biochemical oxygen demand due to deposition of organic material in streams and alteration of populations of terrestrial and aquatic biota that affect the salmon food chain as predators or as competitors. The controversy about the impact of timber harvest on salmon stocks arises because of the enormous complexities of the dynamic relationships of these interdependent effects, which are only partially understood at present. This is clearly indicated in the report by Gibbons and Salo, as follows:

> From the resulting discussions as well as the questionnaire, one can assume we just don't know enough about our fish populations, especially those in logged watersheds. The most frequent question was: "How can changes in populations be measured if the effects are subtle and our knowledge of dynamics is deficient?" Life history research which is directly applicable to land-use problems is definitely needed.[12]

The foregoing statement remains true to the present day, notwithstanding claims to the contrary. The difficulty of securing reliable counts of fish stocks as they move through a multihabitat, multiphase life cycle, especially in the oceanic phase where race-specific, habitat-specific stocks are inaccessible for identifiable counts, is an additional complication.

12. Gibbons and Salo, *An Annotated Bibliography of the Effects of Logging on Fish*, p. 20.

Although a lot is known about the influence on fry production of each of the hydrological effects of logging, the combination of all the interdependent effects operating simultaneously is much more difficult to measure. The most common omission in studying the influence of timber harvest is failure to take into account very complex spawner-recruit relationships. These relationships have been intensively and independently investigated by many researchers, most notably William Ricker, R. Beverton and S. Holt, Gerald Paulik and Jerry Greenough, and Douglas Chapman.[13] These complex relationships can be incorporated into studies that attempt to measure the influence of logging on salmon through analysis of time-series data on *adult* salmon stocks. However, it is incorrect to assume, either implicitly or explicitly, that there is a linear and proportional relationship between reduced fry production in any given year and the resultant reduction in recruitment of adults either in the same year or in the cycle year. The Six Rivers investigators, as well as resource managers on other forests, committed that error.

Platts's work clearly refers to the survival to incubation of eggs and to survival rates of fry in the *immediate vicinity* of the disturbance that produces sedimentation. The work generally does *not* show how localized disturbances affect total fry production in the entire stream. A logical question to ask is whether reduced fry production in a stream segment is offset partially or wholly by increased fry survival in other parts of the stream because of relaxation of the food chain and habitat constraints. This question has not received sufficient research attention to allow a definite answer.

Furthermore, the sediment output index employed in the Six Rivers study was not adjusted to account for the sediment interception performance of streamside protection zones; the question of the optimal gravel spawning substrate composition was not examined;

13. W. E. Ricker, *Handbook of Computations for Biological Statistics of Fish Populations*, Bulletin 119 (Ottawa, Ontario: Fisheries Research Board of Canada, 1958); R. J. H. Beverton and S. J. Holt, *On the Dynamics of Exploited Fish Populations* (London: Her Majesty's Stationery Office, 1957); G. J. Paulik and J. W. Greenbough, "Management Analysis for a Salmon Resource System," in K. E. F. Watt, ed., *Systems Analysis Ecology* (New York: Academic Press, 1966), ch. 9; D. G. Chapman, *Spawner-Recruit Models and Estimation of Maximum Sustainable Catch*, Paper No. 10 (Seattle: University of Washington, Center for Quantitative Science in Forestry, Fisheries, and Wildlife, July 1970); and G. J. Paulik, *Studies of the Possible Form of the Stock-Recruitment Curve*, Paper No. 11 (Seattle: University of Washington, Center for Quantitative Science in Forestry, Fisheries, and Wildlife, July 1970).

and the necessity of some erosion to produce new gravels to replace those scoured out of the river basin during high flows was neglected. Insufficient gravel recruitment reduces the area available for spawning. While sedimentary fines in the streambed can of course be excessive, what is less obvious is that an insufficient amount of fines is deleterious to successful salmon incubation because the spawning substrate requires some fines as a "binder" to keep larger materials immobilized against grinding and tumbling of deposited redds.

The nature of the spawner-recruit relationship and its possible forms were extensively explored by Paulik[14] and by Chapman.[15] It is convenient, though something of an oversimplification, to describe briefly this relationship by separating the salmon life cycle into several more or less distinct phases. Phase I is the "escapement" (from capture by predators and fishermen) and upstream migration of the adult salmon to the spawning site of their origin. Phase II is the deposition, fertilization, and incubation of "redds" or nests of salmon eggs to the point of emergence of hatched "fry."

Phase III is the freshwater phase during which juvenile salmon begin to mature and migrate downstream while undergoing the biochemical changes known as "smolting," which adapt them physiologically to life in the saltwater phase of the cycle. Phase IV may be described as the estuarine or lower river, tidal zone phase of the cycle during which the saltwater adaptation is completed. Finally, Phase V involves the saltwater or oceanic phase of the life cycle during which the stocks might migrate thousands of miles while reaching maturity. This phase culminates in the return of adults and their entry into Phase I, and the cycle repeats itself.

The entire cycle varies from two to six years in length depending on the species. The population (output) leaving each phase of the cycle is thus the input into the following phase. Each phase in this set of "production functions" exhibits diminishing returns to the variable input. Concatenation of all these phases produces the ultimate relationship between spawners in Phase I and the "recruitment" of spawners for Phase I of the subsequent complete cycle. The form of this relationship is given in Figure 7–1, which shows that excessive fry production can in fact reduce production of adult recruits for the next cycle. This in turn suggests that "thinning" during

14. Paulik, *The Stock Recruitment Curve.*
15. Chapman, *Spawner-Recruit Models.*

Figure 7-1.   Form of the Spawner-Recruit Curve.

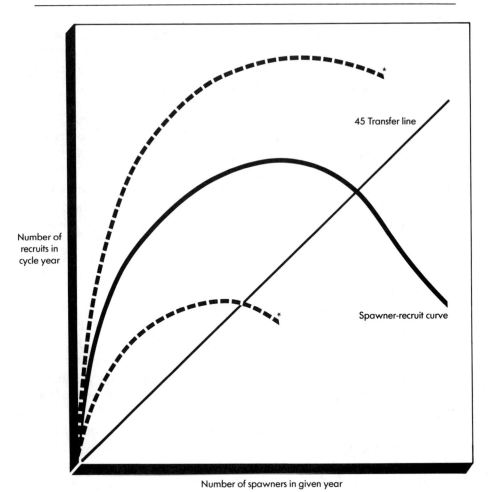

Number of recruits in cycle year

45 Transfer line

Spawner-recruit curve

Number of spawners in given year

*Note: These lines represent wide heteroscedastic dispersion around expected values.

Source: G. J. Paulik, "Studies of the Possible Form of the Stock Recruitment Curve," paper no. 11 (Seattle: University of Washington, Center for Quantitative Science in Forestry, Fisheries and Wildlife, July 1970). Identical to the form found by W. E. Ricker, *Handbook of Computations for Biological Statistics of Fish Populations*, Bulletin 119 (Ottowa: Ontario: Fisheries Research Board of Canada, 1958); R. J. H. Beverton and S. J. Holt, *On the Dynamics of Exploited Fish Populations* (London: Her Majesty's Stationery Office, 1957); and others.

one or more phases of the life cycle can actually be beneficial. The functional relationship between inputs and output in any one phase of the life cycle is, however, unstable. It shifts in response to a large variety of exogenously determined disturbances. It is the unknown and apparently random nature of these exogenously generated shifts that renders salmon population dynamics so unpredictable, even when known influences, such as the effect that sedimentation has on fry population, are taken into account.

The general nature of many forms of biota is to produce far more offspring than are ever expected to survive to maturity. For species of salmon that migrate from one habitat to another during a complex life cycle, great care must be taken in specifying the meaning of "habitat loss" or "degradation," especially if mortality or "thinning" at some point prevents excessive competition in a successive stage. This is even true of adult spawners. In his study William J. McNeil demonstrates that "there is evidence that the capacity of a spawning bed to produce fry is impaired by excessive numbers of adults spawning." [16]

Adult salmon successfully recruited from naturally deposited redds amount to far less than one percent of total eggs deposited. The thinning process takes place at every phase of migration during the life cycle. Many unresolved questions remain with respect to this process for salmon stocks. Paulik suggests:

> The interplay of compensatory and *depensatory* forces can be extremely important; depensation in one stage may be overcome by strong compensation in the next stage. Strong compensating factors in one stage can effectively limit total production. When designing protection facilities such as fishways at dams, or artificial production enhancement facilities such as hatcheries, the interaction of the various life stages must be considered. [17]

Paulik goes on to suggest techniques for incorporating environmental factors into the stock recruitment relationship. He suggests the possible presence of limiting factors or bottlenecks at certain phases in the life cycle that were later identified by other investigators.

The crucial question, then, is precisely where in the salmon life cycle does the environmental "bottleneck" occur that constrains ultimate recruitment? Environmental factors in *all* of the successive

16. W. J. McNeil, "Redd Superimposition and Egg Capacity of Pink Salmon Spawning Beds," *Journal of Fisheries Research Board of Canada* 21, no. 6 (1964): 1385.
17. Paulik, *The Stock Recruitment Curve.*

habitats occupied, including the oceanic migration, must be considered. Too little is known about the oceanic phase to provide much more than speculative answers, but some of the literature suggests that, as long as freshwater fry production exceeds some minimal level, essential limitations may operate strongly in the estuarine and early stages of the oceanic migration rather than during the freshwater life stages.

Stephen Mathews and Raymond Buckley report very high initial mortality rates for Puget Sound hatchery coho smolts (about 75 percent) within the first two and one-half months of saltwater residence.[18] Ultimate recruitment of adults was also shown to be significantly related to smolt *size* at the time of hatchery release. Smolt size of natural stocks is unquestionably related to the density of juvenile population during the freshwater and estuarine stages. But Mathews and Buckley did not study the relationship between mortality rates and the *number* of smolts in the saltwater environment. Compensatory forces undoubtedly operate in this phase, but little or no research is available to document any such effect or to reject its existence.

In studying the Sixes River estuary in Oregon, fisheries biologist Paul Reimers reported that the estuarine density of the fry population "is hypothesized as a major cause of the depressed rate of growth of juveniles."[19] Reimers also showed that, over a considerable range of fry input above a minimal level, smolt output from the estuary was almost independent of fry input. This suggests that the lower reaches of a stream or the estuary may be a very important life-cycle bottleneck.

It is difficult to understand why the possibility of beneficial thinning at various stages in the life cycle has apparently never suggested itself to fishery biologists as a possible management tool. It is again undoubtedly related to the imperfect knowledge of salmon population dynamics, especially in the oceanic phase of the life cycle. Thinning is practiced by managers of many forms of bioculture; it is common in many forms of agriculture and is probably overdone in forestry. Both fishery managers and forest managers could gain from having some discussions along these lines.

18. S. B. Mathews and R. Buckley, "Marine Mortality of Puget Sound Coho Salmon," *Journal of Fisheries Research Board of Canada* 33 (1976): 1677–84.

19. Paul Reimers, "The Length of Residence of Juvenile Fall Chinook Salmon in Six Rivers, Oregon," *Research Report of the Fish Commission of Oregon* 4 (June 1973).

The 1972 workshop reported by Gibbons and Salo reached the following interesting conclusions:

Judging from published research, adequate impact statements (of the impact of logging on salmon) obviously will be difficult to formulate. Consequently, regulations will continue to be conservative, with an increasing amount of field supervision required to monitor whatever environmental impacts are predicted.... Meanwhile, general survey-type research ... has had its day; and the logger, the researcher, and the management agencies must realize that there are no finite answers, no finite guidelines, and perhaps never will be.... This is particularly difficult for the land user to accept, but it is a fact of life and a state-of-the-art for some time to come. On the other hand, the fisheries resource manager has difficulty accepting that which is becoming obvious—i.e., logging (even clearcutting) can be performed without radical damage, in fact, the changes can be so subtle as to defy measurement and at times may, indeed, be beneficial.[20]

One way to attempt the incorporation of environmental factors into the complex spawner-recruit relationship is to investigate time-series data on adult salmon stocks. Where this method has been tried, no statistically significant differences in run attributable to the effects of logging could be identified. The problems of identification are several: (1) very large error terms in the regression equations; (2) spawner-recruitment, density-dependency effects; and (3) possible offsetting effects at different points in the life cycle, as suggested by Paulik.[21]

The first difficulty is illustrated by Gibbons and Salo who state:

Early studies attempted to evaluate the effects of logging on stream environments by comparing the numbers of adult salmon returning to logged watersheds.

These studies were not capable of discerning causes and effects because they were masked by a fluctuating saltwater survival, and freshwater mortality caused by sedimentation, floods, droughts, and temperature changes. For example, it has been reported that changes in an adult salmonid population of less than 50 percent due to any one cause would be difficult to detect within the large natural variation.[22]

These tests provide no basis for rejecting the null hypothesis that logging does not significantly affect salmon. Furthermore, until a

---

20. Gibbons and Salo, *An Annotated Bibliography of the Effects of Logging on Fish.*
21. Paulik, *The Stock-Recruitment Curve.*
22. Gibbons and Salo, *An Annotated Bibliography of the Effects of Logging on Fish.*

way is found to reduce inexplicable variation due to unknown events and fishing pressure, the elimination of the relatively smaller possible influence of logging by regulation of forest practices is futile. In their drive toward "conservatism," those with regulatory authority, however, are willing to adopt extreme measures for protection of the stocks from every conceivable influence except the one factor undoubtedly most responsible for adult stock reductions; namely, excessive fishing pressure. Analytically, the investigator confronted with adult stock data of the type indicated in Gibbons and Salo is loath to follow the scientific canons with respect to drawing inferences. Instead of tentatively accepting the null hypothesis—namely, that logging does not significantly affect salmon stocks—it is instead "concluded" that tests conducted by fishery biologists were inconclusive and that they must try another way to document the adverse impact. An example of this is found in the study by Edie.[23]

Salo, among others, has argued recently that time-series analysis of logging and adult salmon stocks has failed to detect the influence of logging because the study streams are generally "underseeded" from the effects of overfishing.[24] While stocks undoubtedly receive heavy fishing pressure both offshore and in-river, the reference point in the life cycle for definition and comparison of the degree of seeding must be chosen with great care. It may be improper to identify "carrying capacity" of part of a freshwater habitat for populations of juveniles of given age as the criterion for being "fully seeded" because seeding to that level may, by itself, represent overseeding relative to some downstream bottleneck that independently restricts ultimate recruitment. "Carrying capacity" is a dynamic variable, not a static constant, and it changes independently of factors that visibly change parts of the habitat. This makes reliable estimation of the carrying capacity nearly impossible. Thus, stocking artificially to such a carrying capacity estimate, and then attributing observed mortality through all the life-cycle phases including ultimate adult recruitment to habitat changes caused by logging is highly questionable. It ignores constraints that operate independently elsewhere.

23. Edie, "A Census of Juvenile Salmonids."

24. Ernest O. Salo and C. Jeff Cederholm, "Cumulative Effects of Forest Management on Watersheds—Some Aquatic Considerations." (Paper presented to the Edgebrook Conference on Cumulative Effects, University of California at Berkeley, June 2–3, 1980) pp. 2–3. See also Table 7-1.

Richard Lantz has suggested that *resident* cutthroat trout stocks be considered as an indicator species for the influence of logging on *anadromous* salmon stocks.[25] Such an approach is clearly inappropriate because it ignores the multistage, multihabitat life cycle of the anadromous stocks in comparison with a species that is present in a relatively localized freshwater habitat for its entire life. The Six Rivers study cites a 1971 report by Lantz concluding that a 75 percent reduction in the long-term cutthroat trout population occurred because of sedimentation and thermal pollution following logging and, therefore, because of logging. A legitimate issue with respect to these results is the extent to which the resident trout populations might have been reduced by increased recreational fishing pressure facilitated by access improvement provided by the logging road.

There is strong interdependence among the populations of smolt inputs into the oceanic phase of the life cycle from the whole coastal range of streams-of-origin. A potentially fruitful agenda for research in this dynamic interdependence might focus on the probability and consequences of overall recruitment from the simultaneous maximum smolt production emanating from all streams, and the contrary case where low smolt production occurs coincidentally. It is most likely that compensating increases in mortality would occur in the one case, and reductions in the other.

A recent paper by Cederholm, L. M. Reid, and Salo examined the "cumulative effects" of road sediment on salmon stock in the Clearwater River Watershed in Jefferson County, Washington.[26] The study reports a series of massive landslides in 1971 in Stequaleho Creek, a tributary of the Clearwater, and reviews some of the research activity since those events. In the process of separately examining the effects of sedimentation and underseeding and then examining the interdependence between these effects taken together, the authors report that the Queets in-river tribal catch in 1974 (the cycle year following the landslides) reached one of its highest levels in recent years.[27]

25. Richard L. Lantz, *Guidelines for Stream Protection in Logging Operations*, a report of the Research Division, Oregon State Game Commission, 1971.

26. C. J. Cederholm, L. M. Reid, and E. O. Salo, "Cumulative Effects of Logging Road Sediment on Salmonid Populations in the Clearwater River, Jefferson County, Washington," contribution no. 543, Conference on Salmon-Spawning Gravel: A Renewable Resource in the Pacific Northwest?, Seattle, Washington, October 1980 (Seattle: University of Washington, College of Fisheries, 1980).

27. Ibid., p. 25.

This may be coincidental or possibly due to sufficient spawning gravel recruitment in 1971 as a result of the landslides.

ECONOMIC VALUATION OF REDUCED SALMON YIELDS ATTRIBUTABLE TO LOGGING

If the effect that timber harvest has on adult salmon stocks in the cycle year cannot be reliably identified, then it perhaps follows that the loss in value cannot be legitimately counted. But the Forest Service has compounded the errors it committed in assessing the impacts of logging on salmon populations by applying illegitimate techniques of economic valuation. These same errors are being emulated by public agencies responsible for regulating private forestlands. The general application throughout the region of these erroneous analytical methodologies results in grossly exaggerated estimates of the magnitude of external diseconomies generated by logging.

These exaggerated estimates are, in turn, used as a basis for formulating ever more restrictive public policies and regulations governing private forest practices. Exaggerated estimates of the logging damage done to watersheds are also used to justify enormous expenditures of public funds for "stream rehabilitation" projects. The costs of curtailed timber harvest, of elevated logging costs where harvest is permitted, and of expensive and largely futile stream rehabilitation projects are enormous—in the hundreds of millions of dollars per year. The benefits from these adventures are imaginary.

The flaws in the Forest Service valuation procedures are too serious to be left unchallenged. The use of estimates of average annual numbers of spawners as proxies for current catch by applying catch-to-escapement ratios is questionable since catch and escapement move in opposite directions. Also, if a habitat disturbance generates incremental changes in stocks rather than total destruction, then it is not appropriate to apply *average* values per fish to the estimated stock reduction to calculate total loss in value. Rather, demand curve parameters must be employed to estimate the *marginal* change in value for use in calculating total loss.

Smith estimated salmon values attributable to Six Rivers National Forest at $11.1 million.[28] While such cardinal value estimates might

---

28. Smith, *The Economic Value of Anadromous Fisheries.*

be of interest as curiosities, they are of no practical use in trying to evaluate marginal changes.

It may also be of interest, however, to make some gross comparisons of the cardinal value estimates contained in the Smith report with estimates for the same forest at an earlier time. A letter prepared in the Region 5 Office from Edward P. Cliff to Congressman Don Clausen contains the following statement:

> We estimate that approximately 35 percent of the anadromous fish utilized in the Eureka to Crescent City area originate on the Six Rivers National Forest. The average annual direct economic benefits that accrue from use of this resource for commercial and sport fisheries are estimated at a minimum of $720,000 for the Six Rivers National Forest.

The letter does not indicate how this estimate was obtained. But the question of interest is, How could the value have increased so dramatically in eight years? These increased values could perhaps be used to justify reduced timber harvest, but it seems inconceivable that the $11.1 million figure estimated by Smith could be correct. Although this figure includes recreational as well as commercial fishing values, it seems incredible that the total value of salmon attributable to the Six Rivers National Forest is in excess of the value of commercial salmon landed in the entire state. At least, the comparison ought to raise questions about the validity of the latest Six Rivers estimates.

Initially, the valuation of commercial fishery resources appears somewhat simpler than for recreational fishing values because, at least here, there is a set of market transactions at an intermediate stage of production from which the derived demand at the point where fish are taken from the sea theoretically can be estimated. The simplicity ceases at this point however. The cost of harvest at the margin must be subtracted from ex-vessel revenues accruing to the fishery in order to find a point on the relevant derived demand schedule. The theory of open-access resources tells us a priori that we should expect a series of points so derived to be randomly distributed around a price of zero, since the economic rent that would have accrued to the owners of the fish stocks is dissipated in the open-access case to pay the opportunity costs of excess entrants.

Apparently, in order to derive the required demand curve, either we must have the parameters of the relevant economic yield function or the fishing fleet must actually be required to pay a set of market-clearing royalties for access to the stocks, which would permit direct estimation of the demand function. Neither condition applies, since only the general form of the yield function is known, and policy does not provide for the collection of royalties. Large error terms make valid estimation of biological yield function parameters unreliable, which carries over into attempts to estimate economic yield functions.

Other complications relate to the difficulty of identifying that part of the offshore catch attributable to any given stream. Therefore one cannot distribute random change in landings among the large number of racial strains originating from different streams. The change in the total value of landings caused by *small* independent changes in the volume of landings, including those changes perhaps resulting from logging impacts, could be estimated by multiplying ex-vessel price by the change in landings if we assume no induced change in fishing effort and therefore no change in the opportunity costs of harvest. But this procedure, too, is futile if the causes of changes in landings in the offshore fishery cannot be identified.

Salmon management rests heavily on the regulation and control of escapement. The problem of successful management of salmon stocks is compounded by the absence of racial selectivity of the offshore recreational and commercial troll fisheries. Some stocks are more heavily fished than others, so variation in catch-to-escapement ratios is apt to be large. Even if total escapement is optimally managed in any given season, insufficient escapement will be provided for some of the streams and escapement might actually be excessive for others where stocks are fished more lightly. This issue is relevant to the estimation of the value at the margin of salmon spawners in any given watershed in a particular season. Marginal values will be high where escapement is below optimal levels, and marginal value will be negative where escapement is excessive. The universal application of average values is clearly inappropriate.

Spawner escapement can, of course, be estimated by making fish counts at fish ladders, at hatcheries, or after spawning in small streams by using foot surveys. The catch-to-escapement ratio can also be determined after the fact if tagging or fin-clipping studies are conducted. Such studies are usually done only for hatchery stocks and would be difficult at best for wild stocks. Sometimes known escapement is applied to average catch-to-escapement ratios to estimate catch attributable to a given stream where catch is not directly countable. This procedure is not reliable, but the Forest Service uses it.

The valuation of recreational fisheries is more complicated than the valuation of commercial fisheries because no market transactions exist from which the value of recreational fish harvest can be directly derived. A matter commonly overlooked with respect to the employment of various proxies for estimating these values is the separation of the value of the fish from the value of the fishing experience. This separation is of crucial importance in evaluating recreational fisheries because, over some range of fishing success as measured by catch-per-angler-day, the value of the fishing experience may be almost independent of the catch. In any case the value of the catch is subject to the principle of diminishing marginal utility. The value of the fish is probably best indicated by its retail price in the marketplace, or by the retail price of close substitutes. The value of the fishing experience may partially depend on the catch, but is best viewed as a residual between total value of an angler-day and the market value of the catch or its close substitute.

The use of catch-to-escapement ratios to estimate catch for a given stream is often haphazard. In cases such as the Smith report, where escapement has been used as a proxy for the catch by employing the average ratio derived from fin-clipping and tagging studies in hatchery stocks, the actual catch attributable to a particular stream in any given year will be either overstated or understated by an indeterminate magnitude, perhaps of several orders.

The escapement data employed by the Forest Service for making such estimates is highly questionable, largely stemming from guesses contained in the 1965 California Fish and Wildlife Plan. A June 1979 report of the Pacific Fishery Management Council states the following:

> Reliable estimates of past and present spawning escapements for coastal streams are not available, nor do we know at what rates coastal salmon streams contribute to the ocean fishery. Studies are now under way to determine the abundance of salmon in the Klamath River system and their contribution to the ocean fishery, starting in 1979. Estimates of fish produced in other coastal streams can be made once the production of the Klamath system is known.[29]

29. Pacific Fishery Management Council, "Freshwater Habitat, Salmon Produced, and Escapements for Natural Spawning along the Pacific Coast of the United States," a report

More recently, the Pacific Fishery Management Council estimated Klamath River escapement at less than 50,000 adults in 1979.[30] Successful spawners would apparently number far less after in-river recreational and gillnet harvest is deducted. Spawning escapement is thus much less than the 183,000 estimated by the 1965 California Fish and Wildlife Plan for the Klamath system.[31] While reduced escapement in 1979 may reflect higher offshore catches, it probably also reflects lower offshore stock levels caused by reduced recruitment resulting from low escapement in previous years. Thus applying a five-to-one catch-to-escapement ratio to the 1965 figure generates an unreliable estimate of the catch derived from Klamath River runs in 1965 and in subsequent years.

Consider the following hypothetical calculation to illustrate the point. If the five-to-one ratio is applied to the 1965 estimate of 183,000 escaping spawners, the catch would be estimated at 915,000 fish out of a total run of 1,098,000 fish. Suppose the run were identical, but the catch increased to 1,048,000 fish, leaving 50,000 escaping spawners. The actual catch-to-escapement ratio would thus be almost twenty-one to one, but the application of the five-to-one ratio would generate an estimated catch of only 250,000 fish.

The reliable division of the run into landings and spawners is critical to the question of economic valuation of salmon at the margin if such information is to be used for the purpose of making rational salmon management decisions. The value of a mated pair of escaping spawners at the margin, if escapement is small, may exceed significantly the market value or the recreational value of the fish if landed. In other cases where escapement is already excessive, the negative marginal value of a pair of spawners must be considered as a positive benefit of their harvest in addition to values reflected in market or recreational proxy demand curves.

There is no unique value of salmon spawners. Values correctly estimated for one area and applicable to one set of circumstances cannot legitimately be applied to another area and a different set of valuation purposes. This is especially true where recreational fishery values

---

prepared by the Anadromous Salmonid Environmental Task Force of the Pacific Fishery Management Council, Portland, Ore., June 1979.

30. Ibid.

31. California Fish and Wildlife Plan, *Inventory, Salmon-Steelhead and Marine Resources*, Vol. 3, supporting data, part B, Chinook and Coho. (Sacramento, Calif.: California Department of Fish and Game, 1965).

are involved because of complexities of finding an appropriate method of proxy valuation, including the previously mentioned necessity of separating the value of the fish from the vlaue of the fishing experience.

To illustrate the point, consider the following statement by Mathews and Gardner Brown:

> Very commonly, in multiple use of land and water resources, a decision may be made which either permits the continuance of a particular fishery, or brings about its degradation or perhaps its termination. There are numerous examples, such as the choice of a water quality standard which could exterminate a salmon run. In cases where there is a potential loss of an existing sport fishery, a determination should be made as to the amount of compensation which the fishermen would have to receive to be no worse off after being precluded from the recreational opportunity they formerly enjoyed. . . . Our criteria for establishing the net value of sport salmon fishing in Washington was to establish the monetary compensation needed to replace the potential loss of salmon fishing in each of the four previously defined zones.[32]

The four zones included three marine zones: Ocean, Ilwaco north to La Push, Strait of Juan de Fuca, and Puget Sound. Zone Four comprised all freshwater areas open to salmon angling in Washington State. There are several points to be made about this aspect of the Mathews and Brown study and other Forest Service studies that have used it as a basis for recreational fishery valuation throughout the region.

An important implication of the variation in angler-day values from zone to zone is that it is hazardous to translate values from one zone to another. This seems particularly pertinent when applied to an area two whole states away from the zone for which the valuation was estimated, and separated in time by more than ten years.

The Mathews and Brown figures may themselves contain an upward bias. Several estimates were made based on different methodologies, including (1) gross expenditures per angler day, (2) willingness to pay for the right to fish, and (3) willing to *sell* the right to fish assuming an absolute property right exists.

Mathews and Brown correctly rejected the first method as being essentially meaningless. They estimated values for methods (2) and

---

32. S. B. Mathews and G. S. Brown, *Economic Evaluation of the 1967 Sport Salmon Fisheries of Washington*, Washington Department of Fisheries Technical Report No. 2 (April 1970).

(3) from responses to survey questionnaires and rejected method (2) on the grounds that they believed the results to be biased downward. Their belief rests on two considerations: first, willingness to pay is constrained by the financial condition of the respondents, and second, if the respondents believe their answer will have an influence on the size of license fees, they will misrepresent their answer to avoid an increase. Mathews and Brown thus expressed a preference for method (3). But method (3) may contain an upward bias in a manner symmetrical to the downward bias of method (2). Mathews and Brown attempted to deal with this problem by assigning arbitrarily a value of $500 per year to those respondents who answered that they would not sell at any price. While Mathews and Brown argue that this technique understates the total value, it by no means answers the charge of upwardly misrepresenting the price at which the respondents say they would have been willing to sell their rights. Their estimates, in fact, are biased upward. Empirical evidence to support this purely a priori conclusion exists.[33]

The figures in the Mathews and Brown study clearly apply to total elimination of the sport fishery and not to marginal changes in fishing success. The authors underline this with the following statement:

> Although total value is of interest, it is not likely that the salmon fishery in any zone will be suddenly eliminated entirely. More likely is a gradual erosion of average catch per trip. The data yielded a very good relationship between average catch per trip and average value per trip (Figure 2) *which should be useful in determining loss in value from environmental degradation of salmon-producing areas.*[34]

Their Figure 2 contains a curve that purports to show diminishing marginal utility with respect to increased daily catch; the curve is reproduced here as Figure 7–2. Mathews and Brown use this "relationship" between average value per trip and average catch per trip to infer the lost value (of consumer surplus) resulting from a decrease in the average success rate as measured by catch per day. This, in turn, leads them to a value for the fish. (See Table 7–1.)

It is doubtful whether this data can be used to support that analysis and the attendant conclusions. Consider the following: first, when

---

33. R. C. Bishop and T. A. Heberlein, "Measuring Values of Extramarket Goods: Are Indirect Measures Biased?" in *Proceedings of the Annual Meeting* (Pullman, Wash.: American Agricultural Economics Association, 1979).

34. Mathews and Brown, *1967 Sport Salmon Fisheries.* (Emphasis added.)

Figure 7-2. Relationship Between Average Value per Trip and
Average Catch per Trip for Washington Salmon Sport Fishery, 1967.

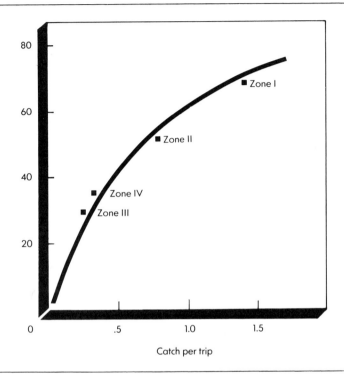

Catch per trip

Source: S.B. Mathews and G.S. Brown, *Economic Evaluation of the 1967 Sport Salmon Fisheries of Washington.* Washington Department of Fisheries Technical Report No. 2 (April 1970). Curve was fitted ocularly to the four data points by Mathews and Brown.

Mathews and Brown plot data points from each of the four zones *and* connect them with a smooth curve, they are tacitly assuming a relationship between the two characteristics measured on the axes. That is, they assume the curve is relevant for decisionmaking and behavior on the part of an average fisherman/respondent. Second, they believe they can infer the marginal value of fishing success from the slope and curvature of the graph. To them this represents a welfare loss, for "in a very real sense, the unreplaced loss of a recreational opportunity leaves a fisherman poorer than before—something of value has been taken away from him."[35]

35. Ibid.

Table 7-1. Angler Days per Salmon Caught by Zone in Washington, 1967.

(1) Zone	(2) Catch per Angler Day	(3) Angler Days per Salmon Caught	(4) Average Value per Angler Day
3	0.29	3.45	$27
4	0.34	2.94	$32
2	0.80	1.25	$48
–	1.00	1.00	$55
1	1.40	.71	$63

Source: Column 3 calculated from data contained in S. B. Mathews and G. S. Brown, *Economic Evaluation of the 1967 Sport Salmon Fisheries of Washington*. Washington Department of Fisheries Technical Report No. 2 (April 1970). Other data as in original, rounded.

There is at least one alternative economic interpretation of the data collected by Mathews and Brown. Suppose, as in Figure 7-3, that one were to plot "fishing days per respondent" per year against "catch per day per respondent." Catch per day, which can be thought of as the expected value of the catch in a given zone, is a parameter to the average fisherman. Like the weather or the price of gasoline, there is nothing the fisherman can do to change it. However, the fisherman can and does decide how many days he will fish per year in each of the four zones. If a line is drawn through the points in Figure 7-3, the resultant curve illustrates that fishermen substitute time (days per year) for success (catch per day) between zones for Zones I, II, and III. Recall that the mean annual values from the Mathews and Brown study are very close to one another for Zones I, II, and III, which have a mean of $196.30 with a range of ±1.5 percent around the mean.

The diagram of Figure 7-3 might be interpreted as follows: suppose fishermen lost the right to fish in Zone II; according to the estimate of Mathews and Brown, they would have lost the sum of $193.31. However, some would fish fewer days per year, shifting to Zone I whose value is $199.19 by the estimate. Others would increase the number of days fished per year, shifting into Zone III, which has an estimated value of $196.41 per year. (See Table 7-2.) In other words, it is possible that the data points from Mathews and Brown lie on an equal value curve wherein the fishermen can adjust

**Figure 7-3.   Fishing Days per Respondent as a Function of Catch
per Day per Respondent, by Zone.**

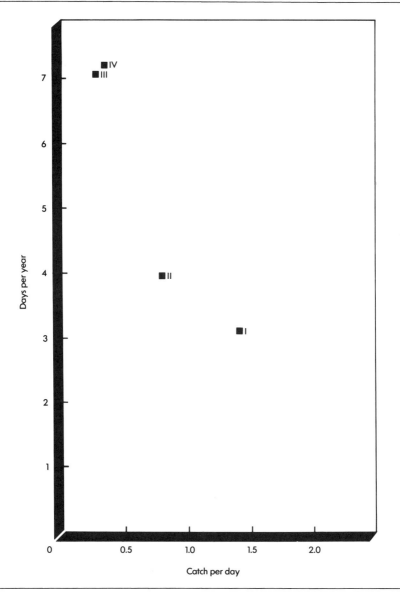

Source: S.B. Mathews and G.S. Brown, *Economic Evaluation of the 1967 Sport Salmon
Fisheries of Washington.* Washington Department of Fisheries Technical Report No. 2 (April
1970).

Table 7-2. Estimated Value per Salmon Caught in the Washington Sport Fishery.

(1) Zone	(2) Mean Annual Value	(3) Annual Fishing Days per Respondent	(4) Value per Day (2)/(3)	(5) Catch per Day	(6) Catch per Year (3) × (5)	(7) Value per Catch (2)/(6)
I	$199.19	3.17	$62.84	1.39	4.41	$45.17
II	193.31	4.04	47.85	0.80	3.23	59.85
III	196.41	7.21	27.24	0.29	2.09	93.98
IV	234.39	7.35	31.89	0.34	2.50	93.76

Source: S.B. Mathews and G.S. Brown, *Economic Evaluation of the 1967 Sport Salmon Fisheries of Washington.* Washington Department of Fisheries Technical Report No. 2 (April 1970). Columns 4, 6, and 7 calculated as indicated above.

the number of days fished per year to the probability of catching fish as measured by catch per day.

Recall that these data were given by fishermen in response to a question about the dollar value they would ask for giving up their right to fish *a year at a time.* They were neither questioned about the value of the fishing experience per day nor asked about the dollar value of different catches per day—or different fishing success rates.

Alternative theoretical frameworks may be used to interpret any set of data; the data of Mathews and Brown are no exception. If their survey data are the result of optimizing behavior, something must be equalized at the margin over the four zones sampled. The mean annual values assigned are remarkably close for Zones I, II, and III, with Zone IV not far off. Consequently, an alternative interpretation is as follows: for this group in the particular period, the respondents valued their annual option to fish as many or as few times as they chose during one year at approximately $196.00 per year. A typical respondent had the option to substitute days fished to compensate for a lower expected catch.

What can be inferred from the behavior of fishermen who release their catch? It may be more than merely an attempt to preserve the fishery perhaps for the benefit of some other fisherman. It may instead indicate that the marginal value of the fish is zero. The derivation of a marginal value curve is necessary to evaluate the loss in value when the catch per angler-day is *reduced* by environmental effects rather than being eliminated altogether. The Forest Service investigators should have employed marginal analysis instead of inferring the total loss of the fishery or inappropriately applying average rather than marginal values.

Where does this leave the Smith report, and by inference, other Forest Service publications that discuss the salmonid-fishery relationship? The answer is obvious. With respect to the economic "analyses" of fisheries contained therein, a drastically altered approach to valuation is called for, and a sound biological data base is needed if anything better than a wild guess is to be made.

SALMON, TREES, AND POLITICS

Some interesting and insightful comparisons and contrasts can be drawn between fisheries biology and forestry as natural resources management sciences. The contrasts help to reveal possible reasons for fundamental differences in ethical perspectives that each field brings to bear in applied practice. Some interesting parallels can also be drawn between political activism and the condition present in most fisheries. Consider, for instance, the absurdity of attempting to regulate access to timber resources in the same manner employed in a typical fishery. This comparison was first drawn by Donald Bevan, as follows:

1. Logging will begin at 6:00 A.M. June 15 and close October 1 at 6: 00 P.M. in even-numbered townships and sections.
2. Logging will be permitted on Tuesdays and Fridays, subject to extension or restriction by field announcement.
3. A logging license to cost $25.00 must be purchased prior to April 1. Thereafter stumpage price shall be zero.
4. It shall be unlawful for any person, firm, or corporation to use, employ, or operate a power-driven saw for the purpose of removing timber.
5. Hand axes must have a blade less than 4 inches but more than 3 inches with the handle to exceed 18 inches.
6. Each axe shall be legibly marked with the registration number and initials of the operator. No axe shall be placed or operated less than 600 feet from any other axe.
7. No logging truck shall be longer than 30 feet overall, except trucks that logged prior to January 1, 1960.
8. Trees with cones can be taken only prior to July 31.
9. Recreational loggers shall not take more than 2 trees per day nor have more than 2 severed trees in possession at any time.[36]

Perhaps even these measures would not be enough to prevent the rapid extinction of trees. Fish are at least mobile, and according to some fishermen, wily, which is probably their only salvation. The control of access to fisheries using the typical methods just mentioned is no less absurd than it would be for trees. Yet the use of bag limits, quotas, licenses, gear restrictions, and the whole range of traditional nonprice rationing devices is taken for granted and rarely questioned in the case of fish resources in spite of the fact that these instruments have not been sufficient to prevent overfishing of the stocks. In the case of much timber, the rule of capture and all of the

36. D. E. Bevan, "Methods of Fishery Regulation," in J. A. Crutchfield, ed., *The Fisheries: Problems in Resource Management* (Seattle: University of Washington Press, 1965). (Emphasis added.)

access restrictions so common in the case of fish, have efficiently been replaced by the simple assignment of property rights. Price is thereby the key means of eliminating excess demand as well as providing for perpetuation of supply. Of course, the assignment of property rights to fish stocks as a means of providing for their conservation in a manner symmetrical to private timber holdings is probably not so simple, if only for the fact of their geographic mobility. However, the possibility exists, and it should not be lightly dismissed as a means of eliminating the problem of the commons.

Fishery managers, recognizing the insufficiency of traditional means of access limitation to fishery stocks, have naturally turned to the preaching of ethics and appeals to altruism in their attempt to reduce the excess demand for zero-access-priced fish as a means of conserving them. Forest managers, by contrast, have found such appeals unnecessary, at least as a means of controlling access to "consumptive" uses of timber resources. The access price is merely raised to clear the market. Appeals to observe the rights of trees are made by druids and their cohorts who (while living in wooden houses) preach the sinfulness of cutting trees. Such hypocritical jawboning is not harmless, however, because it often produces political reactions adverse to efficiency.

The asymmetry between access to timber for consumptive (wood-products) uses at market prices and access to standing timber for recreation and other "nonconsumptive" uses at zero price, has implications for the relative strength of demand for nonconsumptive uses of forest resources over timber harvest. Zero-access price does not mean zero cost in the form of the forgone value of wood products, but it should be no surprise that it leads to the organization of political action groups seeking to shift the allocation of timber in favor of more nonharvested uses. In the process, the cost is shifted to the landowner or, in the case of public forestlands, to the general public. Such behavior constitutes a blatant form of special interest political profiteering, which is always advanced under the guise of serving "the public interest."

Why is it so difficult to inject economic rationality into the management of publicly owned natural resources, particularly forests? It is because the environmental ethic that has gained ascendancy in public policy is fundamentally in ideological conflict with economic efficiency and perhaps also with normative standards of social justice. The acceptance of economic efficiency as a goal rests on the proposition that individuals should be free to act upon their own ethical precepts in contexts where such actions do not forcefully or fraudulently deprive others of their rights.[37] Efficiency is the outcome of free markets where property rights are completely assigned and where, as a result, externalities are nonexistent. Economic efficiency, however, is not widely understood, and it has difficulty competing politically with a superficially selfless philosophy. The logging-salmon controversy is but one example of this dilemma and goes far deeper than a mere lack of biological and economic information. Inefficient regulation of timber harvest, withdrawals of timberlands into wilderness preserves and parks, and the public taking of private timberland for similar purposes constitute self-interested political strategies concealed behind a mask of feigned concern for the welfare of the trees and the salmon.

Politicians may possess the purest of intentions to serve the general public interest, but the structure of incentives involved in the political process usually results in the promotion of narrow interests at the expense of the general public interest, although political practitioners often succeed in deluding themselves to the contrary.

Typically, an "unselfish" environmental ethic is set against the profit-seeking, greedy motives of businessmen ready and willing, if not eager, to wreak environmental destruction. The typical ethically based antimarket argument ignores the external diseconomies generated by misguided government regulation. It neglects the fact that government failure is a more significant problem than "market failure" due to externalities. Indeed, externalities emerge only in the absence of exclusive and transferrable property rights, responsibility for which rests precisely on government failure.

Markets arise spontaneously where exclusive and transferrable property rights have been defined, conferred, and enforced by government. Where government has failed to perform this function or has chosen to exercise public property rights in an economically irrational manner, no market can exist. If a market does not exist, how can it be said to fail?

There is more than one way to catch a salmon, and there is more than one way to make a profit. One way to gain a profit is to gener-

---

37. A brilliant exposition on this point is given by Roger Pilon, "Property Rights and a Free Society," in M. Bruce Johnson, ed., *Resolving the Housing Crisis* (San Francisco: Pacific Research Institute for Public Policy, 1982), ch. 15.

ate "value added" by selling valuable resources or services in the marketplace. This involves purchasing scarce economic resources at full social cost and then deploying these resources to uses that generate sufficient returns from voluntary buyers, to recover all costs plus a possible net economic profit. Pure profits attract additional resource deployment, and losses produce reduced levels of activity and redirection of resources.

Another way to obtain a profit, if profit is defined with sufficient breadth, is to engage in political action, which transfers wealth from nonbenefitted, involuntarily taxed, unwary members of the public to interest groups. This form of profiteering is often a zero-sum, or even negative-sum, game in which "value added" is either zero or negative. This form of profiteering is benevolent only to those who gain, and it is made possible by inherent flaws in the political process that are now well recognized.[38]

Access to private benefits at public expense exhibits many characteristics strikingly similar to the characteristics of open-access resources of a commons, such as a fishery. Attempts at obtaining government grants and subsidies can be likened to "trolling through the public treasury." Indeed, if the problem of overexploitation of open-access salmon stocks is serious, the problem of overexploitation and excessive fishing pressure on the public treasury is much worse. The reallocation of resources from the private to public sector constitutes the same type of problem we find in a salmon fishery. There are simply too few dollars escaping the net of taxation to find their way to the fertile spawning grounds of the private sector. And the dollar escapement that is allowed finds those spawning grounds heavily silted with the sediment of stifling political regulation to the point where mortality rates, especially of small "fry," are dangerously raised.

Attempts at restriction of political profiteering to prevent overexploitation of the treasury also may be likened to fishery management regulations. Restrictions are placed on the type of gear and bait that may be legally employed. For instance, it is illegal to use tables (bribes) under which festoons of dollars are offered much as the fringe on salmon plugs are used to simulate a live bait fish. Political poaching is, nevertheless, apparently common.

---

38. See Charles Wolf, Jr., "A Theory of Nonmarket Failure: Framework for Implementation Analysis," *Journal of Law and Economics* 22(1) (April 1979): 107–39.

For some years environmentalism has evolved into two distinct strains. The one is nothing more than adherence to the economic dictum that optimal protection of the environment consists of setting the level of protection such that benefits and costs are equated at the margin. The other is nothing less than a full-blown religion ready to trade human welfare (accruing to persons other than the practitioners of the faith) for some unspecifiable "welfare of the environment." It is the latter strain that has gained the political bulwarks. The message preached by the environmentalist clergy is strikingly similar to that preached by fire-and-brimstone salvationists; namely, that human survival is at stake. Fear of perdition and hope of ecotopia have been powerful instruments of conversion to the faith, much more appealing than the call for economic optimization, which sounds cold and calculated by comparison.

Some will undoubtedly claim that I am ready to sacrifice the environment to greedy profitseekers willing to permit and abet the total destruction of all that is pure and natural. Nothing could be further from the truth. I propose to apply the economic paradigm to situations in which external diseconomies are the basic source of adverse environmental performance, setting the level of correction at its economic optimum. In other words, environmental protection is not an absolute all-or-nothing proposition. The public interest is served by protection only when the benefits of protection exceed the costs, and if that condition cannot be satisfied, then protection ought to be reduced. There exists a wide range of policy instruments available to accomplish this purpose, not the least of which is the prescription of an all-inclusive set of property rights in environmental resources.

Chapter 8

ECONOMIC ISSUES IN FEDERAL TIMBER SALE PROCEDURES

Dennis D. Muraoka and Richard B. Watson

INTRODUCTION

Federal timber is an extremely valuable resource.* At present, there are 11.266 billion board feet of timber under contract on national forests in western Oregon and Washington alone at an average price of $295 per thousand board feet (mbf) log scale.[1] When ultimately harvested this timber will provide the federal government over 3.3 billion dollars in revenue. Substantial quantities of timber are also found on other federal lands and on state lands and are sold to the private sector. While the economics of efficient management of our timber resources must begin with the more fundamental question of whether the timber should be cut at all, an assumption that a decision has been made to sell a given amount of timber from federal lands aids in determining how such sales should be conducted to most benefit society.

The majority of federal timber comes under the jurisdiction of two agencies, the Forest Service (Department of Agriculture) and the

*Professor Muraoka gratefully acknowledges the cooperation of California State University, Long Beach, in providing academic release time to prepare this manuscript. At the time of its completion, this chapter reflected current sale policies, which are subject to frequent change.

1. U.S. Department of Agriculture, Forest Service, "National Forest Timber Sales, New Timber Sales Procedures," *Federal Register* 47 (January 20, 1982), p. 2886.

Bureau of Land Management (Department of the Interior). Though the sale procedures employed by these two agencies are generally similar, they are not identical.

EXISTING FEDERAL TIMBER SALE PROCEDURES

The timber sale process begins with the Forest Service determining the volume of timber to be offered for sale in a given period and geographic area. This volume is then allocated among a number of specific "sales," which vary in size and quality of resource being offered. Once a specific tract of timber is designated for sale, an appraisal is conducted to estimate the "fair market value" of the stumpage. The "fair market value" is defined by the Forest Service as "the price acceptable to a willing buyer and seller, both with knowledge of the relevant facts and not under pressure or compulsion to deal."[2] The appraisal is normally conducted using a residual value approach. The assumption underlying this approach is that the value for timber is derived from the value for those products that are ultimately produced from it. In terms of the appraisal process, end product market values are determined at the earliest stage of processing where a market price of the product can be observed.[3] In most cases, these primary end products are lumber, plywood, and chips. Having made this determination based on processing facilities found in the general geographic area, selling values of these products are then estimated and output volumes are adjusted to a log-scale basis using predetermined average recovery factors.[4] This amount, expressed in dollars per thousand board feet log scale, represents an estimate of the revenue per unit of log input that a firm could reasonably expect to earn in operating the sale. Subsequent to this, estimated costs of required road construction, logging operations, and mill operation are subtracted to yield an estimated "conversion return."

---

2. U.S. Department of Agriculture, Forest Service, *Forest Service Handbook*, Sec. 2423.12.

3. Ibid., Sec. 2422.31.

4. This overrun factor is based on mill studies conducted periodically. A mill of "average" efficiency is assumed.

A risk adjusted profit margin is then subtracted from "conversion return," giving the "appraised price" or estimated stumpage value. This estimated margin for profit and risk is designed as an aggregate measure of profit, risk, interest on borrowed capital, and income taxes. The government makes no attempt to estimate a competitive rate of return. The rates used are computed as a rate of return on costs and are based on what are felt to be current conditions.

Upon completion of the appraisal phase, a sale is advertised at lease thirty days prior to the designated sale date. Included in the sale announcement are data summarizing the appraisal process as well as relevant contract conditions such as payment methods, contract duration, and performance requirements.

On the sale date, prospective buyers must qualify for the sale by submitting a sealed bid at or above the "appraised price." In addition, a minimum deposit or bond must be posted as evidence of ability to meet stated sale requirements. If the sale in question has been designated as a Small Business Administration setaside, only firms with 500 or fewer employees are allowed to participate.

On the sale date, those who have qualified by submitting an acceptable sealed bid are permitted to participate in an oral auction.[5] Bidding is conducted by species. The level of each bid is determined by multiplying its component species bids, expressed as a rate per mbf, by their respective volumes and summing these amounts across all species.[6] The sale is awarded to the highest bidder.

Sales may be sold under two payment methods: lump sum and log scale. In lump-sum sales, which are favored by the BLM, the buyer pays an amount equal to the level of the bid as described previously. The resulting payment is a fixed dollar amount determined in advance of the harvest, which gives the buyer the right to cut all tim-

---

5. In some cases sales are designated for sealed bids only. On such sales each bidder is allowed one sealed bid at or above the appraised price, and the sale is awarded to the highest bidder.

6. Algebraically the level of each bid is determined as

$$B = \sum_{i=1}^{n} R_i \cdot V_i$$

where B is the bid level

R_i is the log scale species bid for the ith species

V_i is the appraised volume of the ith species

n is the number of species.

ber within the designated sale area. For sales using log-scale payment, as is the case for most Forest Service sales, the buyers agree to pay their winning bid rates per mbf of logs of each species actually harvested. Log-scale sales, therefore, are based on the actual volume of timber harvested rather than estimated or appraised volume.

On winning a sale, a firm is obligated to remove the specified timber prior to a predetermined date. Depending on local policy, sales may be sold using "flat rate" or "escalation" pricing. Under flat rate pricing, payment rates for each species are the bid values recorded at the sale auction. With escalation pricing, bid prices are adjusted to reflect changes in market prices of end products that occur between the sale date and the date in which the logs are removed.[7] Traditionally, under both lump-sum and log-scale payment methods, actual payment to the government is made at harvest. With lump-sum procedures, firms make installment payments during the logging operation. Again, for lump-sum sales, the total payment is fixed and based on estimated volume rather than actual cut. Using log-scale procedures, firms are billed for actual volume cut and removed from the sale site as determined by Forest Service scalers.[8]

Estimated road construction costs are returned to the firm in the form of credits, which may be applied to other sales. This allows firms to finance road construction for one sale using logs currently harvested from another sale.

Failure to complete a contract on time results in a reappraisal of any remaining timber. The firm must then pay this amount plus any bid premium (the amount by which high bid exceeds the appraised price) from the original sale, or the original bid price, whichever is greater. In addition, the government can bar that firm from future

---

7. On these sales, bids are increased by 50 percent of any increase in the assigned index. If the index declines, bid prices are reduced by 100 percent of the decrease to the base rate.

8. The Forest Service has recently altered its long-standing payment policy. Effective April 15, 1982, the winning bidder is required to make a cash deposit of 10 percent of the total bid value of the sale within thirty days of the sale. The deposit may be used as payment for timber removed after 25 percent of the appraised volume has been presented for scaling. For sales of more than three years duration, new payment schedules that either require or provide an incentive for payment prior to the termination date are being implemented on a trial basis. For details on these new procedures see U.S. Department of Agriculture, Forest Service, "New National Forest Timber Sales Procedures: Final Policy," *Federal Register* 47 (April 15, 1982), pp. 16178–16182. These procedural changes do not significantly alter the analysis contained herein.

sales as a punitive action. Until recently, failure to complete sales within the specified period has been rare and punitive action has been limited to repeat offenders. However, concern over more frequent defaults on timber sale contracts has led to recent changes in Forest Service policy. Effective April 15, 1982, purchasers who default a timber sale contract are liable for additional damages in the form of interest charges. "Interest will be charged on the value of the remaining timber for half the resale contract period. In addition, up to 1 year's interest charge will be added for the time from the termination date to the date of the resale."[9]

AN ECONOMIC CRITERION FOR EVALUATING TIMBER SALE PROCEDURES

The government, as trustee for the American people, has the responsibility of wisely managing or, synonymously, conserving publicly held natural resources. While conservation is the appropriate goal for all publicly and privately held resources, the term conservation has taken a variety of meanings. To many, conservation has come to mean a reduction in the use of resources. For example, water is conserved by taking shorter showers, gasoline is conserved by driving more slowly, and electricity is conserved by extinguishing the lights when exiting a room. However, this definition of conservation is logically flawed. Carried to an extreme, it implies that perfect conservation of a resource occurs at zero consumption. After all, as long as any amount of a resource is in use, "conservation" can be practiced by consuming still less of that resource. This definition is logically equivalent to hoarding resources.

A more appropriate definition of conservation is to utilize resources in a fashion that maximizes the value of those resources to both current and future generations. At times, this definition of conservation is consistent with the "use less" definition. However, this alternative definition of conservation may sometimes imply that *more* of a resource should be used!

When applied to public timberlands, the principle of conservation requires that the resource be placed in its highest valued end use, with the production process proceeding at the minimum possible

9. Ibid., p. 16182.

cost. This entails a succession of complex, interrelated decisions including when the timber is to be harvested, how it is to be harvested, and what finished products (i.e., lumber, plywood, paper, particle board, etc.) will be produced.

In general, the government has not harvested, milled, and marketed public timber itself, but instead has chosen to auction uncut stands of timber to private firms. It is private firms, seeking to maximize profits, that determine (within contractual restrictions) the ultimate disposition of a timber stand.[10] However, in transferring public timber rights to private firms, the public is entitled to just or fair compensation. While the "just payment" for a stand of timber is subject to definition, "just payment" for a timber stand is the total gross revenue of the harvested timber less the opportunity cost of the harvest. The opportunity cost of a timber harvest includes appraisal costs, road building costs, logging costs, milling costs, transportation costs, environmental costs, and a competitive rate of return for the firm.[11] "Just value" as defined, is referred to by economists as the economic rent of the resource and is illustrated graphically in Figure 8-1. The total area shown in Figure 8-1 represents the total gross revenue of the timber produced. Because the amount of revenue derived from the timber will vary depending on when the timber is harvested, the revenue (and all other values illustrated in the diagram) is expressed in its present value.[12] The shaded area represents the present value of the total necessary costs of bringing the timber to market, including a normal rate of return for the entrepreneur. The remaining unshaded area is the economic rent of the timber sale.

As stated earlier, the appropriate goal of government timber sale policies is to promote conservation of the resource. An operational criterion for evaluating alternative timber sale methods, consistent with conserving resources, is to compare the extent to which they

10. The transfer of development rights to natural resources from the public to the private sector is widely practiced by government. In addition to timber, notable examples include the vast mineral resources that underlie public lands.

11. The opportunity cost of any activity is defined as the value of what must be foregone to engage in that activity. A competitive rate of return, or normal rate of return, is properly thought of as an opportunity cost, since the entrepreneur must forego a normal return elsewhere to engage in his current activity.

12. The concept of present value is widely used in comparing sums of money received at different points in time. The present value of a future sum of money is the amount of cash that would have to be invested today in order for the investment to grow to the dollar value of the future sum at the time the future sum is to be received.

Figure 8-1.   An Illustration of Economic Rent.

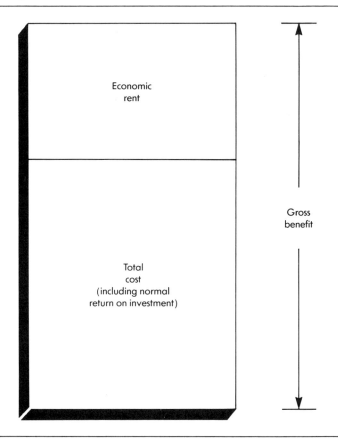

Diagram derived from R. O. Jones, Walter J. Mead, and Philip E. Sorensen. "The Outer Continental Shelf Lands Act Amendments of 1978." *Natural Resources Journal* 19 (October 1979): 894.

maximize and collect economic rent. Timber sale policies affect the available economic rent. For example, a timber sale procedure that results in a tract being harvested too early (or too late) will reduce the total benefit from the acreage. Referring back to Figure 8–1, this is illustrated graphically by a reduction in the area representing gross timber revenues and, therefore, a commensurate reduction in economic rent. A policy that fails to select the most efficient firm to harvest the timber also reduces the available economic rent since costs are increased above the necessary level. Referring again to Figure 8-1, costs that exceed the minimum level necessary increase the size of the rectangle representing the cost of production. Since gross revenues remain constant, this charge falls against economic rent. Similarly, sale policies that require unnecessarily large public administrative costs or private compliance costs also dissipate economic rent. In view of these ways in which timber sale procedures affect economic rent, a socially efficient sale method is one that leads to simultaneously maximizing and collecting the economic rent.

AN ECONOMIC ANALYSIS OF THE EXISTING TIMBER SALE PROCEDURES

Having established a criterion for evaluating current sale practices, the major elements of timber sale policy—appraisal, sale method (e.g., log-scale versus lump-sum, etc.), bid procedure, and payment method—can be considered. Beginning with presale activities, the economic rationale for the appraisal process described earlier is to ensure that the government receives fair value for public timber. Without questioning this intent, it is relevant to ask whether government appraisal procedures are the least costly, hence most efficient, method of achieving this goal.

Public Appraisals

In an auction setting, each competing firm formulates its bid for a stand of timber by estimating what end products will be produced as well as when, how, and at what cost the timber will be transformed into these finished products. In accomplishing this, a firm is faced with two broad options: it may accept published appraisal data from the selling agency or conduct its own appraisal. As noted earlier, federal appraisals involve estimates of both expected revenues and costs based on assumptions for the specific end products to be produced. For example, on a typical Forest Service appraisal, each revenue and cost element is estimated at a rate per thousand board feet for each species present in the offering. In addition, the estimated volume of each species is published, and is used to compute a volume-weighted advertised rate at which minimum bids will be accepted.

In a study commissioned by the Forest Service in 1981,[13] fifty interviews were conducted with firms that frequently vie for Forest Service Region 6 timber. One of the questions asked of these firms concerned the degree to which they utilize data provided in published public appraisals. In all but six of the fifty responses, the firms stated that they make little or no use of the Forest Service data. Most often, firms conduct their own appraisals, then look at the Forest Service data only to see if they are "in the same ballpark."

There is a twofold explanation for this phenomenon. First, statistical analysis and interview results show that firms generally find public appraisals inaccurate in cost and revenue estimates. In its appraisals, the government assumes a firm of "average efficiency." The data used to characterize such a firm are, in most cases, out of date and not typical of current industry conditions. A second problem arises because the Forest Service does not know exactly when the timber will be cut and processed. As a consequence, public appraisals are based on cost and revenue estimates assuming the stand is harvested at the time of the sale. Private appraisals, on the other hand, are based on projected values for the intended date of harvest, which may be as much as three or four years from the sale date.

To illustrate the problem this presents, consider the following hypothetical example. Assume a tract of timber is estimated to yield end products valued at $300 per mbf log scale using current values. If the current dollar cost estimate for this tract totaled $200 per mbf, the stand would be appraised by the government at $100 per mbf. Now assume that a firm considering the same tract agrees with these estimates of current dollar costs and revenues, but plans to cut and process the timber two years after the sale date. Assuming that both costs and revenues are subject to a 5 percent compound annual inflation rate, the private appraisal would forecast estimated revenues at $330.75 per mbf and costs of $220.50 per mbf. This would suggest a time adjusted residual value, and therefore a competitive bid of $110.25 per mbf. It is clearly inappropriate to use current revenue and cost figures to establish the "fair market value" of a resource sold today with harvest and payment in some future period. The in-

13. Walter J. Mead, Mark Schniepp, and Richard B. Watson, *The Effectiveness of Competition and Appraisals in the Auction Markets for National Forest Timber in the Pacific Northwest* (Washington, D.C.: U.S. Department of Agriculture, Forest Service, September 30, 1981), pp. 139–141.

accuracy of Forest Service appraisals is documented in the study of Forest Service Region 6 cited earlier. In that study, actual bids for sales from the Douglas fir subregion (the west side of the Cascade Mountains) were on average twice the appraised price.[14]

The perceived inaccuracy of public appraisals has led most firms to perform their own appraisals. Once individual firms have estimated the potential revenue and costs associated with operating a given sale, profit-maximizing firms are willing to bid amounts up to the total residual value (or as defined earlier, the economic rent) in order to win the sale. In the presence of *competition* and an efficient sale method, the existing public appraisal process is redundant in computing the fair value of a timber sale. Therefore, any costs associated with public appraisal are unnecessary and contrary to the goal of maximizing economic rent. Such is the case in the Pacific Northwest and in California where competition has been found effective in determining the "fair market value" of the timber.[15] The elimination of the minimum bid creates potential problems only in those areas where competition is ineffective. In such instances, a *postsale* appraisal would be appropriate. Our recommendation is to appraise all one-bidder sales and a randomly selected sample of sales with multiple bidders. This policy might be criticized by those who suspect collusive activities among potential bidders, and such criticism might be warranted in view of the strong incentives for such behavior inherent in this type of market.[16]

To deal with this problem, we add another criterion for appraisal. In addition to the number-of-bidders requirement, the government might appraise a sale in which the observed high bid is less than the average bid for similar sales in the preceding six months by a predetermined amount (e.g., 20 percent). While the specific requirements for such a rule would depend upon the local market conditions, this should accomplish the objective of reducing appraisal costs while safeguarding the resource. A system of postsale appraisals would not completely eliminate presale activities because the government would still have to establish general characteristics of each tract to be offered. The savings, and therefore the increase in associated

14. Ibid., pp. 3–5.
15. Richard B. Watson, "The Effectiveness of Competition for National Forest Timber in Region 6" (Ph.D. dissertation, University of California, Santa Barbara, 1981).
16. Ibid., pp. 90–97.

economic rent, would stem from a significant reduction in the time and effort put into such presale activities.

Sale Methods

Turning to the issue of the sale method, the nature of the auction process, that is whether an oral or sealed bid auction is conducted, can also affect the available economic rent. Most timber sale auctions are conducted using a sealed qualifying bid with an ensuing oral auction. Whether the oral or the sealed bid auction is more efficient has received considerable attention in the economic literature.[17] Given that theoretical arguments can be made supporting both methods, the determination of which method is superior in this application becomes an empirical question.

Prior to October 1976 the Forest Service typically used oral bidding for timber sales in the Douglas fir subregion, even though either oral or sealed bidding was allowed. During the thirteen-year period from 1963 through 1975, only 3 percent of all sales were auctioned using sealed bidding in this region. During the same period, the percentage of sealed bid auctions used on the ponderosa pine subregion of Region 6 (the east side of the Cascade Mountains) was even smaller. In October 1976, however, the National Forest Management Act required substantially more sales to be conducted using sealed bidding. This legislation remained in effect until spring 1978 when an amendment restored historical timber bidding procedures. During the eighteen-month period covered by the sealed bid mandate, 57.6 percent of the sales conducted in the Douglas fir subregion and 42.6 percent of the sales in the ponderosa pine subregion used sealed bidding.

This period of mandated sealed bidding provides an opportunity to test the hypothesis delineated above. By controlling statistically for other sale attributes, the impact of sealed versus oral bidding on winning bid levels was examined using multiple regression tech-

17. See Walter J. Mead, "Natural Resources Disposal Policy—Oral Auction Versus Sealed Bids," *Natural Resources Journal* 7, no. 2 (April 1967); Edward M. Miller, "Oral and Sealed Bidding, Efficiency vs. Equity," *Natural Resources Journal* 12, no. 3 (July 1972); Richard W. Haynes, "An Evaluation of Two Measures of Competition for National Forest Timber Sales" (U.S. Forest Service, Pacific Northwest Forest and Range Experiment Station, 1978); and "Competition for National Forest Timber in Northern, Pacific Southwest and Pacific Northwest Regions" (U.S. Forest Service, Pacific Northwest Forest Range Experiment Station, 1980).

niques. The regression analysis was performed separately for the ponderosa pine subregion and the Douglas fir subregion. The results indicate that, holding other factors constant, sealed bidding increased winning bids by $3.34 per mbf in the ponderosa pine subregion and by $13.68 per mbf in the Douglas fir subregion relative to oral bidding.[18] When the analysis was extended to estimate the impact of sealed versus oral bidding within individual forests in Region 6, it was found that in eight out of eleven forests in the ponderosa pine subregion, and in eight out of nine forests in the Douglas fir subregion, sealed bidding increased the level of winning bids. The differences in the winning bids tended to be statistically significant in forests where timber sales were commonly observed to sell at or very near appraised prices.[19] Based on these results, all timber sales should be conducted using sealed bid auctions. While sealed bidding as opposed to oral bidding makes little difference in the level of winning bids in competitive areas, sealed bidding protects the government when competition is lacking.

Bid Procedure

Having addressed the sale method, the bid procedure used at the auction can now be examined. Under the current system, bids submitted for each sale are formulated in log scale rates by biddable species. As noted earlier, the level of each competing bid is found by multiplying the bid for each species by the estimated volume of each species as determined by the Forest Service appraisal and summing across all species.

This process is unnecessarily complicated and may produce inefficient results in that the sale may be awarded to someone other than the true high bidder. This possibility is illustrated in Table 8-1, which outlines a hypothetical timber sale where two species, Douglas fir and hemlock, are eligible for bids. The Douglas fir is estimated to have a volume of 5,000 mbf, and the hemlock is estimated at 2,000 mbf. At the oral auction, firms A and B compete for the sale. If firm

---

18. While in both the ponderosa pine and Douglas fir subregions sealed bidding had the expected positive impact on bid levels, in the ponderosa pine subregion the estimated impact is not statistically significantly different from zero. In the Douglas fir subregion, the impact from sealed bidding is statistically significant from zero at the 0.01 level.

19. A full description of the regression models summarized here is found in Mead, Schniepp, and Watson, *Auction Markets for National Forest Timber*, pp. 217-32.

Table 8-1. A Comparison of Log Species Bids.

	Firm A	Firm B
I. Bid Rates – Log Scale		
(1) Douglas fir	$300 per mbf	$275 per mbf
(2) Hemlock	$250 per mbf	$313 per mbf
II. Appraised Volume		
(1) Douglas fir	5,000 mbf	5,000 mbf
(2) Hemlock	2,000 mbf	2,000 mbf
III. Total Bid		
[(1) · (3))] + [(2) · (4)]	$2,000,000	$2,001,000
IV. Actual Volume (Case 1)		
(5) Douglas fir	5,000 mbf	5,000 mbf
(6) Hemlock	1,950 mbf	1,950 mbf
V. Actual Payment (Case 1)		
[(1) · (5)] + [(2) · (6)]	$1,987,500	$1,985,350
VI. Actual Volume (Case 2)		
(7) Douglas fir	5,200 mbf	5,200 mbf
(8) Hemlock	1,500 mbf	1,500 mbf
VII. Actual Payment (Case 2)		
[(1) · (7)] + [(2) · (8)]	$1,935,000	$1,899,500

A bids $300 per mbf for the Douglas fir and $250 per mbf for the hemlock, while firm B bids $275 per mbf for the Douglas fir and $313 per mbf for the hemlock, firm B will be awarded the sale based on a total bid of $2,001,000 as opposed to $2,000,000 for firm A. Under lump sum provisions, where payment depends upon appraised rather than actual volume, firm B would then pay $2,001,000 in installments and remove whatever volume found on the sale site. In this case the actual volume of each species would not affect the payment. Under a log-scale payment scenario, the actual volume of each species will cause the total payment to vary. This situation is further illustrated in Cases 1 and 2.

In Case 1 the actual volume of Douglas fir was 5,000 mbf, as estimated; however, the actual hemlock volume amounted to 1,950 mbf – 50 mbf or 3 percent less than the appraised volume. Based on actual volume, firm A would have paid $1,987,500 as compared to $1,985,350 for firm B. While firm B bid $1,000 more at the auction and would have been awarded the sale, firm B was not the true high bidder since that bid ultimately returns $2,150 less to the government. This discrepancy is magnified if actual volumes deviate from estimates by greater amounts. If, as in Case 2, actual Douglas fir volume was 5,200 mbf and actual hemlock volume was 1,500 mbf, firm B would pay $35,500 less than firm A would have paid for the same volume.

Clearly, the severity of this problem depends on the accuracy of federal appraisals in estimating available volume. Empirical analysis of appraised versus actual volumes in Region 6 timber sales indicate that this problem is serious. The average absolute error for volume estimates on 842 Forest Service sales closed between October 1, 1977, and September 30, 1979, was an alarming 36 percent.[20] Considering that this error was applied to a total volume of 2,946,642 mbf, the amount of revenue involved is obviously significant.

Another problem inherent in the log-scale payment method stems from the calculus of profit maximization.[21] Profit-maximizing firms will fell and remove a tree from the forest as long as the additional revenue that ultimately results from the tree (or marginal revenue) exceeds the additional cost of production (or marginal cost). A firm will harvest a tree as long as the marginal net benefit (marginal revenue minus marginal cost) is positive. When a firm is required to make log-scale payments to the government for each tree removed from the forest at the time of harvest, that payment is viewed as a marginal production cost by the firm, even though such payments are not actual production costs in the sense that logging, road building, and other costs are.[22] Further, the winning log-scale species bid rates pertain to all of the trees of a particular species in the stand regardless of the quality of the tree or the cost of harvesting the tree. While the high quality or low harvest-cost trees in the sale can profitably be removed from the forest, trees of lesser quality or higher harvest cost may become submarginal given the required payment to the government. This is illustrated in Figure 8–2, which shows the marginal net benefits of harvesting a sale. The reason for the inverse relationship between marginal net benefit and volume is that the trees neither are of uniform quality nor can they be harvested at uniform cost. The

20. Ibid., p. iv.

21. This analysis is based on D. Muraoka and R. Watson, "Improving the Efficiency of Federal Timber Sale Procedures," *Natural Resources Journal* 23 (October 1983): 815–25.

22. Alternative payment methods can be utilized that do not affect marginal decision-making. These include profit-sharing payments (the firm pays a percentage of the net revenue or profit from the harvest) or lump-sum payment due at the sale date.

trees with largest marginal net benefit are those which the firm prizes most and are surely worth removing from the forest. However, as tree quality falls or as harvest costs increase, the marginal net benefit that can ultimately be derived from additional logs declines. It pays the firm to remove an additional tree as long as the marginal revenue from the tree exceeds the marginal cost of harvesting the tree or until the point where the marginal net benefit is zero. At some point it is not worthwhile to remove an additional tree. This is illustrated by volume v^*.

If a firm is required to make a log-scale payment to the government, this has the effect of shifting the marginal net benefit curve down by the amount of the bid rate (the marginal costs perceived by the firm increase by the amount of the bid rate). The additional fee makes some trees that were economically attractive before the fee, submarginal after the fee. The result is a reduction in volume form v^* to v^1. In short, these residual payments entice the firm to destroy or otherwise leave behind some logs that, in the absence of the residual payments, would have been desirable to remove from the forest.[23]

In the extreme, this problem can lead firms to default a sale they would have completed otherwise. This has become a particularly relevant issue during the recent housing slump and the accompanying reduction in stumpage rates. This case is illustrated in Figure 8–3. At the time of the sale, stumpage prices are such that MB^1 is the relevant marginal benefit curve. After the sale, weakening market conditions cause the marginal net benefit curve to fall to MB^2. In the absence of the log-scale payment, this would still allow partial completion of the sale. However, with a log-scale payment rate of ls_1, the marginal net benefit curve falls to the point that none of the sale is harvested.

Log-scale bid payment can also result in socially undesirable distortions and gamesmanship in species bid levels. Suppose a stand is put up for sale with two biddable species; one species is highly valuable and comprises 95 percent of the appraised volume of the sale, whereas the second species is less valuable and constitutes the balance of the appraised volume. Given the method by which the high bid is determined (as explained earlier), this may lead a firm to make

---

23. While this practice is illegal, policing costs necessary to effectively prevent such behavior are prohibitive.

Figure 8-2. Harvest Volume With and Without Log-Scale Payments.

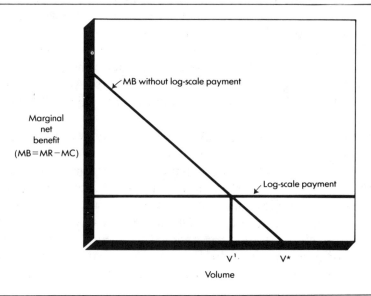

Figure 8-3. Harvest Volume Where Log-Scale Payment Leads to Sale Default.

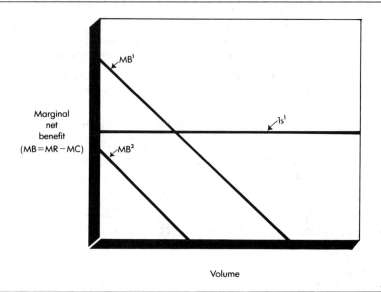

an inordinately high bid on the low-volume species and a correspondingly low bid on the high-volume species. The firm might reason that if their bid wins the auction, they will discard the low-volume species, removing little or none of it from the forest, and therefore making minimal payments to the government for that species. This will leave the firm the high-volume species at a low bid rate.

In this case the government loses in two ways. It does not derive any revenue from the low-volume species, and it receives less than fair value for the high-volume species. Both losses reduce the economic rent collected by the government.

Finally, log-scale species payments are relatively costly to administer. To guarantee the government full receipt of payment from timber sales, it must monitor the actual production from the forest. The cost of the resulting bureau is a burden against economic rent. Even if this payment method were effective in collecting revenue for the government, much of the revenue is dissipated in large administrative costs.

In summation, species log-scale bidding is ineffective in maximizing and collecting economic rent. It can result in the sale being awarded to a firm that is not the true high bidder. It might also result in reducing the total value of the forest in that some socially desirable trees may not be removed from the forest or some contracts, which would be honored in the absence of the residual payments, may be defaulted. This can lead to gamesmanship in bidding whereby firms do not reveal their true valuation of the sale. Finally, it is relatively costly to administer the species log-scale payments. A solution to many of these problems is a change of the bid variable from species log scale to lump sum. As noted earlier, this clears the ambiguity created by differences in actual versus appraised volume regarding total payment to the government for the sale. Further, since the lump-sum total payment is determined prior to the harvest, it is not viewed as a marginal production cost, but rather as a fixed cost. Fixed costs do not affect marginal logging decisions and therefore the problem of abandoning socially desirable trees is circumvented. Finally, since the proposed lump-sum payment is the sole liability of the winning firm, costly policing of output is not required, keeping administrative costs to a minimum. Cash lump-sum bidding is a more effective alternative to log-scale species bidding.

Timing of Payment

Under current sale procedures (either lump-sum or log-scale payment), payments to the government are made as the timber is extracted from the forest. As is the case with log-scale species bidding, the timing of these partial payments obscures the total payment to the government. Paradoxically, the firm that appears to be the high bidder based on the level of either lump-sum or log-scale payment may neither return the highest present value of revenue to the government nor be the most efficient firm in terms of harvesting and marketing the timber at the lowest cost if the payment is made at the time of harvest. By failing to select the most efficient firm, the economic rent is reduced.

The problem stems from the fact that with either lump-sum or log-scale payment, the highest bid determines the winning firm regardless of when the sale is harvested.[24] When comparing bids, no attempt is made to reconcile planned differences competing firms may have for the time of harvest. Firms are not required to disclose when they will harvest the timber. The only requirement is that the harvest occur within the time period specified in the sale announcement. This contract period varies in length from as little as one year to as long as eight years. In the west, the average sale length is 3.5 years.[25] To illustrate the problems this creates, consider the following hypothetical example (see Table 8–2).[26]

Two firms are formulating bids for a stand of Douglas fir. Both firms agree with the government appraisal of the volume of timber in the stand.[27] Firm A plans to harvest the timber two years from now, at which time it will derive $450 per mbf in gross revenue after having incurred $175 per mbf in production costs. Consequently, it is willing to bid $275 per mbf ($450–$175) for the right to harvest the timber. Firm B plans to harvest the timber four years hence. At that

24. The social costs of high-grading and policing high-grading can be avoided altogether if log-scale bids are abandoned in favor of lump-sum bids.

25. U.S. Department of Agriculture, Forest Service, "New Timber Sale Procedures," p. 2886.

26. This example is derived from Muraoka and Watson, "Improving the Efficiency of Federal Timber Sale Procedures."

27. It is further assumed that the timber is no longer growing and that the timber contract contains no escalation clause. These assumptions simplify the analysis but do not alter the results.

Table 8-2.   An Intertemporal Comparison of Two Bids.

	Actual ($ per mbf)	Present Value[a] ($ per mbf)
Firm A [c]		
(1) Estimated Revenue	$520	$355
(2) Estimated Costs	$220	$150
(3) Bid (1) – (2)	$300	$205
Firm B [b]		
(4) Estimated Revenue	$450	$372
(5) Estimated Costs	$175	$145
(6) Bid (4) – (5)	$275	$227

a. Assumes discount rate of 10 percent.
b. Assumes harvest in 4 years.
c. Assumes harvest in 2 years.

time it anticipates $520 per mbf gross revenue, $220 per mbf in production costs, and is therefore willing to bid $300 per mbf for the tract. On the basis of these bids, firm B would be granted the rights to the timber. However, in an economic sense it is not valid to compare $300 per mbf four years from now to $275 per mbf two years from now. The proper basis for comparison of the two bids is their present value.

If the comparison is made assuming a social discount rate of 10 percent, the present value of firm A's bid is approximately $227 per mbf, while the present value of firm B's bid is $205 per mbf. Using a present value criterion for comparing bids, firm A rather than firm B would be the winner. This example is illustrated graphically in Figure 8-4. The diagram shows two "iso-present value" curves. Each curve has the property such that any future value that lies on the curve, when discounted back to the present, has the same present value. The two curves clearly illustrate that if two firms plan to harvest a timber sale at the same time, the larger bid is unambiguously socially preferred (has the larger present value). However, if the two firms plan different harvest dates, the ranking of the undiscounted bids may be different from that of the discounted bids.

Also note in the example above that in terms of present value, firm A foresees a higher valued end use for the timber ($372 per mbf as opposed to $355 per mbf when expected revenues are discounted back to the present) and can achieve this end at a lower cost ($145 per mbf as opposed to $150 per mbf in present value). By not select-

Figure 8-4.   Evaluating Bids.

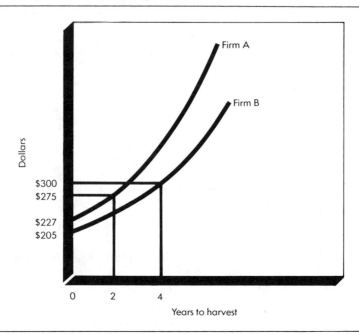

ing firm A, the government receives less than fair market value for the resource because it does not select the true high bidder. It also does not conserve the resource in an economic sense because by selecting firm B, the resource is not placed in its highest valued end use, and production proceeds neither at the lowest possible cost nor at the "right" time.

The problems inherent in payment at the time of harvest can be remedied by changing the payment date. The payment should be due at the time the sale is awarded. Such a payment date, combined with lump-sum cash bidding (as recommended earlier), would reconcile any ambiguity resulting from firms contemplating different harvest dates. This combination would promote the maximization and collection of full economic rent from the resource.

The primary criticism of such a system is that it would place small firms at an unfair disadvantage in competing for sales. The disadvantage stems from the potentially large cash sums necessary to compete for sales. It may be argued that large firms can raise money in capital markets more easily (at less cost) than their smaller counterparts. As a result, the large firms may be able to outbid the small firms and still earn a superior rate of return. The validity of this argument is an empirical question.

While this sale method has not been employed for federal timber sales, the federal government has experience with a similar sale procedure used to issue Outer Continental Shelf (OCS) oil and gas leases. The bid variable for OCS leases is a cash lump-sum payment (called a bonus payment) due at the time the lease is issued. Additional royalty payments of one-sixth any future gross revenue are requisites of these sales. The bonus payments required to win these auctions are extremely large. The average bonus payment for the 1,223 Gulf of Mexico OCS leases issued between 1954 and 1969 was $2,228,000. Even with such large "front-end" payments, empirical analysis of these leases indicates that large firms have not had an unfair advantage at OCS auctions. The profitability of leases owned by the eight largest oil companies is not substantially different (in fact, it is slightly less) than that earned by "non-Big-8" firms.[28]

One approach that has been taken in OCS leasing to lessen the potential barrier to entry posed by the large front-end payment has been to allow coalitions of small firms to submit joint bids. Large firms are not allowed to participate in joint ventures. This approach might also be followed in timber sales. On balance, cash-bonus bidding has been effective in collecting the economic rent from OCS leases. There is no reason to believe it would be less efficient for federal timber sales.

SUMMARY AND CONCLUSIONS

U.S. Forest Service policies for administering the national forestlands are important because they affect the value of the forest resource. Those procedures governing sale appraisals, auction method (oral versus sealed bidding), bid variables, and timing of payment to the government are summarized in Table 8–3.

At present the Forest Service appraises all tracts prior to their sale to ensure the government fair market value. In most cases the "residual value" appraisal technique is used. Where competition is present

---

28. These results are reported in Walter J. Mead, Dennis D. Muraoka, and Philip E. Sorensen, "The Effect of Taxes on the Profitability of U.S. Oil and Gas Production: A Case Study of the OCS Record," *National Tax Journal* 35 (March 1982): 21–30.

Table 8-3. Summary of Timber Sale Procedures.

	USFS	*Recommended*
1) Time of Appraisal	Presale	Postsale
2) Number of Sales Appraised	All	Percentage to Discourage Collusion
3) Appraisal Technique	Residual Value	Regression Model
4) Sale Method	Oral Bid	Sealed Bid
5) Bid Variable	By Species Log Scale	Lump sum
6) Payment Method	By Species Log Scale	Lump sum
7) Payment Date	Harvest Date	Sale Date

these appraisals are unnecessary. Competition can be relied upon to determine the fair value of the timber. Even in those areas where competition is not as intense, presale appraisals are unnecessary. A policy of postsale appraisals on a representative sample of the sales would greatly reduce appraisal costs. Furthermore, the "residual value" approach is inaccurate and should be revamped. While more research is needed in this area, an alternative approach, based on statistical analysis of historical transactions evidence, shows tremendous promise. Such an approach may well be less costly and more accurate than current appraisal methods.

Most Forest Service sales are currently conducted using oral bidding. While oral bidding is effective in situations where competition is present, it may be inferior to sealed bidding where competition is weak. Empirical analysis of timber sales conducted in areas of traditionally weak competition tends to support this result and suggests that sealed bidding should be used on all sales.

The bid variable used at Forest Service auctions is species log scale. This bid variable is flawed in that it can result in the sale not being awarded to the highest bidder in terms of the total return to the government. It can also result in socially desirable trees being discarded as waste, defaults of sale contracts that might otherwise have been completed, and gamesmanship at the auction where firms may not bid their true valuation of the timber. These problems can be avoided by replacing the elaborate species bidding system with lump-sum cash bidding. Such a system not only circumvents the problems mentioned above, but also has the virtue of being much less costly to administer.

The payment for timber sales is currently made at the time the timber is harvested from the forest. The intertemporal nature of the payment makes it difficult to distinguish among the bidders as to which is most economically efficient. The appropriate basis of comparison of competing bids is the present value of the payment ultimately promised to the government. This problem is remedied by moving payment for public timber from the harvest date to the sale date. In this way, all bids are automatically expressed in terms of the present value of sale timber.

Many of the procedures currently employed by the Forest Service dissipate the economic rent from the valuable timber resource. In analyzing existing timber sale procedures, potential flaws have been illustrated and suggestions have been made as to how these procedures might be altered to increase the value of these resources. The public at large and the Forest Service alike should be interested in policy changes that contribute to the conservation of these resources.

Chapter 9

THE ECONOMIC CONSEQUENCES OF THE SETASIDE PROGRAM IN THE DOUGLAS FIR REGION OF THE PACIFIC NORTHWEST

Mark Schniepp

INTRODUCTION

The setaside program provides for the preferential offering of timber sales to timber manufacturing firms that qualify under an appropriate "small business" criterion as designated by the Small Business Administration.[1] By denying large business access to timber sales under the setaside program, smaller firms are ensured a predetermined share of federal timber sold from national forests. However, the program does not formally "trigger" unless small businesses are unable to purchase their predetermined share of national forest timber volume during a given twelve-month period. In some national forests of the Pacific Northwest, this share can be quite substantial based on past small business purchase records covering a five-year period. For example, through the first quarter of 1983, small business shares exceeded 50 percent of the allowable cut in marketing areas within all westside national forests except the Umpqua. In six marketing areas, the share was above 70 percent. The U.S. General Accounting Office (GAO) reported that the small business shares were initially established as

---

1. In Section 2431.12 of the Forest Service manual, a small business eligible under the SBA setaside program is defined as (a) primarily engaged in the logging or forest product industry; (b) independently owned and operated; (c) not dominant in its field of operation; and (d) together with its affiliates, its number of employees does not exceed a 500 person limit.

compromises between Forest Service and Small Business Administration (SBA) efforts to fix them at historical purchase percentage
levels of the 1966–1970 time period.[2]

The procedure used for the recomputation of small business shares
is an analysis of a six-month purchase history between large and
small firms by the marketing area of each national forest. In any six-
month period, if small business fails to win its predetermined share,
the setaside program triggers and remains in effect until small business has purchased its allocation. Each six-month period is reviewed
over a longer five-year recomputation period to determine whether
changes in the small business share allocation should be made. It is
only at five-year intervals that the predetermined small business share
may change in any marketing area.

The program tends to maintain a static or increasing allocation of
timber to small business because the effect of the six-month analysis
and corresponding trigger is such that the purchase history available
at the recomputation will almost always indicate that small firms
have purchased their share or greater. Consequently, incentives are
created for firms to set ceilings on their growth in terms of employee
size in order to meet the SBA criteria.

In recent years the setaside program has been under considerable
attack. Allegations concerning the propriety of the size standard for
eligibility have elicited the greatest critical response by industry and
government interests. Foremost is the call to reduce the eligible size
standard to a one hundred-employee ceiling. Proponents of this revi-
sion cite numerous examples of the failure of the program as currently implemented to help companies in the less than one hundred-
employee range.[3]

Further allegations regarding the economic incidence of the setaside program have been focal points in the expanding literature.
However, few studies have utilized data in a fashion amenable to veri-
fying these allegations unambiguously. While all of the approaches
taken to date have contributed to a consistent set of results, there
remains a need for further investigation of the problem in a more
disaggregated setting, and a need for the application of more power-

2. GAO, "Allegations Regarding the Small Business Setaside Program for Federal Timber," DED–79–8, April 1979.
3. See ibid., or Wesley Richard, "Size Standard Study," prepared for Public Timber
Purchasers Group, Portland, Oregon, 1978.

ful statistical methods to ascertain the independent impacts of the setaside program on timber sale revenues.[4] In the most recent government report on the setaside program, the Comptroller General (hereafter referred to as the GAO) wrote; "We did not determine the magnitude of the revenues denied the Federal Government because we were concerned that the amount calculated would be pure speculation since we could not determine that the setaside sales, if sold as open sales, would have generated similar overbids."[5] To date, no study has attempted to estimate the magnitude of the impact of the setaside program on revenues received by the U.S. Treasury from the sale of public timber.

There are allegations concerning the economic consequences of the setaside sale program as it is currently being implemented in the westside national forests of U.S. Forest Service Region 6, popularly known as the Douglas fir region of the states of Washington and Oregon. The setaside program (1) designates better quality sales to setaside status relative to open sales, (2) generates bid prices for federal timber sales significantly lower than open sales holding competitive forces and sale quality constant, and (3) discriminates against the ineligible firms and their dependent communities.

SALE SELECTION BIAS

The issue of a setaside selection bias is a controversial one among firms in the forest products industry that depend on public timber. Opponents of the setaside program, primarily spokespeople of the ineligible firms, maintain that such a bias exists, which is competitively unfair and effectively discriminates against larger firms. Setaside eligible firms, their trade associations, and the SBA dismiss these accusations and deny that SBA representatives collaborate with the Forest Service to tag particular future sales as setaside sales in the

---

4. In "A Comparison of Open and Setaside Timber Sales on National Forests in the Douglas Fir Region," *Land Economics* (1979), Haynes directed his analysis of the setaside timber sale program over three Forest Service regions, aggregating complete appraisal zones together to arrive at his conclusions. In "Allegations Regarding the Small Business Setaside Program for Federal Timber," CED-79-8, April 1979, the GAO looked at all national forests in the United States for which setaside sales were numerous enough for statistical comparisons.

5. GAO, "Allegations Regarding Setaside Program," p. 57.

event the program triggers. Whether setaside sales are actually chosen from the better quality sales can be assessed using statistical tests on the available data.

Modeling the probability that a sale will be chosen as a setaside sale based on favorable timber characteristics is necessary to determine the existence and nature of the sales selection bias. Measuring the characteristics of setaside sales in contrast to open sales addresses the sale selection allegation. Haynes analyzed the differences between open and setaside sales using discriminant analysis to test hypotheses associated with both the setaside sale selection process and setaside sale impact on overbids.[6] His analysis concluded that setaside sales were characterized by significantly lower logging costs, lengthier sale contracts, and larger timber volumes in both eastern and western appraisal zones of Region 6.

In a followup study, the GAO evaluated fifty-eight national forests for quality differences between setaside and open sales. Eleven quality characteristics such as timber sale volume and the length of the timber sale contract were compared between setaside and open sales over a four-and-one-half-year period. On the basis of a simple comparison of sales characteristic means, the GAO classified fifty national forests as having higher quality setaside sales and only six as having inferior quality setaside sales relative to open sales.

Previous studies of setaside sale bias have not utilized the most powerful statistical methods available in deriving conclusions for policy recommendations. A variety of statistical techniques are available for analyzing a wide range of cases. Nonparametric statistical methods like chi-square tests or comparisons between means are not always well-suited for problems involving a large number of characteristics that must be controlled in determining causality or influence. In general, tests of homogeneity between two means are incapable of measuring differences between discrete situations while independently accounting for all variables or quality differences. For this reason, a more robust method of statistical inference is chosen to test setaside sale selection bias. Furthermore, the analysis covers a wider time period and focuses on a selectively homogeneous appraisal zone.

6. Haynes, "A Comparison of Open and Setaside Timber Sales."

The Model

The present analysis is conducted to identify the particular timber sales characteristics, if any, that are statistically correlated with setaside sales. By constructing a multiple regression model with the status of the sale — setaside versus nonsetaside or open — as the dependent variable and sale characteristics as explanatory variables, estimated parameter values associated with each of the sales attributes can be calculated in orde· to measure the independent influence of each on the probability of setaside sale selection. If in fact the selection method is carried out via some nonrandom process, then those sales characteristics that influence the selection process can be identified using significance tests for the estimated parameters of the model. The interest of this analysis is neither the distribution of the response variable, that is, the probability that the sale is a setaside, nor how that probability changes with different values for the exogenous variables. Rather, the intent of the analysis is to identify those sales characteristics having a significant effect, whether a sale is classified as setaside or open.

The equation can be specified as a linear probability model where the dependent variable is dichotomous, indicating whether the sale is open or setaside. However, discrete dependent variables cause estimation problems in linear probability models, and ordinary least squares estimation methods can lead to biased and inconsistent estimates.[7] If the model equation is solved using the estimated parameters and particular values for the independent variables, the resulting solutions for the dependent variable simply represent outcomes of probable events, those events being the various kinds of physical and cost characteristics indicative of the timber sale. An alternative functional form widely used in the literature on dichotomous dependent variables is based on the logistic distribution, and is utilized here in lieu of the linear probability specification. The logistic distribution function is written as

$$P = 1/(1 + \exp\{-XB\})$$ (1)

---

7. See A.S. Goldberger, *Econometric Theory* (New York: Wiley, 1964); E.A. Hanushen and John E. Jackson, *Statistical Methods for Social Scientists* (New York: Academic Press, 1977); or Robert Pindyck and Dan Rubinfeld, *Econometric Models and Economic Forecasts* (New York: McGraw-Hill, 1980).

where P is the distribution of the response variable ranging from 0 to 1, X is the vector of exogenous variables, and B is the vector of co-efficients associated with X. Rearrangement of Equation (1) yields

$$\log [P/(1 - P)] = XB . \qquad (2)$$

The left hand term is the logit or log of odds ratio. In the present context, $P(s)$ is substituted for P where $P(s)$ is the probability that the sale is a setaside sale, and XB is the implied linear combination of sales and appraisal characteristics used as indicators of the quality of a given sale.[8]

Data

The database consists of all 6,636 timber sales occurring in the Douglas fir region between January 1, 1973, and December 31, 1981.[9] The determinants of timber sale status used in the present study are listed in Table 9-1. These variables have also been commonly used as indicators of timber sale quality in the literature on timber sales and bidding.[10]

The appraised stumpage price measures the minimum bid required to qualify for the timber sale. The stumpage price is the residual value of standing timber derived from an appraised final product selling value less costs of production and allowance for profit. A lower appraised stumpage price would imply, ceteris paribus, a lower required investment pledge needed to qualify for the oral auction phase of the timber sale.

8. In Equation (1), the dependent variable is the logarithm of the odds that the sale is a setaside sale given knowledge of the XB. Large values for B implying substantial importance assigned to particular variables (sales characteristics) in ability to discriminate between open and setaside sales are not to be expected. Rather, the purpose of the logistic regression analysis is to identify attributes among the vector of hypothesized quality indicators that have a statistically significant relationship with setaside sales vis-à-vis open sales, meaning that high or low values of particular sales characteristics have a nonrandom occurrence and thus may be said to influence the setaside sale selection process.

9. There exists a limited amount of quantitative sales information obtainable from timber sale records. All of this information is supplied or derived from the Forest Service timber sales report form 2400-17. These forms have been recorded on tape by the Forest Service computer center in Ft. Collins, Colorado.

10. Haynes, "A Comparison of Open and Setaside Timber Sales"; idem, "Competition for National Forest Timber in the Northern, Pacific Southwest, and Pacific Northwest Regions," PNW-266 (Portland, Ore.: U.S. Forest Service Pacific Northwest Forest Range Experiment Station, January 1980); GAO, "Allegations Regarding Setaside Program."

Table 9-1. Exogenous Variables Used in Logistic Regression Model of Setaside Sale Selection.

Variable Name	Description
APPNET	Appraised net stumpage price ($/mbf)
PCPAM	Percent per acre material
PCDF	Percent Douglas fir
LOGMBF	Appraised logging costs ($/mbf)
ENVMBF	Appraised environmental costs ($/mbf)
MILLMBF	Appraised manufacturing costs ($/mbf)
TOTROAD	Total road costs ($)
TOTVOL	Total estimated sales volume (mbf)
SPLS	Appraised end product selling value ($/mbf)
DURATION	Length of sales contract (months)
HMILES	Haul miles from sale site to average mill
VOLPA	Volume per acre

The percent major species variable indicates the degree of species homogeneity characterizing the timber for sale. In the Douglas fir region, Douglas fir is the most desirable species. Consequently, a better measure of species quality is the percent of Douglas fir comprising the total volume offered. With the exception of the rare westside species known as Port Orford cedar, Douglas fir logs are estimated to have selling value potential as high as manufactured lumber or plywood.

Per acre material (PAM) comprises dead and down stumpage or snags, and is generally considered an undesirable component of a timber sale because of its relatively low value. However, during periods of strong markets it is chipped and exported, selling at profitable prices.

Timber harvest costs normally vary inversely with timber sale desirability. This is not true for manufacturing costs. Higher manufacturing costs are usually indicative of higher appraised end product selling values because grade lumber products and plywood cost more to process than timber going into dimension lumber or studs. Higher manufacturing costs are also associated with Douglas fir since it is appraised within the context of specialty end products, including plywood, whereas certain other types of timber are not.

Larger timber volumes are a favorable sale characteristic in view of the uncertainty in timber acquisition associated with the oral auction process in which the advertised timber stand is awarded to the highest bidder. Given the withdrawals of timberland by RARE II and the decreases in the allowable harvest in Region 6 over the last decade, timber is perceived to be in short supply.

The appraised selling value approximates the contemporaneous market value of products produced from the timber sale stumpage, minus all costs. It is the best indicator of the quality of standing timber estimated by the Forest Service. To account for timber sale density, a variable is included to measure volume per acre, that is, the ratio of total volume to the number of acres spanning the timber site.

Empirical Analysis

To determine the sale characteristics statistically significant in contributing to the probability of a setaside sale, logistic regression using a maximum likelihood estimation procedure is applied to the data. Table 9–2 presents the regression results.

The overall regression is statistically significant as measured by the chi-square statistic. (The probability of a value as high as 298.84

Table 9–2. Parameter Estimates and Significance Tests of Exogenous Variables, Logistic Regression Analysis of Setaside Sale Selection.

Variable	Parameter Estimate	Asymptotic T Ratio	Significance Level
APPNET	-0.008	4.10	0.0001
PCPAM	0.012	4.64	0.0001
PCDF	0.003	2.73	0.0062
LOGMBF	-0.011	-5.02	0.0001
ENVMBF	-0.009	-2.93	0.0034
MILLMBF	0.056	2.63	0.0086
TOTROAD	-1.3E-6	-4.76	0.0001
TOTVOL	7.2E-5	3.97	0.0001
SPLS	0.006	3.44	0.0001
DURATION	0.011	2.96	0.0031
HMILES	0.010	6.24	0.0001
VOLPA	0.004	2.38	0.0175
BIDDERS	0.001	0.10	0.9156
CONSTANT	-3.116	-15.87	0.0001

Model Chi–square: 298.84
DF: 14
-2 Log Likelihood: 6784.48
Number of obs: 6636

occurring by chance alone is less than .0001.) Twelve variables in the model are statistically significant (0.05 level), although as predicted the associated parameter estimates are very small, indicating that the implied probabilities are small. Using the estimated equation to predict setaside sales based on particular attributes without prior knowledge of setaside selection might result in a poor predictive performance. The statistical significance associated with almost all of the parameter estimates, however, does imply that setaside selection is a nonrandom event. The evidence tends to indicate that higher quality attributes are selected for setaside sales relative to open sales.

The signs of the coefficients associated with the various sales characteristics indicate that setaside sales are more likely to have lower appraisal prices (minimum qualifying bid levels), higher percentages of both per acre material and Douglas fir, lower logging and environmental costs, and higher manufacturing costs. Greater manufacturing costs, together with the likelihood of higher appraised end product values implies higher quality timber. Setaside sales are associated with larger volume sales and have longer contract lengths that give operators additional flexibility in timing harvest dates to favorable market opportunities. Other positive relationships include greater timber densities vis-à-vis open sales and, oddly, longer haul distances from sale site to the average point of production.

The allegation that setaside sales are better quality sales cannot be refuted by the statistical evidence demonstrated here. However, if setaside sales are more attractive in terms of net profitability, do they sell for more or less than open sales?

THE EFFECT OF SETASIDE SALES
ON GOVERNMENT REVENUES

The primary focus in analyzing the setaside sale bidding record is the comparison of prices paid for Forest Service timber sales classified as setaside versus unrestricted or open sales. The results of the earlier section on sale selection bias indicated that setaside sales are of better quality and larger size than open sales. Of even greater importance and interest is the size of the bid difference between setaside and open sales. That is, if a significant difference does exist, it is important in reducing revenues going to the U.S. Treasury from the sale of national forest timber?

If a significant difference in overbids between setaside and open sales is observed, ceteris paribus, smaller firms are getting a bargain competing on setaside sales at the expense of the public as owners of national forest timber. It is assumed that no cost differences exist between small and large firms in the timber logging and manufacturing industries because entry barriers in the form of economies of scale are not considered significant beyond the one hundred-employee size firm.[11] If small firms are as efficient as large firms, price differences associated with sale status should decline over time as setaside-eligible firms enter the industry. Ultimately, bid prices paid for federal timber would be the same regardless of setaside classification.

The Model

The model chosen to determine the size of the overbid decrement due to the setaside program and whether the differences between setaside and open sales are maintained over time was initially developed by Schniepp and more formally employed in the literature on the U.S. Forest Service setaside program in Mead, Schniepp, and Watson.[12] The model incorporates fundamental economic relationships to arrive at a final empirical form for testing the hypothesis that setaside sale status significantly affects bid prices for stumpage.

The behavior of firms in the forest products industry has normally been assumed consistent with microeconomic theories of the firm.[13] Profits of the forest products firm are simply total realized revenues less total actual costs, where total costs include the costs to procure stumpage, harvest the timber, manufacture it into finished products, and sell the final products on the open market. The Forest Service estimates revenues and all costs of production including the stumpage, harvesting, manufacturing, and selling costs of an operator of average efficiency. The stumpage value estimate is the residual after estimated costs of production are subtracted from estimated revenues. This residual value is called the appraised price and is the effec-

11. See Richard, "Size Standard Study"; or GAO, "Allegations Regarding Setaside Program."

12. Schniepp, "Analysis of Forest Service Appraisal Methodology"; Mead, Schniepp, and Watson, *The Effectiveness of Competition and Appraisals.*

13. See David H. Jackson, *The Microeconomics of the Timber Industry* (Boulder, Colo.: Westview Press, 1980); or Schniepp, "Analysis of Forest Service Appraisal Methodology."

tive minimum price at which stumpage will be sold. Providing all revenue and cost estimates are accurate in the sense that bidders believe them, the bid price for stumpage will equal the appraised price by definition. However, the bid price is rarely equal to the minimum acceptable bid, that is, there usually occurs a sufficiently large overbid.

The source of part of the difference between the bid price and the appraised price may be attributable to physical timber sale characteristics that bidders perceive to have value above and beyond what the Forest Service has calculated in their appraisal. Other factors including the degree of competition present, institutional considerations such as specific sales policies, and pure inaccuracy by the Forest Service in its cost and revenue appraisals may induce a particular set of bidder incentives and therefore variation in the bid price paid above the appraised price. All of these extraneous components that may affect a positive overbid should be included as part of the final specification of the bid price to form the estimating equation

$$B = f(P, HC, RC, MC, \pi, Z, e)$$

where

$$B = \text{the bid price}$$
$$P = \text{the anticipated finished product price}$$
$$HC = \text{the estimated harvest cost}$$
$$RC = \text{the estimated road cost} \tag{3}$$
$$MC = \text{the estimated manufacturing cost}$$
$$\pi = \text{profit}$$
$$Z = \text{all other timber sale characteristics}$$
$$e = \text{the stochastic component of the equation.}$$

Equation (3) represents the structural model for the firm's bid price decision. The left-hand-side variable is the average stumpage cost (per thousand board feet) or the high bid price. The bid price is the sum of two components—the appraised price plus the bid premium or "overbid." It is the latter part that bidders have discretion over during the oral auction phase of the timber sale. If highbid is used as the dependent variable, then much of the observed variation significantly explained by the independent variables can be traced to the appraised component of the total bid price, which is fixed on a sale-by-sale basis and is unaffected by competition. Consequently, how the exogeneous appraisal value and physical descriptive variables affect the overbid exclusively accounts for bidder willingness to purchase the timber sale. The use of overbid as the measure of bid price enables the parameter estimates of the exogenous appraisal and sale characteristics to be interpreted as the prices that bidders are willing to pay for marginal increments of those characteristics. The use of overbid as a successful empirical measure of competitiveness in the literature of federal timber markets was first introduced by Haynes and more formally employed as a primary decision variable in Schniepp and Mead et al.[14]

The inclusion of Z, the set of additional sale, appraisal, and market characteristics, is important to control for quality differences across sales. The vector Z will include all variables used in the analysis of the Sale Selection Bias section with some slight changes. First, the variable SALVAGE is included to control for sales by the Forest Service that include insect-infested timber and parcels partially burnt from recent fires or damaged in some other way, such as the 1981 Mount Saint Helens eruption. These sales are quite commonly called "salvage" sales and normally have short contract lengths for expeditious harvest.

The collineation between the variables TOTVOL and DURATION is extremely high (the correlation coefficient is 0.83). For this reason, a new variable, REMRATE, constructed as the ratio of sales volume to contract length, is substituted for DURATION in the equation. This variable, which measures the rate at which timber must be harvested or "removed," provides an indirect measure of the relative length of the contract and the flexibility associated with the decision to change harvest rates. It is expected that higher removal rates will depress bid levels relative to lower removal rates that provide the operator with greater discretion over harvest date.

To account for possible temporal variation not captured by cost, production function, and other variables, binary variables for each year represented in the sales data are included. These variables take the mnemonic "Yyr" where "yr" is replaced by the two-digit year

14. Richard W. Haynes, "Competition for Federal Timber" (Paper presented at the 53rd annual Western Economic Association Conference, 1978); Schniepp, "Analysis of Forest Service Appraisal Methodology"; Mead et al., "The Effectiveness of Competition and Appraisals."

73, 74, . . . 81. The number of qualifying bidders is also included in the equation to capture competitive pressure. The use of the logarithmic form for the number of bidders is taken from Mead.[15]

Finally, the price variable (SPLS) is assumed to enter the equation as a quadratic function explaining overbid. The variable SPLS2 is the square of estimated end product value.

The model determines the impact of setaside sales vis-à-vis open sales on bidders' willingness to pay for the timber sale, that is, the overbid. The null hypothesis for the test is that overbids are no different on sales restricted to setaside-eligible firms or open to all firms. To conduct the test by calendar year and to observe any temporal variation of the setaside program impact on overbids, time-oriented interaction terms are constructed with the original binary variable, SETASIDE, used to form the logit in the regression analysis of the Sale Selection Bias section.[16] Nine setaside variables, one for each year, are included along with the vector Z as additional exogenous variables in the model. Each dummy variable measures the independent impact of setaside sales in a particular year on the overbid: negative parameter estimates imply lower overbids due to setaside sales; positive estimates imply higher overbids. The variable names for the nine test interaction terms are "SBAyr" where "yr" is replaced by the two digit year of setaside sale occurrence.

All dollar variables are deflated using the producer price index. Deflation removes the general upward trend in cost and price data over time due to inflation. The results of the complete estimation using ordinary least squares regression methods appear in Table 9–3.

The parameter estimates associated with the SBAyr variables are all negative, indicating that for all years setaside sales generated lower overbids than open sales of comparable quality, given the sales characteristics included in the regression equation. Note that the significance levels associated with the estimated parameters on the setaside variables are all at or below 0.05 except for SBA79, which still

15. Walter J. Mead, *Competition and Oligopsony in the Douglas Fir Lumber Industry* (Berkeley and Los Angeles, Calif.: University of California Press, 1966).

16. Interaction terms are dummy variables in which a multiplication operation occurs between two binary variables. In the present context, the first interaction variable is constructed as

$$SBA73 = SETASIDE * Y73$$

where D73 = 1 if the sale occurred within calendar year 1973, and D73 = 0 otherwise.

Table 9-3. Results of Overbid Estimation Test of Differences in Overbids Due to Setaside Sales, by Year, 1973-1981.

Variable	Parameter Estimate	T Ratio	Significance Level
SPLS	0.2342	8.69	0.0001
SPLS2	-1.23E-5	-6.88	0.0001
LOGMBF	-0.1078	-2.75	0.0060
ENVMBF	0.2049	2.88	0.0040
MILLMBF	-0.5803	-10.83	0.0001
TOTROAD	-8.46E-6	-1.28	0.2009
PROFIT	0.7024	8.01	0.0001
PCDFWS	-0.0249	-1.37	0.1709
PCPAM	-0.2459	-6.33	0.0001
LBIDDERS	27.7992	44.79	0.0001
REMRATE	-0.0238	-5.93	0.0001
SALVAGE	-2.2295	-2.38	0.0172
TOTVOL	1.19E-3	8.27	0.0001
VOLPA	0.0605	3.11	0.0019
HMILES	0.1502	6.97	0.0001
Y74	16.9242	9.36	0.0001
Y75	27.9150	13.04	0.0001
Y76	20.3512	8.84	0.0001
Y77	18.3616	9.23	0.0001
Y78	20.0180	10.37	0.0001
Y79	36.9859	20.29	0.0001
Y80	52.3419	27.63	0.0001
Y81	32.1033	15.42	0.0001
SBA73	-9.7645	-2.58	0.0099
SBA74	-10.3708	-3.83	0.0001
SBA75	-14.5049	-5.14	0.0001
SBA76	-12.0757	-2.80	0.0051
SBA77	-9.5113	-3.46	0.0005
SBA78	-9.1366	-3.54	0.0004
SBA79	-4.5832	-1.86	0.0628
SBA80	-9.8557	-4.34	0.0001
SBA81	-4.3412	-1.95	0.0508

R-square: .4717
MSE: 892.065
Dependent mean: 42.16
Observations: 6636 (1973-1981)

exhibits a sizable coefficient at −4.58. It is important to note that in all other cases the estimates are quite large, indicating that the impact on overbids was nontrivial. (The average overbid in constant dollars over the study period is $42.16.)

However, the impact of the setaside program on bid prices appears to be diminishing over time. The 1981 regression parameter is the smallest of the nine setaside coefficients estimated. Although the first six estimated coefficients are significantly greater than the last three associated with SBA79–SBA81, the latter group of coefficients are not significantly different from each other, indicating a general diminishing trend of smaller overbids on setaside sales since 1979.

The parameter estimates of the remaining variables in the equation indicate that many of the appraisal and sale characteristics influence overbid significantly. For a more elaborate and detailed interpretation of these effects in a similar context, see Mead et al.[17]

Estimated Dollar Loss

The parameter estimates calculated from the regression indicate that in each year examined, setaside sales returned lower bid prices (overbids) for federal timber than open sales of comparable quality. The coefficients of the SBAyr terms can be interpreted as the average dollar amount by which bids were depressed on setaside sales relative to open sales of comparable quality. In 1973 the marginal impact of seventy setaside sales on overbids is estimated to be $9.76/mbf less than on open sales, ceteris paribus. By 1975 this figure peaked at $14.50/mbf, and then dropped to just $4.34/mbf for the 282 sales sold with setaside status in 1981.

To arrive at a total dollar amount of foregone government revenues due to the setaside program, the parameter estimates, which measure the average overbid decrement on setaside sales holding constant other factors in the model, are multiplied by the annual amount of timber volume sold on setaside sales in westside Region 6 over the

17. W.J. Mead, Mark Schniepp, and Richard B. Watson, *The Effectiveness of Competition and Appraisals in the Auction Markets for National Forest Timber in the Pacific Northwest.*

Table 9-4.   Setaside Sales, Timber Volume, and Estimated Revenue Loss Due to the Setaside Program, by Calendar Year, 1973-1981, Douglas Fir Region.

Year	Setaside Sales	Setaside Volume (mbf)	Estimated Dollar Loss (1982 dollars)
73	70	372,408	$ 10,925,914.45
74	161	812,648	25,332,042.24
75	149	979,919	42,711,729.45
76	56	343,983	12,490,875.81
77	156	829,974	23,726,516.54
78	181	984,407	27,046,424.82
79	194	674,243	9,282,627.02
80	247	760,270	22,533,764.17
81	282	810,543	10,574,376.40
73-81	1496	6,768,317	$184,624,270.90

Note: Average overbid deficit per sale during the 1973-81 study period: $27.21/mbf. All dollar volumes are in terms of December 1982 price levels.

Source: Timber sale records and parameter estimates from Table 9-3.

study period. The results of these calculations, inflated to 1982 dollars, are presented in Table 9-4.[18]

Table 9-4 shows that between 1973 and 1981, as a result of the setaside program, Forest Service timber sales revenues in westside Region 6 were lowered by $180 million when measured in 1982 dollars.

18. The results of the calculations in constant 1967 dollars before inflating to 1982 dollars using the December 1982 producer price index value of 3.006 are as follows:

Year	Dollar Loss
1973	$ 3,634,702.08
1974	8,427,159.76
1975	14,208,825.50
1976	4,155.314.64
1977	7,893,052.74
1978	8,997,479.98
1979	3,088,032.94
1980	7,496,262.20
1981	3,517,756.62
1973-1981	$61,418,788.46

The average overbid deficit per sale during the nine-year study period in constant 1967 dollars is $9.07/mbf.

INDIRECT DISCRIMINATION OF THE
SETASIDE PROGRAM

Critics have charged the setaside program with deliberate discrimination against both established large and small firms. In addition to the sale quality discrimination discussed in the Sale Selection Bias section II, and bid price discrimination demonstrated in the Effect on Setaside Sales section, further discrimination in the form of indirect costs resulting from setaside sale policy can be identified. In particular, most sawmills or plywood plants employ one or more small business contractors in the processing of stumpage into finished products. Normally, smaller companies are hired as contractors to harvest and transport timber to the mill as part of the independent logging phase of a typical timber sale operation. Logs are then sorted by species and size. The log diameters and species that are not compatible with the purchasing firm's processing facilities are sold or traded to other installations, many of which are small and totally dependent on scavenger acquisition for their timber input requirements.

The mill then manufactures the logs into lumber or plywood, planes and dries the lumber products, and markets them either through an in-house wholesaling division or by further "subcontract." Many of the contractors who supply goods or services to the mill are small business proprietors with considerable investment in labor and equipment. They can be economically hurt by the setaside program when, for example, the ineligible mill faces closure or even curtailment of operations due to inadequate timber supply. When setaside triggering occurs, timber sales volume, which would normally be sold in open sales available to any qualifying firm, is instead sold to a restricted set of setaside-eligible firms. The setaside trigger normally lasts six months or until small firms have purchased their predetermined share of national forest timber. Consequently, a community dependent upon a program-ineligible firm may be endangered if the mill considers production curtailment or shutdown due to inadequate opportunities for timber acquisition brought about by the withdrawal of federal timber from open sale competition.[19]

19. For example, in interviews with individual firms conducted in the summer and autumn of 1980, it was the consensus of large and small business that the closures of International Paper's Chalatchee plant in Washington State, Edward Hines in the Oakridge

Firms ineligible for setaside sales must not only consider periods of production curtailment or shutdown but also of stagnation or slow growth because significant expansion of operations is precluded by a fixed and limited raw material base. In such cases, the setaside program discriminates against large businesses and subsequent growth, against other small businesses that would otherwise support the ineligible mills, and against the labor force and services industry of the local communities that derive much of their livelihood from large business timber products firms.[20]

The problem has been most acute in recent years with the economic recession that began in 1979. While mill closures have been a common occurrence in all national forests of Region 6 for both small and large firms, the allocation of allowable volume going to small (setaside-eligible) firms has remained relatively constant. Because the small business base share of national forest timber sale volume is fixed by the purchase history of the 1966–70 initial period of computation with few significant changes made since, installed mill capacity of an area today may have little relationship to this historical small business base percentage. Severe allocative distortions can occur in areas where the historical small business share is allowed to continue despite significant changes in local firm composition from small to large size over time.

In the Rogue River National Forest in southern Oregon, the Forest Service estimates that 70 percent of the installed wood-manufacturing capacity in the area is operated by large businesses, yet the small business share of national forest timber volume is approximately 70 percent. In instances such as this, less competition is assured on sales "setaside" in the short run because allotted timber exceeds the capacity of those small operators still in business. In the long run, however, and in the absence of entry barriers, other new small firms will enter the industry if existing small firms are getting a bargain. The bid price differentials between open and setaside sales will then

---

Ranger District of Oregon, and Cabax Mills in Eugene, Oregon, were due in large part to the withdrawal of significant timber supplies from open sale competition due to the triggering of the setaside program.

20. Transportation and search costs are nonzero and imply that labor is not completely free to move to other firms or industries upon shutdown of a large lumber mill in a relatively isolated community. Such cases, however rare, contribute to the potential indirect costs of the setaside program. In more realistic applications, the local labor force and supporting services will simply move to other firms, large or small, in the industry.

diminish. The industry will support enough small firm capacity to accommodate the small business share of national forest timber volume. If there exist size diseconomies with small (setaside-eligible) firms, then the setaside program creates further social costs by encouraging the entry of higher cost firms.

Moreover, as installed capacity of large business is reduced over time by the entry of small firms, the remaining large firms will not be forced to compete as vigorously on open sales as they now do because the number of large bidders vying for "scarce" open sale volume will be less. This is not to say that large firms compete less vigorously against small firms – the maintenance of open sale timber volume shares critically depends on the purchase record of open sales by large firms. Bid prices of open sales should decline to levels approximating those of setaside sales. The relationship between overbids and a perceived shortage of open sale timber appears to be a critical cause of the observed difference in bid prices paid for open sales relative to setaside sales. This is particularly true when the total installed capacity of large firms exceeds the allocated national forest open sale volume in a well-defined bidding area.

CONCLUSION

In the Sale Selection Bias section it was demonstrated that setaside sales were characteristic of lower harvesting costs, longer sale terms, larger appraised volumes, higher estimated end product prices, and higher manufacturing costs, implying better quality timber grades and species. The results of the statistical analysis cannot be considered unambiguous proof that SBA representatives, in collaboration with small business trade association representatives, conspire with the National Forest Supervisor to select sales for the setaside sale program. However, favorable characteristics of setaside sales are, with high probability, not the product of pure chance, and some nonrandom mechanism was operating in the selection of setasides over the 1973–81 time period in the Douglas fir region of the Pacific Northwest. It follows indirectly from these results that the mills operated by large business are not only precluded from bidding on the same volumes of timber available to program-eligible firms, but also face the less attractive timber stands that remain in open sale competition.

The direct economic consequences of the setaside program show that government revenues were significantly lower for setaside sales than for open sales of comparable size and quality. It is estimated that between 1973 and 1981 overbids measured in 1982 dollars on setaside sales averaged about $27/mbf less than open sales, resulting in a $185 million loss to the U.S. Treasury over the nine-year period.

Small business contractors who provide support services to large forest products firms are economically hurt if the mill installation is forced to suspend or curtail operations due to the trigger of the setaside sale program. Incentives to limit growth are also created by the setaside program as firms attempt to stay under the 500-employee limit to maintain eligibility. The setaside program therefore acts to control growth among firms that might otherwise expand operations to enhance efficiency in production or raw material procurement.

The composition of firms classified as setaside eligible may change over time in a marketing area. However, installed capacity of an area today may have little relationship to the small business base percentage of national forest timber volume still used to trigger the setaside program. As a result, small businesses may have a significant overallocation of setaside timber, depriving large ineligible firms of necessary stumpage for normal mill operations. Over time, the composition of the industry will change to one supporting more small firms. If diseconomies of scale are associated with setaside-eligible-sized firms, further social costs will result.

Between 1973 and 1975 the setaside sale percentage of total sales offered in the nine national forests of westside Region 6 increased from 9.4 to 22.8. The increase in the amount of timber withdrawn from open sale competition (980 mmbf in 1975 as opposed to 372 mmbf in 1973) is the likely cause of the substantially higher prices paid for open sales that would have been generated otherwise. In 1975 large firm percentage purchase of open sales reached its all time high of 38.9 percent for the nine-year study period.

For this same year, the regression equation yielded the largest setaside sale deficit in terms of overbid relative to open sales ($14.50/mbf). Furthermore, in 1981 large firms purchased fewer sales (23.41 percent) than in the previous eight years, and according to the regression parameter estimates associated with the setaside test variables, the impact on overbids in 1981 declined to an all time low ($4.34/mbf). The competitive vigor demonstrated by large firms from 1973 to 1980 by open sale purchase percentage and higher average overbid relative to setaside sales was significantly reduced in 1981. These data suggest that the setaside program has been a contributing cause of Region 6 timber price inflation indicative of the years following the 1973–74 economic recession. This was particularly true with the advent of RARE II, and the reduction in national forest annual allowable harvest, creating conditions approximating a shortage for federal timber since the autumn of 1976.

Chapter 10

THE ECONOMIC IMPLICATIONS OF LOG EXPORT RESTRICTIONS
Analysis of Existing and Proposed Legislation

Richard W. Parks and Judith Cox

INTRODUCTION

Prohibitions on exports have generally played a relatively minor role in U.S. trade policy in contrast to tariff and quota restrictions on imports. In many instances the export restrictions have been imposed for strategic or political reasons, as for example in the case of prohibitions on the export of wheat to the Soviet Union in response to the invasion of Afghanistan, the limitations on the export of high technology items to Warsaw Pact nations, and the export of Alaska oil. Export restrictions motivated primarily by economic considerations are apparently rare. The only examples found are the prohibitions on the export of softwood logs by certain classes of owners. Policies involving restrictions on log exports have expanded during the last decade and now are an important feature in forest products markets. Almost every recent congressional session has seen attempts to expand the scope of the restrictions or to extend them to different forest products or different jurisdictions.

We would like to thank Brandt K. Stevens for extensive comments and suggestions on an earlier version of the paper. We would also like to thank Randal Heeb for his diligent research assistance.

CURRENT AND PROPOSED RESTRICTIONS
ON LOG EXPORTS[1]

The first log export ban was imposed in 1926 on logs taken from federal lands in Alaska.[2] The law prohibited exports both to foreign countries and to the lower forty-eight states. In 1960 the Alaskan legislature extended the ban to include timber taken from state-owned lands.[3] Logs taken from state-owned lands in Oregon and California were covered by bans in 1961 and 1972 respectively.[4]

In 1968 Senator Wayne Morse (Democrat, Oregon) added an amendment to the Foreign Assistance Act of 1968 limiting log exports from federal lands administered by the U.S. Forest Service and Bureau of Land Management in the western states to a quota of 350 million board feet per year.[5] In 1974 the quota feature was dropped and all log exports from these federal lands were banned. At the present time, the export of softwood logs harvested on all federal lands[6] west of the hundredth meridian (a line running roughly from the middle of North Dakota south to Texas) is prohibited.[7] In addition, the federal law contains important antisubstitution provisions designed to make the ban on exportation of federal timber effective, for without some form of antisubstitution provisions, timber owners not subject to the ban could expand exports from their own holdings and subsequently use timber purchased from federal lands as a replacement or substitute in domestic uses.

1. See John W. Austin, "Log Export Restrictions of the Western States and British Columbia," United States Department of Agriculture, Pacific Northwest Range Experiment Station, Forest Service Research Paper PNW–91 (1969); and Robert E. Wolf, "Background Paper on Softwood Log Export Issue," Appendix 18 in U.S. Congress, House, *United States Trade with Japan: Public Lands Timber Export Bill (HR 7972). Hearings Before the Subcommittee on International Economic Policy and Trade of the Committee on International Relations*, 95th Cong., 2d sess., April 4 and 21, 1978.

2. U.S. Congress, Act of April 12, 1926, Exportation of Timber, 44 Stat. 242, 16 U.S.C. 616 (1926).

3. Alaska Administration Code, title 11, 76.130 (1974).

4. Or. Rev. Stat. 526.805 (1961). Cal. Pub. Res. Code §4605.1 (West, 1973).

5. U.S. Congress, Foreign Assistance Act of 1968, Pub. L. No. 90–554, Part IV, 82 Stat. 966, 16 U.S.C. 616 (1968).

6. Although hereafter we refer to the ban as applying to federal lands, only those lands administered by the Forest Service and the Bureau of Land Management are subject to the ban.

7. U.S. Congress, Department of the Interior and Related Agencies Appropriations Act of 1974, Pub. L. No. 93–120, Title III, 87 Stat. 447 (1973).

In addition to the current prohibition on the export of logs from federal lands and from state-owned lands in California and Oregon, there is a ban on exports from the Crown lands in British Columbia.[8] Given the existing export restrictions, private owners in Washington and Oregon and the Washington Department of Natural Resources (DNR) are virtually the only sources of softwood log exports, most of which go to Japan.[9]

There have been many attempts to enact legislation that would impose further export restrictions. Particular attention has been given to an extension that would cover state-owned lands in Washington. Washington's public timber resources are administered by the Washington DNR. An initiative that would have restricted exports from DNR lands was turned down by Washington voters in 1968, but similar proposals have been presented to almost every session of the state legislature since then.

The key features of the proposed legislation[10] would require that timber sold from DNR lands in the state of Washington after January 1, 1982, be given "primary processing" in the United States. Primary processing involves the conversion of logs into plywood lumber or some other finished forest product. Effectively the legislation would prohibit the export of raw logs or of crudely squared off logs called cants.

During the first year of a four-year phase-in period the act would require that 200 million board feet of DNR timber sold from the Washington public lands be given primary processing in the United States.[11] This limit would rise to 400 million board feet during the second year, to 600 million board feet during the third year, and to 800 million board feet during the fourth year. After January 1986 the law would require that not less than 80 percent of the timber sold annually from Washington State public lands receive primary processing in the United States. Given the 1978 volumes of DNR timber sales and exports, it appears that the act would be fully effec-

8. Forest Act, British Columbia Rev. Stat., Chapter 140 §135–37 (1979).

9. In addition to restrictions on softwood log exports, there is recent legislation prohibiting the export of red cedar logs in unprocessed form from public lands. See U.S. Congress, Export Administration Act of 1979, Pub. L. No. 96–72, 93 Stat. 521 (1979).

10. House Bill No. 218 for the 1981 regular session of the Forty-seventh Washington Legislature.

11. Since logs are not typically hauled great distances before being processed, the restriction would mean that most of the processing would occur in Washington. There would probably be some "leakage" into Oregon.

tive within three years. In addition, the law involves strict nonsubstitution provisions that would prohibit the purchase of DNR timber by anyone who exports from his/her own lands more than 15 percent of the average annual log consumption of his/her own processing facilities.

ECONOMIC ANALYSIS OF EXPORT BANS: BASIC RESULTS[12]

Some basic economic ideas and results will be used subsequently in the detailed analysis of the effects of a Washington export ban extension. Although none of the legislation considered above provides for a complete log export ban, analyzing the effects of a total ban is helpful because many of the key ideas are easiest to understand in that context.

The Effects of a Total Export Ban

The analysis of the effects of the total export ban represents an elementary extension of some simple results in international economics involving import tariffs and quotas. The analysis focuses on two trading regions: an exporting region (Washington) and an importing region (Japan), with a single traded commodity (logs). This viewpoint represents an extreme simplification of the actual trade situation because, in fact, Washington sells logs to other countries besides Japan, and Japan imports logs from sources other than Washington. Some of these details will be incorporated in a more elaborate model used to analyze the Washington ban extension because there is a connection between the log and lumber markets.

There are separate supply and demand conditions in the two regions that show the motive for exchange between them and the re-

---

12. For further literature on the economics of log export restrictions, see Jeff Harkins and Frank Selto, "The Regional Income Effects of a Log Export Policy: A Cost-Benefit Study," University of Washington, 1975 (mimeo); A. Clark Wiseman and Roger A. Sedjo, "Effects of an Export Embargo on Related Goods: Logs and Lumber," *American Journal of Agricultural Economics* 63 (August 1981): 423-29; and David R. Darr, Richard W. Haynes, and Darius M. Adams, "The Impact of the Export and Import of Raw Logs on Domestic Timber Supplies and Prices," USDA, Forest Service, Pacific Northwest Forest and Range Experiment Station, Research Paper PNW-277 (November 1980).

sulting free trade solution. Figures 10-1 and 10-3 show the domestic supply and demand curves for logs in Washington and Japan, respectively. At prices above P_2, Washington supply is greater than Washington demand and the difference is available for export. In Japan domestic demand for logs is greater than domestic supply at prices less than P_3. This difference between domestic demand and supply for prices below P_3 represents Japan's import demand. Figure 10-2 explicitly shows the export supply and import demand curves implicitly shown in Figures 10-1 and 10-3. At a price of P_2, for example, Washington export supply is zero—Washington consumers of logs are purchasing the entire output that producers are willing to offer at that price. At prices higher than P_2, the horizontal difference has been plotted between Washington demand and supply at each price to trace out the Washington export supply curve.

The Japanese import demand curve was derived in a similar fashion, starting from the price P_3 where Japanese demand equals Japanese supply and where the demand for imports is zero. In a world of free trade, the equilibrium price is P_1, the price at which the quantity of imports demanded equals the quantity of exports supplied.[13] At this point, Washington producers supply a quantity X_1 of logs per year. The quantity X_2 is sold in the domestic market, and the quantity $X_1 - X_2$ is exported. Japanese consumers purchase the quantity M_1 of logs, M_2 from domestic sources, and $M_1 - M_2$ from Washington. In Figure 10-2 the quantity of traded logs, Q_1, equals Washington exports, $X_1 - X_2$, and Japanese imports, $M_1 - M_2$.

If a total ban on log exports is imposed by Washington, the elimination of Japanese demand in the Washington market causes the Washington price to fall to P_2, the price at which Washington demand and supply are equal. Washington production falls to X_3. In Japan the price rises to P_3, and the quantity of logs consumed falls to M_3, the amount that Japanese producers are willing to supply.

These same diagrams can be used to show the welfare effects on the market participants in the two countries resulting from a complete ban on trade in logs. Washington consumers of logs, the wood-processing firms, have a gain in consumer surplus shown by the area

13. In this discussion transportation costs are zero. With positive transportation costs the free-trade equilibrium price in Japan will be greater than P_1, and the corresponding free-trade price in Washington will be less than P_1, with the difference being transportation costs.

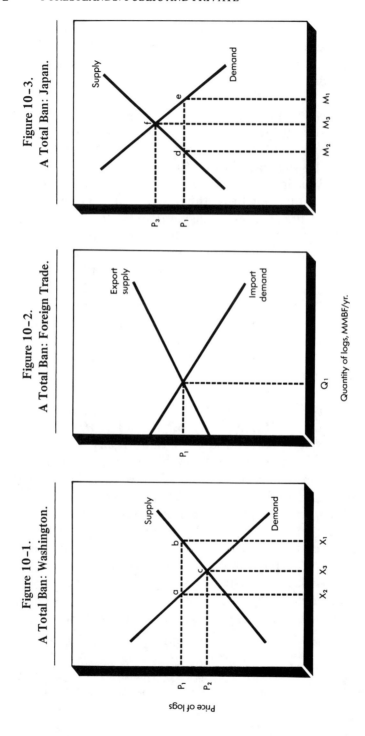

Figure 10-1.
A Total Ban: Washington.

Figure 10-2.
A Total Ban: Foreign Trade.

Figure 10-3.
A Total Ban: Japan.

$P_1 acP_2$ in Figure 10–1. Producers of logs, who receive a lower price for a smaller quantity of logs, lose producers' surplus equal to the area $P_1 bcP_2$. The loss to producers is greater than the gain to consumers by the amount shown by the triangle *abc.* For the Washington economy as a whole, there is a net loss resulting from the ban. In addition, Japanese log consumers must pay a higher price for a smaller quantity of logs.

The loss in consumer surplus to Japanese consumers is shown in Figure 10–3 as the area $P_3 feP_1$. Japanese log producers gain because they are able to sell more logs at a higher price. The increase in their producer surplus is $P_3 fdP_1$. As in the case of Washington, however, the gain to suppliers of logs is smaller than the loss to consumers, and the net effect in Japan is a welfare loss represented by the area *def.* The results are explained by the fact that Washington has a comparative advantage in log production, and when trade in logs is prohibited both countries suffer a net loss in welfare.

The Effect of a Partial Export Ban

Although the discussion of a complete ban is useful for understanding the economic effects of export restrictions, the analysis does not capture the characteristics of the present situation in Washington where there is a partial ban covering federal timber but where exports from private and DNR lands are permitted. If a bill banning the export of DNR logs were passed, private timber would still not be covered. Therefore, in order to understand the situation both before and after a DNR ban, the effects of a partial ban must be understood. In many contexts, a partial ban may be ineffective. In the present case it is important to understand when a partial ban would be effective in lowering prices to domestic processors and when it would not.

First consider the case where a federal ban would be ineffective. In the preban situation, domestic mills and Japanese purchasers would be buying logs from federal, state, and private sources. After the imposition of a ban on exports from federal lands, the Japanese would have to buy exclusively from the private sector and DNR. If the quantity of exportable logs supplied by them is large enough to meet Japanese demand at the existing price, the partial ban would have no major effect. It would switch the sources from which some

Figure 10-4. A Partial Ban.

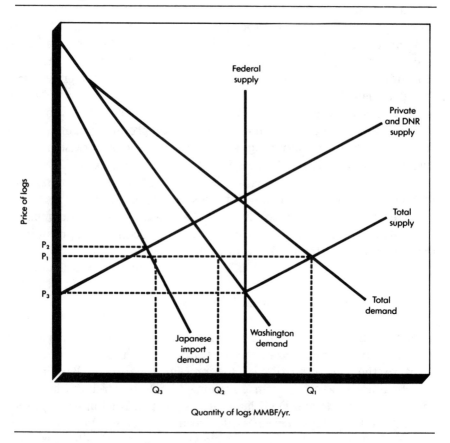

domestic processors and Japanese buyers obtain their logs. There would be some dislocation costs but no major price effect.

Figure 10-4 shows the conditions under which a ban would be effective. The supply function for logs from federal and DNR lands is assumed to be perfectly inelastic. (The justification for this assumption is provided in the next section.) The supply function for logs from private lands is assumed to be price responsive and the sum of supplies from federal, DNR, and private lands gives total supply. Total demand is the sum of Washington demand and Japanese import demand. With no ban in effect, the market equilibrium occurs where total quantity demanded equals total quantity supplied, at price P_1 and quantity Q_1. Of this quantity, Q_2 represents the quantity purchased by Washington processors and Q_3 the quantity purchased by Japan.

Now assume that the export of federal logs is prohibited. The quantity demanded by the Japanese at P_1 is greater than the amount produced by the private and DNR suppliers, and the export price is bid up to P_2. Federal supply is greater than domestic demand at P_1 and the domestic price falls to P_3. Figure 10-4 shows that for a ban to be effective, Japanese demand at P_1 *must* exceed nonrestricted supply. It is obvious that federal revenue declines while both domestic processors and private log exporters gain. It appears that the 1974 ban on the export of federal logs has been effective and has resulted in higher prices for export than for domestic logs in Washington.

This analysis ignores several real-world complexities. Figure 10-4 does not attempt to take into account the antisubstitution provisions of the federal ban and implicitly assumes that all logs are of the same quality. In fact, Japanese importers appear to be interested primarily in high quality, old growth timber.[14] If Washington processors are relatively indifferent to quality as long as differences in relative prices compensate for quality differences, Japanese demand for high quality timber will be greater than Washington DNR and private supply.

ANALYSIS OF A PROPOSED WASHINGTON DNR EXPORT BAN[15]

The Structure of Washington Log and Lumber Markets

There are three major groups of market participants and data on aggregate prices and quantities based on 1978 market data, which

---

14. In Japan the building construction methods involve greater use of *exposed* wooden structural elements and trim than is common with the cellular 2 X 4 methods used in the United States. This difference means that in Japan there is greater concern for the wood grain and color and other aspects of quality than there is in the United States.

15. See Barney Dowdle, "The Economics of Log Export Restrictions" (Seattle: University of Washington College of Forest Resources, 1979). (Mimeo.); idem, "Log Export Restrictions: Causes and Consequences," in Roger A. Sedjo, ed., *Issues in U.S. International Forest Products Trade* (Washington, D.C.: Resources for the Future, 1981); Roger A. Sedjo and A. Clark Wiseman, "The Effectiveness of an Export Restriction on Logs," *American Journal of Agricultural Economics* 65 (February 1983): 113-16.

provide a quantitative description of the participants' relative importance.

Timber Owners. Timber owners who ultimately provide the log flowing through the markets can be usefully categorized as follows:

Washington State Public Owners. The Washington DNR manages the state-owned timber. DNR is currently under legal mandate to sell state timber to the highest bidder. Logs harvested from DNR lands currently flow into both export and domestic log markets, and the stumpage prices paid for the rights to harvest from DNR lands reflect the opportunities to sell in both markets. The flow of logs from DNR lands is determined by DNR sales decisions. There is typically a variable one- to three-year lag between DNR stumpage sales and the ultimate harvest of logs from those lands. Over any extended period the supply of logs from DNR lands is under DNR's direct control despite the fact that some variation in timing can be effected by the successful bidders. The quantity of DNR sales is subject to administrative control, but the rules governing this administrative behavior are not entirely transparent to outside observers. It appears that DNR's sales roughly follow a sustained-yield policy that involves no supply response to changes in the market price. A few other state public timber owners, who together account for only a small fraction of the total supply of logs, have been included with DNR.

Private Timber Owners. This category includes both industrial and nonindustrial timber owners, some large and some small, and distinguishes between those timber suppliers who participate in export markets and those who do not. The major private timber owners normally participate in both domestic and export markets. The industrial owners may purchase timber from both DNR and from the Forest Service. Nonsubstitution provisions of the federal log export ban precludes participation by some private timber owners in the export market because of their need to purchase federal timber.

Private timber owners appear to be price sensitive in their supply response. Some private timber owners sell timber into both export and domestic markets. The stumpage price that affects these timber owners' supply decisions will reflect prices in both domestic and export log markets minus the relevant harvest and transport costs.

Other private suppliers of logs participate only in the domestic market. These private nonexporters include small farmers for whom the transactions costs of exporting are prohibitive, timber owners for whom transport costs to the nearest port are prohibitive, and timber owners who need to buy federal timber for their mills and are therefore restricted by the antisubstitution provisions of the federal export ban.

U.S. Federal Agencies. Federal timber in Washington State is managed primarily by the United States Forest Service. Federal timber makes up a major portion of the timberland located in the state of Washington, but since 1974 federal timber has been subject to an export ban and is sold only in the domestic market. Federal timber is cut according to a sustained-yield management policy that is insensitive to market price variations; hence, in the formal model, the assumption that federal timber is supplied perfectly inelastically is made.

Harvesters. The harvesting of timber is viewed as a competitive activity that converts standing timber into logs transported either to port or to processing mills. This activity is carried out by integrated firms as well as by independent harvesting contractors.

Processors. Processing encompasses the activity of turning logs into lumber, plywood, or other finished wood products. Processing is carried out both by integrated firms and by independent processors. Lumber and other final wood products flow into both Washington and non-Washington domestic markets as well as into export markets. In modeling the processing sector both in the United States and Japan, the simple but restricted view that processing involves some combination of capital and labor resources, which then combines in fixed proportions with logs to produce final wood products (which will be loosely referred to as lumber), will be adopted.

Prices and Quantities for 1978: The Dual Log Market. Table 10-1 shows total Washington State output of logs for 1978, the latest year for which reasonably complete market data are available. The output is broken down by major timber producers and also shows the allocation of total output between domestic and export markets. The log prices were roughly $295 and $210 per thousand

Table 10-1. Washington Timber Harvest, 1978 (million board feet scribner).

Destination	Export	Domestic	Total
Source:			
Private	1677	2359	4036
Washington public	520	435	955
Federal	8	1733	1741
Other public	37	13	50
Total	2242	4540	6782

Sources: State of Washington, Department of Natural Resources, *Timber Harvest Report* (1978); U.S. Forest Service, Pacific Northwest Forest and Range Experiment Station, *Production, Prices, and Employment, Fourth Quarter, 1979*; and State of Washington, Department of Natural Resources, *1973 Washington Mill Survey.*

board feet in the export and domestic markets respectively. Harvest and transport costs were approximately $100 per thousand board feet.

A comparison of the export and domestic prices reveals a real price differential that remains even after an adjustment for the quality and species differences in the material flowing through the two markets.[16] Normally, in a freely operating market, supply and demand adjustments eliminate any log price differential between the log prices in domestic and export markets. Given the free movement of logs between the two markets, the only price differentials that could be expected to persist would be those associated with quality or species differences. It was shown earlier, however, that a price differential can arise with the partial export ban in combination with strong Japanese preference for old growth timber. Although to some extent Japanese purchasers respond to price and alter the cutoff point in the quality of the timber that they buy, their actual behavior suggests very limited ability to substitute on the demand side. The substitution possibilities between size, species, and quality in domestic markets appear to be greater.

Given the fixed selection criteria for logs flowing into the export market, timber owners supplying the export market can be viewed as producing a joint product consisting of two kinds of logs. When an

16. Wesley Rickard, "Impact Analysis of a Complete Ban on Exportive Logs Originating From Lands Administered by the Washington State Department of Natural Resources— Long Term Revenue Impact" (Gig Harbor, Wash.: Wesley Rickard, 1981). (Mimeo.)

acre of standing timber is cut, it will yield a certain fraction of logs with the species, size, and quality characteristics desired by the export market. The remainder of the timber can be sold only in the domestic market. The Forest Service ban (with its nonsubstitution provisions), together with the inability or unwillingness of the Japanese to substitute in the quality spectrum, creates a situation in which an export price premium can arise because of the inability of the private suppliers to provide as many logs as the Japanese would like to buy.[17]

The dual price log market represents the starting point for any analysis of the consequences of a ban on the export of DNR timber. A DNR ban would be an extension of the existing Forest Service ban and would have the effect of further restricting the flow of exportable material into the export market and placing that material instead in the domestic market. The easily predictable consequences of such a ban extension are that export log prices would rise and domestic log prices would fall, thus increasing the export premium. The more difficult part of the analysis involves the behavior of the lumber market.

Japan currently imports both logs and lumber from Washington State. Imported logs are converted through Japanese processing into lumber and other final products. Since imported lumber must compete with lumber produced by Japan from Washington logs, it is clear the Japanese demands for lumber and logs are interrelated. An extension of the log ban to include DNR timber would, as indicated previously, lead to higher prices for logs sent to Japan. Higher prices for logs would have the effect of increasing the Japanese demand for imported lumber, a proportion of which would come from Washington. The size of this lumber feedback is crucial for determining the effects of a DNR export ban. The following model developed for predicting the consequences of a DNR ban attempts to describe the Japanese markets in enough detail to provide an estimate of the size of this feedback effect.

---

17. Roger A. Sedjo and A. Clark Wiseman, "On the Effectiveness of Log Export Restrictions."

A Washington-Japan Trade Model
for Logs and Lumber [18]

The model is constructed to focus on the consequences of the ban from the point of view of producers, consumers, and taxpayers in Washington. Although Washington and Japan are the primary actors in the model, other regions of the United States and other countries have roles, as well. Since the vast majority of Washington's log exports go to Japan, Japan is treated in the model as if it were the only destination in the model.

In the absence of export bans, it would be possible to model the trade between Washington and Japan by considering only two integrated markets: the log market and the lumber market. For each commodity, there would be a single price, apart from transportation costs, that would prevail in both countries. As explained above, the existing export restrictions have resulted in a split market for logs; therefore, three interrelated markets—the lumber market, the domestic log market, and the export log market—have been examined. These three markets are fully interdependent in the sense that quantities supplied and demanded in each market depend not only on the price in that market but also on the prices in the other markets.

The Japanese Import Demand for Logs and Lumber. The total quantity of lumber demanded by Japanese users is assumed to be inversely related to the market price of lumber in Japan. Japan produces the majority of its own lumber, using logs that come from Japanese forests, from Washington, and from other foreign sources. (The USSR is the chief other source for softwoods. A large quantity of hardwoods are imported from Indonesia, Malaysia, and the Philippines.) Table 10–2 shows the size and source of recent Japanese log imports. Japan also imports some lumber from Canada, the United States (including Washington), New Zealand, and the USSR. Table 10–3 shows the size and source of recent Japanese lumber imports.

Japan's total demand for logs is a derived demand that rests ultimately on its lumber demand (excluding lumber imports). The Japanese demand for Washington logs can be viewed as the difference be-

18. The complete algebraic specification of the model is presented in Richard W. Parks and Judith Cox, "The Effects of a Log Export Ban on Timber from Washington State Public Lands" (Seattle: University of Washington, 1981). (Mimeo.)

Table 10-2.   Japanese Log Imports by Source, 1978.

Origin	Volume Cubic Meters	c.i.f. Value 1000 Yen[c]	Volume MMBF Scribner
U.S.A.[a,b]	10,338,513	254,389,605	2585
USSR	8,834,238	108,752,988	1686
Canada	311,581	7,254,767	59
New Zealand	812,725	10,156,542	155
Indonesia[d]	9,217,769	148,976,860	1760
Malaysia[d]	10,517,824	158,648,058	2008
Philippines[d]	1,805,292	33,630,396	345
Other[d]	815,430	24,009,014	156

a. Imports from the USA are invoiced in Scribner units, then converted to cubic meters by multiplying by the factor 4. For USA imports column (3) is column (1) × (0.25). Imports from other countries are invoiced in cubic meters. They have been converted to Scribner units using the more standard .1909 multiplication factor.

b. Imports from Washington represent 1907 MMBF Scribner of total imports from USA.

c. 1978 exchange rate 210.49 yen/$U.S.

d. Log imports from Indonesia, Malaysia, Philippines, and Other (mainly Africa) are largely hardwoods.

Source: Japan Lumber Journal 21 (September 30, 1980): 4-5.

Table 10-3.   Japanese Softwood Lumber Imports by Origin, 1978.

Origin	MMBF Lumber Tally
United States	554
Canada	1026
USSR	72
New Zealand	126

Note: Washington's lumber exports represent 141 MMBF of the U.S. total.
Source: Japan Lumber Journal 21 (September 30, 1980): 4-5.

tween its total log demand and the supply of logs from Japan and other non-Washington sources.

The link between the lumber demand and the log demand comes through the processing technology. A simple, fixed-coefficient production relation in which lumber (the output) is produced using logs (the raw material input) and processing or "manufacturing" has been assumed. The manufacturing input is actually a combination of capital, labor, and other inputs. The Japanese lumber technology can be described by specifying the input-output coefficients for logs and for manufacturing (the quantity of log inputs per unit of lumber and the quantity of manufacturing inputs per unit of lumber). From this perspective, the supply price of lumber produced in Japan is simply a weighted sum of the prices of the log and manufacturing inputs, with the input-output coefficients as the weights.

The Japanese demands for lumber and logs imported from Washington are interrelated in the following way. For any given log price, the import demand for lumber will be a declining function of the lumber price, and the higher the log price the larger will be the lumber import demand. The lumber import demand takes into account both the availability of lumber from other foreign sources and the self-supplied lumber because of its dependence on the log price. Similarly, the Japanese demand for logs imported from Washington, allowing for the availability of logs from Japan and other foreign sources, depends inversely on the log price and positively on the lumber price.

Washington Log and Lumber Markets.   In Washington the domestic log and lumber markets are connected because the logs are the main input into lumber production. In addition, since some timber owners supply logs to both the domestic and export markets, their supply decision will depend on the prices available in both markets.

The total supply of logs from Washington DNR lands is exogenously determined and price inelastic. Recent observations suggest that approximately 60 percent of DNR logs are of export quality. The remaining 40 percent flow into the domestic log market. The total quantity of logs supplied by the Forest Service and other federal agencies is also assumed to be exogenously determined and price inelastic. All of these federal logs must be sold in the domestic market.

Some private suppliers of logs sell in both export and domestic markets, and as with DNR, roughly 60 percent of their logs are of export quality. These private suppliers are responsive to price. The total quantity of logs supplied by them will be an upward sloping, linear function of a stumpage price that is a blend of the log prices in export and domestic markets adjusted for the costs of harvest and transportation.

Private nonexporters are also assumed to be price responsive in their supply decisions, and their supply function is assumed to be linear and positively sloped. The stumpage price to which they respond is based entirely on the domestic log price adjusted for harvest and transportation costs. Based on these supply assumptions, the total supply of logs into both export and domestic markets will depend jointly on the prices observed in these two markets.

In the lumber market the demand for Washington lumber by all buyers except the Japanese is a simple, downward sloping function of the Washington lumber price. For Washington's lumber processing sector, as for Japan's, logs—the raw material input—combine together with manufacturing inputs in fixed proportions to produce lumber.

From these assumptions the demand for the domestic Washington logs used in the production of Washington lumber can be derived. This demand function will depend inversely on the domestic log price and positively on the domestic lumber price. Finally, the supply of Washington lumber depends positively on the lumber price and negatively on the log price.

By assembling the basic supply and demand functions, a complete specification for the export and domestic log markets and for the Washington lumber market where these markets include the net import demand for logs and lumber by Japan can be obtained. The solution of the model provides the set of prices in these three markets that equate the quantities supplied with quantities demanded. The ban would result in a shift of the currently exported DNR timber into the domestic market. The model then predicts the price *changes* in each of the three markets that would result from imposition of the ban.

A Graphical Analysis of a DNR Ban.   Some aspects of the model are difficult to convey graphically because of the interrelations among the variables, but the graphical analysis helps to demonstrate most key aspects of the model.

Figure 10-5 represents the export log market. Before imposition of the ban, the DNR supply to the export market is shown as being perfectly inelastic. Total supply to the export market is the sum of the DNR export supply and the exportable component from private exporters. (For both the DNR and for these private exporters, approximately 60 percent of the harvested logs are export quality.)

The Washington domestic log and lumber markets are represented in Figures 10-6 and 10-7.[19] Since there are no restrictions on lum-

19. The horizontal scales of Figures 10-6 and 10-7 are linked to show the assumed fixed relation between the quantity of logs and the quantity of lumber. In Washington the proportion is about 1.3 board feet of lumber per board foot of log.

Figure 10-5.   Export Log Market.

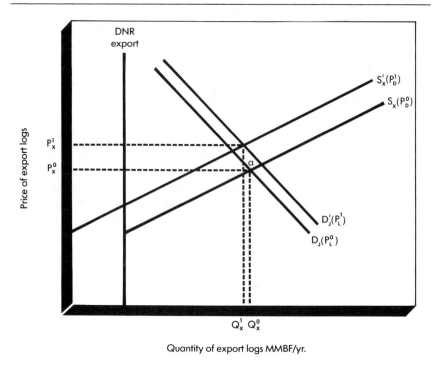

Quantity of export logs MMBF/yr.

ber exports, both domestic lumber demand and the Japanese lumber demand combine in the same market. The domestic log and lumber markets are interrelated because the domestic log demand is derived from the total lumber demand given the fixed relationship assumed between logs and lumber.

The demand for Washington-produced lumber, D_L, is shown as a downward sloping function of the lumber price, but its position depends on the price of logs in the export market. The derived demand for logs in the domestic market depends, in turn, not only on the domestic log price but also on the lumber price. The supply function for domestic logs is represented by S_D, and includes the inelastic supply from federal lands and the nonexported portion from DNR lands in addition to the price-responsive supply from both private exporters and nonexporters. The lumber supply function is shown as the positively sloped S_L, but its position also depends on the domestic log price P_D.

Figure 10-6. Domestic Log Market.

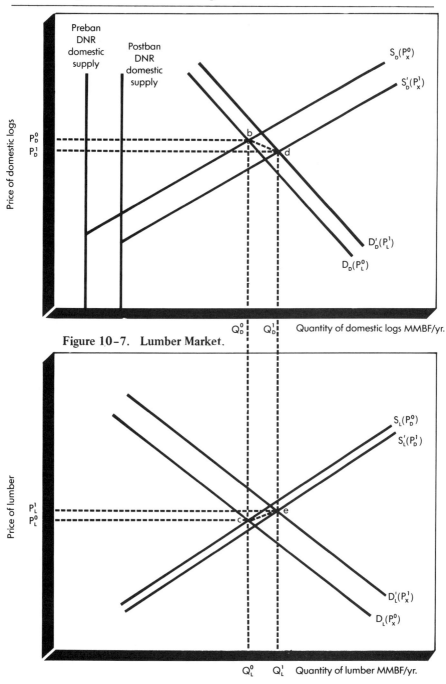

Figure 10-7. Lumber Market.

An initial equilibrium position is shown in these three figures at points a, b, and c with prices P_D^0 and P_L^0 in the domestic log and lumber markets, and with price P_X^0 in the export log market. Notice that to be fully consistent, the positions of the interdependent functions that have been drawn must correspond with the actual equilibrium prices. In 1978 the prices in export and domestic log markets were $295 per thousand board feet (MBF) Scribner and $195 per MBF Scribner, respectively, and in the lumber market the price was $226 per MBF lumber tally. Total exports of logs were 2242 million board feet (MMBF) Scribner, of which 520 MMBF came from DNR lands. Domestic log supply was 4540 MMBF.

If a DNR export ban were imposed, the initial consequence would be a reduction in the supply of logs going into the export market and an increase by the same amount in the supply going into the domestic market. This shift is shown in Figures 10–5 and 10–6 by the functions S_X' and S_D'. Although these supply changes are represented by shifts in the export and domestic supply functions, the actual changes implied by the rest of the model are a bit more complicated because of the interrelations among the functions. The shifted demand functions in the figures represent those consistent with the new equilibrium after the interrelated changes have been completed. The new equilibrium involves a higher export log price P_X^1 and a lower domestic log price P_D^1. Japan's import demand for lumber has shifted outward because of the higher export log price so that the new lumber demand is D_L'. Lumber supply has also shifted outward to S_L' because of the lower domestic log price. The net effect on the Washington lumber price depends critically on the parameter values, but for many reasonable values it rises slightly to P_L^1, as shown in Figure 10–7.

Quantitative Results of a DNR Ban

Predicting Price and Quantity Changes.   In order to develop quantitative predictions of the effects of a DNR ban, a formal, locally linear version of the model is used. All of the supply and demand functions were written to be linear in terms of the price and quantity variables. Equating supply and demand in the three markets results in a set of equations that, in principle, could be solved for the set of initial prices in the three markets. Actual 1978 prices and quantities were used to represent this initial situation, and were then solved for the *change* in prices that would result from the shift of DNR timber from the export to the domestic market. The price *change* solution involves only the slope parameters of the basic supply and demand relations together with the input-output coefficients. The values used for parameters were taken from what were judged to be the best published studies and industry estimates.

The principal results include an increase of $10.55 in the export log price, a decline of $7.31 in the domestic log price, and an increase of $.08 in lumber prices. This small lumber price change represents the offsetting effects of a decline in domestic wood costs on the one hand and the increase in our net lumber export demand on the other. At the same time log exports would decline by 502 MMBF Scribner while domestic log sales would increase by 491 MMBF Scribner. Domestic lumber production would rise by 701 MMBF (lumber tally) with net exports (exports minus imports) rising by 711 MMBF.[20] A detailed discussion of the parameter estimates used for the study is given in Parks and Cox.[21]

Gains and Losses to Groups in Washington.   Having determined the price changes expected to result from a DNR export ban, gains and losses to groups in the state of Washington are calculated in a fairly straightforward manner. Price and quantity data for 1978 provide the reference points from which the changes are computed.

Forest Service.   The Forest Service sells all of its stumpage in the domestic market where a DNR ban is predicted to produce a price decline of $7.31 per MMBF Scribner. The amount of stumpage

---

20. A number of sensitivity tests varying the elasticity assumptions underlying the slope parameters, were undertaken. The results of the model are quite robust for different values of the elasticities of non-Japanese demand for Washington lumber, Japanese lumber demand, non-Washington lumber supply, and Washington exporters' and nonexporters log supply. Raising or lowering the elasticity of each of these items by 50 percent gives predicted price changes for export logs, domestic logs and lumber that differ from the results by very small amounts. The results are more sensitive to changes in the supply elasticity of processing inputs in lumber manufacturing and the Japanese log supply elasticity.

The elasticities of the predicted price changes with respect to changes in the underlying parameters are generally well below unity. The exception is the lumber price change, which is quite sensitive. In all cases, however, the actual magnitude of lumber price changes is small and makes a minor contribution to the overall welfare measure.

21. Richard W. Parks and Judith Cox, "The Effects of a Log Export Ban on Timber from Washington State Public Lands."

auctioned by the Forest Service is assumed to be insensitive to changes in market price; therefore, if a DNR ban had been established in 1978 the Forest Service loss would have been $7.31 × 1733 MMBF = $12,668,000.[22] One quarter of the Forest Service stumpage revenue goes to Washington counties in lieu of property taxes. Thus, the loss to Washington from the decrease in Forest Service revenues would have been .25 × $12,668,000 = $3,167,000.

Department of Natural Resources. For the Washington DNR, as in the case of the Forest Service, the amount of stumpage put up for auction is determined by an administrative rule that is largely insensitive to the market price. The loss from a ban on the exportation of DNR logs is twofold. First, DNR loses the export premium ($85 per MBF) on the 520 MMBF previously exported, and it must now sell this material at the new domestic price, which is $7.31 per MBF lower than before the ban. The loss on previous exports is 520 MMBF × $92.31 per MBF = $48,001,000. Second, the 435 MMBF of nonexportable DNR logs that were originally in the domestic market would now sell at a lower domestic price, producing a loss of 435 MMBF × $7.31 per MBF = $3,180,000. The total loss in DNR revenue is $51,181,000. Since this revenue forms part of the state's school trust funds, it is clearly not the agency—the Department of Natural Resources—that suffers the loss, but rather the citizens and taxpayers of Washington.

Private Nonexporting Timber Owners. The loss to these price-responsive producers is shown schematically in Figure 10–8. As the domestic log price falls from P_D^0 to P_D^1 per MBF as a result of the ban, the nonexporters' stumpage price, P_N, falls by an equal amount, and the quantity supplied falls from Q_N^0 to Q_N^1. Their loss is the hatched area and is equal to $\Delta P_N Q_N^0 - 0.5 \Delta P_N \Delta Q_N$, where Δ denotes the change in the variable from preban to postban situations. For 1978 the measured loss is ($7.31) (1241 MMBF) − (0.5) ($7.31) (41.24 MMBF) = $8,921,000.

Washington Lumber (And Other Wood Products) Consumers. Previously the demand curve for Washington-produced lumber was included in the specification of the model. In calculating the gains and losses to citizens of Washington State, only the demand for lumber by Washington citizens must be considered. The quantity

---

22. All the welfare calculations are rounded off to the nearest thousand dollars.

Figure 10-8. Nonexporters.

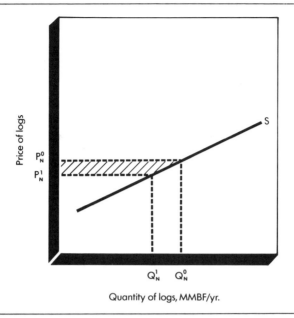

Figure 10-9. Lumber Market.

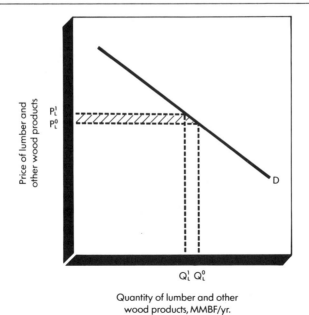

Figure 10–10. Exporters.

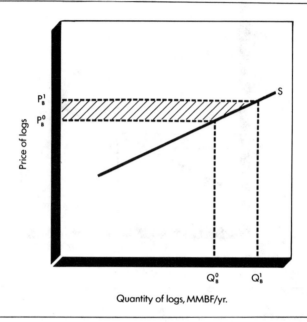

demanded differs from the output of Washington-*produced* lumber because in 1978 Washington was exporting finished lumber products. *Net* consumption was 975 MMBF. The changes in domestic log and lumber prices should also result in a change in the prices of other wood products made from softwood logs such as plywood, shingles, shakes, poles, and pilings. The effects of these price changes should also be included in welfare calculations. Their prices should rise also by $.08 per MBF lumber equivalent, but the demand response to this price change is negligible. The change in the price of lumber and other wood products results in a loss of $\Delta P_L\, Q_L^0 - 0.5\Delta P_L\, \Delta Q_L$, = (2292 MMBF) ($.08) – (0.5) ($.08) (.104 MMBF) = $183,000. This loss is shown as the shaded area in Figure 10–9.

Private Exporters. Private producers who currently participate in both the export and domestic market respond to the blend price, $P_B = [(0.6P_X - \text{harvest costs}) - (0.4\,P_D - \text{harvest costs})]$ when making their supply decisions. As a result of the ban, the blend price rises from \$161.00 to \$164.40 per MBF and the quantity produced rises from Q_B^0 = 2795 MMBF to Q_B^1 = 2825 MMBF. The gain to private exporters is thus $\Delta P_B \, Q_B^0 + 0.5 \, \Delta P_B \, \Delta Q_B$ = (\$3.40) (2795 MMBF) + (0.5) (\$3.40) (29.5 MMBF) = \$9,553,000, shown by the hatched area in Figure 10-10. They lose by having to sell in the domestic market at a lower price than before, but gain on their sales in the export market. This net gain will mean an increase in private timber companies' stumpage values. Twenty-eight percent of this figure will go to the federal government in the form of capital gains taxes, with the remainder (\$6,878,000) being a gain to Washington.[23]

Washington Processors. Washington processors gain because of the decrease in domestic log prices and the increase in lumber prices. Referring back to Figure 10-6, the initial equilibrium in the domestic log market is at point b with price P_D^0 and quantity Q_D^0. The new equilibrium after the ban, including the lumber feedback effects, is at point d, with price P_D^1 and quantity Q_D^1. The gain to processors from lower log prices is $P_D^0 \, bdP_D^1 = \Delta P_D \, Q_D^0 + 0.5 \, \Delta P_D \, \Delta Q_D$ = (\$7.31) (4540 MMBF) + (0.5) (\$7.31) (490.6 MMBF) = \$34,981,000.

In Figure 10-7 the initial equilibrium for lumber and other wood products is shown at point c, where the price is P_L^0 and the quantity is Q_L^0. After the imposition of the DNR ban, the new equilibrium in the lumber market is at point e with price P_L^1 and quantity Q_L^1. The gain to processors from higher prices for lumber and other wood products is $P_L^1 \, ceP_L^0 = \Delta P_L \, Q_L^0 + 0.5 \Delta P_L \, \Delta Q_L$ = (\$.08) (5902 MMBF) + (0.5) (\$.08) (702 MMBF) = \$500,000. The total gain to processors, therefore, is \$35,481,000 – the sum of their gains in the log and lumber markets.

Table 10-4 summarizes the gains and losses for all the groups in the state of Washington.

CONCLUSION: THE POLITICAL ECONOMY OF EXPORT BANS

Two interesting political economy issues emerge from the discussion of log export restrictions. The first issue concerns the conditions necessary for the formation of coalitions and for their success in influ-

---

23. Twenty-eight percent represents the 1978 capital gains tax. It has since been lowered.

Table 10-4. Gains and Losses to Groups in the State of Washington Resulting from a DNR Export Ban.

Losses:		
Forest Service		$ 3,167,000
DNR		51,181,000
Private nonexporters		8,921,000
Washington consumers		183,000
	Total losses	$63,452,000
Gains:		
Private exporters		$ 6,878,000
Washington processors		35,481,000
	Total gains	$42,359,000
	NET LOSS	$21,093,000

encing public policy. Over the past twenty-five years a number of authors have addressed this issue.[24] They point out that in the political marketplace, small groups with concentrated interests, whose wealth will be significantly affected by a particular piece of legislation, may be able to mobilize the political process to transfer wealth from the public at large to themselves. Groups with a small number of participants and concentrated interests are predicted to be more highly motivated and more successful at organizing and financing such an endeavor. When the number of losers are many and losses to each individual are small, the opposition is likely to be ineffective.

The development of the log export ban issue fits this general model of the political process. The primary beneficiaries of a log export ban (and the only beneficiaries of a total ban) are the lumber mills. The number of processors is relatively small and potential gains to each from a successful export ban are substantial. Thus their financial interests are concentrated enough and the transactions costs of organizing and eliminating free riders is small enough for them to lobby for further export restrictions.

24. Some of the seminal work on this topic has been done by Anthony Downs, *An Economic Theory of Democracy* (New York: Harper & Row, 1957); Mancur Olson, Jr., *The Logic of Collective Action* (Cambridge, Mass.: Harvard University Press, 1965); George J. Stigler, "The Theory of Economic Regulation," *Bell Journal of Economics and Management Science* 2 (Spring 1971): 3-21; and Sam Peltzman, "Toward a More General Theory of Regulation," *Journal of Law and Economics* 19 (August 1976): 211-40.

The primary losers are the taxpayers. Although the public agencies involved, such as the Forest Service and the DNR, represent taxpayer interests to some extent, they are less likely to be as vigorous in their opposition to the bans as would a private firm.

The theories mentioned above explain why there are likely to be export restrictions on intermediate goods, such as logs, rather than on final consumer goods. The theories do not explain why export restrictions have been used so infrequently as a tool of U.S. commercial policy. Part of the explanation may lie in the fact that export taxes are prohibited by the Constitution; although there surely are cases, other than logs, where domestic processors would benefit from an export ban.

In focusing on the identity of the gainers and losers from the ban, the large, integrated forest products firms seem to represent a paradox. As major private exporters, they would benefit substantially in the short run from the DNR ban. These companies, however, have consistently opposed the ban extension. The explanation appears to involve the distinction between short-run profit and long-run wealth maximization. These companies seem to hold a domino theory of log bans. Given the existence of the federal ban, if processors are successful at extending the ban to DNR lands, their next target will be private lands. Many Washington lumber mills have old and inefficient facilities, so the prospect of further reductions in their raw materials costs from a complete export ban is attractive. For integrated companies with large inventories of timber, the potential long-run loss in wealth from further export restrictions appears to dominate the prospect of a short-run gain from the DNR ban.

The second issue involves the role of an individual state in formulating foreign trade policy. With all of the other bans in place, DNR exports accounted for 12 percent of Japanese softwood log imports in 1978. Banning DNR log exports would have an important effect on Japan, but one whose welfare consequences have not yet been measured. In trade negotiations with Japan over concessions sought by the United States, such as "voluntary" export quotas on Japanese cars, the consequences of a Washington State export ban could be an important issue.

Chapter 11

THE SIMPLE ANALYTICS OF FOREST ECONOMICS

Robert T. Deacon

The allocation of forest resources in the United States is affected by public policy in a variety of ways. Direct control is exercised over public forestlands owned by the federal government and managed by the U.S. Forest Service and the Bureau of Land Management, as well as forests owned by state and local governments. The national forests, under Forest Service administration, account for about 18 percent of the commercial forest acreage in the United States and for over 45 percent of the softwood growing stock, as figures in the first two rows of Table 11–1 show. Holdings of other public agencies amount to an additional 10 percent of forestland acreage and 11 percent of growing softwood inventories.

Public policy also influences timber supplies from private lands by altering the rules and incentives under which private owners operate. Both the magnitudes of tax rates and the form of taxation (i.e., whether levied on yields, property values, or forest products income) affect the relative profitability of alternative rotation and reforestation strategies. Environmental regulations impose direct constraints on the construction of roads and the application of herbicides, and often prescribe both logging and reforestation practices to protect habitats.

Without implicating them for any errors or conclusions this chapter may contain, I wish to thank Margriet Caswell, Perry Shapiro, and John Sonstelie for valuable comments on an earlier draft.

A general economic framework for analyzing allocations of timber resources can be developed in nontechnical terms. The economic decisions of private timber producers are influenced by a wide range of factors including input and output prices, interest rates, tax policy, and environmental and other regulations. To accurately assess the effects of public policy on the decisions of private foresters, an understanding of these economic relationships is clearly important. At the same time, an economic analysis of the costs and benefits of alternative strategies is necessary for evaluating management policy on public forests.

Most treatments of the economics of forestry have been either mathematical in nature, or incorrect in certain important respects.[1] The use of mathematics in the present survey is minimal; rather, important points are demonstrated graphically and explained intuitively wherever possible. The general principle of comparing benefits and costs provides a unifying theme. When benefits and costs are defined to include only factors that enter the profit calculus of the private forest owner, the result is a description of self-interested behavior, a useful guide to the positive analysis of market outcomes. When suitably adapted, the benefit-cost framework also provides a natural vehicle for the analysis of alternative public management strategies.[2] The classic economic problem of when, or at what age, a private owner will harvest a forest is the starting point for the analysis. The concepts and terms developed are then used to examine the sustained-yield forestry practices currently mandated for public lands.

---

1. Examples of rather mathematical presentations are M. Gaffney, "Concepts of Financial Maturity of Timber and Other Assets," *Agricultural Economics Information Series*, No. 62 (Raleigh: North Carolina State College, 1957); J. Hirshleifer, *Investment, Interest, and Capital* (Englewood Cliffs, N.J.: Prentice-Hall, 1970); C. W. Howe, *Natural Resource Economics* (New York: John Wiley and Sons, 1979), ch. 14; and Paul A. Samuelson, "The Economics of Forestry in an Evolving Society," *Economic Inquiry* 14 (1976): 466–92. Relatively nontechnical accounts may be found in Irving Fisher, *The Theory of Interest* (New York: Macmillan, 1930), pp. 160 ff.; and in G. K. Goundrey, "Forest Management and the Theory of Capital," *Canadian Journal of Economics and Political Science* 62 (1960): 124–42. However, both presentations contain important analytical flaws; see Samuelson, "The Economics of Forestry," for a discussion. For an excellent nontechnical analysis of selected topics, see Y. Levy, "An Economic Alternative to Current Public Forest Policy," in *Economic Review* (San Francisco: Federal Reserve Bank, 1978), pp. 20–39.

2. The benefit-cost approach has been widely applied to public sector decisionmaking and has been legally mandated for the analysis of federal water resource projects. Hence, its potential relevance for public forest policy is clear. See Howe, *Natural Resource Economics*, for further discussion of the uses of benefit-cost analysis.

Table 11-1. Growth, Productivity, and Growing Stocks on Public and Private Forestlands, 1977.

	National Forests	*Forest Industry Forests*	*Total, All Ownership*
Land area of commercial timberland (1000 acres)[a]	88,718	68,782	482,486
Softwood growing stock (millions of cubic feet)	207,699	74,382	455,779
Annual net growth of growing stock (millions of cubic feet)	2,465	2,866	12,285
Ratio of growing stock to annual growth	84.25	25.96	37.10
Annual growth per acre (cubic feet)			
actual	35	59	45
potential	74	87	74
actual as percent of potential	47%	68%	61%

a. The other major ownership categories are "other public" and "farmer and other private." The latter group consists primarily of small individual holdings, which, though an important source of commercial timber, are often managed for objectives not compatible with timber harvesting.

Source: USDA, Forest Service, *An Analysis of the Timber Situation in the United States, 1952-2030*, Forest Resource Report no. 23 (Washington, D.C.: Government Printing Office, December 1982).

The same tools are used to study the competitive market supply of timber and the relationships between supply and costs, prices, interest rates, and alternative tax instruments.

THE HARVESTING DECISION

How long will a private entrepreneur allow a stand of trees to grow before harvest? This is, of course, only one of many economic decisions the owner must make. Other economic choices involve outlays for disease control, for the labor and equipment used in thinning, fire suppression, and reforestation, and for research directed toward genetic enhancement. However, the long-lived nature of the resource and the long-run character of timber production make the harvest age problem particularly interesting.

Although actual forest harvest decisions result from long-run planning, and are presumably decided well in advance of the actual harvest date, it is useful for expositional purposes to imagine the forest owner re-examining the harvest decision anew each year. When considering whether or not to allow the stand to mature an extra year before harvesting, a rational decision requires a comparison of the benefits and costs of waiting. The benefits to the private forest owner are reflected in the value of salable timber that will be grown during the waiting period. The amount of new growth obtained per year will depend on the age of the stand and will eventually decline as the stand matures.

The costs of delaying the harvest are represented by the value of receipts that are forgone when the stand is allowed to grow for an additional year. The stock of growing timber is a "capital" asset. If, instead of being allowed to grow, it was harvested and the proceeds invested, it would earn interest for the owner. Thus, the forgone return on the stock of standing timber is a cost of allowing the forest to mature. A second cost is associated with the use of forestland to support an additional year of growth in a standing forest. This cost equals the forgone return from the highest valued alternative service the land could have provided during that period.[3] In some cases the highest valued alternative use will be in growing future stands of timber, an activity that requires the existing stand be cut. In other cases the highest valued alternative may lie in some nonforest use such as farming or residential development.

If in a particular period the benefit of waiting an extra year outweighs the cost, then the rational forest owner will postpone the harvest. As the stand matures, the rate of growth will decline, and the benefit from further delays in harvesting will diminish. Eventually, the benefit to waiting an extra year will fall to the point where it just equals the cost of waiting, and no further postponement is profitable. At that age the stand has reached "financial maturity" and will be harvested.

---

3. The stock of timber capital and the parcel of land the forest occupies may be viewed as two inputs. Use of those inputs for a year is required to produce one year's growth. Accordingly, the marginal cost of waiting is simply the cost of using two inputs for one year.

A Simple Harvesting Problem

To illustrate the preceding concepts and to develop notation that will be useful in subsequent analysis, consider a highly simplified situation in which both the real rate of interest and the real price of timber net of any harvesting cost are expected to remain constant in the future. Furthermore, the only economically scarce input needed to grow timber is the capital embodied in the growing stock. Whatever land is required for growth is assumed to have no opportunity cost.[4] At issue is the age at which a given stand of trees will be harvested by a rational owner. The following notation can be used to address this question:

T the age of trees in the stand;

$f(T)$ the volume of timber available for harvest, if left to grow until age T;

$\Delta f(T)$ the annual growth of the stand, at age T;

r the real rate of return (interest) on alternative investments;

p the real price of timber, net of any harvest costs.

The term T has been incorporated into the above notation for f and Δf as a reminder that both the volume of timber in the stand and its annual rate of growth will change as the stand ages. Where no confusion will result, the T will be dropped to simplify expressions.

With the preceding notation, the benefit from waiting an extra year before harvesting—denoted *MB* (waiting)—is simply the value of new growth, the product of annual growth, and the net price of timber,

$$MB \text{ (waiting)} = p\Delta f .$$

If the owner decides to wait, the opportunity to earn the market return on the net value of harvested timber will be forgone. Thus, the

---

4. To the private entrepreneur, an absence of opportunity cost would be reflected in a zero market price for bare timberland. This may have been relevant at some historic time when timberland was so plentiful that it could not command a positive price. At present it may apply, at least approximately, to acreage that is either sufficiently unproductive or remote from market centers that no significant rent can be charged for its use.

marginal cost of waiting is the product of the rate of return and the value of the harvested stand,

$$MC \text{ (waiting) } = rpf \ .$$

If these terms represent the only costs and benefits relevant to the problem, then the rational decisionmaker will continue to postpone harvesting so long as the benefit of doing so exceeds the cost. At some age, however, the two will be equal,

$$p\Delta f = rpf \ , \tag{1}$$

and the forest will be harvested. Any additional delays beyond that critical age would involve costs that exceed benefits. If the net price p is cancelled from both sides of this expression, one obtains a benefit-cost condition expressed in physical units,

$$\Delta f = rf \ . \tag{2}$$

This form of the harvest age criterion is particularly useful for a diagrammatic analysis.

A third representation of this condition can be obtained by dividing both sides of equation (2) by the volume of the stand, f,

$$\Delta f/f = r \ . \tag{3}$$

This is a condition that figured prominently in Irving Fisher's analysis of the forest-harvesting decision.[5] The left hand side of equation (3) is the proportionate rate of growth of the forest, and it represents the physical rate of return on the stock of growing timber. With this interpretation, the benefit-cost decision rule indicates that the owner will liquidate the stand when its own rate of return falls to equality with the return available on other investments.

The preceding analysis has a ready diagrammatic interpretation. Figure 11-1 depicts a growth function for the stand of trees in question. On the horizontal axis is the age of the stand (T); the volume of timber (f), measured in thousands of cubic feet per acre, is shown on the vertical axis. The shape of the curve in Figure 11-1 is representative of growth characteristics for Douglas fir.[6] The exact pat-

5. Fisher, *The Theory of Interest*, pp. 163, 164.

6. See R. McArdle, "The Yield of Douglas Fir in the Pacific Northwest," *U. S. Department of Agriculture Technical Bulletin*, No. 201, Washington, D.C., 1949.

Figure 11-1. Typical Growth for Douglas Fir.

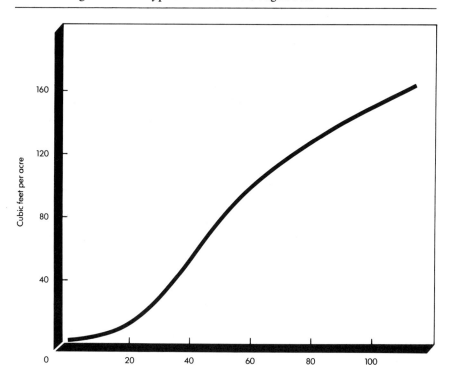

tern of growth for a particular forest would, of course, depend on the species in question and prevailing growing conditions.

The growth function in Figure 11-1 was used to derive two of the curves in Figure 11-2, those labeled Δf and rf. (The third curve, denoted $rf + R/p$, is discussed in the next section.) The vertical dimension of Figure 11-2 has been expanded to permit easier inspection. The curve labeled Δf is simply the annual rate of growth, that is, the annual change in f at each age. Consequently, it shows the marginal benefit of waiting expressed in physical units. The curve denoted rf in Figure 11-2 is proportional in height to the growth function f in Figure 11-1. If, for example, the real rate of interest (r) were 2 percent (the interest rate used in drawing Figure 11-2), the curve would at each age be exactly 2 percent as high as f in Figure 11-1. In the harvesting decision discussed above, rf represents the marginal cost of waiting for the stand to mature, where cost is measured in physical units. The solution to the harvesting problem occurs where the two curves intersect. At this age, denoted T^1, the benefit-cost condition in equation (2) is satisfied.

Due to the simplifications present in this problem, particularly the assumption that the use of timberland has no opportunity cost, its analysis is of limited interest. Before examining more general cases, however, this simple example may be used to illustrate the sensitivity of the harvest age to the real rate of interest. If r were higher, the curve labeled rf in Figure 11-2 would lie above its present position, and the equilibrium harvest age would be lower. The effect of a higher rate of interest is to increase the marginal cost of waiting at all ages and to commensurately reduce the amount of time the owner will find it profitable to wait. Using a symmetric argument it is easy to show that a lower rate of interest would have resulted in a longer waiting time and older age at harvest.

Figure 11-2. Determination of the Harvest Age.

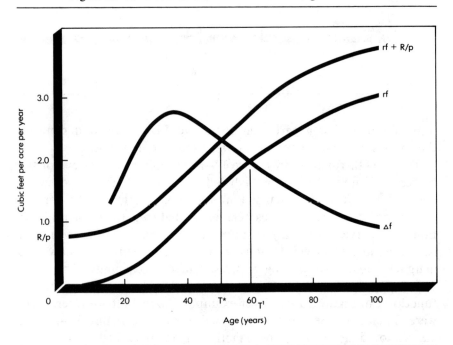

Harvesting and Reforestation

Land used to support growth of standing forests generally has economic value in alternative uses.[7] These alternatives might range from reforesting and growing a new crop of timber to clearing the land for farming to subdividing into residential parcels. The opportunity cost of allowing a standing forest to occupy the land for an additional year is the value of these forgone uses. In the market, this opportunity cost would be reflected in the rent charged or imputed for use of the land. Letting R denote this per period cost, the benefit-cost criterion for the optimum harvest age becomes

$$p\Delta f = rpf + R \ . \tag{4}$$

The marginal cost of waiting, represented by the right-hand side of the equation, now has two components. This reflects the fact that two economically scarce inputs, timber capital and timberland, with per period opportunity costs of rpf and R, respectively, are required to produce new growth. As before, it is advantageous for graphical analysis to express this benefit-cost condition in physical terms. This is accomplished by dividing both sides of equation (4) by the price of timber to yield

$$\Delta f = rf + R/p \ . \tag{5}$$

The term R/p now represents the opportunity cost of land expressed in units of timber per period.

At an intuitive level the introduction of an additional component to the marginal cost of waiting reduces the age at which trees are harvested. This is confirmed in Figure 11–2 where the new marginal cost function is drawn as $rf + R/p$. The vertical distance between old and new marginal cost curves is R/p, the opportunity cost of using the land, and the introduction of this cost reduces the equilibrium growing span from T^1 to T^* years. It is also true that at T^* the percentage rate of growth of the forest exceeds the real rate of interest. Thus

---

7. The investment problem addressed in this section was first successfully analyzed by Martin Faustmann, "On the Determination of the Value Which Forestland and Immature Stands Possess for Forestry," 1849, trans. M. Gane, *Oxford Institute Paper* 42 (1968). The following discussion is rather brief, and the reader who wishes more detail or rigor should consult Gaffney, "Concepts of Financial Maturity"; Hirshleifer, *Investment, Interest, and Capital*, ch. 3; and Samuelson, "The Economics of Forestry."

the simple harvesting rule attributed to Irving Fisher does not apply in this more general setting.[8]

How is R determined, and what economic factors influence it? Consider a parcel of bare timberland just after harvest and assume that the land is expected to remain in foresting over an indefinite sequence of future growing cycles or rotations. (Nontimber uses of the land are temporarily ignored.) The present value of net receipts from these future harvests will clearly be related to the future course of real timber prices, replanting costs, and interest rates. Let this present value be denoted by V. If the forest was allowed to grow and occupy the parcel for an additional year, the entire stream of future receipts would be delayed by exactly one year. As a result, the opportunity to earn the annual competitive return (r) on the value of the stream (V) would have been forgone. Consequently, the opportunity cost of allowing the standing forest to occupy the parcel of land for an additional year is

$$R = rV . \tag{6}$$

For clarification, the relationship shown in equation (6) may be viewed from a slightly different perspective. Suppose the timber grower rented the parcel of land from its owner. With land allocated competitively, the equilibrium rent will equal the largest annual charge that any grower would willingly pay. This maximum annual payment is rV. The present value of an infinite stream of such annual rents would equal V and hence would just exhaust the net economic profit from foresting.

The general benefit-cost condition stated in equation (5) can be used to analyze how equilibrium land rents and harvest ages will change in response to changes in timber prices, harvesting or refor-estation costs, interest rates, taxes, and other economic parameters.[9] For clarification, changes in economic parameters are introduced one at a time, and the parameter changes considered are confined to simple shifts from one constant level to another. Thus, for example,

---

8. Fisher, *The Theory of Interest.*

9. The value of future forest receipts will also be affected by the harvest age chosen for future stands. With timberland allocated competitively, the rotations used will maximize the present value of future receipts. Moreover, if levels of real price, replanting costs, and interest rates persist indefinitely, then future stands will also be cut at T^*, the age that maximizes profit from the stand currently growing.

Table 11-2. Qualitative Relationships Between Economic Conditions and Profit-Maximizing Forestry Decisions.

	Net Price of Timber: p	Replanting Cost: c	Interest Rate: r
Land rent from future timbering: R	+	−	−
Age at harvest: T^*	−	+	−
Long-run supply:			
Acreage in timber	+	−	−
Supply per acre	−	+	−
Net supply effect	?	?	−

Note: The price of timber is net of any harvest costs per unit. All prices, costs, and interest rates are interpreted to be in real (inflation-adjusted) terms.

the effect of price on the rotation age is analyzed by comparing equilibrium rotation ages under different constant price regimes.

Consider first how changes in prices, costs, and other factors would alter R, the equilibrium rent on land devoted to growing timber. Clearly, a higher timber price would increase the annual return to land devoted to forestry, and increases in costs would tend to reduce it. Changes in the interest rate, r, would also affect R, though the direction of this relationship is less straightforward. Here it is useful to view R as the maximum amount a potential user would be willing to bid for use of the land for one year. If the interest rate is increased, the discounted value of future receipts from any given harvest and reforestation plan will decline. Accordingly, the amount of current income a forester would pay to obtain this stream of receipts falls, as well.[10]

The preceding qualitative relationships are listed in Table 11-2. In this table the column headings are economic parameters that influence returns to forestry and the harvest-replanting decision. The term c is defined to be a per acre replanting or reforestation cost incurred at the beginning of each growing cycle. The row headings

10. Recall that $R = rV$ in equation (6). The argument in the text only demonstrates that an increase in r will cause V to decline. To conclude that it causes R to decline, it must be shown that the fall in V more than offsets the associated increase in r. This follows from the fact that the effect of r on V is more than proportionate, due to the compounding of interest in the present value relation. A formal demonstration of this point is available from the author on request.

are variables that result from forest management decisions, such as the rent on forestland and the rotation age. The signs in the first row of cells in this table indicate directions of relationships between the equilibrium rent on forestland and the price of timber, the replanting cost, and the interest rate. Thus, the first row of entries indicates that R responds positively to increases in price and negatively to both increases in replanting cost and increases in the interest rate. Recall that price is defined net of harvesting costs (i.e., it is a stumpage price). Hence, increases in harvest costs will, ceteris paribus, reduce p and cause R to decline.

Examine next how economic conditions will influence the rotation age, T^*.[11] As shown in Figure 11-2 (and in equation (5)), T^* is determined by the rate of growth (Δf) and by the opportunity cost of using both the stock of timber and land to support growth (rf and R/p, respectively). Consider first the relationship between c, the initial reforestation cost, and the optimum harvest age. From the results represented in the first row of Table 11-2, an increase in c will reduce R. From Figure 11-2, a reduction in R would cause the curve labeled $rf + R/p$ to shift down, increasing the equilibrium rotation age. Hence, the relationship between c and T^* is positive, as shown in the second row of Table 11-2. At a more intuitive level, the forest manager can mitigate the impact of increased reforestation costs by reducing the number of replantings undertaken in any given time period. To do so, the length of each rotation must, of course, be increased.

The relationship between p and T^* is somewhat more complicated. The net price, p, enters the benefit cost condition in Figure 11-2 through its effect on R/p. Because p is positively related to both the numerator and the denominator, it is not immediately clear how this expression would change if p were increased. To clarify this question, it is useful to write out the present value of a single rotation's net receipts, denoted N, where discounting is to the initial period of the rotation,

$$N = \frac{pf}{(1+r)^T} - c .$$ (7)

11. An analysis of the effects of prices and costs on the length of rotations is also presented in Howe, *Natural Resource Economics*, pp. 225 ff.

In this expression,

    c is the cost of reforestation incurred at the beginning of each rotation;

$1/(1 + r)^T$ is the present value of a receipt received T periods in the future.

The terms p, f, r, and T were defined earlier. From equation (7) it can be seen that, so long as c is positive, a change in p will cause a more than proportionate change in profit per rotation (N) and hence a more than proportionate change in R. For example, a 10 percent increase in price will increase *gross* receipts by exactly 10 percent. If replanting costs are positive, however, the resulting rise in *net* receipts, and hence R, will exceed 10 percent. Thus, increases in p will cause R/p to rise, since the numerator is increased relative to the denominator. From Figure 11–2, an increase in p will shift the curve $rf + R/p$ upward, and a shorter rotation time will result.

For a less mechanical and more intuitive explanation of this relationship, recall the monetary expression of the harvesting condition in equation (4). There it may be seen that a given increase in price causes proportionate increases in both $p \triangle f$, the marginal benefit of waiting (since any timber grown will be worth more), and rpf, the opportunity cost of allowing the stand to mature an extra period (since the return would be greater if the stand was harvested and the proceeds invested). If the opportunity cost of land (R) also increased in proportion, then both marginal benefit and marginal cost would be increased proportionately, and no change in rotation times would be indicated. With positive replanting costs, however, the increase in land cost is more than proportionate, and the costs of waiting rise relative to the benefits. As a result, the rotation time is reduced.

Regarding the last entry in the second row of Table 11–2, note that the real rate of interest enters the marginal cost of waiting in two ways. An increase in r will raise rf, the opportunity cost of using "timber capital" to produce new growth. At the same time, however, a higher interest rate reduces the present value of future harvests and hence lowers the opportunity cost of occupying the land. (Recall the relationship between r and R in the first row of Table 11–2.)

Hence, the net effect of a change in the interest rate on the marginal cost of waiting and the chosen rotation age would seem ambiguous. It can be shown, however, that the change in rf dominates, so that higher interest rates increase the marginal cost of waiting and reduce the rotation age.[12] Without delving extensively into the algebra of the present value relation, it may be noted that increases in interest rates signal increases in the premium that current consumption commands over future consumption. Forest management decisions respond to that signal by reducing rotation times and thus moving future consumption closer to the present.

FORESTRY AND PUBLIC POLICY

The analysis to this point has been exclusively concerned with private forest management practices. However, the general benefit-cost framework developed earlier can be applied, with suitable modification, to questions of public policy, as well. The competitive outcomes analyzed previously may well diverge from an appropriately defined social norm, due perhaps to the presence of externalities. However, the market solution still provides a very useful benchmark for policy analysis since, as Arrow and others have pointed out, if markets existed for all goods and services that affect society's welfare, then equilibrium-competitive outcomes would be socially efficient.[13] In this case, application of the private benefit-cost criterion developed above would yield results that pass a social benefit-cost test, as well.

An understanding of the relationship between competitive outcomes and socially efficient forest resource allocations may be gained by reinterpreting terms in the private benefit-cost framework developed earlier in order to transform that rule into an appropriate criterion for social policy. To do this, it is most convenient to work with the monetary form of the condition stated in equation (4) as $p \Delta f = rpf + R$. First, the price of timber, p, must be reinterpreted as the marginal benefit society receives from the use of timber in housing, paper products, and so forth. Any postulated difference between

---

12. As in the case of the relationship between r and R, this result follows from the effect of compounding in the present value relation. A formal demonstration will be provided by the author upon request.

13. K. J. Arrow, "The Organization of Economic Activity," in Haveman and Margolis, eds., *Public Expenditures and Policy Analysis* (Chicago: Markham, 1970), pp. 59–73. By "socially efficient" it is meant that the competitive equilibrium would be a Pareto optimum, an allocation from which any departure will necessarily make one or more members of society worse off.

this marginal benefit and the competitive price would imply socially optimal rotations that diverge, in a predictable fashion, from those chosen by private forest managers. Second, it might be necessary to modify r, the real rate of interest relevant for competitive investment decisions, in order to reflect the socially appropriate rate for discounting future consumption. Third, the opportunity cost of land used to grow timber (R) might need to be altered to allow for possible nonmarket benefits (or costs) that the presence of standing forests confer.

One potential reason for a divergence between price and the marginal benefit of consuming timber products arises from external damages imposed in harvesting timber or in processing it into paper and wood products. On the one hand, if these external effects are large relative to the externalities associated with other forms of consumption, then the market price revealed to forest managers would be too high from a social point of view. On the other hand, favorable tax treatment of income earned from growing timber might result in timber supplies that are excessive in a social sense, and market prices that are accordingly too low. If the net difference between price and marginal benefit could be determined, then the preceding analysis and the qualitative relationships shown in Table 11–2 could be used to determine the direction of bias in privately chosen rotation ages. Clearly, however, careful empirical analysis in several areas would be needed to determine the presence and magnitude of any discrepancies between market prices and social benefits, and hence an appropriate policy toward private rotation practices.

The possibility of divergences between social and market rates of discount has been debated for decades in the academic literature.[14] Some noted economists have asserted that, due either to the effects of corporate income taxation or to a public good aspect of bequests to future generations, the discount rates applied to private investment decisions are too high from a social perspective. Others, most notably Hirshleifer, have argued against any such distinction between private and social rates of discount.[15]

If one agrees with the proponents of a lower discount rate for evaluating private investments, the implications of this position for pri-

14. For a brief discussion of this literature, see Samuelson, "The Economics of Forestry," p. 488.

15. J. Hirshleifer, "Investment Decisions Under Uncertainty," *Quarterly Journal of Economics* 80 (1966): 252–77.

vate forestry are not entirely clear. The ambiguity arises because the social discount rate reasoning offers a prescription to subsidize all private investment. To apply it to forestry decisions alone would result in a misallocation of capital between forestry and other sectors of the economy. As a result of these considerations, Samuelson was led to conclude, "It is not necessarily an argument for programming . . . [the choice of timber rotations] with a hypothetical interest rate much lower than interest rates that prevail elsewhere."[16]

Possible divergences between social and private measures of the opportunity cost of occupying land with standing timber (R in the benefit-cost equations) might arise from a variety of sources. In the forest policy literature, references to external benefits from recreation, watershed enhancement, and habitat protection are very common, though attempts at actual measurement appear to be rare.[17] If these external benefits are important at the margin, then a market allocation system will tend to overstate the opportunity costs of occupying land with standing timber. Here it is important to stress that it is the marginal effect, the contribution of an extra acre of standing timber to these nonmarket benefits, that is significant for policy. On the one hand, if these nonmarket demands were already largely satisfied by private allocations of forest resources, then the divergence between social and private opportunity costs might be quite small.[18] On the other hand, if this divergence was significant, then the benefit-cost rule stated in equation (4) would indicate the nature of the difference between competitive and socially efficient rotation plans.

This brief survey is not the appropriate context for a full discussion of the externality issue or application of the benefit-cost approach to actual policy problems. Even from this limited discussion, however, it should be clear that the comparison of benefits and

16. Samuelson, "The Economics of Forestry," p. 488.

17. For discussions regarding the claim that standing forests promote flood protection and commercial fisheries, see Nelson and Grobey, Chapters 2 and 7, respectively, in this volume. As Hartman has shown, the presence of such nonmarket considerations tends to lengthen optimum rotation times, a result that confirms the relationship between R and T^* in Table 11-2. See R. Hartman, "The Harvesting Decision When a Standing Forest Has Value," *Economic Inquiry* 14 (1976): 52–58.

18. Grobey (Chapter 7 in this volume) has made precisely the same point regarding the importance of marginal values for policy analysis in the area of fishery enhancement. He also points out that the average benefits are often used for actual policy recommendations, while marginal benefits are generally lower.

costs is an essential part of any acceptable public policy toward forests. To approach public policy problems by simply placing forests in the public sector and then relying on the good intentions of public managers is clearly not adequate, as a growing body of research has demonstrated.[19] Rather than confront the difficult economic comparisons that must be made in allocating such resources, public forest managers have traditionally attempted to base policy solely on physical criteria.

A general neglect of economic considerations is exemplified by policy concerning choices among alternative uses of public forestlands. In recognition of the fact that forests can often serve a variety of purposes, current public forest policy stresses the principle of multiple use. A formal mandate for this policy was first stated in the Multiple-Use Sustained-Yield Act of 1960. This act also provided that "due consideration shall be given to the relative values of the various resources in particular areas, . . . latitude for periodic adjustments in use to conform to changing needs and conditions; that some lands will be used for less than all the resources."[20] Despite the economic guidance in this clause, the Forest Service's implementation of the multiple-use philosophy has often resembled an attempt to require all uses to be represented on all public forestlands. Such a practice accentuates conflicts between uses and often has the effect of unnecessarily reducing the levels of important forest outputs. Any economically efficient policy of public forest management would require an examination of conflicts among alternative uses and a determination of the economic merits of alternative uses in situations where conflicts exist. In general, a correct benefit-cost analysis would not prescribe the coexistence of all uses on all forestlands. As is common in other contexts, certain forest resources would best serve society's interests if they were specialized, for example, for either timbering or recreation, rather than managed to accommodate all uses simultaneously.

19. See, for example, Marion Clawson, *The Economics of National Forest Management* (Baltimore: Johns Hopkins University Press, 1976). In the present volume, see Nelson (Chapter 2), Johnson (Chapter 4), Nelson and Pugliaresi (Chapter 6), Grobey (Chapter 7), and Muraoka and Watson (Chapter 8).

20. Quoted from Howe, *Natural Resource Economics*, p. 225. More recent statements of policy for national forests appear in the Forest and Rangeland Renewable Resources Planning Act of 1974 and the National Forest Management Act of 1976.

Clawson has found that the Forest Service does not allocate management expenditures among forests in a way that maximizes the value of services produced.[21] Rather, expenses for promoting timber growth are often directed toward forests that are relatively unproductive at growing wood, thus short-changing the more productive national forests. Accordingly, Clawson has recommended a policy of dominant use, really an application of the principle of specialization, that would allocate the least productive timber growing forests to wilderness and recreation use and concentrate timber management efforts on the most productive sites. The result, according to Clawson, would be a two to threefold increase in annual timber growth, and a two to fourfold increase in recreational and wilderness opportunities.

Another area where public forest management has largely ignored economic considerations and attempted to base policy on physical principles is in the choice of rotation ages and harvest schedules. Here the dictum of maximizing sustained yield and the more recent requirement for nondeclining even-flow harvest schedules have formed the basis for public forest policy. Citing again the Multiple-Use Sustained-Yield Act of 1960, the goal in planning harvests is "the achievement and maintenance in perpetuity of a high-level annual or regular periodic output of the various renewable resources of the National Forests, without impairment of the productivity of the land."[22] In practice, this directive has been interpreted to call for rotation schedules that would maximize the sustainable yield of timber from public forestlands.

If harvest ages are chosen to maximize sustainable yields, then forests will be cut when cumulative growth per year of growing time is largest. This age has been described as the "culmination of the mean annual increment" of growth, and harvesting at this age is explicitly mandated by the National Forest Management Act of 1976. In terms of the notation developed earlier, a maximum sustainable yield policy amounts to setting the harvest age to maximize f/T, the mean annual increment or average growth per year. This policy has a ready graphic interpretation from the growth curves used earlier.

In Figure 11–3 the growth function from Figure 11–1 has been reproduced, and a line segment has been drawn between point A on

21. Clawson, *The Economics of National Forest Management.*
22. Quoted from Levy, "An Economic Alternative," p. 23.

Figure 11-3. Maximum Sustainable-Yield Harvest Age.

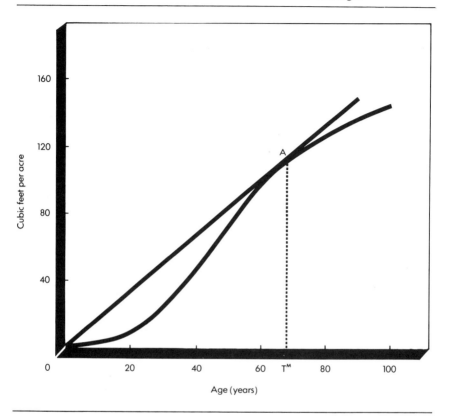

the growth curve and the origin. The slope of line OA equals the
ratio of the volume of wood grown by that age (AT^M) and the age
of the stand (OT^M). The slope of this line is, therefore, the mean
annual increment for a stand of age T^M. There will, of course, be a
different mean annual increment for each harvest age. The mean
annual increment is maximized, however, at age T^M. Thus, a policy
that specified rotations at intervals of T^M years would maximize the
sustainable yield from the forest shown in Figure 11-3.

This criterion has no economic content and is completely independent of such economic considerations as prices, costs, and interest
rates. Only in a very special set of circumstances, where the real rate
of interest is zero and replanting costs are nonexistent, would such a

policy coincide with an economic optimum.[23] If the rate of interest was zero, society would be indifferent regarding the timing of forest outputs. That is, a dollar's worth of present or future benefits would have equal value, and a socially efficient policy need simply maximize the average annual value of net benefits. If replanting costs were also zero, then net benefits would be dependent only on the average annual volume of wood produced.

Accordingly, a policy that maximizes f/T would also maximize net benefits in this case.[24] However, in a world where the interest rates and replanting costs are positive, a forest management policy that maximizes annual timber output will not maximize the net present value of the resource to society. Likewise, a socially efficient forest policy will not maximize the long-term undiscounted volume of wood produced. Though this may seem anomalous at first glance, it simply reflects a social preference for present to future consumption and a recognition that the process of growing timber uses socially valuable resources.

Although it is clear that the maximum sustainable-yield criterion will not, except coincidentally, result in a social optimum, it cannot be determined from theoretical considerations alone whether the disregard for economic values results in rotation schedules that are too long or too short. To see this, recall from Table 11–2 that positive replanting costs tend to extend the present value maximizing rotation age, while positive interest rates tend to reduce it. As an empirical question, however, it is widely agreed that rotation ages adopted by the U.S. Forest Service for softwood timber substantially exceed those employed on industry forestlands, and most economic analysts

---

23. In keeping with the practice of comparing alternative steady state equilibria, it is assumed that all economic variables (prices, costs, and interest rates) are expected to remain constant over time.

24. The result can also be shown using the benefit-cost condition stated earlier in equation (4). Interpreting p as the marginal social value of timber, $(pf - c)/T$ is the undiscounted average value of net receipts per period. If the interest rate were zero, this would equal R, the rental payment required to occupy the land with standing timber for one period. Incorporating this into the benefit-cost condition of equation (4), with r set equal to zero, results in the harvest criterion

$$p \Delta f = (pf - c)/T \ .$$

If $c = 0$ also, this reduces to $\Delta f = f/T$. This rule indicates that the forest should be cut when the last year's growth (Δf) just equals the average annual growth of the stand over the entire rotation (f/T). In terms of Figure 11–3, this occurs at age T^M.

have concluded that these rotation ages are excessive from a social viewpoint as well.[25]

An indication of the divergence between harvest practices on public and private forestlands may be obtained from Table 11-1. Figures in the fourth row show the ratio of growing stock to annual growth under different ownership regimes. As shown, this ratio is over three times as high in national forests as in industry forestlands. In a fully regulated forest this ratio would equal the rotation age.[26] Because actual forests are not fully regulated, this finding is best interpreted as indicating only the relative magnitudes of rotation ages under different ownership regimes.

The other growth indicators in Table 11-1 show that, at least in terms of timber yields, private forestlands vastly outproduce national forests, even if corrections are made for differences in natural productivity. These disparities in growth are no doubt due to a variety of factors, including differences in the use of such high-yield practices as thinning, weed and disease control, and genetic improvement, plus differences in the allocation of such efforts among individual forests. But important causes of low growth on public lands remain the choice of harvesting schedules and the Forest Service practice of retaining extensive volumes of old growth timber until even the age of maximizing physical yields is exceeded. As Clawson points out,

> The only way in which more timber can be grown on many national forest areas is to cut the timber now standing. . . . [Few] people seem to realize that growth of timber cannot proceed indefinitely unless timber harvest also goes forward, since inventory cannot accumulate beyond some maximum volume per acre.[27]

TIMBER SUPPLY IN THE SHORT AND LONG RUN

The supply of timber over the long run may be expressed as the product of yield per acre and the number of acres in commercial for-

---

25. See Clawson, *The Economics of National Forest Management*, and Nelson and Pugliaresi (Chapter 6 in this volume).

26. Annual growth in a regulated forest would be f/T per acre, and the size of the growing stock per acre would be f. Hence the ratio of growing stock to annual growth would be T, the rotation age.

27. Clawson, *Man, Land, and the Forest Environment* (Baltimore: Johns Hopkins University Press, 1976).

ests. Changes in economic conditions in timber markets will, in general, cause private timber producers to alter both components of supply. The per acre yield on forestlands can be altered by changing the rotation schedule or by varying the intensity with which certain growth-enhancing activities are pursued. The amount of acreage in commercial timbering is sensitive to decisions of whether to continue harvests and reforestation on marginal timberlands and to the possibility of reforesting lands that are currently used in other ways. In total, then, there are three sources of potential timber supply response: choices of rotations, growth enhancement, and land use. The rotation problem has already been treated in some detail, though the implications of alternative rotations for short- and long-run timber supply levels has not been stressed. This section incorporates the results of the rotation problem with a simple treatment of the land use component of timber supply. The growth enhancement aspect of supply is not directly addressed.

The possibility of nontimber uses of the land can affect both the choice of harvest ages for current stands of timber and the decision of whether or not to reforest after harvest. To address these questions let all possible uses be collapsed into two categories: the growth of forests and some nonforestry alternative such as residential development, denoted F and A, respectively. The opportunity cost of allowing a standing forest to mature an extra year now depends on the future use to which the land will be allocated. Let R^F denote the forgone return if the future use is growing new forests and let R^A represent the return the land could earn if allocated to the nonforestry activity. Then the true opportunity cost of allowing a standing forest to grow an extra year will be the higher of these foregone returns:

$$R = \text{maximum} (R^F, R^A) .$$

In this broader context, R enters the decision of when to harvest a standing forest in exactly the same way that it did in equations (4) and (5).

Recall the benefit-cost rule developed earlier for the decision of when to harvest, $\Delta f = rf + R/p$. This rule continues to apply for the choice of harvest ages, even in the case where the nonforest alternative will occupy the land in the future (i.e., where $R^F < R^A$). Although the land will not be reforested in such instances, the qualitative relationships shown in the second row of Table 11–2 still indicate the age at which the current stand will be harvested. Although it has not been included as a separate parameter in Table 11–2, the per period value of nontimber outputs the land could produce (R^A) also is important in determining forest management decisions. For example, an increase in R^A on land that is occupied by an economically marginal stand will tend to increase R. As a result (using the apparatus in Figure 11–2), the age at which this forest will be cut is reduced, and once cleared the land will be withdrawn from timber production and devoted to the nonforestry alternative.

When analyzing the effects of shifts in prices, costs, or interest rates on timber supplies, the steady state characterization adopted earlier is retained. Thus, for example, a price change refers to a discontinuous shift in price from one level to another, with the new level expected to remain in effect indefinitely. Such movements will cause changes in long-run rotation ages and land use decisions. They will also give rise to transitory or short-run changes in harvests and timber supplies as inventories of standing timber shift from one long-run equilibrium level to another. These short-run supply impacts are discussed further later.

With land allocated to forest and nonforest uses in a competitive fashion, any change in economic conditions that increases R^F (ceteris paribus) will tend to increase the amount of acreage devoted to growing timber. Likewise, changes that reduce R^F will cause some marginal forestland to be withdrawn from production in the long run. Consequently, the qualitative relationships shown in the third row of Table 11–2 coincide with those shown in the first row. If, for example, net price (p) were to increase, it would tend to bring more acreage into production and thereby increase long-run supply.

Over the long run, the per period volume of timber grown on an acre of forestland will equal f/T. Accordingly, long-run supply per acre will depend on the rotation age chosen. The qualitative relationship between the rotation age (T^*) and f/T depends on whether present value of maximizing rotation periods tends to exceed or fall short of T^M, the rotation that would maximize sustainable yield. It is evident from Figure 11–3 that if T^* exceeded T^M, then a small decrease in T^* would cause f/T to rise. On the other hand, if $T^* < T^M$, then a reduction in the rotation age would decrease timber grown per period.

As noted earlier, the relationship between T^* and T^M cannot be determined on theoretical grounds alone. Rather, it depends on the force of discounting and replanting costs, and these two factors tend to pull the privately chosen rotation age in opposite directions. It was also noted, however, that private harvest decisions tend to result in rotation ages that are far below those found on national forests. Since the latter are at least nominally guided by yield maximization, it seems reasonable to conclude that $T^* < T^M$ in most situations.[28] Correspondingly, the qualitative effect of changes in economic parameters upon long-run timber supplies per acre coincides with their effect on T^*, that is, increases in T^* tend to increase supply per acre, and vice versa. For this reason, the signs in the fourth row in Table 11-2 are the same as those reported for T^*.

The last row of relationships in Table 11-2 shows the net qualitative relationships between economic parameters and the long-run supply of timber. Surprisingly, perhaps, the effects of permanent changes in net price and replanting costs on long-run supply are ambiguous. That is, they cannot be predicted on theoretical grounds alone; rather, empirical analysis would be required to determine the directions of these effects in specific cases. If, for example, the net price level rises, more land will be brought into production and long-run supplies will tend to increase. The anomaly arises, however, because this increase may be more than offset by the lower long-run yields per acre caused by shorter rotations. Exactly the same kind of ambiguity surrounds the effect of replanting costs on long-run supply. Only in the case of interest rate changes is the qualitative shift in long-run timber supply determinate. An increase in the interest rate will, ceteris paribus, force some marginal land out of production and induce private foresters to liquidate future stands at earlier ages. It is appropriate to recall that one dimension of supply response, the enhancement of growth per acre through disease control, genetic improvement, and other means, has been omitted from the preceding analysis. It is expected that such efforts, and the additional supplies

28. For additional evidence in support of this conclusion, see P. Berck, "The Economics of Timber," *Bell Journal of Economics* 10 (1979): 447-62. This relationship is, of course, dependent upon replanting costs and may therefore be different for different forests. Interestingly, Clawson has found that the Forest Service sometimes spends resources actively replanting land on which private investment in reforestation would be unprofitable. If the absence of private reforestation is interpreted as a very long private rotation period, then the Forest Service practice may reflect a situation in which its yield-maximization policy leads to shorter rotations than present value maximization. In this case, it is the neglect of replanting costs that is crucial in determining the relationship between T^* and T^M. See Clawson, *The Economics of National Forest Management.*

they bring forth, would respond positively to price and negatively to replanting costs. If so, this would reinforce the land use component of long-run supply and thus make the anomalous supply response cases less likely.

The preceding discussion has focused exclusively on timber supplies in the long run by comparing the attributes of different long-run equilibria. Accompanying any actual shift, however, will be a period of transition from one steady state to another, a short-run situation in which timber supplies may move in a direction that differs from the long-run shift. Suppose, for example, that price increased and rotation times were lowered as a result. A portion of the growing stock that was previously below the optimum harvest age would now be above the new optimum harvest age. In the transition period between long-run equilibria, there would be an increase in short-run supplies as standing forests are placed on the new rotation schedule. This short-run impact may also be viewed as an inventory adjustment. A reduction in T^* is equivalent to a reduction in the optimum inventory of standing timber. The liquidation of this timber inventory increases the supplies of timber that reach the market in the short run. Similarly, increases in T^* tend to increase equilibrium inventories and to decrease supplies in the short-run transition period.

TAXATION AND TIMBER SUPPLY

By employing the relationships developed in Table 11–2 and retaining the long-run, partial equilibrium approach applied above, it is possible to explore the resource allocation effects of alternative forest taxation policies.[29] Consider first a severance tax levied as a fixed percentage of the *net* price of timber. In terms of the preceding supply analysis, imposition of this tax has the same effect as a reduction in p. That is, rotation times are lengthened and the return to marginal land is reduced. From Table 11–2 the net effect of the tax on long-run supply is ambiguous. By reducing R^F, the tax leads to the withdrawal of marginal land from future production. Gaffney has

29. The effects of alternative tax instruments on forest management decisions have also been examined by M. Gaffney, "Taxes on Yield, Property, Income, and Site" (University of Victoria, B.C.: Institute for Policy Analysis, 1975). (Mimeo.)

termed this phenomenon "invisible high grading," that is, only high grade forestland will be restocked.[30] It occurs principally because the present value of reforestation costs cannot be deducted from the forester's tax liability. In practice, it appears more common for severance taxes to be levied against the *gross* price of timber, that is, the price at the mill rather that on the stump. In these cases where harvest costs are not deductible, the severance tax has the additional effect of discriminating against the harvest of marginal resources, stands for which net price is low. In this case, the high grading would be quite visible, and marginal stands would remain uncut.

Consider next a property tax levied annually as a fixed percentage of the market value of standing timber on a parcel of land. The effects of such a tax on rotations and timber supply are symmetric to those accompanying an increase in the interest rate.[31] The tax imposes a per period cost on standing timber in much the same way the interest rate does, and thus encourages shorter rotations.[32] A property tax also lowers the equilibrium return to foresting and thus reduces R^F and the incentive to employ land in growing timber. Assuming that the tax does not have an equivalent effect on the return to alternative uses of the land, the effect of this reduction in R^F would be to remove some land from growing timber. Qualitatively, then, the property tax affects the long-run supply of timber in the same way as an increase in the interest rate.

Finally, consider a tax levied as a fraction of the value of forestland alone, or the annual rent received from its use. So long as the tax is levied on the land only and is independent of the use in which the land is employed or the amount of capital (standing timber or otherwise) that occupies it, it will be impossible to avoid the tax by altering the pattern of resource allocation. As a result, such a tax would have no effect on rotation times, the choice of activity that occupies the land, or long-run timber supply. In other words, it would be perfectly neutral.

Although completely neutral taxes are possible, all commonly applied taxes distort investment and production decisions and there-

30. Ibid.

31. They are not, however, identical, as V. Gamponia and R. Mendelsohn have shown in "The Economics of Forest Taxation" (Seattle: University of Washington, Department of Economics, 1983). (Mimeo.)

32. Gamponia and Mendelsohn provide a formal demonstration of this effect in "The Economics of Forest Taxation."

fore reduce the present value of forest outputs. In general, the magnitudes of such losses will depend on the type of tax levied and the price, reforestation cost, and growth characteristics of the taxed species. An important policy issue is the choice of taxes to minimize such losses.

Tax-induced shifts in rotation age have been examined empirically by Gamponia and Mendelsohn.[33] They compared the social losses that result from alternative property and severance taxes designed to produce equal tax revenues. For the tax rates and timber species they examined, their analysis indicated that severance taxes were vastly preferred to equal yielding property taxes. To complete the analysis it would be necessary to examine the magnitude of land use distortions as well, and perhaps to extend the comparison to a multitude of different species and economic conditions. Nevertheless, Gamponia and Mendelsohn's approach clearly indicates the role of economic analysis in answering important policy questions.

CONCLUSIONS

In the private sector, the choice of profitable management strategies was seen to depend on prices, costs, and interest rates. A potential use of the private decisionmaking model presented in this chapter lies in the choice of alternative tax instruments and a comparison of their potential impacts on private rotation decisions. The same approach could also be extended to permit analysis of the impact of public regulations on private management decisions. Elsewhere, it was noted that any public management policy designed to maximize the net benefits that society receives from public forestlands will also be sensitive to values, costs, and interest rates. The optimizing decisions reached by unregulated private entrepreneurs and enlightened public managers may well differ due to the presence of nonmarket costs and benefits, but the principle of comparing benefits and costs, and even the structure of the benefit-cost calculus, is common to both settings.

In actuality, the management practices applied to public and private forestlands differ dramatically, and the divergence does not appear to arise from any careful application of economic principles to treat externalities or market failure. Rather it seems to stem from

33. Gamponia and Mendelsohn, "The Economics of Forest Taxation."

an unwillingness on the part of public forest managers to confront economic issues and the difficult choices and tradeoffs they often imply. Disparities in public and private management practices might not be remarkable if they were confined to such nontimber uses of forestlands as recreation or watershed protection. However, most of the criticism directed toward federal forest management, including the multiple-use philosophy, maximum sustained-yield harvest policies (cutting at the culmination of mean annual increment), and the nondeclining even-flow constraint on harvest schedules, has regarded the way public forests are used to grow timber. As several analysts have shown, these policies unnecessarily constrain the production of timber on public lands without generating offsetting increases in nontimber benefits. The public forests of the United States are a great national asset. Without a management strategy based on careful consideration of costs and benefits, however, the return society receives from this asset will remain below its full potential.

SELECTED BIBLIOGRAPHY

American Petroleum Institute. *Analysis of the Processing of Permits to Drill on Federal Lands*, Research Study 029. Washington, D.C.: American Petroleum Institute. 1982.

Anderson, Terry L. *Water Rights: Scarce Resource Allocation, Bureaucracy, and the Environment*. San Francisco: Pacific Research Institute for Public Policy, 1983.

Arrow, K. J. "The Organization of Economic Activity: Issues Pertinent to the Choice of Market versus Nonmarket Allocation." In R. Haveman and J. Margolis, eds., *Public Expenditures and Policy Analysis*, pp. 59–73. Chicago: Markham, 1970.

Baden, John, and Richard L. Stroup, eds. *Bureaucracy vs. Environment: The Environmental Costs of Bureaucratic Governance*. Ann Arbor: University of Michigan Press, 1981.

Barlow, Thomas; Gloria Helfand; Trent Orr; and Thomas Stoel. *Giving Away the National Forests: An Analysis of U.S. Forest Service Timber Sales Below Costs*. Washington, D.C.: Natural Resources Defense Council, Inc., 1980.

Barney, Daniel R. *The Last Stand: Ralph Nader's Study Group Report on the National Forests*. New York: Grossman, 1974.

Benson, Bruce L. "Why Are Congressional Committees Dominated by 'High-Demand' Legislators? – A Comment on Niskanen's View of Bureaucrats and Politicians." *Southern Economic Journal* 48 (July 1981): 68–77.

Berck, P. "The Economics of Timber: A Renewable Resource in the Long Run." *Bell Journal of Economics* 10 (1979): 447–62.

Bevan, D. E. "Methods of Fishery Regulation." In J. A. Crutchfield, ed., *The Fisheries: Problems in Resource Management*. Seattle: University of Washington Press, 1965.

Beverton, R.J.H., and S.J. Holt. *On the Dynamics of Exploited Fish Populations.* London: Her Majesty's Stationery Office, 1957.

Bishop, R. C., and T. A. Heberlein. "Measuring Values of Extramarket Goods: Are Indirect Measures Biased?" In *Proceedings of the Annual Meeting.* Pullman, Wash.: American Agricultural Economics Association, 1979.

Breton, Albert and Ronald Wintrobe. "The Equilibrium Size of a Budget-maximizing Bureau: A Note on Niskanen's Theory of Bureaucracy." *Journal of Political Economy* 83 (February 1975): 195–207.

Brooks, William M., and Richard G. Cline. "Linear Program Management Alternatives Using Literature-Land-Form-Based Sediment Values: A Method." Notes, U.S. Forest Service R-1. February 1979.

Buchanan, James M., and Gordon Tullock. *The Calculus of Consent.* Ann Arbor, Mich.: University of Michigan Press, 1962.

California Department of Fish and Game. "Inventory, Salmon-Steelhead and Marine Resources." *California Fish and Wildlife Plan*, vol. 3, supporting data, part B. Sacramento, Calif., 1965.

Cartwright, Philip W. "The Management of Federal Timberlands." In *Agenda for the 80s: A New Federal Land Policy.* Proceedings of the National Conference on States' Rights, the Sagebrush Rebellion, and Federal Land Policy, Salt Lake City, November 20–24, 1980.

Cederholm, C. J.; L. M. Reid; and E. O. Salo. "Cumulative Effects of Logging Road Sediment on Salmonid Populations in the Clearwater River, Jefferson County, Washington." Contribution No. 543 for conference on Salmon-Spawning Gravel: A Renewable Resource in the Pacific Northwest? Seattle, Washington, October 1980. Seattle: University of Washington, College of Fisheries, 1980.

Cederholm, C. J.; R. Stokes; and E. Salo. "Salmonids, Forestry, and Economics on the Clearwater River, Washington." Paper delivered at Western Economic Association Meeting, University of Washington, Fisheries Research Institute, July 3, 1981.

Chapman, D. G. *Spawner-Recruit Models and Estimation of Maximum Sustainable Catch.* Paper No. 10. Seattle: University of Washington, Center for Quantitative Science in Forestry, Fisheries, and Wildlife, July 1970.

Clawson, Marion. *The Bureau of Land Management.* New York: Praeger, 1971.

Clawson, Marion. *The Economics of National Forest Management.* Resources for the Future Working Paper EN-6. Baltimore: Johns Hopkins University Press, 1976.

Clawson, Marion, and Burnell Held. *The Federal Lands: Their Use and Management.* Baltimore: Johns Hopkins University Press, 1957.

Clawson, Marion. *Man, Land, and the Forest Environment.* Baltimore: Johns Hopkins University Press, 1976.

Congressional Budget Office. *Forest Service Timber Sales: Their Effect on Wood Product Prices*, 1980.

Cooper, A.C. "The Effect of Transported Stream Sediments on the Survival of Sockeye and Pink Salmon Eggs and Alevins." *International Pacific Salmon Fisheries Commission Bulletin* 17 (1965): 16.

Crowell, John B., Jr. "Current Public Policies on Natural Resources: The Symbiosis of Environmental Quality and Economic Efficiency." Oklahoma State University, Nat Walker Lectureship, 1983.

Crutchfield, J. A., and G. Pontecorvo. *The Pacific Salmon Fisheries: A Study of Irrational Conservation.* Baltimore: Johns Hopkins University Press, 1969.

Culhane, Paul J. *Public Lands Politics.* Baltimore: Johns Hopkins University Press, 1981.

Cummings, R. G., and R. N. Johnson. "Welfare Analysis of Long-Term Forest Products Price Stabilization: Note." *American Journal of Agricultural Economics* 60 (November 1978): 689-90.

Dana, Samuel T., and Sally K. Fairfax. *Forest and Range Policy: Its Development in the United States.* 2nd ed. New York: McGraw-Hill, 1980.

DeWitt, John; B. F. Emad, Stephen J. Leiker; and others. "Fisheries Aspects" in *Review and Analysis of Smith River Draft Management Plan and Appendices,* pp. 33-35. Special study under contract for the county of Del Norte. Eureka, Calif.: Terrascan Environmental Consultants, 1980.

Edie, B.G. "A Census of the Juvenile Salmonids of the Clearwater River Basin, Jefferson County, Washington, in Relation to Logging." M.S. thesis, University of Washington, Seattle, 1975.

Emad, Bruce; F. Jewett, J. Grobey; and others. "Socio-Economic Base Study on Six Rivers National Forest." RFP-R5-10-79-39. Submitted to U.S. Forest Service, Six Rivers National Forest. Eureka, Calif.: Terrascan Environmental Consultants and Planners, December 21, 1979.

Emad, Bruce, F. Jewett; John Grobey, John DeWitt; and others. *Review and Analysis of Smith River Draft Management Plan and Appendices.* Submitted to County of Del Norte, County Planning Department. Eureka, Calif.: Terrascan Environmental Consultants and Planners, 1980.

Everest, Fred. *An Economic Evaluation of Anadromous Fishery Resources of the Siskiyou National Forest.* Grants Pass, Ore.: USDA, Forest Service, Siskiyou National Forest, 1975.

Everett and Associates. *Withdrawal of Public Lands from Access to Minerals and Fuels.* Washington, D.C.: Everett & Associates, 1980.

Everett and Associates. *Analyses of Delays in the Processing of Applications for Permits to Drill and Prestaking Clearance Applications.* Washington, D.C.: Everett & Associates, 1981.

Fairchild, Fred R. & Associates. *Forest Taxation in the United States.* USDA Miscellaneous Publication 218. 1935.

Faustmann, Martin. "On the Determination of the Value Which Forestland and Immature Stands Possess for Forestry." 1849. English translation edited by M. Gane. *Oxford Institute Paper* 42, 1968.

Fernow, Bernhard E. *Economics of Forestry*. New York: Thomas Y. Crowell, 1902.

Fisher, Irving. *The Theory of Interest*. New York: Macmillan, 1930.

Frome, Michael. *The Forest Service*. New York: Praeger, 1971.

Gaffney, M. "Concepts of Financial Maturity of Timber and Other Assets." *Agricultural Economics Information Series*, No. 62. Raleigh: North Carolina State College, 1957.

Gaffney, M. "Taxes on Yield, Property, Income, and Site: Effects on Forest Revenues and Management." University of Victoria, B.C., Institute for Policy Analysis, 1975. (Mimeo.)

Gamponia, V., and R. Mendelsohn. "The Economics of Forest Taxation." Seattle: University of Washington, Department of Economics, 1983. (Mimeo.)

Gaskill, Alfred. "Whither Forestry?" *Journal of Forestry* 32(2) (1934): 196-201.

General Accounting Office. *Accelerated Onshore Oil and Gas Leasing May not Occur as Quickly as Anticipated*, EMD-82-34, 1982.

General Accounting Office. *Actions Needed to Increase Federal Onshore Oil and Gas Exploration and Development*, EMD-81-40, 1981.

General Accounting Office. "Allegations Regarding the Small Business Setaside Program for Federal Timber." CED-79-8, April 1979.

General Accounting Office. *Federal Leasing Policy—Is the Split Responsibility Working?*, EMD-79-60, 1979.

General Accounting Office. *Interior's Minerals Management Programs Need Consolidation to Improve Accountability and Control*, EMD-82-104, 1982.

General Accounting Office. *Minerals Management at the Department of the Interior Needs Coordination and Organization*, EMD-81-53, 1981.

Gibbons, Dave R., and Ernest O. Salo. *An Annotated Bibliography of the Effects of Logging on Fish of the Western United States and Canada*. USDA, Forest Service General Technical Report PNW-10. Portland, Ore.: Pacific Northwest Forest and Range Experimental Station, 1973.

Glasner, David. *Politics, Prices, and Petroleum: The Political Economy of Energy*. San Francisco: Pacific Institute for Public Policy Research, 1985.

Goldberger, A.S. *Econometric Theory*. New York: Wiley, 1964.

Gordon, Scott. "Economics and the Conservation Question." *Journal of Law and Economics* 1(1) (October 1958): 110-21.

Gorte, Ross. "An Analysis of Forest Service Timber Management Costs." Washington, D.C.: National Forest Products Association, 1982. (Unpublished.)

Goundrey, G.K. "Forest Management and the Theory of Capital." *Canadian Journal of Economics and Political Science* 62 (1960): 124-42.

Grobey, John H. "An Alternative Public Policy for Regulating the Impact of Forest Practices on the Northern California Salmon Fishery." Ph.D. dissertation, University of Washington, Seattle, 1975.

Hall, George R. "The Myth and Reality of Multiple Use Forestry." *Natural Resources Journal* 3 (October 1963): 276-90.

Hanushen, E. A., and John E. Jackson. *Statistical Methods for Social Scientists.* New York: Academic Press, 1977.

Hartman, R. "The Harvesting Decision When a Standing Forest Has Value." *Economic Inquiry* 14 (1976): 52-58.

Haynes, Richard W. "A Comparison of Open and Setaside Timber Sales on National Forests in the Douglas Fir Region." *Land Economics* 55, no. 2 (1979): 277-84.

Haynes, Richard W. "Competition for Federal Timber: The Effects of Sealed Bidding." Paper presented at the 53rd annual Western Economic Association Conference, 1978.

Haynes, Richard W. "Competition for National Forest Timber on the Northern, Pacific Southwest, and Pacific Northwest Regions," PNL-266. Portland, Ore.: U.S. Forest Service Pacific Northwest Forest Range, January 1980.

Hirshleifer, Jack. "Investment Decisions Under Uncertainty: Applications of the State-Preference Approach." *Quarterly Journal of Economics* 80 (1966): 252-77.

Hirshleifer, Jack. *Investment, Interest, and Capital.* Englewood Cliffs, N.J.: Prentice-Hall, 1970.

Horak, Francis J. "An Economic Analysis Series for Screening Proposed Timber Management Projects: Report No. 1 – Analytical Considerations." BLM Technical Note. 1977.

Howe, C. W. *Natural Resource Economics: Issues, Analysis, and Policy.* New York: John Wiley and Sons, 1979.

Hyde, William F. "Compounding Clear-cuts: The Social Failures of Public Timber Management in the Rockies." In John Baden and Richard L. Stroup, eds., *Bureaucracy vs. Environment.* Ann Arbor: University of Michigan Press, 1981.

Hyde, William F. *Timber Supply, Land Allocation, and Economic Efficiency.* Baltimore: Johns Hopkins University Press, 1980.

Jackson, David H. *The Microeconomics of the Timber Industry.* Boulder, Colo.: Westview Press, 1980.

Johnson, M. Bruce, ed. *Resolving the Housing Crisis: Government Policy, Decontrol, and the Public Interest.* San Francisco: Pacific Research Institute for Public Policy, 1982.

Johnson, Ronald N. "Budget Maximization and Agencies Control: The Case of the U.S. Forest Service." Bozeman: Montana State University, 1982.

Johnson, Ronald N., and Gary D. Libecap. "Efficient Markets and Great Lakes Timber: A Conservation Issue Reexamined." *Explorations in Economic History* 17 (1980): 372-85.

Kaufman, Herbert. *The Forest Ranger.* Baltimore: Johns Hopkins University Press, 1960.

Kunkle, C., and P. Janik. *An Economic Evaluation of Salmonid Fisheries Attributable to Siuslaw National Forest.* Siuslaw National Forest, Region 6, Pacific Northwest. USDA, Forest Service, April 1976.

Lantz, Richard L. *Guidelines for Stream Protection in Logging Operations.* A report of the Oregon State Game Commission, Research Division, 1971.

Le Master, Dennis C. "Forest Service Funding Under RPA." *Journal of Forestry* 80 (March 1982): 161-63.

Leman, Christopher. "Resource Assessment and Program Development: An Evaluation of Forest Service Experience Under the Resources Planning Act, with Lessons for Other Natural Resources Agencies." Discussion paper, U.S. Department of the Interior, 1980.

Levy, Y. "An Economic Alternative to Current Public Forest Policy." *Economic Review.* San Francisco: Federal Reserve Bank, 1978.

Libecap, Gary D. *Locking Up the Range: Federal Land Controls and Grazing.* San Francisco: Pacific Research Institute for Public Policy, 1981.

MacKay, Robert J., and Carolyn L. Weaver. "On the Mutuality of Interests Between Bureaus and High Demand Review Committees: A Perverse Result." *Public Choice* 34 (Fall/Winter 1979): 481-91.

Mathews, S.B., and G.S. Brown. *Economic Evaluation of the 1967 Sport Salmon Fisheries of Washington.* Washington Department of Fisheries Technical Report No. 2, April 1970.

Mathews, S.B., and R. Buckley. "Marine Mortality of Puget Sound Coho Salmon." *Journal of Fisheries Research Board of Canada* 33 (1976) 1677-84.

McArdle, R. "The Yield of Douglas Fir in the Pacific Northwest." *U.S. Department of Agriculture Technical Bulletin*, No. 201. Washington, D.C., 1949.

McNeil, W.J. "Effect of the Spawning Bed Environment on Reproduction of Pink and Chum Salmon." *Fishery Bulletin* 65, no. 2 (1966): 495.

McNeil, W.J. "Environmental Factors Affecting Survival of Young Salmon in Spawning Beds and Their Possible Relations to Logging." U.S. Bureau of Commercial Fisheries. Manuscript Reports 64-1, 1964.

McNeil, W.J. "Redd Superimposition of Egg Capacity of Pink Salmon Spawning Beds." *Journal of the Fisheries Research Board of Canada* 21(6) (1964).

Mead, Walter J. *Competition and Oligopsony in the Douglas Fir Lumber Industry.* Berkeley and Los Angeles: University of California Press, 1966.

Mead, Walter J.; Dennis D. Muraoka; and Philip E. Sorensen. "The Effects of Taxes on the Profitability of U.S. Oil and Gas Production: A Case Study of the OCS Record." *National Tax Journal* 35 (March 1982): 21-30.

Mead, Walter J.; Mark Schniepp; and Richard B. Watson. "An Analysis of Bidder Response to Forest Service Appraisals in the Pacific Northwest." Paper presented at the 55th Western Economic Association Conference, San Diego, Calif., June 15-19, 1980.

Mead, Walter J.; Mark Schniepp; and Richard B. Watson. *The Effectiveness of Competition and Appraisals in the Auction Markets for National Forest Tim-*

ber in the Pacific Northwest. U.S. Department of Agriculture, Forest Service. Final Report, Contract No. 53-1-43 and PSWG-34, September 30, 1981.

Migue, Jean-Luc, and Gerard Belanger. "Toward a General Theory of Managerial Discretion." *Public Choice* 17 (Spring 1974): 27-47.

Muraoka, Dennis D., and Richard B. Watson. "Improving the Efficiency of Federal Timber Sale Procedures." *Natural Resources Journal* 23 (October 1983).

Nelson, Charles W. "Broader Lessons from the History of Lake Superior Iron-Ore Taxation." In Richard W. Lindholm, ed., *Property Taxation – USA.* Madison: University of Wisconsin Press, 1969, pp. 237-61.

Nelson, Robert H. "Ideology and Public Land Policy: The Current Crisis." In Sterling Brubaker, ed., *Rethinking the Public Lands.* Washington, D.C.: Resources for the Future, distributed by Johns Hopkins University Press, 1984.

_____. "A Long Term Strategy for the Public Lands." In Richard Ganzel, ed., *Resource Conflicts in the West.* Reno: Nevada Public Affairs Institute, University of Nevada, 1983.

_____. "The Public Lands." In Paul R. Portney, ed., *Current Issues in Natural Resource Policy.* Washington, D.C.: Resources for the Future; distributed by Johns Hopkins University Press, 1982.

Nienaber, Jeanne, and Daniel McCool. "Agency Power: Staking Out Terrain in Natural Resources Policy." Tucson: University of Arizona, Department of Political Science, 1980.

Nienaber, Jeanne, and Daniel McCool. "For Richer or for Poorer: A Comparative Approach to the Study of Bureaucracies." Paper presented at Western Political Science Association meeting, Denver, Colo., 1981.

Niskanen, William A. *Bureaucracy and Representative Government.* Chicago: Aldine & Atherton, 1971.

Niskanen, William A. "Bureaucrats and Politicians." *Journal of Law and Economics* 18 (December 1975): 617-44.

Pacific Fishery Management Council. "Freshwater Habitat, Salmon Produced, and Escapements for Natural Spawning along the Pacific Coast of the United States." A report prepared by the Anadromous Salmonid Environmental Task Force of the Pacific Fishery Management Council, Portland, Ore., June 1979.

Pacific Fishery Management Council. "Proposed Plan for Managing the 1980 Salmon Fisheries off the Coast of California, Oregon, and Washington." Portland, Ore., January 1980.

Paulik, G.J. "Studies of the Possible Form of the Stock-Recruitment Curve." Paper No. 11. Seattle: University of Washington, Center for Quantitative Science in Forestry, Fisheries, and Wildlife, July 1970.

Paulik, G.J., and J.W. Greenough. "Management Analysis for a Salmon Resource System." In K.E.F. Watt, ed., *Systems Analysis Ecology.* New York: Academic Press, 1966, Chapter 9.

Pilon, Roger, "Property Rights and a Free Society." In M. Bruce Johnson, ed., *Resolving the Housing Crisis: Government Policy, Decontrol, and the Public Interest*. San Francisco: Pacific Research Institute for Public Policy, 1982.

Pinchot, Gifford. *Breaking New Ground*. New York: Harcourt, Brace and Co., 1947.

Pincyck, Robert, and Dan Rubinfeld. *Econometric Models and Economic Forecasts*. New York: McGraw-Hill, 1980.

Platts, W. S. "Time Trends in Riverbed Sediment Composition in Salmon and Steelhead Spawning Areas: South Fork Salmon River, Idaho." USDA, Forest Service, Intermountain Forest and Range Experiment Station, n.d.

Platts, W. S., and W. F. Megahan. "Time Trends in Riverbed Sediment Composition in Salmon and Steelhead Spawning Areas: South Fork Salmon River, Idaho." In *Transactions of the Fortieth North American Wildlife and Natural Resources Conference*. Bethesda, Md.: American Fisheries Society, 1975.

Regier, H. A. "Mary, Mephistopheles, Machiavelli, and Menhaden." In *Transactions of the American Fisheries Society* 4 (1971): 804-12.

Reimers, Paul. "The Length of Residence of Juvenile Fall Chinook Salmon in Six Rivers, Oregon." *Research Report of the Fish Commission of Oregon* 4 (2) (June 1973): 36-39.

Rickard, Wesley. "Size Standard Study." Prepared for Public Timber Purchasers Group, Portland, Ore., 1978.

Ricker, W. E. *Handbook of Computations for Biological Statistics of Fish Populations*. Bulletin 119. Ottowa, Ontario: Fisheries Research Board of Canada, 1958.

Robinson, Glen O. *The Forest Service: A Study in Public Land Management*. Baltimore: Johns Hopkins University Press, 1975.

Samuelson, Paul A. "Economics of Forestry in an Evolving Society." *Economic Inquiry* 14 (December 1976): 466-92.

Schniepp, Mark. "Analysis of Forest Service Appraisal Methodology in the Pacific Northwest." Ph.D. dissertation, University of California, Santa Barbara, 1981.

Shapley, S. P., and D. M. Bishop. "Sedimentation in a Salmon Stream." *Journal of the Fisheries Research Board of Canada* 22 (4) (1965): 919.

Shelton, J. M., and R. O. Pollock. "Siltation and Egg Survival in Incubation Channels." *Transactions of American Fisheries Society* 95 (2) (April 1966): 183-87.

Shepard, Ward. "The Bogey of Compound Interest." *Journal of Forestry* 23 (1925): 251-59.

Silcox, F. A. "Forward Not Backward." *Journal of Forestry* 32(2) (1934): 202-07.

Smith, Dean. *The Economic Value of Anadromous Fisheries for Six Rivers National Forest*. USDA, Forest Service, Region 5. February 1978.

Steen, Harold K. *The U.S. Forest Service: A History*. Seattle: University of Washington Press, 1976.

Stroup, Richard L., and John A. Baden, eds. *Natural Resources: Bureaucratic Myths and Environmental Management.* San Francisco: Pacific Research Institute for Public Policy, 1983.

Thompson, Earl. "Book Review" of *Bureaucracy and Representative Government* by William Niskanen." *Journal of Economic Literature* 11 (September 1973): 950-53.

Truluck, Phillip N., and David J. Theroux, eds. *Private Rights and Public Lands.* Washington, D.C.: The Heritage Foundation; San Francisco: Pacific Institute for Public Policy Research, 1983.

Tullock, Gordon. "Competing for Aid." *Public Choice* 22 (Summer 1975): 41-51.

U.S. Comptroller General. "Projected Timber Scarcities in the Pacific Northwest: A Critique of 11 Studies." EMD-79-5 (December 12, 1975).

U.S. Congress, House Hearings, Subcommittee on Forests of the Committee on Agriculture. *National Forests – Multiple Use and Sustained Yield.* 86 Cong., 2d sess., 1960.

U.S. Congress, House Hearings, Subcommittee on Forests of the Committee on Agriculture. *National Timber Supply Act of 1969.* 91st Cong., 1st sess., 1969.

U.S. Congress, Office of Technology Assessment. *Management of Fuel and Nonfuel Minerals in Federal Land.* 1979.

U.S. Congress, Senate. *Administration of National Forests for Multiple Use and Sustained Yield.* 86th Cong., 2d sess., Rept. 1407, 1960.

U.S. Congress, Senate. *Congressional Record.* Chief McGuire to Senator James A. McClure. August 24, 1976, pp. S14352-53.

U.S. Congress, Senate. National Forest Management Act of 1976. Report of Senate Committee on Agriculture and Forestry. Report No. 94-893.

U.S. Department of Agriculture, Forest Service. *An Analysis of the Timber Situation in the United States, 1952-2030.* Forest Resource Report No. 23. 1982.

U.S. Department of Agriculture, Forest Service. *An Assessment of the Forest and Rangeland Situation in the United States.* 1980.

U.S. Department of Agriculture, Forest Service. *Douglas Fir Supply Study.* Pacific Northwest Forest Region Experiment Station. 1969.

U.S. Department of Agriculture, Forest Service. *Forest Service Handbook.*

U.S. Department of Agriculture, Forest Service. *Forest Statistics of the United States, 1977.*

U.S. Department of Agriculture, Forest Service. *Forest Statistics of the United States.* Unnumbered publication. 1978.

U.S. Department of Agriculture, Forest Service. *Guidelines for Economic and Social Analysis of Programs, Resource Plans, and Projects: Final Policy.* Federal Regulations, Part III 47 (80). April 26, 1982, pp. 17940-54.

U.S. Department of Agriculture, Forest Service. "National Forest Timber Sales, New Procedures." *Federal Register* 47 (January 20, 1982).

U.S. Department of Agriculture, Forest Service. "New National Forest Timber Sale Procedures: Final Policy." *Federal Register* 47 (April 15, 1982).

U.S. Department of Agriculture, Forest Service. *The Outlook for Timber in the United States.* FRR-20. 1973.

U.S. Department of Agriculture, Forest Service. *Price Trends for Forest Products.* 1956.

U.S. Department of Agriculture, Forest Service. *Report of the Chief Forest Service, 1970-71.* 1971.

U.S. Department of Agriculture, Forest Service. *Report of the Forest Service Fiscal Year, 1980.*

U.S. Department of the Interior. *Final Report of the Task Force on the Availability of Federally Owned Mineral Lands.* 1977.

U.S. Department of the Interior. *Public Lands Statistics.* 1980.

U.S. Laws and Statutes. National Forest Management Act, PL 94-588 (1976).

U.S. Laws and Statutes. National Forest Management Act Amendment, PL 95-233 (1978).

Watson, Richard B. "The Effectiveness of Competition for National Forest Timber in Region 6." Ph.D. dissertation, University of California at Santa Barbara, 1981.

Wildavsky, Aaron. *The Politics of the Budgetary Process.* Boston: Little, Brown, 1964.

Wolf, Charles, Jr. "A Theory of Nonmarket Failure: Framework for Implementation Analysis." *Journal of Law and Economics* 22 (1) (April 1979): 107-39.

Wooldridge, D. "Review—Timber Harvest Scheduling Study: Six Rivers National Forest." USDA, Forest Service, Pacific Southwest Region, May 1979.

INDEX

ABOUT THE EDITORS

Robert T. Deacon is Professor of Economics at the University of California at Santa Barbara. He received his B.A., M.A., and Ph.D. degrees from the University of Washington. Dr. Deacon has been a consultant to the Department of Commerce, the Department of Energy, the Department of Housing and Urban Development, and was a National Fellow at the Hoover Institution in 1975–1976.

Dr. Deacon is the author of *Price Controls and International Petroleum Product Prices* (with W. Mead) and a contributor to the volumes *Economic Analysis of Pressing Social Problems, State and Local Government Finance and Financial Management*, and *U.S. Energy Policy: Errors of the Past, Proposals for the Future*. His articles have appeared in such scholarly journals as *American Economic Review, Journal of Energy and Development, National Tax Journal, Natural Resources Journal, Public Choice, Review of Economics and Statistics*, and *Water Resources Research*.

M. Bruce Johnson is Professor of Economics at the University of California at Santa Barbara. He is Chairman of the Board of Advisors and former Research Director of the Pacific Institute. He received his B.A. from Carleton College and his M.A. and Ph.D. from Northwestern University. In addition to serving as President of the Western Economics Association (1981–1982), Dr. Johnson has been

Associate Professor of Economics, University of Washington; Acting Director, Institute for Economic Research, University of Washington; Chairman, Department of Economics, U.C.S.B.; Visiting Professor of Economics, U.C.L.A.; and Associate Research Director and Professor of Economics, Law and Economics Center, University of Miami.

A contributor to over a dozen scholarly volumes, he is the author of *The Economics of America's Third Century, Energy and Jobs: A Long Run Analysis* (with J. Cogan and M. Ward), and *Household Behavior: Consumption, Income, and Wealth.* Dr. Johnson is the editor of *Advertising and Free Speech* (with A. Hyman), *The Attack on Corporate America: The Corporate Issues Sourcebook, The California Coastal Plan: A Critique, Resolving the Housing Crisis: Government Policy, Decontrol, and the Public Interest,* and *Rights and Regulation: Ethical, Political, and Economic Issues* (with T. Machan).

His articles and reviews have appeared in the *American Economic Review, American Spectator, California Real Estate Magazine, Economic Inquiry, Economic Studies, Economica, Econometrica, Environmental Law, Expressways and Automobiles, Journal of Economic Literature, Law and Liberty, Policy Report, Quarterly Journal of Economics, Reason, Southern California Law Review,* and other popular and scholarly journals.

ABOUT THE AUTHORS

Judith Cox received her B.A. in economics and history from Northwestern University and her M.A. from Stanford University. She was Visiting Associate Professor of Economics at Williams College in Williamstown, Massachusetts in 1983–84, and has now resumed her position as Lecturer in Economics and Undergraduate Program Director at the University of Washington.

Barney Dowdle is Professor of Forest Resources and Adjunct Professor of Economics at the University of Washington. Professor Dowdle received his B.A. from the University of Washington, and his M.A. and Ph.D. from Yale University. He specializes in natural resource economics, forest management, and economic theory.

Dr. Dowdle is a contributor to the volumes *Bureaucracy vs. Environment, Logging and Pulpwood Production, Private Rights and Public Lands, Recreational Use of Wild Lands, Timber Policy Issues in British Columbia*, and *Timber Supply and the Environment.* His articles have appeared in *Forest Industries, Journal of Economic History, Journal of Forestry, Society of American Foresters Proceedings, University of Washington Business Review, Washington Public Policy Notes* and other journals. He is a former advisor of the States' Rights Coordinating Council, an organization which promotes the "Sagebrush Rebellion."

John H. Grobey is Professor and Chairman of the Department of Economics at Humboldt State University. He received his B.S., Master of Forestry, M.A. in economics, and Ph.D. degrees in forest economics from the University of Washington. Dr. Grobey has been a consultant for numerous studies of forest economics, especially as related to the use of public lands and has testified on fisheries and forestry issues before numerous legislative committees.

The author of *An Economic Analysis of the Hardwood Industry of Western Washington* and *An Alternative Public Policy for Regulating the Impact of Forest Practices on the Northern California Salmonid Fishery*, Dr. Grobey's studies have appeared in *California–Nevada Proceedings* of the American Fisheries Society (Wildlife Society), U.S. Fish and Wildlife Service, and U.S. Department of the Interior publications.

Steve H. Hanke received his B.S. and Ph.D. degrees from the University of Colorado at Boulder. He is currently a Professor of Applied Economics at Johns Hopkins University. Dr. Hanke is also a Senior Advisor for the Joint Economic Committee of the U.S. Congress, and a Senior Fellow at The Manhattan Institute for Policy Research. In addition, he serves as financial advisor to several private firms in the U.S. and Europe.

In 1981–82, Dr. Hanke was a Senior Economist on the President's Council of Economic Advisors, where he was the architect of the President's program to privatize public lands. He has also served as a member of the Governor's Council of Economic Advisors in Maryland.

Dr. Hanke's academic experience has included faculty appointments at the Colorado School of Mines, and the University of California at Berkeley. He has also held positions at research institutes and universities in Austria, France and Sweden. In 1983 he was a Senior Fellow at the Heritage Foundation in Washington, D.C.

He is Associate Editor of the *Water Resources Bulletin* and serves on the editorial boards of several economics journals. Dr. Hanke has contributed to many edited volumes and written numerous articles in scholarly journals, including *American Economic Review, Cato Journal, Journal American Water Works Association, Land Economics, New England Journal of Medicine, Policy Analysis, Policy Review, Public Policy, Review of Economics and Statistics, Techniques et Sciences Municipales, Water Resources Research*, and the *Water Resources Bulletin.*

Ronald N. Johnson is Associate Professor of Agricultural Economics and Economics at Montana State University. He received his B.S. from Utah State University, his M.A. from California State University at Long Beach, and his Ph.D. from the University of Washington. Dr. Johnson specializes in natural resources and property rights as well as applied price theory and industrial organization.

Dr. Johnson's articles and reviews have appeared in *American Economic Review, American Journal of Agricultural Economics, Economic Inquiry, Explorations in Economic History, Journal of Economic History, Journal of Labor Research, Journal of Law and Economics, Journal of Political Economy, Natural Resources Journal, Review of Economics and Statistics*, and *Southern Economic Journal.* In addition, Dr. Johnson has contributed to the volumes *Bureaucracy vs. Environment*, and *Water Rights: Bureaucracy, Property Rights, and the Environment.*

Gary Libecap is currently Associate Professor of Economics and Director of the Karl Eller Center for Study of the Private Market Economy at the University of Arizona. He received his B.A. from the University of Montana, his M.A. and Ph.D. from the University of Pennsylvania. He has been Assistant Professor of Economics, University of New Mexico and Assistant Professor of Economics, Texas A&M University.

Dr. Libecap is the author of *The Evolution of Private Mining Rights: Nevada's Comstock Lode, Locking Up the Range: Federal Land Controls and Grazing*, and a contributor to *The Environmental Costs of Government Action, Public Lands and Private Rights*, and *Emergence of the Modern Political Economy.* His articles and reviews have appeared in *Agricultural History, American Economic Review, Business History Review, Economic Inquiry, Explorations in Economic History, Natural Resources Journal*, and *Southern Economic Journal.* Dr. Libecap is a member of the Board of Advisors for the Pacific Institute.

Dennis D. Muraoka is an Associate Professor of Economics at California State University, Long Beach. He received his B.A. in economics and mathematics, his M.A. in urban economics, and his Ph.D. in economics from the University of California at Santa Barbara. Dr. Muraoka has provided economic analysis of municipal and industrial projects concerning natural resources and energy related issues.

Dr. Muraoka has authored or co-authored articles for professional journals such as *Contemporary Policy Issues, National Tax Journal, Natural Resources Journal*, and *Oil and Gas Tax Quarterly*, as well as for several local and federal government publications. He is a co-author of the forthcoming Pacific Institute book *Leasing Offshore Lands: A Critical Analysis of Federal Oil and Gas Leasing Policies.*

Robert H. Nelson has been a member of the Economics Staff in the Office of Policy Analysis, U.S. Department of the Interior since 1975. He received his B.A. in mathematics from Brandeis University and his Ph.D. in economics from Princeton University. Dr. Nelson was Senior Economist of the Commission on Fair Market Value Policy for Federal Coal Leasing in 1983–1984, and Staff Economist for The Twentieth Century Fund. He has been a consultant to the Puerto Rico Planning Board and Assistant Professor of Economics at the City College of the City University of New York.

Dr. Nelson is the author of *The Making of Federal Coal Policy*, and *Zoning and Property Rights: An Analysis of the American System of Land Use Regulation*, and has contributed to the volumes *Current Issues in Natural Resource Policy, Land Reform, American Style, Resource Conflicts in the West, Rethinking the Federal Lands*, and *Western Public Lands*. He has authored or co-authored numerous articles and reviews appearing in professional journals such as *Environmental Law, Journal of Industrial Economics, Journal of Policy Analysis and Management, Journal of Regional Science, Journal of Political Economy, Land Economics, Natural Resources Journal, Public Finance, Southern Economics Journal, Urban Studies*, and *The Urban Lawyer*, as well as many unpublished government papers. Dr. Nelson's articles have also appeared in popular publications such as *Forbes, Forest Planning, Planning, Regulation, Technology Review, Urban Focus, Urban Land*, and the *Washington Post.*

Richard W. Parks received his A.B. from Harvard University, his M.A. in statistics, and his Ph.D. in economics from the University of California at Berkeley. Dr. Parks was an Assistant Professor of Economics and Director of Undergraduate Studies, University of

Chicago. He is currently Professor of Economics at the University of Washington where he has also served as Director of the Institute for Economic Research. He is the recipient of many awards, including the Fulbright Lecturership in Argentina, National Science Foundation grants, and a Hoover National Fellowship at Stanford University.

Dr. Parks has authored or co-authored numerous articles which have appeared in the *American Economic Review, Economic Inquiry, Economic Journal, Econometrica, Inter-American Economic Affairs, Journal of the American Statistical Association, Journal of Business and Economic Statistics, Journal of Econometrics, Journal of Money, Credit and Banking, Journal of Political Economy, Property Tax Journal*, and the *Review of Economics and Statistics.*

Lucian Pugliaresi is Senior Member of the Policy Planning Staff, U.S. Department of State. He has held directorial positions since 1974 in the U.S. Department of Energy, the Environmental Protection Agency, and the Department of the Interior. Mr. Pugliaresi received his A.B. in economics and undertook graduate studies at the University of California at Berkeley where he also served as Senior Analyst in the Office of the President. He is the author (with R. Nelson) of *Timber Harvest Policy Issues on the Oregon and California Grant Lands*, and a contributor to the *Public Interest*, and *Deutsche Studien.*

Mark Schniepp received his B.A. and Ph.D. from the University of California at Santa Barbara where he is currently Lecturer of Economics. He is also Senior Economist with Applied Economic Systems. Dr. Schniepp has been an economics and computer consultant to legal and economics firms and served as co-investigator for a three-year U.S. Department of Agriculture study on "The Effectiveness of Competition for Timber in the Pacific Northwest."

Dr. Schniepp is the author of *Analysis of Forest Service Appraisal Methodology in the Pacific Northwest*, and has presented papers at meetings of the Western Economic Association, and co-authored an article for the *Journal of Natural Resources.*

Richard B. Watson is presently Lecturer of Economics at the University of California at Santa Barbara and Research Associate for the Community and Organization Research Institute at U.C.S.B. He received his B.A. in quantitative analysis from Southern Methodist

University, his M.B.A. from Valdosta State College, and M.A. and Ph.D. degrees in economics from the University of California at Santa Barbara. Dr. Watson has been a statistical and economic consultant and has conducted research for the U.S. Department of Agriculture.

Dr. Watson co-authored a research study for *Natural Resources Journal* and his papers have been presented at meetings of the Western Economics Association.

PACIFIC RESEARCH INSTITUTE
FOR PUBLIC POLICY

The Pacific Research Institute produces studies that explore long-term solutions to difficult issues of public policy. The Institute seeks to facilitate a more active and enlightened discourse on these issues and to broaden understanding of market processes, government policy, and the rule of law. Through the publication of scholarly books and the sponsorship of conferences, the Institute serves as an established resource for ideas in the continuing public policy debate.

Institute books have been adopted for courses at colleges, universities, and graduate schools nationwide. More than 175 distinguished scholars have worked with the Institute to analyze the premises and consequences of existing public policy and to formulate possible solutions to seemingly intractable problems. Prestigious journals and major media regularly review and comment upon Institute work. In addition, the Board of Advisors consists of internationally recognized scholars, including two Nobel laureates.

The Pacific Research Institute is an independent, tax exempt, 501(c)(3) organization and as such is supported solely by the sale of its books and by the contributions from a wide variety of foundations, corporations, and individuals. This diverse funding base and the Institute's refusal to accept government funds enable it to remain independent.

OTHER STUDIES IN PUBLIC POLICY BY
THE PACIFIC RESEARCH INSTITUTE

URBAN TRANSIT
The Private Challenge to Public Transportation
Edited by Charles A. Lave
Foreword by John Meyer

POLITICS, PRICES, AND PETROLEUM
The Political Economy of Energy
By David Glasner
Foreword by Paul W. MacAvoy

RIGHTS AND REGULATION
Ethical, Political, and Economic Issues
Edited by Tibor M. Machan and M. Bruce Johnson
Foreword by Aaron Wildavsky

FUGITIVE INDUSTRY
The Economics and Politics of Deindustrialization
By Richard B. McKenzie
Foreword by Finis Welch

MONEY IN CRISIS
The Federal Reserve, the Economy, and Monetary Reform
Edited by Barry N. Siegel
Foreword by Leland B. Yeager

NATURAL RESOURCES
Bureaucratic Myths and Environmental Management
By Richard Stroup and John Baden
Foreword by William Niskanen

FIREARMS AND VIOLENCE
Issues of Public Policy
Edited by Don B. Kates, Jr.
Foreword by John Kaplan

WATER RIGHTS
Scarce Resource Allocation, Bureaucracy, and the Environment
Edited by Terry L. Anderson
Foreword by Jack Hirshleifer

LOCKING UP THE RANGE
Federal Land Controls and Grazing
By Gary D. Libecap
Foreword by Jonathan R.T. Hughes

THE PUBLIC SCHOOL MONOPOLY
A Critical Analysis of Education and the State in American Society
Edited by Robert B. Everhart
Foreword by Clarence J. Karier

RESOLVING THE HOUSING CRISIS
Government Policy, Demand, Decontrol, and the Public Interest
Edited with an Introduction by M. Bruce Johnson

OFFSHORE LANDS
Oil and Gas Leasing and Conservation on the Outer Continental Shelf
By Walter J. Mead, et al.
Foreword by Stephen L. McDonald

ELECTRIC POWER
Deregulation and the Public Interest
Edited by John C. Moorhouse
Foreword by Harold Demsetz

TAXATION AND THE DEFICIT ECONOMY
Fiscal Policy and Capital Formation in the United States
Edited by Dwight R. Lee
Foreword by Michael J. Boskin

THE AMERICAN FAMILY AND STATE
Edited by Joseph R. Peden and Fred R. Glahe
Foreword by Robert Nisbet

DEALING WITH DRUGS
Consequences of Government Control
Edited by Ronald Hamowy
Foreword by Dr. Alfred Freedman

CRISIS AND LEVIATHAN
Critical Episodes in the Growth of American Government
By Robert Higgs
Foreword by Arthur A. Ekirch, Jr.

THE NEW CHINA
Comparative Economic Development in Mainland China, Taiwan, and Hong Kong
By Alvin Rabushka

ADVERTISING AND THE MARKET PROCESS
A Modern Economic View
By Robert B. Ekelund, Jr. and David S. Saurman
Foreword by Israel M. Kirzner

HEALTH CARE IN AMERICA
The Political Economy of Hospitals and Health Insurance
Edited by H.E. Frech III
Foreword by Richard Zeckhauser

POLITICAL BUSINESS CYCLES
The Political Economy of Money, Inflation, and Unemployment
Edited by Thomas D. Willett
Foreword by Axel Leijonhufvud

WHEN GOVERNMENT GOES PRIVATE
Successful Alternatives to Public Services
By Randall Fitzgerald

THE YELLOWSTONE PRIMER
Edited by John A. Baden and Don Leal

TO PROMOTE THE GENERAL WELFARE
By Richard E. Wagner

For further information on the Pacific Research Institute's program and a catalog of publications, please contact:

PACIFIC RESEARCH INSTITUTE FOR PUBLIC POLICY
177 Post Street
San Francisco, CA 94108
(415) 989-0833